Preface to Modernism

Preface to Modernism

Art Berman

University of Illinois Press
Urbana and Chicago

Parts of this book were written during a professional leave
granted by Rochester Institute of Technology.

© 1994 by the Board of Trustees of the University of Illinois
Manufactured in the United States of America
1 2 3 4 5 C P 5 4 3 2 1

This book is printed on acid-free paper.

Library of Congress Cataloging-in-Publication Data

Berman, Art, 1938–
    Preface to modernism / Art Berman.
        p.   cm.
    Includes bibliographical references and index.
    ISBN 0-252-02103-7 (alk. paper). — ISBN 0-252-06391-0 (pbk. :
alk. paper)
    1. Modernism (Aesthetics) 2. Philosophy, Modern—19th century.
3. Philosophy, Modern—20th century. I. Title.
BH301.M54B47   1994
190—dc20   93-36653
                                                                  CIP

Contents

Introduction

This book posits and elaborates a set of hypotheses intended to aggregate into an extended conceptual definition.

"Modernism" names an aesthetic movement; its definition rests on certain premises about empiricism and its dilemmas, as well as about the alternatives to empiricism. I am attempting neither a history of modernist art or literature nor a "reading" of certain visual and literary works of modernism. I have not included biographical synopses, critical aesthetic assessments, or reviews of the critical and scholarly literature, although such studies have encouraged me to write this one. Rather, I introduce a collection of associated hypotheses about where modernism has come from, where it fits into the scheme of things, and what it means.

The large ideas that influence intellectual and aesthetic movements are, in my view, first introduced into the community of writers and artists through philosophy. Philosophical texts codify the definitions and the boundaries for the concepts that have influenced Western thought, art, science, and politics since the days of Plato and Aristotle, concepts that even influence those who possess little knowledge of or little interest in the technical considerations of philosophers. Yet while I privilege philosophy in this way, this book is hardly meant to be a work of philosophy or a treatise on philosophy, as any real philosopher would readily testify. I take an assortment of terms—*modernity, modernism, empiricism, idealism, romanticism, classicism, transcendentalism, psychoanalysis, humanism, formalism, capitalism, fascism, Renaissance, Enlightenment,* and others—and consider each as falling into certain juxtaposable alliances. Modernism can best be understood as having emerged from the theoretical conflicts inherent in these various oppositions.

I customarily separate groups of ideas into two poles and then walk back and forth between them, so that by the end of the book I will have worn down a visible path. The virtue of this approach is that I can touch upon a wide variety of subjects. The drawback is that far more is asserted than demonstrated. I accumulate perspectives, not evidence. (On Picabia's painting titled *A Little Solitude amidst the Suns* are written the words "A picture to tell and not to prove.") My intention has been to outline a speculative position.

I use the term *modernity* to identify the process through which rationalism is channeled into empiricism, which in turn provides the theoretical foundation for the Enlightenment, whose outlooks, goals, and predispositions characterize the "modern" world. The most important factor here is, then, the rise of empiricism—that credo of modernity—and the subsequent reactions, confrontations, adaptions, and rejections. *Modernism* is the name of an aesthetic movement inside modernity, yet one that sees itself as counteracting certain negative aspects of modernity—the inability, for example, to yield a contented and equitable society, despite its promises, or fully to account for the aesthetic experience as a guide to and an authorization of value, as romanticism had been able to do. Modernism can account for the aesthetic experience, but only by sustaining certain romantic proclivities, such as the belief in the preeminence of art as affording a verifiable access to truth. There is, then, a tension, even an incompatibility between modernity and modernism, although modernism is inside modernity. Ultimately modernism, not modernity, capitulates to the opposition.

The preeminence of art as insight into truth, which emerges in the writings of Kant, in the idealists, like Schelling, and in the romantics, is a solution to a basic problem that has existed for two hundred years. It could once be believed that rationality, logic, and science were compatible with theological and religious speculation. Medieval and Renaissance philosophers had purported to find a reconciliation; so had the rationalist philosophers and theologians in the seventeenth and eighteenth centuries. By the late eighteenth century, when religious thought and secular thought had separated sufficiently that reconciliation between them seemed improbable, even impossible, "Art" was ingeniously placed in the gap between them: such is the origin of aesthetics. Experiencing art can then become the "aesthetic experience," now situated in its intermediary position between the physical and the metaphysical. By way of new definitions of art and the artist, this offers the notions of intuition, inspiration, and imagination that seem to validate the possibility of transcendence and to provide some verification that empiricism alone cannot provide a complete understanding of the world.

Of course, empiricists themselves have no need to elevate art or the aesthetic experience in this manner. Empiricism experiences no doubts in regard to its methods and abilities; it is not intimidated by what it can either dominate or make obsolete. The aesthetic tactic, from Kant onward, is repeatedly a reaction against empiricism: an attempt to preserve the transcendent by those for whom its disappearance is intolerable, for whom human life would lose much of its meaning should transcendence wane. The aesthetic strategy is always—at least so far—unsuccessful.

In the first chapter, I briefly define what I mean by *modernity* and *modernism*, draw the distinctions between naturalism and transcendentalism, identify how certain broadly defined intellectual movements (the Enlightenment and romanticism) are affiliated with the empiricism that evolves from naturalism and the idealism that evolves from transcendentalism, and provide a preliminary overview of where modernism fits into these philosophical notions.

While chapters 2 and 3 present four stages of modernism, I must again emphasize that this is not a history of modernism but a way of thinking about that history. I am quite casual (perhaps unthinkably so, to a historian) about dates and sequences. Directions are described, but chronological periods are not; and in fact the "phases" cannot really be identified as precisely equivalent to "periods."

Modernism shifts away from its romantic influences as these become less tenable—especially as German thought, and metaphysics generally, becomes less attractive after the Germans lose World War I. The movement is toward formalism, which characterizes literary "high" modernism. High modernism gradually competes with and augments the earlier modernism of the prewar painters, which nevertheless continues in painting, although eventually formalism becomes critically central to the visual arts, too, especially after modernist painting moves to the United States, empiricism's mighty fortress.

This movement from the original romantic influences determining modernism into formalism underlies the notion of "classicism" that the literary high modernists set in opposition to "romanticism." Chapters 2 and 3 also expand upon the consequences of these transitions for abstraction, realism (and photography), and formalist theory.

Chapter 4 more closely addresses the connections and antagonisms between empiricism and modernism. The empiricism that initially receives its most influential form in Locke and Hume is responded to by Kant and later by the idealists, who believe they are following in Kant's footsteps, a belief I share. (Kant is no representative of modernity or the Enlightenment to me.) Kantianism and idealism I then affiliate, as so many others have done, with romanticism. *Modernism*, a term I employed in the first chapter to refer only to an aesthetic movement (neither "modern times" nor the "modern world" of the twentieth century), arises from a dilemma: How might writers and visual artists retain their romantic heritage in an environment where the strength of empiricism (its mechanistic view of the world, its science, its technology) is steadily increasing? (Especially because of the alliance of empiricism and capitalism.) In this chapter, as in the first and periodically throughout, I note how by the late nineteenth century the artist and poet had come to believe that art might offer the modern world what religious transcendence had been forced or would clearly be forced to relinquish. Art is not to refurbish, replenish, or substantiate transcendence in the old sense, as in the midnineteenth century amalgamation of religion, idealism, aesthetics, and conservative or reactionary politics. It is too late for that, and the modernists reject that amalgamation. Modernism is not simply romanticism extended. Nevertheless, even when quite secular, art is situated on the site religion used to occupy. In the long run this displacement proves infeasible, which partly accounts for modernism's most important transition—to the formalism that now so commonly characterizes criticism as well as art and literary history. Modernism ultimately fails in its original mission.

In Chapter 5, I discuss scientific ideas. For example, in astronomy and physics since Copernicus and Newton, certain general patterns of thought are now often taken for granted, patterns the modernist must somehow both accept and react against. Of particular importance are questions of human freedom and determinism. I also suggest that quantum physics attempts to reintroduce the Kantian ideas that classical physics had consciously excluded; like modernism, physics is involved in the attempted resolution of conflicts between empiricism and idealism.

Really?!

The diverse issues discussed in chapters 6 and 7 are all connected by time, a theme already raised periodically during the preceding discussion of science as well as in part 1. How have the concepts of time and the timeless been affected by the spread of empiricism, accompanied by the decline of a theology attached to idealist metaphysics? What is modernism's relation to the history that has preceded it, from which it attempts to detach itself? I consider the idea of nature, which solves a certain problem for the Renaissance and which takes on different meanings for succeeding generations; the notion of rebirth; the idea of the unconscious; and other matters that shape modernism's response to form, style, and content. Since art and literature have been so strongly influenced by romanticism, artists and writers constantly struggle with the linear, even-paced, vast, infinite, and empty time of empiricist science, for which neither religion nor metaphysics seems any longer to offer remedy or consolation.

Time.

+ nature

Big ✗ claim

In chapter 8, the first of three chapters on modernism and politics, I introduce a consideration of capitalism, followed by a schematization of the politics of the modernists: right and left, elitist and popularist. Chapters 9 and 10 compare capitalism, socialism, and fascism. As before, my approach is to conceptualize the terms, to theorize their basic attributes as ideas, and to examine how they pertain to the themes of the earlier chapters, without analyzing the specific operations of each system as a political scientist might. In particular, I am concerned with how universalizations are posited or denied in the various systems, how will and intellect are envisioned in them, and how evolutionary biology has been an influence.

Doesn't want to get into specifics (?)

Chapters 11 and 12 concern issues of the self. Between the time of romanticism and modernism a new type of ego emerges, and personality and individuality become distinct in new ways. The personality of the modernist artist and writer is fundamentally unlike that of the Renaissance, neoclassical, or romantic artist and writer. Nor are the egos of the rest of us exactly what our selves were in time past. These chapters are not written as a technical analysis of selfhood; rather, I attempt to elaborate on what the changes have meant, to describe what has happened (not how), to discuss some of the implications (not the mechanisms). Insofar as modernism carries forth romanticism

Big claim!

This is where Nicholls' book begins.

genius?

while transforming it inside the empiricist environment, it makes available certain generalized beliefs about talent and aptitude. This affects what it means to go to work in capitalism. Marx wrote without foreknowledge of modernism, yet part of the change brought about by modernism has diverted the class struggle Marx described.

Most of the names and places I refer to concern painting and literature; architecture, music, and the other arts are only occasionally mentioned. Similarly, my attention has been given to the European and Anglo-American environments, although modernism has been played out over a much wider territory—in Latin America, for example.

I do not so much expand the factual information about the various subjects as increase the possibilities about how the facts can be organized, should one attempt such an organization. I ultimately decided not to use quotations from modernist writers and artists in the narrative. For every supporting quotation there could be another to contradict it; modernism is not a coherent set of beliefs, although one can have a coherent set of beliefs *about* modernism. "Wise man was he," writes Thomas Carlyle in *Sartor Resartus,* "who counseled that Speculation should have free course, and look fearlessly towards all the thirty-two points of the compass, withersoever and howsoever it listed." I do presume that it will be readily apparent what kinds of facts, substantial in number, the book rests upon.

Part One

The Configurations of Modernism

Modernity and Modernism

1

Defining Terms

The word *modernity* is used here to signify particular values, beliefs, and dispositions concerning the theoretical foundations, practices, and aims of society. Modernity includes certain intellectual movements, political directions, and socioeconomic trends and involves the setting of optimistic social goals. Recognizable by the midseventeenth century, modernity is founded on the assertion that the present inaugurates an unprecedented era: not simply a continuation or modification of the past, but an incomparable age. A new form of human self-consciousness is to intervene in history, not only as a mode of awareness, but as a mode of power. Human rationality will predominate, subordinating irrationality, custom, and superstition, with the efficacy to plan for and attain progressive improvement in all social institutions through the free exercise of will. Humans have the ability to understand nature as it is—real, solid, and lawfully dependable—which diminishes dependence on theological or transcendental concepts.

The mechanisms of the mind function to receive directly, through the senses, the objects of the world. Furthermore, the mind has sufficient power to deduce the real relationships among these objects, which can be formulated as laws independent from either the human mind that observes and analyzes these relationships or the divine mind that may have originally invoked them. Human nature, mentality, and consciousness are part of nature as a whole.

Personal, familial, and social values can be derived from rationally objective analyses and decisions. Society and human behavior can be based on natural principles. While human beings have hostile, selfish, greedy, and antisocial impulses and desires, these can be subordinated to cooperation, honesty, ethical responsibility, and altruism; even selfish behavior can be made beneficial if properly contextualized, especially in free commerce (capitalism). Through science, applicable to every domain of knowledge, natural forces can be understood, even mastered; there will be continual scientific invention (technology) leading to an enhanced standard of living, the elimination of disease, and increased freedom of choice and action. Wealth will continually grow and be judiciously apportioned. The rationality capable of changing the world is to be trained by universal education and exercised through democratically representative political institutions; an ultimate peace and harmony between people, between nations, and between humans and nature will be achieved. The arts will function to improve mental well-being through rational and normative insights into correct judgment and integrated emotion, presented in a vivifying and beautiful way.

Although each of these distinct ideas has its own history, they converge during the early seventeenth century, at the time of Francis Bacon and Descartes, to command a strong and influential advocacy as a unified worldview. This worldview is fully formulated as a philosophy (empiricism) and integrated into the European intellectual environment by the mideighteenth century, around the time of David Hume, following the acceptance of scientific procedure as the predominant model for all valid reasoning concerning causal relations.

As a set of hypotheses and practices, modernity still provides the foundational assumptions for contemporary life and expectations, even though these have undergone transformations in what is now called "modern life," which is not equivalent to modernity. Modern life is usually described by emphasizing the hecticness and diversity of its profuse activities; its stresses, novelties, and complexities; its insecurities, because every idea is temporary and every belief tentative; its intricately changing relationships, whether financial, social, marital, sexual; its drives for money, power, importance, or self-definition; its abundance of products (especially those driven by electricity and fossil fuel), people, cities, media, facts, and technological innovations; its crime, selfishness, pollution, anxiety, secular materialism; its internationalism; and its own sense of its unprecedented modernness.

The word *modernism* is used here specifically to signify the suppositions of an aesthetic-artistic movement clarified toward the end of the nineteenth century, permeating the outlook of the twentieth, and now in the process of concluding. Artistic innovation, creativity, exuberance, and insight into the human condition are to act as a critique of modernity and as a social, political, and aesthetic corrective to it.[1] Modernism is, however, also intended to advance modernity, in particular its optimistic belief in material, social, and intellectual progress. This advancement of modernity is originally to be accomplished by introducing, promulgating, and assuring, through artworks, the acceptance of the aesthetic values of beauty, intuition, and spirituality. An elevation both resembling and substituting for religious transcendence is awakened by lyric poetry and metaphor, music, harmonious visual and literary form, and vibrant color. (Only much later will outright disharmony, as distinct from unfamiliar new varieties of harmony, become a value, especially in the visual arts and in music.) Modernism envisions the improvement of human life based on values derived from the artistic culture. The uniquely aesthetic experience of art is taken to guarantee its value and insights—and to subsume, not refute, rationality and science in order that these might be directed elsewhere than toward the selfish and often pernicious ends of commerce, nationalism, industrialization, and an impersonalizing urbanization.

The modernist critique evolves from the romanticism of the early nineteenth century but differs from it in temperament. While romanticism originated as a response and alternative to empiricism, modernism's transformation of the romantic aesthetic occurs inside empiricism. Because modernism occurs inside modernity, it fights its battles while depending for support on what it most attacks: the middle class in a capitalist environment. (Although chastised by modernism, the middle class provides its only audience.) Modernism originally opposes "materialism" in both its senses. Like romanticism, it opposes materialism as a set of assumptions about the ontological constitution of the world (philosophical and scientific materialism). But it also rejects the materialism of the bourgeois ethic of material comfort. It rejects the social and commercial values of a conservative and complaisant middle class, and it abhors the way the middle class defines value in commercial and monetary terms.

Modernism participates in the transition from a reliance on philosophy to a reliance on psychology to produce knowledge about the human mind. (What Schelling is to romanticism, Freud is to modernism.[2]) Psychology is positioned as a borderline discipline between the aesthetics of philosophical idealism and empiricist science, as if it might reconcile them. This ambiguous positioning is caused by two distinct lineages in philosophy, with Kant a central figure in both.

First, Kant's critical philosophy argues that the forms in which the world appears to us are imposed upon "things-in-themselves" by the structures (categories) of the mind. This can be viewed as an incipient idealism, not fully developed by Kant. A later, more completely evolved idealism eventually assumes (by retaining the Kantian categories of thought but discarding the things-in-themselves) that the world need not exist in some unapprehensible form independent of its appearance in human thought. Rather, the world is a manifestation of a universalized thought or reason that is the basic ontological reality (Fichte's Ego; Hegel's Absolute[3]) from which the individuated mind issues and in which the individual mind participates.

Second, contrary to the first, the Kantian critical philosophy can be viewed (as the neo-Kantians, reacting against idealism, viewed it[4]) as both a critique and the culmination of empiricism in a psychology that identifies the conditions for individuated mentality, conditions that make possible empiricist knowledge of a world that exists fully independently of the mind that knows it. Innate categorical structures are empirically present in each mind separately (here is where alienation historically originates), and there need be no grounding Absolute or encompassing World-Soul.

Modernism evolves during the time when both of these positions have strong arguments for their superiority. Modernism at first inclines both ways at once, as if art might reconcile what philosophy alone cannot. From Kant onward, as religious and secular thought move apart in the eighteenth century and even threaten to sever all connections in the nineteenth century, art is repeatedly offered as an intermediary bond. It is as if art might both preserve and give evidence for the connection between the physical and the metaphysical, as Schelling, Hegel, and the romantics like Schiller, Novalis, and Friedrich Schlegel had proposed.[5] (Of course, the romantic theorists also favored the philosophy of idealism, which the modernists cannot sustain.) Modernism at first situates itself somewhere between empiricism and idealism: both phenomena and the idea of a noumenal substratum to visible reality become implicated in notions of consciousness, subjectivity, and creativity. Modernism will inhabit this location until around the time of World War I, when idealism is forced to relinquish its claim to a share of the partnership and psychology becomes, or claims to become, fully empirical. The idealist romantic influence falters and yields, even if never totally, to the dominant empiricist influence in all areas of thought.

In modernism, a segment of modernity turns its critical attention upon itself. Modernity's critique concerning the betterment of humankind becomes self-reflexively applied when modernity recognizes its failure to bring about the conditions that had once seemed not only desirable but, once reason took charge, inevitable. The history of modernity had extended through time long enough to be surveyed, to become a "history" to itself—the history of the Enlightenment. This history can then be subject to the particular form of historical determination that causes an era's blindness to its own inadequacies, a blindness that historical analysis both reveals and corrects. Numerous intellectuals, writers, and artists share the supposition that if modernity remains bound to unconstrained capitalism, it will fail;[6] the supposition underlies not only modernism's aesthetic critique but Marx's economic one. (Modernists are not necessarily Marxists, for revolutionary art and revolutionary politics need not—although they frequently do—go hand in hand.) The idea of progress assumes that the past, whatever its virtues, involved an ignorance that we nowadays perceive and hence need not share; we are the future our ancestors envisioned. The Enlightenment presumably erred in privileging rationality at the expense of intuition and feeling—even while serving the worthwhile purpose of defeating religious superstition. (The intensity of faith exhorted by Fenelon and Mme Guyon in the late seventeenth century—living in perpetual devotion and prayer for a God who is pure love—cannot likely entice the world of modernity.) For modernism, as once (naively) for the Enlightenment, historically embedded ignorance might end altogether; history might soon reach its fulfillment.[7] Not that the modernists believed humanity might soon *know* everything; there would certainly be new discoveries, inventions, and artworks. But with the romantic corrective to the Enlightenment set on firmer ground than could be offered by the romantics themselves, hypotheses and insights concerning how civilization could offer maximum fulfillment to its members might be illuminated and confirmed, subsuming unconstrained capitalism and industrialization (even while collaborating with them).

Modernism accuses modernity of a shortsightedness, of which

modernism is the overcoming. Modernity had failed to recognize its limitations, its intellectualized onesidedness; overcoming this deficiency is both to rectify modernity and to accelerate it. Modernism is modernity's deconstruction of itself: some portion of modernity expresses its self-doubt, its apprehension about weaknesses in the very principles once designed permanently to cure doubt. One transient form of this apprehension is that of *la fin de siècle*, the sudden onset of insecurity and even dread (modernity's night terrors) as it becomes apparent that science and economics cannot cure the ontological loneliness following upon God's, or the soul's, obsolescence. Modernism intends, however, not to become a rescuing alternative to modernity, but rather a component of it, its informing structure.

There is a distinction between modernism as a critique of modernity and the eighteenth-century "battle of ancients and moderns"—a long dispute over whether the moderns were the equals of, and in many areas undoubtedly superior to, the classical Greeks and Romans.[8] The earlier battle was not a movement of aesthetic theory or practice but of content. The "moderns" maintained classical forms, whether in literature or architecture, but argued for modern content (knowledge) to fill those forms. That the ancients had wisdom does not confirm the authenticity of their information. From the viewpoint of aesthetic form, the movement was conservative, neoclassic. Underlying the argument for the superiority of modern content was the assumption that certain universal truths exist perpetually—the truths about human nature, for example. While particular areas of knowledge were expanding, moral and ethical knowledge as well as standards of taste presumably remained universal.

The nineteenth-century modernists change and reconstitute aesthetic forms. While there is a standard truth, that truth is (at least to begin with) the romantic spiritual truth, which is not a set of empiricist propositions about facts but statements about the source of meaning. Empiricism must always turn to external sources for meaning—both Descartes and Locke, for example, admit the God of the old theology[9]—and meaning is quite distinct from the facts empiricism generates. In an empiricist society, the fundamental dilemma is that life examined closely (which modern hecticness is meant to prevent) appears meaningless. For the modernists, since empiricism cannot generate meaning and the traditional meanings of theology can no longer command assent, the function of embodying meaning is transferred to art. Like the idealists, the romantics had assumed that art affords access to encompassing truths that have the same source as values. ("'Beauty is truth, truth beauty,'—that is all / Ye know on earth and all ye need to know.") But in modernism the truth is *generated by* art, not simply *contained in* art. An encompassing meaning does not subsume events; rather, events of a certain kind, art in particular, determine meaning. For the modernist, the event called art is always fundamentally a personal event occurring in an individual mind, whereas for the classicist it is equally or more a communal or societal event. The modernist personality (ego, individuality) intensifies in proportion to the amount of responsibility for creating both meaning and its container that is given to the unique individual, whose chief exemplar is the artist.

The modernists can no longer rely upon the classic forms, since these have become allied with empiricist modernity in its social guise—with the academies, money, and power. Even eighteenth-century neoclassicism had, after all, been accepted and financed by royalty: the perpetuation of enduring truths and aesthetic forms simultaneously stabilized both the aristocratic hierarchy and, for the middle class, a universally applicable conservative moral and political code. The modernists seek a new theoretical constitution not resembling classicism—combined with a procedure permanently to revivify (not, however, to replicate) the ideals and aesthetic values of romanticism. Romanticism had, after all, been co-opted by conservative forces, by Victorianism, by German conservatism following the Napoleonic wars, and by the French Third Republic. Each of these forces had transformed romanticism into a reactionary movement:[10] a union of sentimentality, an often orthodox spirituality, and nationalism. (The combination contributes substantially to fascism.) Modernism intends to rejuvenate a society in which capitalism had arrogated classical formalism, had devitalized romanticism by subordinating it to formalist criteria or rules of technique. At the outset the modernists intended to reconfigure modernity so artworks could generate the values of modernity, not vice versa. During the late 1920s, its original mission left incomplete, modernism will issue in its own critical formalism.[11]

Naturalism and Transcendentalism

Two different philosophical predilections yield a continuing polarity in philosophy: naturalism and transcendentalism. The tensions, interactions, and confusions between them have influenced artists, writers, and thinkers since the debate between empiricism and idealism began. Modernist principals are influenced by the same contentions.

Naturalism assumes "nature": that all things living or inert constitute a single system, an aggregation ordered by rules, laws, or principles that are intrinsic to and among individual objects, as qualities and relationships. The rules, laws, or principles are discoverable through special methods of thought (logic) and scrutiny applied to information that is categorized both anatomically (facts) and causally (relations). Naturalism supposes atomism. The world is built of small units, collections of which comprise what we know as common objects: the system is the sum of its parts. The inevitable order of deductive logic can be applied to the inevitable order of phenomena: the truth will never be illogical. Consequently, naturalism promptly leads to determinism. In response, the exclusion of human intellect and will from the domination of natural causation is often proposed; free will is defended, an enduring paradox.[12]

Naturalism is a realism. Knowledge of reality is achieved through the senses, which are formed with the specific capacity to receive and transmit to the mind the basic qualities of objects. Reality *is* the aggregation of natural objects and their interrelations. This leads to a forthright materialism: all qualities of objects have observable and rule-dominated physical consequences. Human reason is trustworthy and is its own supervisor, providing internal monitoring and correction. (The system of democratic "checks and balances" is based on this model of the self-governing mind.) If there is a supernatural cause of reality, a universal intelligence or will, the qualities of this cause cannot be directly known.

For those naturalists who do posit a supernatural cause, the "facts" about ultimate causes are deductions made necessary by a consideration of nature, not vice versa. One reasons from what is known about the natural (its orderliness, its beauty) to what might be properly deduced concerning the supernatural, rather than beginning with a theory of supernatural causality and transferring that meaning to all natural facts. From Descartes forward, the strategy is to begin with a fastidious consideration of the rudimentary data about the mental interior supplied by introspection. One must then order these data into a causal theory of how the mind operates on information presumed to come through the senses.

Once mind is thus understood, the mind must observe itself work in order subsequently to deduce, first, how the information from the senses might or might not correspond to real objects and, second, what might or might not authorize metaphysical propositions, which are neither about objects nor about the mind.[13] The mind has the surprising ability to explore itself as if it were an object. A naturalist concept of God, then, if God is posited, comes from first understanding the qualities and structure of the physical world and of the human mind, and afterward considering (which is neither to intuit nor to have revelation) what might be their necessary antecedents.

In the long run, however, it will not be to God that naturalism will attribute the source of mentality.

Empiricism is a specific philosophical form of naturalism, arising in the seventeenth century and finding its definitive expression at first in Hobbes and Locke.[14] Empiricism provides an epistemological validation of naturalism, in a theory of sensation and perception that accounts both for knowledge and, equally important, for the limitations of knowledge. Its epistemology is mechanistic: operations of the mind function like the internal workings of a machine, as does the universe as a whole. Mentality operates in the head; the description of this inner space develops just when engines and small clocks (watches), devices depending on internal parts, become mathematically comprehensible, manageable, precise, and even self-regulating.

Empiricism makes clear the limitations of knowledge, which are the limitations of empiricism itself. This fact encourages empiricism repeatedly to move into a temporary skepticism, as first with Hume.[15] Skepticism occurs when it is recognized that the products of reason do not confirm but refute common assumptions. Earlier in empiricism, reason and common sense could presumably become equated by assuming that the goal of reasoning is the unmasking of irrational biases and prejudices; but in skepticism, discarding bias and prejudice is where one begins, not where one ends. One does not reason to clear the mind, but first clears the mind in order to reason. Skepticism takes what empiricism has shown to be the limitations of human reason and makes those limitations the foundation of the system, rather than the place into which the system cannot reach. In other words, in skepticism the limitations are the *bases* of knowledge, not the *boundaries* of knowledge. The goal of empiricism is to overcome the skepticism that its method necessarily generates. It aspires to define with certainty not only what mentality can know, but how mentality can know about the material universe, organic and inorganic, and do this without having the doubts about its method turn into doubts about its findings.

Sensation, perception, emotion, and even deduction become themselves physical phenomena. By making them physical, a correspondence between intellect and everything else in the world can be accounted for. Such a materialistic monism (just the opposite of Eastern nonmaterialist monism[16]) affords a solution to the mind-body dilemma. Language can mediate between the mind and the world, acting as the site where the conversion from one to the other takes place. While language had been basically a property of a metaphysical entity (the soul, the Cartesian subject), it now becomes an applied procedure of a physical entity: sounds are assigned to objects and then the sound is conveyed between minds. This transfers the metaphysical problem from consciousness to language. Language is transformed from an event inside the body to a product externalized by the body.

When it passes into France, the political, social, and aesthetic project of empiricism becomes the Enlightenment. Maintaining the application of reason and sound judgment in human affairs generally admired in the polities of England and Holland, the French add an evolutionary optimism—the idea of progress. The largest structures of human society, its institutions, compose history; the history of humanity is, accordingly, fully enclosed within this institutional history. In the Enlightenment, the cultural history of humankind becomes a secular intellectual history (institutions are thoughts), rather than a religious history: religion becomes but one institution among many. History is not the sum total of biography; rather, biography is generated by the encompassing institutional forces of history, which, like other phenomena, are rule governed. Moreover, history is progressive: history moves linearly "forward." Human society has a natural tendency to will its own improvement, and progress will occur if that tendency is permitted to operate. Rationality must be liberated from any subordination to irrationality, from superstition and ingrained but indefensible customs that are usually maintained and defended by those they benefit. Enlightenment empiricism takes the optimistic and paradoxical strategy of finding exclusions for human intellect and will from materialistic causality. The goal of society is to maximize free will within the ethical boundaries that universal reason makes apparent.[17]

Transcendentalism is the alternative to naturalism. As a specific response to empiricism in the eighteenth century, it takes the form of

Kantian transcendental logic and, subsequently, philosophical ideal-ism. Transcendentalism presumes a realm of immaterial supersensory reality that grounds the reality known by the senses; and only through knowledge of the existence of the former does one gain a full under-standing of the latter. While the existence of this transcendent realm can be deduced logically, the deduction is not equivalent to a confir-mation. To achieve confirmation requires special intuitive modes of knowing, modes inadmissible in naturalism. These additional meth-ods of knowing are more than supplementary; once identified, they are declared to provide the principal access to the most important knowledge, not only about the transcendent realm but also about the meaning and purpose of the physical world. Naturalism feels no obli-gation to provide such meaning and purpose for the universe as a whole, or even to admit of their existence. But such meaning and purpose are always components of transcendentalism.

In Judeo-Christian theology since about the fifth century, a theolog-ical transcendentalism had been consolidated by an alloy of Greek neo-Platonism with Old and New Testament theology stabilized by Augus-tine of Hippo. In neither testament is any transcendence performed by subjectivity: communion with God does not require transcendence when God inhabits the world or can visit it or act upon it or speak to the creatures inhabiting it. The later theological transcendence, howev-er, presumes a special faculty of communion distinct from any of the senses. The senses are no longer sufficient for such communion, as they once had been (God spoke directly to Moses), although the senses may sometimes be employed in a subordinate way by that special faculty (seeing visions, hearing voices). There is a realm that transcends the earth and that is ontologically unlike earth, without matter or time, for example; nevertheless the realms of heaven and earth are connected in a comprehensive system of logic and belief, including revelational evi-dence and faith. Both realms are integrated insofar as one is the cause and origin of the other, but the human capacity for thought and for feel-ing is presumed to be placed between the two realms, partaking in both and, with the addition of the special faculty of transcendence, serving as the link between them. In addition, mediation between the two realms is provided by God through periodic personal intervention or through special earthly delegates.

In theological transcendentalism—and obviously before an empiri-cist physics—all motions of matter depend upon the constant sustaining presence and persistence of God's will constantly applied, without which everything would stop.[18] Through its scientific method, empiricism eventually proposes that the motions of matter ("nature" as a whole) can be accounted for by forces internal to the system of matter; this irrevocably separates nature, as an operating system, from the realm of God. Human mentality is subsequently incorporated into nature, as minds become discrete entities with autonomous internal mechanisms. Because human intellect depends on the senses for all information (the basic premise of empiricism), that intellect is limited. Traditional theology can no longer offer, even in principle, verifiable knowledge based on evidence.

The limitations empiricism places on human knowledge call forth the need for a *philosophical* transcendence. A new advancement of logic must ground, yet supersede, the earlier *theological* transcendence whose philosophical underpinnings (scholasticism) had been weakening since the Reformation moved westward in Europe. Because the limits of mind imposed by empiricism are also imposed on the mind's ability to know itself, one becomes trapped inside mentality, which provokes skepticism. Empiricism assumes that the structure of knowledge corresponds to the structure of the world, although it cannot prove this. (Ultimately all one can think about are ideas in the mind.) The tactic of philosophical transcendence, originally set forth in Kant's writings, is to overcome the empiricist limitation by allowing subjectivity to transcend its self-knowledge, arguing that subjectivity itself can understand the necessary conditions for the existence of its knowing. These conditions are then used to explain the limitations—in effect, to overcome them by accounting for them, by discovering the principles that necessitate them in the first place.

This transcendence is atemporal: time is inherent in the process of perception, only contingently real. Although these conditions are the conditions for a historical being, they are not themselves part of history. The relationship of subject to object is based not on a correspondence but on a transformation. While a world external to the mind exists, the structures of human knowledge about that world are innate structures of mentality imposed upon what the senses receive. The empiricist errs by assuming that all information comes through sensation. The idea of infinity occurs to us; yet infinity cannot be a perception or a simple totalizing of perceptions. Structures of mentality (Kant's categories) are the conditions for the world appearing to us; the world cannot be known unless knowledge has formal qualities, which (for Kant) mentality must supply or else nothing could be known. Yet since the *conditions* for knowledge cannot be made the *object* of knowledge, deriving their existence in the mind requires a "transcendental" deduction, which Kant determines to provide.[19]

What is transcended in the Kantian philosophy is not, at first, the secular material world of mortality and transience transcended by religion and theology, but the limitations on thought imposed by empiricism. Yet eventually Kant employs this strategy to introduce ideas that, he claims, pure reason is inevitably led toward by the necessities of its own operations. Nothing can be proven about the soul, God, or the world as a unified whole, since they are ideas outside the range of the understanding. To attempt proofs leads only to paradoxes, antinomies. Nevertheless, these attractive ideas may be true and certainly are not preposterous, and Kant finds adequate reasons for consenting to them. Those who view Kant as culminating the exercise of reason in the Enlightenment, because he refutes the traditional proofs of God's existence, are mistaken. The transcendental logic is a reaction against the Enlightenment, assuming the Enlightenment's procedures only to undermine its directions by creating internal faculties and capabilities to substitute for what was once unabashed revelation. By placing God beyond any "proofs," Kant is less reason-able than either the rationalists or the earlier scholastics. Still later, Kant argues that moral consciousness, "practical" reason, also yields assumptions (called postulates) necessary to ground moral action. The postulates are human freedom, immortality, and God. Even if the truth of these postulates is, like the ideas of pure reason, undemonstrable to the understanding, Kant argues for a commitment to them.[20]

The form of transcendentalism that arises in the eighteenth century as a response to the successes of empiricism is, then, an epistemological transcendence. Subjectivity is redefined so that what was once the knowledge incorporated in a theological transcendentalism becomes a natural, inherent, and necessary tendency and capability of human mentality. The Platonic realm of Ideas had been moved inside the mind of God by Christianity. Because scientific empiricism threatens to place God at a very remote distance from the earth, the realm of Ideas is transferred entirely into the mind of humanity by Kant and a subsequent idealism. This retains the connection between two ontologically dissimilar realms. The procedure for transcendence is not an achievement of a regimen (ritual) or revelation or communion or acceptance of belief through authority; rather, it is the exercise of a natural faculty. That this faculty is named "reason" (*Vernunft*), which is then made to subsume "understanding" (*Verstand:* empiricist knowledge, science in particular), is a strategic co-optation and inversion of the Enlightenment vocabulary; what Enlightenment "reason" was supposed to name ends up being subsumed to Kant's "Reason," which to the empiricists would certainly not be a category of "reason." This natural faculty ostensibly requires no external supernatural authorization. The logic of transcendence is to be completed *within* its own system of reasoning—although one can reach a knowledge of, or at the very least the supposition of, the supernatural (the metaphysical) *through* that system of reasoning. Both to accept the Newtonian celestial mechanics and to reduce its stature by subsuming it to subjectivity permits God, or the evidence for God, to be removed from the former and placed in the latter.

In this way philosophical transcendentalism and the old theological transcendentalism, conceptually quite distinct, are bonded. Kant attempts to complete the interiorization of revelation that Protestantism begins, but without yielding to the authority of the fundamental revelatory biblical text. As the troublesome shared use of the term *transcend* indicates, a logical strategy is linked to a potential of consciousness that had traditionally surpassed logic, as if the shifting of logical levels can now correspond to the shifting of ontological realms. No need for this philosophical transcendence arose until the strength of empiricism erected an epistemological barrier between two realms whose theological connection was once quite obvious and comprehensible. By undermining theological transcendence, empiricism provided what it was that philosophical transcendentalism, ultimately a conservative act of recuperation, aspired to transcend. The very existence of subjectivity is used to authorize the transcendental conditions for the possibility of subjectivity.

Moreover, the knowledge of the conditions for subjectivity is presumed to transcend their operation, as if self-consciousness could know the conditions for its own existence. Like the later psychoanalysts, Kant believes that the conditions hidden behind manifestation (the categories of cognition for Kant, the unconscious for Freud) can be disclosed, even if subjectivity has been constructed on the logical necessity of their hiddenness. (Kant does this by transcendence;

Freud, by descendence.) While the underlying substructure or substratum of existence may be fundamentally unknowable, the observed order of the perceived world is presumed to reflect an underlying ontological order. The self (subjectivity individuated) and the known exterior world are posited simultaneously, and each is one condition for the other.

Idealism and Romanticism

In the philosophical idealism that develops after Kant, Kant's things-in-themselves (existence as it is, distinct from the categories of thought in which it is known) becomes an infeasible hypothesis. Since a representation in consciousness is what makes a thing a "thing," an object, what could a "thing" be in itself? Evolving through Fichte, Schelling, and Hegel, idealism presumes that the world known as an object to humans originates as an act of, an emanation from, or a self-imposed resistance to an ontologically grounding universal reified thought, mind, ego, world-soul, spirit, the Absolute, Reason, or God, from which each individual mentality arises. The world is produced by thought, albeit a universalized thought. (Idealism is not a solipsism.) Although Kant claimed to demonstrate the conditions for and the structures of mentality, the ultimate causes of mentality could not be demonstrated, even if they might be illuminated. Even the notions of freedom or God are suppositions, not conclusive deductions, arising out of the predilections of rationality inherent in the logical processes of reason itself—specifically, its need for encompassing coherence. The idealists assume that the material world and human mentality are not only the manifestation of the qualities or forces that cause them but also formal correlates of these qualities and forces. The empiricist qualifications placed on human knowledge are overcome by assuming that the conceptual structure both of the material world and of the world-soul or Absolute that transcends it correspond, either positively (in which case the material world incarnates the Absolute) or negatively (in which case the spirit does its work by overcoming the inert resistance of the material world, which it has, however, itself produced).[21] In idealism, knowledge enters an area restricted by both empiricism and Kant. Eventually Hegel attempts to absorb empiricism into idealism by treating certain concepts, specifically "Freedom," as the empiricist treats physical laws and forces. Reified concepts are given a physical although somehow not fully material reality. Since these reified concepts can interact or conflict, they yield, through a direct causation, the history and transformations of material reality, including human life.[22]

The idealists transcend the Kantian transcendence by positing that the fundamental ontological causation can be known, since the human mind is both inside it and a component of it. The knowledge held by the aggregate of human minds is the knowledge that absolute reason has of itself, because absolute reason evolves to know itself through the agency of human minds. Kant correctly asserted that the notion of God or the soul (the unified, enduring entity in which self-consciousness is a property) cannot be demonstrated directly through the empirical understanding; but while Kant was not dissatisfied by this dilemma (because God and humankind were totally distinct), the idealists posit a natural mode of immediate knowledge about the metaphysical absolute. That mode, usually called "intuition," is made possible by the fact that human mentality is encompassed by the universal mentality.

Art becomes affiliated with these intuitional modes of knowing. Even for Kant, art provided not knowledge but a suggestion—a pointing toward, rather than at—the numinous substratum of the world. Kant's various "ideas" and "postulates" are actually quite close to the idealist's intuitions (although presumably Kant would deny this). Schelling and Hegel give art even more substantial powers. As the physical world of objects derives from the encompassing universal thought or reason, so correspondingly do artworks (also objects) derive from individual mentality. Art is an exercise and a proof of intuitional knowledge and of its object and, consequently, of the idealist's general suppositions. Art serves to splice the severance between physics and metaphysics opened by empiricism: art is placed, like a coupling, between them. Furthermore, as revelation has been interiorized, so also is the source of artistic inspiration. Once an external "gift," in the Renaissance and earlier, Plato's *daemon* now becomes a faculty of the psyche.[23]

Idealism bears with it the older theological transcendentalism. The physical world, including humanity, is presumed to result from qualities, potentials, and relationships internal to an order of reality that is not itself physical or material, yet that can cause these. The use of transcendentalism as an epistemological strategy by which mentality subsumes itself to (by elevating itself above) its own method is equated with an ontological transaction. To know reality is to understand the relationship of materiality to its cause. The cause is "higher" than and logically prior to materiality, which is a collection of transient, momentary phenomena. The cause is inseparable from purpose, from telos. Any mechanical or organic orderliness in nature results from an order imparted to nature, because there is a source of order, neither mechanical nor organic, that is intelligent.

Although idealism and traditional Western religion may be compatible, certain differences between them are striking, especially because in Judeo-Christianity the individual human and God are quite distinct. In traditional religious thought, the human spirit can commune with the source of creation, either through certain immediate experiences—meditation, insight, mysticism, and transcendence (this latter term names both what is done and what is achieved), and perhaps even art[24]—or through being personally or communally selected as a recipient of revelation. The former is an interiorization of transcendence and usually founds religious practices; the latter is an exteriorization of transcendence and usually founds religious institutions. The more the source of order is conceived of as undefinable, unknowable, or unapproachable, the more spiritual attainment becomes an awareness of the source that is not equivalent to a knowledge of it (as in mysticism). Such understanding and awareness is, accordingly, not the justification for establishing a regimented discipline but the anticipated outcome of discipline, its goal. Regimen and discipline authenticate knowledge. Alternatively, the more precisely God is understood as bearing traits corresponding to those that humans have or ought to have (goodness, justice, inventiveness), the more is a God defined who requires specific forms of institutional devotion and obedience. Knowledge authenticates regimen and discipline.

The aesthetics of idealism are somewhat transformed and intensified as idealism and romanticism interact. Theological transcendence and epistemological transcendence are fused in a theory of artistic creativity, which then becomes simultaneously superior knowing, superior being, and transcendent contact with the beyond.[25] For writers and artists, romanticism unites the aesthetics issuing from idealism and notions derived from a quite traditional theological transcendence. God can appear very close or very far away to the romantics, who feel, at times, completely comfortable in the universe, yet at oth-

er times isolated (not alone, but shunned).[26] In romanticism, to be a
poet, artist, or musician is to possess a refined intuitional capacity that
leads to idealist knowledge of the union of the world-soul or spirit
with the individual soul.[27] But at the same time, the artist is also described as a recipient of revelation, in the traditional religious and pro-
phetic sense. The romantic reconciliation between the idealist and the
theological worldviews is accomplished by reintroducing an objective
natural world, a world that is neither the inert material of the empiricist nor the idealist's product of a universalized thought. In a world
that is simultaneously spiritual yet materially external to thought,
"nature" is redefined, reconceptualized. The specific approach is the
revitalization of Spinoza's philosophy as a pantheism.

Romanticism engenders a political, social, and aesthetic project. The
mind studies the operations of its own mentality as if every act of subjectivity is intrinsically contained within those operations, but not as
if mentality as a whole can ever be an empirical object for itself. The
mind knows itself intuitionally. The goal of romanticism is to ground
human knowledge not on the quantity of experience and information
(the basis of empiricist induction) but on its quality, which can only
be assessed through the involvement and confirmation of the intuitive emotions. The intensity of emotion then becomes a new quantitative criterion to replace the empiricist's aggregation of experience.

Intuitive emotions are not equivalent to physical desires, which are
physically determined and are, consequently, simple empiricist causes. *Passion* (deriving from *passive*) enlarges its meaning and comes to
denote something intermediary between emotion and desire, connecting intuition to desire, physicalizing the former and spiritualizing the
latter. In empiricism, the world can be understood, although in itself
it has no meaning. (Meaning is an attribution derived from human
needs—empiricist ethics is a "humanism.") In romanticism, however,
the world carries transcendental meaning as the necessary content of
subjectivity, a meaning internal to subjectivity yet externally grounded (whether in a personal God, an impersonal God, or nature). This
insistence upon transcendental *meaning*—which evolves in idealism
after Kant, who sought transcendental *knowledge*—characterizes the
romantic response to empiricism.

Generating a theory that might provide common ground for idealism, romanticism, and empiricism motivates much nineteenth-century thought. By the early twentieth century, empiricism confidently

dismisses all the others, declaring its adequacy to develop an ethics on its own. (Such an ethics is usually based on a biological theory of evolutionary altruism.) But in the nineteenth century, the Hegelian system often seemed a plausible reconciliation of scientific determinism and free will. In Hegel, freedom is reified as a metaphysical force. Consequently, world advancement can be built into the world system from its origins. Human freedoms need not be gained at the expense of the spiritual (so the Enlightenment had also argued), quite unlike the customary situation for the ego in Judeo-Christianity. Once, freedom was prodigality and obedience was piety; now, on the contrary, freedom is the fulfillment of the spirit. Freedom and obedience are amalgamated, since the institutions that demand allegiance—the state in particular (for Hobbes as for Hegel, since empiricists and idealists both demand political loyalty)—are now purported to be the very structures that are evolving to maximize freedom.[28] Idealism's Golden Age of the spirit can then be placed in the future, just where the empiricist idea of progress had also envisioned it, rather than in the past, where the Greeks had placed it. Over time, the promise of the future Golden Age displaces both the achievement in Deuteronomy of the land of Israel (since the Holy Land—and how explain this?—was within the Ottoman Empire) and the Christian relinquishing of secular domination in the New Testament (the rendering unto Caesar) compensated for by acquiring the preferable Kingdom of Heaven. In the union of Hegelianism and the idea of progress, the future holds freedom instead of, while also as a form of, salvation.

Romanticism bequeaths to modernism its theory of the artist's special status and of the unique artistic derivation of truths about the world. The *image*, a term derived from Hobbes to indicate a purely mechanical product of perception actually inferior to immediate sensation, is in romanticism elevated to metaphor, something indubitably superior to sensory functioning. Modernism later issues from the resurgence, within the strongholds of empiricism, of the romantic transcendental impulse. Empiricism, nevertheless, will prevail, even if it will not entirely subdue this impulse. Although modernism restores romanticism, it must function inside the empiricism that discomforts and will eventually reintegrate modernism.

Unlike the idealists and the romantics, the modernists require that their aesthetics be compatible (or at least not incongruous) with the empiricism from within which modernism emerges. Modifications of

Hegelian philosophy initially provided the modernists with what seemed a semiscientific metaphysics, an often unobjectionable idealism even in an empiricist stronghold like England (in F. H. Bradley, for example).[29] At the end of the nineteenth century, however—during the years when Bertrand Russell's generation reached maturity—the positivists reject the Hegelian mediation between empiricism and idealism.[30] The writings of Henri Bergson also become instrumental in positioning modernism both as a critique of modernity and as an example of it. Bergson encourages the retention of an intuitive subjectivity that classical empiricist epistemology cannot account for, but which is compatible with aesthetic intuition (compare Benedetto Croce). Metaphor is an example of direct intuition.[31] But Bergson, an empiricist by temperament as Hegel a century earlier was not, further offers a quasi-metaphysical quality or force—the *élan vital* of vitalism[32]—that seems to allow the material world and the nonmaterial yet nevertheless physical world to correspond in an acceptably scientific way. By Bergson's time, advanced theories of the electromagnetic field offer a more sophisticated model than Hegel could have used for the force, called freedom, that he had reified.[33]

Admittedly, modernism becomes a variety of aesthetic practices rather than a coherent shared philosophical system. Nevertheless, modernism can be understood as a practice depending for legitimation on the romantic aesthetic and on the empiricist environment. It would be appropriate to call modernism, even if as an oxymoronic aphorism, a *transcendental realism*, at least when it began. Modernism detaches or uncouples romanticism from its source in idealism and attaches it to a realism that is at least not incompatible with the empiricist environment in which modernism must operate. While, for the romantic, intuition yields access to a higher truth that has a Platonic form, the modernist can eventually sustain no intuited truth higher than psychological truth, *our* truth. Even prior to modernism, the predisposition toward a philosophical "scientific" realism, in France especially, had provoked an escape from traditional classicism. Impressionism demanded scientific exactitude in the study of light, which was claimed to be a new and immediate interaction with the world. Like so many other credos in the history of art, impressionism claims there will be a greater "truth to nature," freed from the past prejudices that had stood between the pure exercise of vision and the object of vision. For similar reasons, the literary realism called naturalism emerged in literature.

For modernism, this freedom from bias is claimed as a spiritual or a psychological act not requiring a representational mimetic act, whereas for romanticism the two could be, even ought to be, the same. Freedom from mimesis separates modernism both from impressionism and naturalism, both of which demanded an exactitude of representation. Meaning is expressed, not reported. The results in visual modernism are, first, a burgeoning of exquisite color not only distinct from linear confines but from the surface of objects, and second, a juxtaposition of shapes defined by their formal properties without regard to their mimetic ones. (Various movements in painting use either one or both of these, for formal relations need not—as they do not in sculpture—require color relations, or vice versa.) In literature, there emerges a sensory and tactile metaphor. In both fields, the psychic mechanisms by which the artwork was produced erupts in and is disclosed by the work. A theory of psychology—and a variety of them become available as modernism evolves—usually also verifies for the modernist a convenient linkage between empiricism and modernism. Cubism, expressionism, and surrealism are each accompanied by a rudimentary epistemology, a cognition theory. (Writers, for example, experiment with automatic semiconscious writing.[34]) Just as the impressionists had relied on the optical theories of Chevreul,[35] so do the modernists eventually absorb the ideas of William James, Sigmund Freud, the Gestaltists, and even the behaviorists to validate various techniques like the fictional stream of consciousness and visual abstraction, or certain ideas like those concerning the function of poetic image and metaphor, or the link between dream, psychic pathology, and art, or the relation of the personality of the artist to the faculties of creativity.

Modernism

Modernism is, then, the aesthetics of a transcendental realism—although this apothegmatic term binds irreconcilables. Here is the source of the central tenet of the modernist theory of poetry and art: the union of irreconcilables is a principle aesthetic goal.

This aesthetic is promulgated by artists for whom romanticism has already contributed the materials for their self-image. Modernism incorporates notions of spirit, genius, self-expression, and inspiration as instruments of world change. But modernism will eventually produce, in a more comfortably empiricist guise, critical formalism. The transition during which modernism yields its romanticism and adopts a critical formalism is the most important change that occurs in the history of modernism. In fact, the later formalism is frequently used nowadays to definitively classify modernism. Even early in modernism, some artists call their works "experiments" or "researches"; later, notions of the impersonality of art emerge. Art becomes the record of one's psychological processes rather than, as in romanticism, the expression of a personality that precedes the experiencing of those processes. Formalism ultimately comes to be the most essential feature of the movement called modernism, because modernism consistently retreats from the founding romanticism that it must ultimately find untenable. When the retreat is completed, when romanticism, after nearly two hundred years, becomes a concluded segment of past history (a long chapter in the textbook), postmodernism begins.

The combination of transcendence, philosophical realism, and romanticism (in the symbolist movement, for example) originally establishes modernism's aesthetic approaches and solutions.[36] This is "early" modernism, for which romanticism is still the most obvious artistic tendency. But idealism is put on a philosophical defensive from which it cannot recover, mainly for political reasons. The most significant political factor is quite apparent: the Germans lose a war. (For Hegel, the German state should have proved the most conspicuous manifestation of the evolving Absolute.) After World War I, the military, political, and economic domination by countries where empiricism flourishes is accompanied by a turn to the high modernist literature of the twenties, prevailed over by those who write in English, to the logical positivism that comes to be headquartered in England, and to the Bauhaus of the Weimar Republic—each based on the empiricist principle that immediate sensory stimulation (sensation) is the only sure foundation of knowledge.

The subordination of the idealism inherent in modernism's aesthetic romanticism enervates idealism. Economic conditions also contribute: the stupendous economic inflation in postwar Germany undermines the aggrandized self-confidence that idealism requires. Idealism is no longer a suitably formidable adversary of a prospering empiricist modernity; it is reduced to an internal discontent. Thereafter, romanticism will always be summoned forth in discomforting times, when modernism periodically recognizes the potential failure of its own aspirations to reorient the values of contemporary life.

By the end of the nineteenth century, modernism has emerged to impede or prevent modernity from proceeding along the path dictated solely by empiricist principles. The consequences of these principles will appear to be the bleak economic dominance of urbanized, industrialized capitalism. Science and technology had once promised better. As for science, the modernists are quite willing to let empiricism, as a cognitive method, have it completely; modernism is a movement that concerns itself with defining value, not with facts. The scientist would provide the technology to change the world; the artists and writers would (as the Futurists in particular argue) rejuvenate the spirit or psyche that would inhabit that world. (Contrast this with Saint-Simon, who had granted the artist and writer equal moral leadership with the scientist.) The modernists claim a separate territory, the aesthetic-emotional leadership necessary to give value to science. The scientist can dominate the method, if only the artist and the writer might dominate the context; for the scientific project had not been misconceived, but misemployed.

Modernism will not retard or halt the economic advance of capitalist modernity. The vision of artists will not prevail; instead, it will increasingly become either isolated inside the practice of art or transformed into elements of other industries, like entertainment or fashion. Modernist art forms will decorate all of contemporary life by the midtwentieth century, but the original modernist aspiration for the arts fails. Modernism may even be said to have had the opposite effect of that intended: rather than liberating people from the economy, it helped liberate them only to participate more fully in the economy. The modernist vision will become increasingly sheltered, either within the haven of a separate art world or as part of a university curriculum, often appealing most to those who are discontent with the triumph of modernity through its technology and its international economics. The modernist protests that the cost of economic prosperity has been the homogenization of humanity. But artists alone are inadequate to counteract all this, not because they lack genius but because they lack an audience of sufficient magnitude and influence. If there had been such an audience (if romanticism had succeeded), they would not have needed to convince it. Modernism has never created an audience of the requisite magnitude and power, aside from the audience that uses modernism only to adorn its surroundings.

Eventually the proponents of modernism will be forced to understand that, despite their reluctance and resistance, art has been moved inside the category of entertainment, which is itself a component of commercial business. Coming to understand this repositioning of art (a repositioning incompatible with modernism's original assumptions, whether these assumptions were tenable or not) yields a disillusionment, sometimes disabling and certainly contributing to the dwindling of the vestiges of romanticism. In capitalism, pleasure is a product originating in what is itself classified not as pleasure but as work: the work of making the object that causes the pleasure that then is to serve as a recreation, as an escape from work. Creating pleasure as a product is but one form of the work from which the product is to offer release. In capitalism, the use of the product negates the production of the product: pleasure as a product is an emotional negation and denial of its pleasureless origin in rational work. This is exactly the opposite of what is often proposed as the origin of art by the romantics, for whom the source of art and the source of commerce were set in opposition.

As the twentieth century progresses, conflicts escape any boundaries that art or reason can provide for them. By the seventies, the ability of art to contain, include, or advance either the life of reason or the opposition to reason is under suspicion. The subject matter of art becomes a critique of its own premises, a challenge to the legitimation of the endeavor: every work is, at some self-reflexive level, its own worst critic. The recognition that there is no avoiding the failure of modernism's assault on modernity initiates postmodernism, an animated disillusionment with modernism (not with modernity) accompanied by an upsurge of ironic creativity, ironic because it creates artifacts that bear no promises.[37] Of course, the social hope for continued economic prosperity lingers: even artists are now entrepreneurs. So does the hope for equality under the law. What will be the nature of the human recipients who will enjoy these things? This question does not disappear. But it will no longer be assumed, except by a minority even less substantial than before, that artists have the answer.

Modern Art and Literature: Early Phases

2

Modernism and Modern Life

Before discussing the phases of modernism, it is important to make a distinction between the aesthetics of modernism and the analysis of modern life. Ibsen, Balzac, Dostoevski, Zola, Flaubert, George Eliot, Dickens, Meredith, Henry James, Galsworthy—each addresses issues pertinent to modern life, invoking the dilemmas of moral decision-making in an era that provides no assured principles on which to base those decisions. In that era such decision replaces custom, personal biography replaces lineage, individual action is in disharmony with community ethics (and often must be so to be meaningful). The psyche senses its dislocation from the haven it cannot quite identify or believe in. The longing for commitment arises in the face of its implausibility. The range of possibility increases for the average person in cosmopolitan life, freed from attachments to the agricultural soil; cities offer the best of pleasures—but only at the cost of the worst of vices.

Earlier literature had avoided the unattractive and even repugnant side of life except perhaps as a subject for satire or moral condemnation, whereas writers who analyze modern life often show how humans, as a species, may be irremediably greedy, immoral, selfish, vain, stupid, perverse, corrupt, and sexually driven, despite the Enlightenment. (Painters and photographers, too, peer into the tavern and the brothel; nudity and beauty no longer coincide.) The novel and drama particularly lend themselves to disclosing modern life, portraying characters meant to resemble those who readers and their acquaintances imagine under certain circumstances they themselves might be.

The literary experience presents possibilities for behavior, not only the vicarious experiencing of behaviors outside the reader's expectations.

But such analyses are not all equivalent to modernism. To qualify as modernism, the consideration of aesthetic form must take precedence over content. Not that form is simply necessary to display content, or that some forms are better suited to certain contents than others, for these have always been the case. Rather, form and content must be understood to be indistinguishable. Worldview is not simply placed inside form; worldview is equivalent to form. Not only is the content of the work the content of the psyche, but the form of the work is also the form of the psyche. Creativity at its best requires formal innovation.

Practical concerns about the audience aside, all external rules for composition theoretically disappear. Where once the most admirable art demonstrated a mastery of rules, it now demonstrates the creation of rules. While Dostoevski, Dickens, and Zola are certainly "modern," it is Ibsen, Flaubert, James, and Conrad whose work contributes to (or, in the case of the latter two, is part of) modernism.[1] The modernist must consciously invent the rules of personal discourse, not as a renovation of style (like Dante's triplets or Milton's blank verse) but as a simultaneous innovation of insight. One of the lessons learned from Baudelaire is that what one has to say is precisely how one must say it, both as an inner compulsion and as a labor of craft.

One follows self-generated rules because one's volition itself has the form of those rules. The same strategy had long been applied to ethics as a general theory both of "the conscience" and of capitalist self-reliance, although both had acknowledged limits, the former set by the Bible and the latter set by the law of contracts. The transfer of the rules of art from external criteria applied to genre into the creative imagination of the artist is, like the Protestant ethics of conscience, part of the general interiorizing of law. In Kant it appears as the transferring of revelation to a mental faculty. Physics, similarly, had transferred natural law from the external compulsions of the deity into matter itself.

New truths cannot be conveyed in the old forms. For modernism, both meaning and form are unprecedented and unorthodox, simultaneously and inseparably. Where meaning and form are inseparable but not unorthodox, one has politics or religion, not art. Of course, the genres and the relevant techniques remain: there are still novels, plays, and poems, and the customary tricks of those trades. The audience for literature, especially for fiction, demands the preservation of certain conventions for holding the reader's attention over a number of hours, conventions unnecessary in painting, in poetry, or for the most part in music.

Form has a wider import in modernism than the notion of genre. Genre is an inherited codification of form, the rules of a subdiscipline within which skills are refined. But form is also an emanation of the psyche, to which it corresponds. Form is more than the boundaries of practice; form is the contour of genius. The borders between traditional genres erode. Not only is form situated between the artist and the world. Indeed, form is the means by which the artist exists in the world and the world exists in the artist.

By the end of the nineteenth century, received truths had been challenged, threatened, and often discarded in geology, biology, cosmology, psychology, physics, and even, with the strengthening of socialism (the word had come into general usage around 1830), political theory. The old theology, which had for so long leaned upon the gradually discredited premises of these disciplines before their modernization, could hardly reconfigure its alliances quickly enough to maintain equilibrium. Besides, the educated and economically prosperous class was not seeking that kind of equilibrium. No knowledge was secure from the rapid modification of knowledge: any fact might have resulted from a causal process previously unimagined. Like the universe itself, knowledge was mostly emptiness. Artists and writers are not the only ones to recognize this, although one strategy available to them is to make the emptiness itself a form of knowledge: nothingness—and the entire medley of anxieties it generates—becomes an aesthetic perception. Filled by God for the pious and by the field of gravity for the scientist, this nothingness is now filled by art.

The Phases of Modernism

Visual artists and writers undergo a sequence of four phases, the course of which is "modernism." The description of these phases is offered here not as a history of modernism but as a hypothetical construct that can qualify to stimulate, perhaps to generate, a history of modernism. The phases are conceptual or logical sequences; sometimes they fit well with a chronological narrative, sometimes not.

While sequences occur in the various arts, the dates, places, and rates of change are different, and not always of the same explicatory value. Between the 1880s and the 1970s, possibilities accumulate, any of which might be exercised.

Modernism is more an aggregative self-reflection than an order. Although the sequence of phases is narrated here as a progression of ideas and attitudes, no artist or writer is obliged to any particular set of these because of the year in which a work is produced. Transitions occur so rapidly in modern history that the lives of major figures (Picasso, Stravinsky, Pound, and Matisse, for example) often span many generations of change. Only in the past twenty years or so, as the very last of those famous modernists born in the nineteenth century have died, has modernism become self-conscious of the necessity for its own conclusive definition. An almost general homogeneity of mood has emerged, shared by artists and critics even when they dispute the details.

Modernism's predecessors served modernism by defining the modern condition—that best of worlds, that worst of worlds—and by indicating what sensibilities the artist and writer might cultivate in response to it. There is, first, the maintenance of the *transcendental ideal*, the continued reliance on the numinous substratum of ordinary reality that the urban world itself eagerly relinquishes in favor of city life. There is, second, the maintenance of an *ethical ideal*, a personal commitment, exercised through an aesthetic, in a society whose shared ethical bonds are rapidly being replaced by political and economic structures that function not as a universal ethics, theologically justified, but as utilitarian law making. And there is, third, the *aesthetic ideal*, the insistence on the autonomy of art, as a self-sustaining realm fully satisfying the artist, the world at large being now incapable of so doing. Transformations of each of these three approaches occur within early, mid-, and high modernism. Late modernism, a fourth phase, summarizes, competes with, reduplicates, parodies, and also exhausts the earlier phases, in a flourishing of novelty and ingenuity following World War II, an exuberantly prosperous time, especially in the United States.

The modern condition results from placing Enlightenment optimism in doubt or jeopardy, although no other vision or faith can replace it. All the social enthusiasms and optimisms remain, but without the unchallengeable security. Social insecurity is at first converted into personal challenges to self-reliance, so that dilemmas can be seen as personal, without calling into question the possibility of a rational foundation for society. There is no retreat for the individual the Enlightenment has generated; that modern purposeful individual takes the idea of social progress as if it might also be a personal psychological condition and then assumes that the meaning of one's life is a personal destiny. Fiction usually portrays the modern condition, and poetry illustrates what sensibilities are available to respond to it. The novel of contemporary realism provides the strongest confirmation of the existence of the world that the poets (at least those who influence modernism) often lament or denounce.[2]

Early Modernism

The early modernists received from their predecessors the already elaborated disjunction between the real and the ideal, between the world that was to have emerged from the Enlightenment and the world that actually emerged. One might retain optimism, even if bounded by caution. Those less enthusiastic might replace optimism with cynicism, condescension, or humor, combined with a purportedly objective analysis, since the claim of objectivity in literature always includes the claim of distance and even superiority. Each of these was an option for Victorian novelists and poets. Early modernism would add the possibility of outright desperation, although such desperation is itself regarded as a victory over its cause. Art and literature might be placed either alongside social progress or in opposition to it or as a retreat from it. Taking a position, having a platform, in regard to "modern life" as a whole is one of the defining characteristics of modern life.

In painting, the predecessor of and prelude to modernism is impressionism. Beginning in the late 1860s, Renoir and Monet work together at La Grenouillère, exploiting the colors of shadows and transient light, the effect of adjacent colors, and the use of patches of primary color mixed by the eye. The first impressionist exhibition in 1874 met with substantial ridicule, which later provides modernism with its primary instruction—to deploy art as adversarial and unorthodox. The "true" must be issued as a challenge, rather than a confirmation. The impressionists themselves had learned this lesson from Degas and from the reception of Manet's exhibition in 1863, the year when the

Salon des Refusés was established.[3] Manet had as his precursor Courbet, who in 1850 exposed to the public the "realism" that made him first notorious and afterward famous. Based not on standardized conventions but on direct and immediate sensory perception, art would be an alternative to commonplace prejudices and customary aesthetic values. Realism in art (which impressionism claimed to be) had formerly been based on a naturalism of body and shape, the visual perception of linear clarity, volume, solidity, and distance, the *primary* qualities also identified by science: qualities presumed to be fully real properties of the independent object, perception aside. Unambiguous clarity of line had been defended from Pliny in the first century through Kant, who argued around 1790 that drawing alone was sufficient to represent the object, color being superfluous.[4] Impressionism, however, is a realism of light and color. (One recalls the contention between the followers of Poussin and the followers of Rubens, one arguing for the predominance of line, the other for color.) In traditional physics, color is one of the *secondary* qualities, resulting (like smell, temperature, and sound) from the interaction of sensory mechanisms and the real properties of the objects that cause these qualities to occur for the senses but are themselves quite unlike these qualities. Secondary qualities have no independent reality outside the perceiving organism.[5] Impressionism shifts what is "real" in perception, at least for art, from the qualities of the object to the qualities equally determined by the observer. Modernism would not be possible without this transference.

In early modernism, the transcendental ideal—inherited from romanticism—can still be considered an alternative to the mundane, and the spiritual may still envelop the secular. To early modernism can be assigned those writers for whom the transcendent has not yet vanished: the symbolists (Verlaine, Mallarmé, Laforgue, and Jean Moreas's *Symbolist Manifesto* of 1886; Arthur Symons's book on symbolism caught the attention of English poets[6]), Hardy, Yeats, Frost, Lawrence, William Carlos Williams, and, let us grant, T. S. Eliot. In painting, there is Gauguin, Redon, Puvis de Chavannes (and perhaps the English pre-Raphaelites should be credited with influencing symbolism in France[7]), also Munch, Kandinsky, Klee, and Mondrian. For these, as for Brancusi, the spiritual permeates the world even when, as Kierkegaard had forewarned the modernists, the majority have by their actions repudiated it.

The ethical ideal, expressed so forcibly by Ibsen and by Matthew Arnold, can be offered as both sanctuary and remedy in a world where values are disintegrating. This outlook is sustained especially among the English in the novels that cross the line between late Victorian and early modernist—James, Hardy, Conrad, Forster, Ford, Bennett, Wells—where the possibility of an ethical dignity might compensate for cosmological assurances forever lost. In painting, Van Gogh represents this facet of early modernism, as not only his paintings but also his letters attest.[8]

The aesthetic ideal, the notion of art's autonomy, is received by the early modernists from the art for art's sake movement, which detaches art from what was for the romantics an aesthetic *religion* of commitment. The bonding of art to philosophical idealism has been weakened, so the modernists can afterward transform art into an aesthetic *politics* of commitment. The devotion to art no longer necessarily entails transcendent spiritual avowals—although, of course, it does not exclude such avowals. Art is sufficient; art might itself be what transcendence means. The world is transcended not by the spirit but by the imagination, although "spirit" is often used as a metaphor for "imagination." The popular aesthetic theory of Benedetto Croce, for example, retains the concept of an "intuition" not reducible to simpler psychological terms, albeit confined for the most part to artists.

At the same time, art is more than the cultivation of (the cult of) sensibility and emotion, which too easily degenerates into dandyism or neurotic sensitivity. The devotion to art is a devotion to arduous labor, the reward for which is the masterpiece. The labor in art is not performed on behalf of the traditional social, religious, or political institutions (patronage will have to change accordingly), but for the artwork itself, which no longer requires any validating affiliations or authentications. (The artist or writer may, at the extreme, even withdraw from society altogether, never work for hire, perhaps never publicly show work.) Cézanne substantiates this specific variety of dedication for the modernist painters. If the form of art is equivalent to the form of life, the meaning of the life is equivalent to the meaning of the work.[9] This makes biography critically superfluous. The criticism of the work exhausts its meaning. Such logic will also underlie the formalist criticism of visual art that arises in the twentieth century. In literature, this stance is passed on to the modernists by Baudelaire, Rimbaud, and Lautréamont, for example, and found early in James and Yeats; it eventually issues in the high modernism of Eliot, Pound, and Joyce.

In painting, early modernism begins with Van Gogh, Gauguin, and Cézanne. The avowed "realism" of the impressionists, their use of color as direct and accurate representation, is discarded by freeing light and color to disclose what is not quite meaning in the ordinary sense, but the acknowledged presence of meaning. The essence of an art object is both the perception of it and the meaning inherently erupting from that perception. Perception is cognition.[10] The psycho-physiological processes of vision cannot be distinguished from the essence of the things perceived. Sensory vision does not precede knowing (and knowing is both information and its meaning), but vision is itself a knowing.[11] While artists individually perceive "nature," nature looks different to each of them. Yet the unique appearances are truths—as odd as this may sound to an empiricist.

Since the presence of meaning can be fully signified by the presence of color and light, as modernism progresses the insides of things disappear. The shape and solidity of ordinary objects are demoted and bypassed, and the term *realism* becomes no longer germane. Light and color, released from line and solid mass,[12] become manipulable according to a meaning and an effect distinct from representation, even when accompanied by a representation. (Not all modern art is abstract.) Meaning and symbol can be irradiated by shaped color, rather than by drawn allegory or metaphor. Such color undoubtedly rests on the surface of the canvas, not on the surface of an object. Accordingly, while much of romantic painting possesses an internal luminosity (Delacroix or Corot), much of early modernist painting displays an external brilliance: the former glows, the latter shines. This surface brilliance will characterize a significant portion of modernist painting. Even where color is not emphasized as an essential component of the aesthetic act or experience, most commonly where structural relations are primary (as in cubism for Picasso and Braque), the often severe limitation of color can only be accomplished because color has already been released from its adherence to the surface of solid objects. To reduce or discard color in painting requires color's independence from form. (This applies even to monochromatic painting. An all-white painting is the color white, not the absence of color; a white painting, or a black one, is not the same as an etching or photograph.) The greater the abstraction, the more arbitrary the association of any specific form with a specific color, a major source of modernist artistic freedom.

(When formalism becomes the dominant mode of criticism in the visual arts by the 1950s, color will be demoted as a "romantic" aspect of painting, in favor of a "classicism" of structural relations. Cubism will then be designated by many critics as the most significant visual modernist innovation.)

The visual art object appeals to sight, the same sense in the viewer that has been exercised by the artist. In a descriptive literary work, however, truth to nature cannot duplicate a sensory process. Eyesight, smell, taste, and tactility are converted into language. According to classical empiricism, words are markers representing real individual things in the world; words offer a medium for exchanging these things in thought. In contrast, just as visual perception is cognition for the modernist visual artist, so for the modernist literary artist language is cognition. In art, the effect (the artwork) defines, and indeed creates, the true nature of its cause, exactly reversing the procedure in science. One does not say what one knows; rather, one knows what one says. The issue of "point of view" then becomes essential both to literary criticism and to criticism of the plastic arts. Point of view is not simply opinion or outlook. Specifically, the linguistic reality in the literary work cannot be transcended by some external sensory confirmation. The project of naturalism is an impossibility because although one can be absolutely loyal to perception, the world will still appear different from one author to another. The ego has become exceedingly individualized and autonomized by the time of modernism (a topic discussed at length in part 4), largely because of democratic capitalism. In literature, point of view is not an arguable position; point of view is not the position one *takes,* but the position one *is.* Consequently, the term *realism* is no more germane to literature than to painting.

Literature can record speech and be a speaking. In general for modernism, the novel does the former, poetry the latter. The sense exercised by the reader and the sense exercised by the writer (sound) correspond—assuming that writing is speech written down. Meaning is on the surface of language, not behind language, just as color rests on the canvas, not the object. The inside of language disappears in writing, just as the insides of objects had disappeared in painting. Language has been released from the solidity of things just as color has been. The exuberance this causes produces an extraordinary diversity of lyric poetry, a greater array than at any other time in European history. In the novel, dialogue becomes absolutely paramount. Like authors, characters speak their existence, rather than act it.

To be sure, there is something real behind language for the early modernists; they are hardly post-structuralists. But the reality behind language recedes in importance compared with the intrinsic possibilities of meaning. The Platonic realm of Ideas, of such importance to the romantics, is replaced by a source of the as yet unsaid: unformed linguistic energy (like the energy the late nineteenth century released from petroleum and electricity) from which ideas issue through the human mind, their only avenue. Language exists all at once, although it is uttered piecemeal. In its entirety language possesses an encompassing potential for the meaningful which cannot itself be said: the meaningfulness of the very existence of meaning.

Consequently, nature itself appears laden with interior meaning, although the meaning is now interior not to things, but to our saying them. Literature is an intermediary between objects and the conditions of their existence for us. Art remains situated between the realm of ordinarily experienced reality and some other realm, a (higher) reality of another kind, an idea inherited from idealism; in this regard, modernism reinvigorates while it also reconfigures romanticism. (Modernism is hardly itself an idealism.) Modernist art reveals not a metaphysical geography, but an aesthetic state.

For modernism, the higher reality lacks the metaphysical solidity attributed to it by the romantics. The ground of reality is the inchoate possibility of that reality. The transcendent is—like energy, the *élan vital*—a universal potential, which artistic creativity corresponds to and verifies. The potential is not a volition, like God's will or some reified "urge" in the universe, but an energy that exercises itself through the laws of its own nature. The highest form of that energy is human consciousness, most particularly creative (artistic) consciousness. The laws discovered by science are the logical internal order of materiality, laws that both describe the movements of matter and, in an admittedly odd sense, cause it. Like art, these scientific laws connect two separate realms. While the laws are situated inside matter, they are not subordinated to matter but, instead, are at once the conditions for and the causes of the behavior of matter. Whether the laws might have been caused by operations in an ontologically separate realm (by a god who is elsewhere or a spirit that is everywhere) is irrelevant.

But while art and science can both be said to connect two separate realms, science is limited to dealing with cause and effect. For the early modernists, however, art is situated between cause and effect and the ground of cause and effect. This both subordinates science and overcomes Humean skepticism by providing a quasi-transcendent ground for mentality. While mentality can deduce what it cannot observe (it can think what it cannot find), art can directly display the truth of what deduction itself may suggest but cannot confirm. Art discloses and circumvents the limits of observation by appealing to a special aesthetic faculty evidenced, perhaps incontrovertibly, by the aesthetic experience. That faculty, once legitimated by Kant and by the idealism that will in the midst of modernism rapidly wane, eventually falls into disrepute.

Midmodernism

By midmodernism, the conditions of modern life overwhelm any possibility of sustaining the transcendental ideal, even while transmuted romanticism continues in the work of those born early enough to remember its vitality. (Recall that these categories are only an approximate chronology, since most early modernists live through more than one of these "phases.") Romanticism becomes less of a philosophical influence and more of a temperament, a predisposition rather than a creed, an advocacy of value rather than any specific set of values. Art is society's saving grace. Early modernism's maintenance of transcendence is short-lived because, in part, literary modernism depends so heavily on Anglo-American authors. For them, transcendence constantly weakens in an intellectual environment characterized by the empiricist suspicion of it, especially because of the antagonism toward Germany. The shift in painting from a physiology of sensation to the psychology of perception to the phenomenology of perception is matched in literature by the transition from the presumed scientific objectivity of naturalism to a psychological realism that is not a determinism but a quandary of choice to a phenomenological subjectivism.

For phenomenology the issue is *consciousness* and how it achieves subjectivity. Why and how can consciousness be individuated into personhood? This involves the "meaningfulness of the very existence of meaning" already referred to. For psychology, however, the issue is *mind*, or the content and mechanisms of subjectivity and personhood. For example, the Gestalt psychology beginning in the twenties with Wertheimer, Kohler, and Koffka[13] argues that, in perception, psychological mechanisms operate to compose forms that are greater than the sum of their parts. The overall form is not the total of the perception of the parts, but a configuration that mentality imposes upon the parts. (Gestaltism seems to be an empiricistlike recuperation of idealism during the same years when quantum physics has undertaken the same mission; this will be discussed further in chapter 5.) Yet such a Gestalt psychology cannot lead to transcendence in the former sense; it offers instead a physiologically based substitution for the idealist's intuition. The aesthetic unity of the artwork, too, can be declared over and above its constituent elements.

The transcendental ideal weakens as modern considerations of the human ethical dilemma intensify. Under the pressures created by an outmoded theology, humanity may appear small, lost, abandoned, or ineffectual, as in the fiction of Kafka or Musil or the paintings of expressionists like Munch or George Grosz or Max Beckmann. Nevertheless, the ethical ideal is often enhanced by this alienation (although rarely in Germany). In Joyce, Lawrence, and Woolf, heroism remains a possibility even where salvation does not; subjectivity is both ground and battleground of meaning and challenge. Daily life (not the celebrated exploits of champions) yields valor—a valor that is, however, often nothing other than the forceful extraction of meaning from a world that repeatedly declines to yield it.

Literary midmodernism is weighted with the ever-present immediacy of moral decision. The subject matter of art and literature becomes the everyday: the small town, the long conversation, the brief love affair, the single day, the predicament, the passing reflection or momentary insight. The furniture, transportation, clothing, food, and weather take on symbolic values and austere meanings never before assigned to them. Even when set in the midst of stupendous historical events, especially war, the characters often play minor roles. Despite the magnitude and intensity of the personal feelings or insights events produce, they often seem ludicrously beyond the control of anyone in particular, even of the people who can be said to have caused them. Crane, Gide, Mann, Malraux, Faulkner, Hemingway, Wolfe, and even

Mailer may be cited here. Despite the span of years involved, almost the entire history of the modernist novel can be assigned to literary midmodernism insofar as the large majority of those novels focus on a single major character who faces significant choices with no resources other than psychological strengths and weaknesses. The premodernist confidence in normative ethical criteria in the midst of chaos gives way to the exhilarating yet guilt-laden ethically relative and even the ethically preposterous, where every possible action is the implementation of an error sensed but insufficiently apprehended. It is a matter of discovering not encompassing values, but what one personally values: value is a mode of behavioral motivation. It is not a matter of discovering principles—for where might these be found?—but of being principled in the midst of one's insecurities, of knowing that one's personal behavior or fulfillment might not matter in the grand scheme of things, although nothing else *can* "matter." This personal freedom is the source of human grandeur as well as of human inadequacy. The valiant pretend to ethical meaning, which thereby comes, miraculously, to exist.

As for the aesthetic ideal in midmodernism: art is not meant to be a retreat from modern life, but a mastering of it. To know life well enough to transform it into art is to overcome it. Uniqueness of aesthetic form is equivalent to uniqueness of ego, and so the best artist is the most authentic human, the least co-opted by the common crowd, by the preacher, politician, or salesperson. Overview is wisdom, and worldview can even be genius. One's vision of the world is a rebuttal to being passively fashioned by the world. Art is the alternative both to conformity and to madness.[14] In painting, the movements from the fauves through cubism and Futurism[15] (the seven or eight years preceding World War I) are attempts to capture, summarize, and encapsulate modern life, attempts to control it by incarcerating it inside the artwork, by trapping the world in the paint. The aesthetic command of modern life can equally be the release from it, by taking modern life as the raw material on which freedom can be exercised, rather than as the limits imposed on behavior and freedom. Of course, modern life cannot be trapped in this way for more than a second or so; but even as it eludes the canvas, the tenor of its dynamic forces coalesce within the frame, achieving a momentary harmony. Its compelling certainties inside the frame stave off the incessant commotion, itself the origin of inspiration, that strives to rush in.

By midmodernism, God and immortality are no longer vital issues to the cosmopolitan, nor is Hegel's Absolute quite so absolute. But although religion has been placed in jeopardy, the need for the transmundane does not abate. Theology had given transcendence its dualistic cosmography of heaven and earth; for two hundred years, through the midnineteenth century, theology had been comfortably reconciled with the Cartesian duality of the realms of matter and mind, with humans possessing both and therefore connecting both. The topology of the mind and the topology of the universe corresponded. When this harmony disintegrates, the relationship between the transcendental and the mundane becomes not the underlying source of human existence but the psychological predicament of human existence. Transcendence exists through the awareness of its absence; "transcendence" no longer names the achievement of it, but the longing for it. The transcendental is not a separate ontological realm but a mental procedure or enactment. Cartesian dualism has been placed fully inside psychology, which increasingly purports to be on the verge of accounting for that apparent dualism. A human being strives to transcend its experiences by knowing it is having them (transcendence is proportional to self-awareness) and consequently by hoping to overcome, impossibly, the various structures in the form of which experience occurs. These structures of experience are the what of experience, not the why of it. The why that would yield meaning remains just out of reach.

Human existence may still be described as essentially a duality, so that human life remains an internal struggle, perhaps irreconcilable; but human duality can no longer continue to imply the older ontological bifurcation. There are neither two realms nor two types of being, but one realm within which is a certain type of being (us) with a double nature.[16] That double nature is itself a unity: the human body and the human mind are not two things joined, but one thing fused, no longer requiring an accompanying parallel cosmography. "Higher" and "lower" are, when the terms are severed from metaphysics, degrees of the integration of this human duality. The more integration, the higher the achievement and the better the quality of one's life, since this quality relies on the soundness of self-knowledge. Because there are no longer separate ontological realms, mortality and time cannot be transcended. Transcendence, now as an overcoming, includes the courageous acceptance of time-bound mortality, recognizing finitude not simply as a fact about (attached to) human existence, as if finitude were a contingency, but, as Heidegger will detail, an absolutely necessary condition of human existence.[17] Immortality is a quest, but not a possibility.

Whereas for the romantics nature (the organic countryside) had spiritually expanded to fill the spaces a retreating personalized deity had left behind, for the modernists these same spaces are filled by the expanding cosmopolitan city. The secular dualism of nature and city life intensifies, in a very different way than for the romantics: because the metropolis is where artwork flourishes, even in opposition to it. The modernist artwork is always produced to hang on the walls of (stand in the courtyards of, be in the bookstores, theaters, and hallways of) the largest and most prosperous cities. (Even projects in remote locations—from earthworks to avalanches—gain reputations only through photographs and films brought to the city.) A city was once the sum of its inhabitants; now each inhabitant is a small summation of the metropolis, for urbanity as a set of human relations dominates the older relations based on extended family, town, agricultural land, or church.[18] At the beginning of the nineteenth century, only one-fifth of the population in Europe and the United States lived in cities; within the first two decades of the twentieth century, only one-fifth of the population does not live in cities. Formerly a comparison of customs, manners, and sophistication, the urban-rural duality has now become congruent to the composite dual nature of human beings. Urbanity becomes a configuration of psyche. City life seems, for the initiated, an entirely new mode of existence.

While both literature and painting contribute equally to early modernism (through, say, 1905), and while literature generally dominates the third phase, high modernism (from the early twenties through the early fifties), painting dominates midmodernism. The two art forms do not function in the same way. Unlike painters, literary modernists cannot be readily grouped under a few major classifications and well-known movements. The practical conditions of displaying art required the visual modernists to show their work as part of a group, usually with a shared manifesto, which frequent personal interaction fortified as a mutual influence. This does occur in literature, particularly in poetry, when the potential audience is so small that group affiliation enhances the possibility of publication. (Imagism, under Pound's mentorship, gave literary modernism its foremost example in this regard.) But the availability of novels and dramatic works are commonly determined by potential profitability: unlike a painting, a literary work can be sold (either as volumes or as tickets) in great numbers. In high modernism, literature advances together with the publishing business and with the cost reductions in an urban market avidly seeking "culture," especially as electric lighting extends the day for reading and for urban pleasures (the theater, concert, film, restaurant) now enjoyed even by those with moderate incomes. Because playwrights and novelists are only one work away from prosperity, they can write directly for an audience, rather than for their literary peers. Visual artists form "schools," and poets comprise factions; in drama and the novel, critics create the categories, retrospectively.

A literary work is not a physical object in the same way as a painting. The printed work is a transcript not itself of value; a poem, for example, could exist in memory and be recalled. The painting is itself the object of value; a memory of it cannot serve as a substitute for it. A physical aesthetic object is at one with its meaning, just as body and mind are one; but verbal art can always assert its independence of materiality—which is why the poet was for so long considered superior to the visual artist. (Through the early Renaissance, painters of murals and painters of saddles belonged to the same guild.) Visual art displays and confirms the interlocking of body and spirit as a single entity, which is why the stature of visual art becomes so important in modernism. Color and form are bonded like body and psyche: figures are not painted, the paint is the figure.

Since form and content, like soul and body, are no longer separate entities, modernist painting must confirm the very mortality the negation of which often motivates the production of the work. Yet there is an optimistic side to irremediable mortality. The escape from religious orthodoxy, from a morality grounded in theological metaphysics, and from an art and politics (monarchy in particular) whose subject matter has historically been determined by these orthodoxies liberates humanity to reconsider its fundamental definition. Everything is permitted. At the same time, the price of this exuberance—the uneasy admission that human life has no comprehensive meanings beyond what might be self-assigned—suffices for some, not for others. Art transcends the human limitations of the artist by facing these limitations as irrevocable, by going to the edge of what it is impossible to go beyond. The artist can see, looking back, the entire con-tents of the world that both entraps human beings yet provides, like a prison yard, the only area for the exercise of freedom. Maximum free-dom is gained only by knowing the conditions under which freedom can be maximally exercised, an exercise which is art.

By the time of midmodernism in painting, the artwork presents the artist rather than re-presents an object or incident. Vision as per-ception through eyesight is subsumed to vision as perception through insight. An artistic envisioning is not the creation of the portrait of a narrative (i.e., what addresses the eyes in a way corre-sponding either to the world, objectively viewed; or an illustration of its social, political or mythical history; or a narrative about the meanings either inherently contained in the world or granted by its creator) but the visual equivalent to the psyche in forms derived from, but not congruent to, the seen qualities of objects. Between impressionism and modernism, the emphasis shifts from the physi-ology of sensation to the psychology of perception and then moves into the phenomenology of perception, particularly the unique qual-ities of the perception of the individual artist. Theory based on the physiology of the senses is replaced by theory based on the univer-sal cognitive and emotional structures of mentality, which is in turn replaced by theory based on the formation of mentality in individu-al *self*-consciousness (selfhood): a shift from the body-mind relation to the self-world relation. For the symbolist, the dreamer is the soul; as modernism progresses, the dreamer is the psyche. The primary dictum is to be true to what one sees, although what one sees is also what one knows as well as who one is. Such originality in the mod-ernist artist is, of course, an aberration to the empiricist, for whom the mechanics of clear perception yield universal consensus.

The modernist search is not for the universal in the particular (the classical aesthetic) but for the particular in the universal. What is ex-pressed is not *the* meaning, but my meaning, not human vision (only) but my personal vision (particularly). There are no imposed limits on the creative imagination. Limits are simply conventions; conventions are the consensus of the untalented. Insofar as vision is private al-though objects are public, abstraction becomes a legitimate strategy. To embody meaning in what can be perceived (art) is to create an object that offers a meaning inherent in its source, since objects issuing from the imagination are the only ones that can have meaning. The art object is imbued with meaning by its creator, who need not derive that meaning from any object represented. The physical properties or qualities of objects are detached from actual objects to become autonomous artistic materials. The properties of objects are like phonemes in language: not meaning, but the material from which meaning is constructed. The world's actual objects are but one way of assembling these properties (one vocabulary, as it were), which the imagination reconstitutes into an alternative vocabulary of its own.[19]

Nevertheless, the midmodernists also believe themselves to be expressing truths of universal import, insofar as every unique vision has its source in potentialities of consciousness common to all artists, perhaps to all humans. Otherwise, what would distinguish the uniqueness of genuine creativity from personal mania or dementia? Admittedly, a number of artists do believe that they are connected to what transcends them and exists independently of them. Like the symbolists preceding them, some believe spirit suffuses the work by passing through the artist to the canvas.[20] In some movements, like De Stijl and suprematism, even a simple geometry often carries a mystically Platonic import. It does not take long for such beliefs to be dismissed by the many who do not share them. One of the functions of formalist criticism, which eventually comes to dominate modernist criticism in high modernism, will be to make such beliefs irrelevant to understanding even those works which without such beliefs would not have been produced in the first place. (What formalist accepts Mondrian's theosophical beliefs, even while praising his genius?) For the entire course of modernism generally, the grounding of the suprapersonal in a basis for ego that is fully internal to a consciousness that no longer requires a transcendent cause is, again, the function of any phenomenology. There is a human spirit, although humans are no longer spirits. The transcendent in art is displaced by the elevation of the self-contained aesthetic experience, without the signification of any external spiritual source of it. The content of the mind can *hold* meaning for us without itself actually *having* some meaning in a more encompassing sense. The universal truths are existential truths. To account for the origin of meaning reveals only that origin, not some overriding significance of meaning—even when the artwork seems to radiate such significance. The unconscious does not contain significance; it is itself significance.

That the midmodernists increasingly forfeit the possibilities of romantic transcendence yields a progressively widening freedom of verbal and visual display. If exalted language no longer need correspond to exalted metaphysical realms, then exalted language can be attributed to the reaches of the human imagination. The purpose of art is imagination's full exercise, no longer bound to any truth "higher" than humanity's knowledge of its own capabilities. Since the artist (like the rest of humanity) is fundamentally a psychological entity, a personality rather than rarefied subjectivity, artworks are excursions to the psychological depths. Art becomes an inward journey, rather than an outward journey.

Art has always revealed the content of the human mind, but since antiquity the content of the mind had been assumed to consist of patterns of thought aligned with the structures of external reality. Emotions were placed between the two (thought and reality), with judgment somehow above them both. In modern art, thought, emotion, and judgment are inseparable; it becomes possible to discuss the writer's or artist's interpretation of reality. This is the opposite of the scientific method, which claims to generate not individual interpretations of reality but consensual objective descriptions of it.[21] Placing art in opposition to science in this way allows art to claim a separate and legitimate cognitive ground for itself.

The modern artist provides no explanations. Artists whose work is purported to consist of interpretation without explanation become exemplary figures, often artists whose individual beliefs seem either elusive (Shakespeare, Chaucer, Rembrandt; Keats's phrase "negative capability" is frequently heard[22]) or, for modern readers at least, irrelevant to accepting their artistic greatness (Dante, Giotto, Milton). To know the world is not to judge it or to mirror it but to be turned into it through the production of an artwork so that ego and world, self and other, are permanently amalgamated. The living artist is transformed into an inert object, dead matter, as if such an object could preserve life in aesthetic form. This secular similacrum immortality appears in an age that discovers the vast cosmological time that will consume the earth and the once immortal sun. Lyricism takes precedence over epic, the sensation or the description (recall the Bloomsbury aesthetic) over the analysis or the explication.[23] Interpretation is received as a form of truth: the mind's organization of the world composes the world for each person individually. Hermeneutics becomes a methodology: if the work is to be properly understood, there is no place outside it for the interpreter to stand.[24] The early empiricist belief, in Hobbes and Locke, that some purely mechanistic relation assures a natural correspondence between an external reality and internal mental processes may be the truth, but not the whole truth.

Only when modern art is freed from acknowledging, reflecting, or representing transcendence, by turning inward to the psyche, can it also be freed from representing ordinary reality. Yet since the content of the psyche must originate in the world, art is objective too. Art is any intentional configuration of materials in an arrangement designed to transmit a meaning whose existence does not preexist the specific arrangement through which it is transmitted.[25] The objective description of the visual world can be left to science (and photography), which can subsequently claim this as its sole and unchallengeable prerogative. On the other hand, the "ordinary" reality left to science can no longer be equated with what is the emotionally real for the modernists. Science is granted undisputed authority only over what modernism believes it has subordinated—the ordinary reality that is, after all, middle-class reality, whose truths are only facts and whose interpretations are only ideologies. (Deep psychic processes elude them.) Better to free the imagination to roam among these processes than to copy the world as it superficially appears. In painting, abstraction intensifies; in literature, abstruseness of meaning intensifies.

The imagination achieves complete autonomy: in art, absolutely nothing is now prohibited. This yields more than the multifariously fanciful—although that, too. The artwork is the most real of realities for the modernist, who confronts the viewer in some inescapable and uncancelable way. Yet with midmodernism the firmly grounded selfhood that inspired romanticism to liberate the creative imagination, a transcending selfhood within which personality had once been subsumed, is relinquished. Transience, contingency, and a contextless mortality are the prices paid for complete freedom. The self that creates artistic reality does so at the expense of its own reality; the work is permanent, the self irretrievably ephemeral. One is free to do anything except escape this ego, although an escape from ego has traditionally been precisely the aim of the disciplines, East and West, that propose to give life meaning. But life can no longer have meaning; it can only produce meaning.

In high modernism, the dual-truth aesthetic theory will eventually (around the forties) grant separate "truths" to art and science: the objective truth about subjectivity is also to be the subjective truth about objectivity. Except to its often devoted adherents, this double truth will seem a mystification, since the avowed "truth" of art (its distinctive legitimate cognitive ground) can never be pinned down. The only verification is to believe in it. No consistent empiricist can possibly find dual-truth theory plausible. Yet dual-truth theory is not designed to please empiricists: it is a compensation for empiricism.

Abstraction

The movement toward abstraction in modern painting might at first seem an attempt to escape the "real" world, to replace it with ideal form or imaginative fabrication. It is not the real world that disappears, however, but the ordinary interpretation of a world external to the mind—an interpretation for hundreds of years associated with the Renaissance technique of vanishing-point perspective. (Narrative history and naturalist prose fiction are perspective's literary counterparts.) This commonplace view of external reality had become more than familiar; it had become distasteful, having been arrogated by science and the middle class—explained by the former, shaped by the latter. Modern visual art does not display reality but augments reality; it does not reflect the real but expands the real, spilling over its pedestrian boundaries. One is not meant to look through art to that to which it corresponds, as if it were a window or a guidebook.

Abstract art is always in the immediate present, conveying no narrative but creating a statement. In contrast, a narrative always tells a story that is already over. Abstract art creates the present of the observer by converting that proposed special aptitude of mentality called imagination into an object directly perceivable. In abstract art, imagination need not organize the external world; rather, it directly presents the organizing function itself. The formal relationship among constituent parts proclaims itself the content and purpose of the work, struggling for dominance with the narrative left untold, with the story one might have anticipated the work to tell, a struggle without which there is only design, not art. Any ostensible subject matter is the means the imagination uses to reveal itself, not the subject. We learn not what *it* is, but what art is, how the work's subject exists in and for the artwork. The world that stimulates the production of the artwork is transferred into the imagination; the artwork is not a subsequent reexternalization of the object in artistic form, but an externalization of the imaginative interior with the object captured inside it.

Abstract art is structured not according to the structure of a represented object but according to the structure taken by the imagination as it enfolds the object. The margin or partition between that inner space and some obvious or naively undeniable external reality (which is precisely what empiricism was invented to describe) is excluded from the painting. There is no procedure, or the work is devised to prevent one from finding a procedure, for "translation" of the artwork back into what is represented; "representation" becomes an inappropriate term. Even where realistic techniques are employed (as in those aspects of surrealism that display a mastery of Renaissance perspective) there is no longer a reality external to the mind into which the painting can be transformed by some familiar grammar or code of correspondence. Nor is there a table or index of iconography. The grammar resembles that of psychoanalysis—not a way of making the interior mental world comprehensible as a "mind" that knows impersonal reality, but of making reality what the personal interior world creates in tension with a reality also knowable from other viewpoints. The artist's personal construction of the world is always surrounded by numerous denials of it or alternatives to it, the most important being the public consensus.

When photorealism eventually evolves in painting in late modernism, that realism will actually be hyperreal and hence completely unreal: although every detail is, in some sense, a copy, the painting is somehow not a copy.[26] Surprise was once the reaction to a photograph; but once photography becomes familiar, surprise is the reaction to the recognition that a photorealistic painting is so obviously not a photograph. The most precise (apparent) copying of external reality has not presented external reality at all. This is exactly the opposite of nineteenth-century naturalism and the limit of visual modernism. What appears at first pictorially synonymous with the real world is, remarkably, also an abstraction. The commonplace has been fully co-opted by the imagination. This was the original intent of Duchamp's found objects, the urinal and the bottle rack; but only by passing through abstraction and exiting into a new (quite unreal) "realism" could this modernist intent reach its culmination. During the course of modernism, the imagination that yielded abstraction in painting has ingested the entire world. Replicating the external world ultimately becomes itself a form of abstraction—a lesson quickly learned by advertising.

During its three hundred years or so, modernity has been based primarily on heard, spoken, written, and read language. The visual is never considered cognitively primary, even though it may be sensorially primary. The visual is the raw material of what language alone can transform into "knowing." The visual is explained by language or a technical adumbration of language, namely mathematics; the visual yields the data. Platonism and Augustinianism, however, were both based on the priority of vision as access to truth, as was the Renaissance art influenced by these.

For the first time in modernity, modernism reintroduces the idea that the visual attests to an a-linguistic knowledge or cognition of reality, not simply a sensory awareness of reality. The argument is made that the visual can provide direct and even prelinguistic knowledge, since the psyche presumably has operations that precede or take logical precedence over the formation of language. (This is also the assertion of psychoanalysis.) If language serves to provide "markers" or labels that, according to empiricist theory, are attached to the real objects in the world, then images must be originally in the mind, as the "impress" of objects. Contact with the world must, in this view, be made before language sets in; even if language organizes the world, the mind has content preceding this organization. Modernism, like psychoanalysis, grants this content prelinguistic *meaning*.[27] This visual content is directly available to the imagination, which manipulates it even prior to the mediation of language. Even in poetry, a theory of metaphor-as-truth makes vision logically prior to expression: metaphor is image-ry. A modern poem is interpreted by adding (critical) language to the metaphor that in the poem has no need of it.

Admittedly, metaphor can have no meaning except as that meaning occurs for creatures (us) who already possess language. The import of metaphor is that meaning seems to erupt from it; but to know that one is in the presence of meaning (to even be a "one") requires language. Visual art is, after all, something that occurs only for a linguistic being; any purported prelinguistic visual meaning occurs only for a postlinguistic being. In modernism, metaphor seems, enigmatically, at once logically prior to but temporally posterior to language.

The effect logically precedes the cause. The aesthetic experience is the sense that one is experiencing as a result of the work what itself has preexisted and engendered the work.

In modernism, the need for the narrative caption diminishes. Even though artists continue to use titles, the function of the title changes as abstraction increases. The older form of title, better called a caption, informs the viewer what the artwork is about. The modernist titling of a visual artwork tells the viewer where to begin the aesthetic response. No longer required to have any obvious connection to the work, the title is a formal device for structuring interpretation. The title (even the title "Untitled") does not describe or annotate the work; it is part of the work. (Although a modern artwork may be commissioned, the commission does not, as in the Renaissance, stipulate the caption.) The title issues from the work it seems to name.

Throughout the history of art, prior to modernism, the caption had provided directions about where one would conclude; the caption will later be found to organize and to summarize the content of the experience. The painting is subordinated to the narrative implanted in the caption. In modernism, however, the title informs the viewer where to begin. The modernist title is *given* meaning by the artwork in which it participates, not vice versa. The genius of technique becomes an end, not a means. Genius does not fulfill the challenge of some momentous caption (the Crucifixion, for example); rather, genius creates the import of the title, which is another reason why no subject matter whatsoever needs to be excluded from modern art. The classical concept of decorum is obsolete. Of course, for many viewers a work without an easily recognizable identifying caption is puzzling and even meaningless, but in modernism this signifies an uninitiated viewer. Since the caption had for so long been attached to the specific Renaissance device of perspective, that device can also be summarily dismissed by modernism, in favor of abstraction.

Architecture has an empty interior. Only in architecture is the artwork intentionally constructed not only to be observed but to be "occupied," inhabited according to instructions given by the owner who furnishes it, rather than by the work itself. In modernist architecture, representation is discarded through the development of styles that do not allow one to tell from the outside exactly what "business" the building is being used for. Like a painting, each building must be given a title, a sign attached to the outside to initiate the observer's viewing. When the sign is unclear to the observer—the corporate name might be unfamiliar—the building remains a mystery. These signs are modernist titles, rather than captions. The meaning of the corporation or hospital or church is not transmitted by the building, as was the case when meanings were not constantly in jeopardy; rather, the corporation or hospital or congregation is to be given meaning by the building. The modernist sign is not meant to tell us what is occurring inside the building but to disclose what the building itself is, as a work. It is the kind of building that is eligible to carry that kind of sign. The sign is meant to unify structure and function in the architectural version of the reconciliation of opposites.

One does not learn what goes on in the modernist building ("products" are manufactured elsewhere), only who or what entity is doing whatever it is that goes on. Nor are there specific architectural forms that themselves serve as captions rather than titles, like the special forms each associated with churches, steel mills, ballparks (instead of sports stadiums), stores (the display window, for example) and homes (the porch). The purported early modernist intent was to have form and function coincide, as if that coinciding was equivalent to beauty: the factory would be like a cathedral, the municipal building a welcoming rather than foreboding presence, the home a family's little Eden rather then the place of its nightly entrapment. But modernist architecture eventually yields the deployment of forms that have multiple and ambiguous functions, erected with the supposition (as formalism and Le Corbusier instruct) that the internal aesthetic relationships of the object supplant what some use of it would dictate—the use being what in architecture would otherwise be, unacceptably, some meaning preexisting the work. By the fifties and sixties, the metropolitan landscape in the wealthier cities is increasingly dominated by those all-purpose, flexible, airy spaces of glass and steel and preformed concrete, indebted especially to Mies van der Rohe. Of course, the traditional forms are still sometimes attached to or incorporated in a modernist facade (the cross on the church; the fireplace chimney extending from the roof of the house; the high-rise balconies, infrequently used) to serve as comfortable reminders.

Function does not, then, dictate form. Rather, the functions of modern life have accommodated themselves to the architectural forms in which they occur. Frequently the function is actually hidden by the form. During the years when psychoanalysis describes mentality as

resting on what is hidden, just as Marxism describes the social structure as resting on what remains hidden (the underlying exploitive
economic relations), machinery, automobiles, and large appliances are
designed, like buildings, to cover up the functioning parts. Their
mechanisms too become hidden—unlike, say, the cotton gin, the water wheel, the loom, or even the typewriter.[28] The Eiffel Tower had
placed in plain audacious view the structure of the steel it celebrated;
so did many buildings, like the original Pennsylvania Station in New
York. But as modernism progresses, walls hang from the steel to hide
it; the expanses of seemingly weightless windows are a denial of what
supports them. Compared to the classical structures of stone, the modern building is not what it seems; its strength is hidden, the ugliness
(internal beams, pipes, tubes, wires, heating or elevator parts) encased
in a beautiful shell. The building hides even as it purports to expose.
Even the curvilinear forms used (from art nouveau forward) in emulation of organic shapes disingenuously substitute for the organic nature now placed at a distance from the city. Guimard's florid entranc-
es to the Paris Metro are modern gates to the depths, as if one had
found the gates to hell. The way of life the underground trains make
possible hardly corresponds to organic nature, for there are no seasons and no day and night there.

One can guess fairly accurately what is happening inside the shop
with the shoemaker's sign, and one is welcome to see for oneself, since
that sign is a caption. But one knows not exactly, or even approximately, what is happening inside a corporate headquarters, aside from
common functions like meetings, bookkeeping, telephone calls. In
fact, since capitalist business is based on secrecy, trying to discover
exactly what happens inside can be a crime. Private life is also sequestered, despite the glass. Can one easily tell, for example, where to find
the front door in one of Wright's "prairie" houses? Glass, whose value
was once that it was invisible, now becomes tinted or mirrored, the
most visible material of all. Even where its transparency is maintained,
this is either to promote business (most often as a storefront) or to
demonstrate that the inhabitants need not fear the intrusions of the
snoop or meddler. (The picture window of the suburban tract residence, on the contrary, serves to expose the lives of those with the
least power.) The titled modernist office buildings stand completely
open to vision, and one can often walk inside at will and take the elevator here and there. Yet while open to vision, the buildings are

mute: nothing can be heard beyond the trivial, since the important matters occur in plain square rooms.

Photography and Realism

Photography's visual conservatism, its "realism," qualified it as a link between empiricism and romanticism. It was simultaneously a "science" (and officially applauded as such by the French government[29])—dependent upon technology to develop emulsions, chemicals, lenses, and shutters—and an "art." Presumably photography would always keep a firm grip on reality, since its mechanical process assured veracity. The photograph does not represent the facts, it is the facts, at least so the public assumes.

In "fine art" photography, it has been unnecessary to introduce the strategy of a dual-truth theory. Such theory is a compensation for the diminution of aesthetic authority and influence in an empiricist age. But photography can be, even must be, empirically true. Even as an art, photography long ago accepted the invitation to participate in the empiricist methodology that the other arts were devising ways to cast aside. (The finest lenses are those causing the least "distortion.") This technical discipline nevertheless achieves status as an art, and the photographic artist can be included among the geniuses.[30] This then becomes a substantial criterion for what an art is, especially as distinct from a craft: that at least some of its practitioners can be included among the geniuses. In a similar way, six hundred years earlier, one segment of the painting crafts of the medieval guilds was slowly modified and positioned as an art, which allowed Renaissance humanists later to argue that the new artists could be set alongside the geniuses of poetry.[31]

But even while admitting photography into the arts, in order to explain why the photographic process works it must be assumed that an image is impressed upon the emulsion atomistically, mechanistically, that each point on the coated surface is activated by light. The light itself need not be atomistic: continuous nongranular phenomena can be displayed by grains. The electromagnetic field, for example, can be viewed by sprinkling over it iron filings, which assemble into a looped pattern that duplicates the patterns of the invisible, weightless, and completely "empty" field. (If a tacky paper is laid on the filings, one obtains a granular photograph of the invisible.) But even if light may not be atomistic—and nowadays it is considered both a particle and/or a wave[32]—matter must be, since it is divisible. Photography depends upon advances in a theory of chemistry that explains the divisibility of matter based on a permanent array of distinct elemental atoms and their compounds. Not until this particular notion of an atomistic reality is a testable theory can a permanent, controlled, and replicable recording of the image cast by the long-familiar camera obscura be thought possible. Photography is invented in the 1820s and 1830s, when elements were being variously classified according to their atomic "weights," culminating in Mendeleyev's periodic table of 1869.[33] Even in recent experimentation, the very smallest known particles are detected by scrutinizing the traces left on film emulsions by particle collisions—another, more advanced, connection between photography and the ultimately granular constitution of things according to the scientists.

In photography the "visions" of science and art meet cognitively: one knows the same (sort of) world in both cases. That which impresses itself on the emulsion has its fundamental source in the real, while in the other modern arts implements like brushes or chisels or pens are used with no technical warrantee of veracity. A painting or poem might be a fantasy, but a fantasy in a photograph is a photograph of a fantasy. The photographer is fundamentally a traveler acquainted with the world firsthand. Photography is the least methodologically innovative of the arts, since the means of its production allow little flexibility.[34] (This is not meant pejoratively.) Aside from the speed of the exposure and the qualities of the materials—using pliable base instead of glass to hold the emulsion,[35] introducing color, improving lenses, increasing film speed, automating the exposure—contemporary cameras allow little more than the early cameras, although they do it more easily. Much of the innovation in recent photography is a modification of subject matter.[36] The formal characteristics of photographs have remained relatively stable for eighty years. In the other visual arts and in literature numerous formalist movements have come and gone; photography does not have such "movements."

Considered both science and art, photography (including the motion picture) becomes for the general public the most important, most prolific, most stimulating, and most attended-to art form of modernism. Its literary competitor is the realistic novel, since realism proposes to generate accurate mental images. From a photographic viewpoint, a novel is a proposal for a movie.

It has often been argued (even by modernists, like Matisse) that photography outmoded realism in the visual arts because the camera effortlessly matched or surpassed what required the painter's exacting skills and abundant time.[37] But photography is introduced as an art form after painting and sculpture have completed their work in the domain of realism. Between the Renaissance and the nineteenth century, painters had already achieved unsurpassable adroitness using compositional and technical effects. The techniques that characterize photography had become standard and repetitive techniques in painting: the few customary variations on portraiture lighting; the framing of an image so that its "world" extends invisibly beyond the frame (like cutting objects in half at the edge of the image), common in Dutch painting by the late seventeenth century; the use of unusual perspective, especially exaggerated foreshortening; the placing of large partial masses in the forefront; the internal framing (doorways, arches); the seclusions of small radiant lights in dark areas. Photography does not demonstrate the deficiencies of realistic painting. Rather, having taken Renaissance perspective and realism to its limits, painting defines what photography will have to do to be successful: it must be at least as accurate as the work of Louis Le Nain and George de La Tour in the seventeenth century, or of Vermeer (who used the camera obscura), and Rembrandt and Velazquez.[38] And fifteenth-century intaglio engraving had first made possible a "run" of identical works in black and white that many people could own at small expense. Photography recapitulates what painting has already perfected and is no longer pursuing, even if photography apparently does this effortlessly. (Of course, photography takes a further step: the painting takes time, while the photograph halts time, a modern transcendent act.)

The function of the lens is to cast an image that resembles reality in the way a painting does ("photo-graphy" is "light-drawing"), presenting three dimensions in two. Renaissance artists originally mastered this technique by sighting through flat grids (flattening the image into two dimensions is what the ground glass does in the camera) and by studying the projections of the camera obscura (pinhole projection). The task of preserving images is transferred to, not appropriated by, photography when painting is about to find its work elsewhere. Techniques from the days of Turner and Delacroix through Van Gogh and Cézanne had given objects a volume (an expansiveness or capaciousness) not identical to solidity, through color effects and texture alone. Photography lacks precisely this surface texture.[39] That a modernist painting, no matter how abstract, is not simply as flat as the canvas can be demonstrated by viewing a full-size photograph of it. Modernist painting relies on its texture, at least until late modernism is well advanced. The dimensions of the painted object are what space is filled by, as if the object has palpably expanded into it, while earlier the painted object (as in photography) had been tightly bound by its drawn perimeter.

Reproduction of an external reality can only become a mechanically solvable problem when what is to be reproduced is already unambiguously defined. One had to know what the photograph was supposed to look like even before photography is invented. A lens can be said not to distort only when we think we already know what the world looks like undistorted. Even so, a photograph does not present us what we see looking at the scenery. Much of our usual vision is peripheral blur; our eyes physically respond to a photograph differently than to a scene.

The process of photography causes but does not explain its effect. What chemically occurs can be explained, but what a photograph appears to be is something different. The effect can only be explained by circumstances external to the process. In the Renaissance, one had to learn both to see and to admire perspective; this trick works only after one learns to consent to it.[40] Even if vision yields corresponding effects (railroad tracks do seem to converge), it would be equally plausible, when drawing things, to dismiss these simply as aberrations of the visual process (since the tracks do not converge). Why reproduce an aberration caused by perception? Furthermore, the peripheral blur is not reproduced; perception as clarity becomes important to reproduction, just at the time when "clarity" of knowledge is coming to acquire a sensory base, during the transition from the Middle Ages to the Renaissance. For perspective to be valued, one must believe that the way reality appears to the senses is of substantial enough importance not to be subordinated to how the world in itself might be, the senses aside. Perception itself becomes an interest, a knowledge, not simply a means. In empiricism and in Kantianism, the reality that can be known will become defined as, limited to, only what the senses can perceive.

As photography proliferated, painters were discovering visual dimensions alternative to the customary three-dimensional perspective. In Japanese art (its Parisian popularity began in the 1860s), spatial representation could be achieved in ways other than through traditional perspective, which not only signifies depth but also creates the illusion of volume. Asian art revealed to the West, or again reminded the West, that the potential for maximizing two-dimensionality could still evolve innovatively. This had been quite familiar in the International Gothic of the late fourteenth century, where depth is indicated by setting visually two-dimensional planes behind one another without any real sense of space between them.[41] In the nineteenth century there was a renewed promising future for a reinvigorated two-dimensionality, sometimes confined to a single plane but often consisting of a sequence of planes for which the viewer provides the intervening volume. Even where there are significations of depth relationships, this can be accomplished by the comparative size even of somewhat flattened objects or by overlapping planes.[42] Rounded solid volumes are no longer necessities. Nor must all the depth be represented as in perspective—by, say, a continuous landscape, a retreating road or courtyard or city street, or walls. The intervening space may even be canceled, yet without totally discarding depth—as in cubist painting, which seems to be composed of overlapping tiles. Collage—which the cubists suddenly invent—similarly accomplishes this.

Modernist painters emphasized various principles and strategies to overcome the traditional alliance of skillful drawing and perspective. In the classic empiricist epistemology, extension and mass are *primary* qualities of objects, while color, sound, and smell are *secondary* qualities, results of the human sensorium. But the modernists give color a status equal to extension. After all, color does not merely coat the mass and shape of things; what has absolutely no hue would be invisible, purely transparent or purely dark, like a hole. Color is not bound by a shape to which it adheres; it is equivalent to shape. (Berkeley had made this point around 1715.[43]) The modernists can, going further, take color to be prior to shape, an independent phenomenon. In modern art, color is more real than volume. This central assumption of modern art is where it parts company with empiricism. Color becomes liberated from solid mass, from volume; its properties are deployed as visual ends in themselves, as color rather than coloring. Mass defined by line (extension) and an expanse of color (a field) need no longer coincide in painting; color can also create or suggest a mass whose discrete boundaries (its edges) are altogether obscured. Perspective replicating solid mass through the use of line is no longer the chief illusion; rather, brushstrokes of color applied in a certain way—so that the single brushstroke cannot (except by the inattentive) be overlooked—and viewed from a certain distance yield mass. Viewed up close, the placing of the strokes is not congruent with a "literal" drawing of the object.

Much modern art is actually more, not less, of a trompe l'oeil than traditional perspective, since mass or shape only coalesces when the work is viewed from no less than a certain distance. In a photograph or a detailed drawing, no matter how close one gets, the drawn figuration does not disappear.

Three approaches are widely used to overcome traditional drawing and perspective. In each of these, aesthetic considerations increasingly involve not only technique but, equally important, the theory of technique. First, just discussed, straight line (edge) and color need not coincide. Eventually, even the illusion or suggestion of three-dimensional mass is no longer requisite for the modernist. When the painting flattens out (as the volume between consecutive planes evanesces), color can be allowed to spread like a pool across the canvas, specifically in the work of the fauves, Matisse in particular, and of the German expressionists, by way of Kandinsky, through the days of the abstract expressionists. (This was neither an aim nor an effect, at least not originally, of cubism.) As color flows and spreads the canvases grow to accommodate it. For some, the goal seems to be pure extension and pure abstraction: perfect color, like Flaubert's ideal literary work that would be pure language but no content.

A second alternative to traditional representation is to treat mass as if it were composed of ideal geometrical forms, either two-dimensional forms (squares are the suprematist's perfect form) or three-dimensional forms. The forms are related through Euclidean geometry, since the three-dimensional figures are ideal assemblages or projections of the two-dimensional figures, and the smooth two-dimensional curves (circle, ellipse, parabola, hyperbola) are conic sections, generated by slicing the cone with a plane. Pure and ideal forms are not to be considered practical abstractions from the rough and irregular configurations of mass in the real world. Rather, in a Platonic gesture, the pure forms are given ontological priority over mass: the ideal form is more real than the mass or volume. (The approach characterizes the purists, Chirico, Mondrian, Klee, De Stijl, the constructivists, and lasts through the minimalists.) One often finds the belief that society will simplify or ought to simplify its common forms—whether in clothes, furniture, household items, machines, or art. The pure, the simple, the efficient, and the beautiful can be conjoined in the basic geometrical curves, and art and manufacturing might be allied.

A third approach to rejecting traditional drawing is to usurp those methods, using them for purposes for which they had not been originally intended. Frequently, there is extreme distortion. At other times, the customary techniques by which the external world had been accurately represented are used to display what cannot possibly exist in the external visible world: dream, fantasy, hallucination, the symbolic, the "psychological," or psychopathological. These are frequently subjects in expressionism and surrealism. (Of particular interest is the fastidious use of perspective by Magritte and Dali.) Photorealism, as mentioned earlier, is the furthest extension of this method, where exactitude of representation becomes, strangely, a completely interior vision.

Each of these visual approaches has counterparts in literature. The release of color from mass is, in poetry, the escape of the sound of language from the meaning of language. The Platonic idealization of form corresponds to the elevation of the structure of a work above its content—namely, formalist criticism itself. The techniques of objective realism found in literary naturalism are applied to interior subjectivity: its "stream of consciousness," its illusions and delusions, its illogicalities, its often random or bizarre connections, its dreams, are all projected out into the world to appear externally real. Similar comments can be made about the other arts. In music, for example, tone is released from harmony (by Stravinsky, for example); form is idealized (Arnold Schoenberg's twelve-tone scale, repeated, inverted, reversed); a turn to the abstract and the fantastic translates into a tonal disorientation that is the musically uncanny (Webern, Berg, and Bartok).

Modern Art and Literature: Later Phases

3

High Modernism

In literature, the most notable phase of modernism, "high" modernism, matures in the early 1920s, at the time of Eliot's *The Waste Land* and Joyce's *Ulysses*. It also includes the prose of Proust, Woolf, Musil, and Lawrence, and in poetry (the later) Yeats, Rilke, Pound, Crane. So much talent has literary modernism yielded: Gide, Lawrence, Malraux, Wolfe, Hesse, Mann, cummings, Huxley, Marianne Moore, Auden, Schnitzler, Hofmannsthal, and Faulkner, not to mention those still writing. The writers address a wider variety of distinct audiences than do the painters. The history of literary modernists born in the United States—Eliot, Pound, Stevens, Frost, Robinson, cummings, Williams, Aiken, Lindsay, Lowell, Masters, Moore, Sandburg[1]—differs greatly from the appearances of modernism in Vienna (Musil, Schnitzler) or in Prague (Rilke, Kafka), to which must be added Berlin, Zurich, and even Moscow before the revolution.

High modernism is not a style, a theme, a form, or a school. Rather, a certain attitude predominates about how literature is produced, the purpose it serves, and the function of the writer. The writer undertakes a mission of utmost seriousness: to increase society's self-conscious realization of the unique dilemmas that had emerged as knowledge in every area had been called into question. Literature does not answer those questions; it provides a way of living among them, of having courage, ethics, dedication, purpose, and even truth, since the most significant truths concern this very condition. Cosmological and terrestrial insecurity were experienced by a generation whose earliest members were born in the 1880s, by which time Darwinism was no longer just a reasonable hypothesis but the only feasible explanation. Hopes for an altruistic humankind carried invariably forward by optimistic progress were shattered by World War I, ending a halcyon tranquility in the midst of this generation's youthful maturity.

High modernism completes the disillusionment with and rejection of the romantic admixture of transcendentalisms, which earlier modernism had gradually outmoded but never repudiated. Tracing the recurrence and decline of the once nearly ubiquitous term *spiritual* from the 1880s through the mid-1930s would readily illustrate this point. Furthermore, by the time of high modernism, the primary philosophical source of romanticism and metaphysical transcendence, Germany, has lost the war to the empiricist nations.

The high modernist work gives structure to the world, since the world itself cannot give structure to the work. Art excepted, all structure is frail and temporary, including selfhood. Art succeeds where the world itself fails, even though that victory is also ever-present proof of the tremendous loss: the success of art signals the failure of everything else. For centuries the elevation obtained from art and religion had been allied; the field of "aesthetics" was initially a tightening of this bond, weakened by empiricism. But the literary figures can neither sustain nor serve as the last defense of the spiritual, as the earlier modernists, particularly the painters, had done. The concepts that held the world order together lose legitimacy, rather like the royal dynasties that toppled or grew enfeebled after World War I. While visual artists are affected by this, writers need to address it directly.

The work of writers is made of words, the same material as the concepts that comprise worldview. If the world is reorganized, that reorganization happens in literature because in a profound sense the reorganization is literature. How to create the sublime, when the sublime myths are dwindling—that is, how to make the sublime interior to the artwork? (To recreate the sublime myth politically is another approach, inspiring fascism.) The internal compositional harmonies of art were once static because they were based on the eternal. This is true of the Sumerians and the Egyptians, for whom the earth was eternal, as well as of the medieval and Renaissance painters. But when the timeless wanes, the harmonies internal to the artwork must come from organic life; they are dynamic, not static, and every work is filled with a movement that its structure can enclose but not hold still. The interior of the work is always in tension. The work does not envelop us, it carries us; we are not calmed (no Aristotelian catharsis here) but agitated.

These circumstances increasingly predominate during the time that the transition occurs between dada (Tzara, Picabia, Arp, Duchamp) and surrealism (Breton, Aragon, Ernst, and eventually Picabia and Duchamp, Magritte, and Dali), the first two components of visual high modernism. Dada arises from the anticipation, during and after World War I, of the demise of German idealism and German intellectual leadership. For the dadaists, immersed in German culture, this seems equivalent to the irremediable collapse of a meaningful Western civilization. With no conceivable alternative to German culture (for example, without the alternative that the English literature of high modernism will later provide for so many), Germany's defeat appears apocalyptic, albeit necessary and just. For the dadaists, to conclude that the origin of meaning is only a psychic contrivance is a ludicrous substitute for those once majestic meanings now becoming obsolete, since it makes meaning preposterous. And for the personality to stand alone, ungrounded by any Absolute, makes action equally preposterous; for action can have no ultimate meaning either, which provokes modern anxiety. (Modern anxiety is the absence of ultimate meaning; once, anxiety was an inadequacy felt in the presence of ultimate meaning.) Action literally makes no sense, and consequently dadaist behavior becomes nonsensical, a form of existential bravery.

For the surrealists, however, the same recognitions give meaning its bedrock: the truth is about what meaning means. The human mystery and profundity is that meaning can be assigned to the world, rather than be found in the world. This is reason for exuberance rather than for anxiety, at least for surrealist artists. Surrealism transforms dadaism by discovering that a psychological theory can again make the world as meaningful as the now defunct Hegelian philosophy had done, even if not in quite the same way. The earlier dada, deprived of theory altogether, had no replacement for meaning besides pure behavior. For the surrealist, meaning can emerge from the unconscious, free and unchecked. One can even forgo conscious control over the painting (or poetry), because meaning and mental structure are innately congruous. (Some surrealists explore, even admire, the artworks of the insane.) The course of modernism in its entirety shows, in part, how the idea that meaning in the world needs to be assigned, since it cannot be discovered, comes to be celebrated.

In surrealism, the content of the artwork images the content of the unconscious. Subjectivity is its ideational content, which is why surrealism is recognized as so often relying on literary elements. Surrealism was, of course, founded in 1919 by poets—Breton, Aragon, Soupault, all influenced by Apollinaire, coiner of the term *surrealism*, who died in 1918, two years after being wounded in the war. By the time of abstract expressionism (Pollock, de Kooning, Still, Newman, Rothko: the last phase of visual high modernism, beginning in New York City in the 1940s) individual personality, the creative unconscious, and visual formalism are unified in a pure abstraction. The formal properties of artworks and the formal properties of the unconscious become correlated but are no longer the same, because a consciously formalist technique is interposed between mind and canvas. The abstract expressionist exercises dominance and control at exactly the point where the surrealist lets go. A conscious stylistic choice determines the form subjectivity will take: the painting then has a subject that is not the same as the transmuted mental content. The unconscious fuels meaning but is not, as the surrealists thought, identical to meaning; the unconscious is an energy, not a collection of thoughts. To use it spontaneously is not the same as to use it unconsciously. The literariness of painting (the symbol as ideational content) that characterized surrealism is abandoned, along the lines once taken by Picasso, whom the abstract expressionists venerate. Images are replaced by abstractions, without the residue of ordinary eyesight, sensory prejudices, or dreams and hallucinations.

Dada and surrealism, together with abstract expressionism, comprise the stage of visual high modernism, which will flourish (in surrealism and abstract expressionism; dada endured briefly) for forty years. The term *high modernism*, usually applied to literary modernism after World War I, is justified for surrealist and abstract expressionist painting insofar as the term names a process during which the properties of the artwork and the psychological properties of the artist move apart and eventually become severed, by interjecting formalism between them. Formalist criticism then becomes as autonomous an academic discipline as art history, both estranged from psychology.

By the time of literary high modernism, modernist painting—particularly French painting—had already celebrated its important victories. It had become no longer just a critique of the modern world but the official critique. Modern visual art had come to decorate the very aspects of modernity it once disavowed; its innovations in painting and sculpture begin to become confused with cultural novelty, where the interesting and the entertaining become synonymous. This will prove especially true of the architecture of the international style, through which visual modernism will finally be irreversibly legitimated as compatible with the corporate model of political and economic organization that finances the construction.[2] As with painting, the literary high modernist's social protest is increasingly incorporated into modernity as a functional, even when unconventional, feature of the social milieu. The vaunted isolation or alienation of the artist and writer, or at least the aloofness (since many of them take on a dignified eminence that artists and writers had not enjoyed since the heyday of the Salon Carré in the late 1840s[3]), are excused as a quite understandable psychic condition, likely necessary for inner aesthetic vision, perhaps even a professional qualification.

High modernism does not develop completely new principles. High modernism is modernism become self-conscious of itself as a historical event, decades into its progress, rather than as the new event announced in the early modernist manifestos. From the perspective of literary criticism alone, high literary modernism may appear completely new, but from a larger view it involves the transfer of the avant-garde from painting to writing. (Writing is itself a "belated" modernism at its origins, following painting.) Modernism turns its attention to itself; its subject matter is frequently about what modernism as a whole ought to amount to. The artist considers, frequently with no trace of humility, what it is to be a modern artist or writer in an environment where (obviously) almost everyone else is not. Or perhaps it is more exact to say that since modernism had been self-conscious from the beginning, since it always operated in a purported opposition to the status quo, high modernism is the historical self-consciousness of the aesthetic self-consciousness. For the literary modernist, the consequent multiple distancing is a type of knowing: accordingly, irony flourishes. Writers and artists are to some extent reappropriated by the conditions of history from which modernism had meant itself to be the escape. The high modernists no longer need to rebel against history; they are not newly forging modernism but have taken possession of modernism. Modernism advances itself by assessing itself, paying tribute to itself. High modernism has become society's authorized and permanent critique.

Certain poets assert extensive influence, but, to judge by the size of the readership, the novel becomes the principle literary genre. In the novel of the internal, psychological narrative, significant actions and accomplishments can occur not as deeds but as thoughts in the minds of acutely self-conscious characters. The fictional characters emulate the history of modernism itself—as if all these novels are allegories of modernism. Such novels appeal to a new readership, a generation seeking the same release from its historical precedents and determinants that modernism began by seeking. That class defines itself educationally, professionally, and politically rather than nationally, ethnically, and religiously. It is a class whose education will include learning about modernism, and which will develop an intensity of self-awareness (half self-confidence, half anxiety) to substitute for the now untenable convictions, prejudices, and misinformation of their parents and grandparents.

Truth becomes timebound and impermanent. Absolutist truth is demoralized, replaced by opinion, outlook, worldview. Science aside, knowing is not knowledge in any ultimate sense—it is not a state, but a procedure. The best one can do is to have a moral commitment to a vulnerable position. The aim of positivist philosophy is to clarify an argument without resolving it or for the clarification to be received as the resolution. Like pragmatism, positivism in philosophy is designed to replace what phenomenology regards as meaning (not what humans find, but what humans are) with the logical conditions for stating knowledge as propositions. Essence is forfeited in exchange for process. This leads to a certain cynicism, since while everything can be clear, nothing can be certain.

In response to this dilemma, artists and critics begin to propound versions of the dual-truth theory, claiming that art, too, contains "truth"—not a propositional truth, like science, but nevertheless a valid "truth" deserving of the name. Art reflects reality through an organization of experience in linguistic and visual structure that corresponds to human reality, even if does not objectively describe that reality. The form of the work and the form of the world correspond; emotional structures serve as the means of translation between the two.[4] For the eighteenth-century neoclassicist, truths, however expressed, were ultimately statable as declarative sentences. In dual-truth theory, the truths of art repose in a different cognitive dimension from the truths of science. As high modernism progresses, the theory becomes a doctrine.

Some versions of dual-truth theory (which has its remote origins in the debates over the compatibility of religious revelation and Aristotelian logic in Aquinas, Averroes, and the Italian humanists) have permeated all the aesthetic movements from romanticism forward, through symbolism, through the New Criticism,[5] to the present day. Earlier, however, any theory of the duality of truth depended on an accompanying belief in either revelation or "intuition." In high modernism, on the other hand, transcendence has disappeared from the analysis: the comparison is horizontal, not vertical. Under the influence of psychology, factual truth and "emotional truth" (once a meaningless term) can confront one another. For the first time, as a result of empiricism, human factual knowledge no longer can fulfill human emotional need. We have come to know that whatever once made us blessed or sacred was likely a delusion.

For some modernists in the twenties and thirties, particularly in England, dual-truth theory will not be sufficient compensation for the loss of transcendence. Eliot undergoes religious conversion; so does Auden. And there is the literary Christianity of C. S. Lewis, G. K. Chesterton, and Hilaire Belloc.

Romanticism abides in high modernism (as it still does today), not as the romantic worldview but as the romantic personality. There is, of course, also the prominent claim of some literary high modernists that "classicism" ought to be the guiding principle, that romanticism has been obviated, that what is needed is not so much human yearning but human limitation, not so much unbounded emotion released into art but measured experience proportioned in art, not so much an exuberant freedom but a scrupulous discipline.[6] Nevertheless, artists still envision themselves as unique, sensitive, privileged, both elites and exiles.[7] Romanticism is deeply ingrained in the artistic personality, and the intuitional aesthetic faculty empiricism cannot substantiate is surreptitiously maintained, even if transformed. But the old justifications for it have evanesced. Seeking an explanation for creativity that sustains the uniqueness of the artist (for a modernist to discover that the artist is merely human is a humiliation), writers and artists frequently turn to psychology, romanticizing that discipline by giving literature and art a conspicuously elevated prominence.

In high modernism art is a refuge and a haven. Modernism had not pulled the switch that would transfer the train of empiricism from one track to another; all the work still remains to be done. But if the modernist goal was not simply a delusion, should it not already have been achieved? Renewing the effort to demonstrate how art can be used to refashion the personal experience of one's own life and society, surrounded by the collaborations of politicians and investors, the high modernists elevate art to the highest human experience.

Formalist criticism follows. The history of art becomes autonomous, internal to itself, even while artists continue to defend their role as essential to the social condition generally. A severance grows between the formalist criticism of artworks and the lives of the artists who produce them. The work comes from the artist, but by producing it the artist releases it from the self. The self is not transformed into the visual or literary artwork for the high modernist: creativity is not the creation. The self is the medium in which the artwork coalesces, not the "materials" out of which the work is made. (The materials, on the empiricist model, come directly from outside through the senses). The artwork evolves as it passes through the self. For the romantics, and generally for the early and midmodernists, creativity was autonomous selfhood in expressive action. For the high modernist, the self is not entity but act, as it was for certain early modernist French poets.[8] The self is not exactly exercised in creativity, but evolved through the act of creativity; the self does not simply have experiences, it is, more accurately, composed of experiences. The artist positions the self at a critical junction of external events; at that junction, the external events integrate into an authentic artwork. The artist's personality has been the catalyst for the work, not its subject.

Although the artist may profess that self or personality is not the content of the work,[9] this is usually received by the public as an interesting aspect of the artist's personality. Knowing the artist's opinions, tastes, and personal habits become part of the public's critical assessment—as if the unity in the artwork corresponded to the configuration of the artist's selfhood. Novice artists, trained in the imitation of style, also imitate the personalities of well-known artists. The artist becomes a recognizable "type"—not always the same type, for the bohemian on the Left and the personage of mighty distinction on the Right are competing models. Those who most appreciate modernism pride themselves on their differences from people who cannot: to understand the work properly is to some degree to be as unique as the work is.

Psychic forces are considered inherent in a biological mind, just as science had placed all forces of motion inherently in matter. While self, or even soul, was once the unity of subjectivity to which personality adhered as a set of contingent traits, personality and ego now become what the "individual" essentially is. Any substratum is not spiritual, but a rudimentary psychobiological inheritance, raw material for personhood. Beginning early in the thirties, the only form of transcendence will be fame.

As high modernism progresses (and therapeutic psychologies become popularized concurrently), intellectual or propositional or objective content of the self gradually become subordinated to the personal features of the individuated ego. The artwork eventually becomes confessional. Appreciation of it is an empathetic emotional condition, for to appreciate the work is also a type of confession. Criticism, on the contrary, which had increasingly proclaimed itself to be an objective discipline (professionally established in the universities), now becomes completely formalized, emphasizing the very opposite of appreciation or emotional rapport, even if such rapport motivates undertaking the criticism. Critics and artists become two very different kinds of people, just as the work and the artist are segregated.

Formalism

The transition to literary or high modernism is characterized by a move toward formalist theory and criticism, first in literature and afterward in the other arts, especially painting. The process takes thirty years. As modernism loses the efficacy of its meanings, it triumphs in its forms. Newer developments do not obviate earlier ones. While formalism becomes the method of professional criticism (it is why criticism is "professional"), the emphases on the personality of the artist and the psychology of the imagination are not discarded elsewhere. The artist and the aspiring artist cling to them, and so do many patrons as well as the generally interested public.

Formalism is modernism's assessment and valuation of an artwork according to the presumed unified interrelationship between its structure, the devices of its "language," and the materials from which it is assembled. Whether in the literary arts (from Russian formalism through Prague structuralism and French structuralism, the New Criticism, and Northrop Frye), the visual arts (from the German formalist-historicist critics to Roger Fry to Clement Greenberg and his contemporaries), or the musical arts, formalism's central question is not (only) what the work means but how the work means, not what the work can do or has done to the observer but how it has done this.[10] The "how" is different from the "why," because one can know how art functions without knowing why—leaving the why to physiology or psychology, to a theory of color or linguistics or tonal perception. Formalism asks both about the work's rhetoric (semantic devices that yield meaning) and about its syntax (the conceptual and the spatial relationships of its parts). The meaning of an artwork is not like the meaning of ordinary declarative sentences, which are propositions convertible into another form (into formulas, for example, or by re-wording). The work of art does contain statements, and it does manifest an outlook or viewpoint—otherwise it would only be design. Yet content and form, although not the same, are inseparably bonded inside the specific materials of the artwork (paint, stone, words). The unification of emotion in what is called the aesthetic response is taken to demonstrate the unification of content and form. Insofar as the emotion cannot be partitioned at the most intense level of response, neither can the components of the work. While the components can be isolated for the purpose of analysis (this isolation is analysis), the whole is more than the sum of its parts, a Gestaltist principle. The meaning and its manifestation are inextricable. While the components of art are the sounds, shapes, colors, and gestures by which meaning is ordinarily constituted, these elements of ordinary meaning assume an extra-ordinary meaning inside a particular artwork.

Formalism assumes the work of art to be an object of study whose properties are objectively discoverable through analysis, like the properties of natural objects investigated by science.[11] Criticism can therefore be legitimated as a professional discipline, since a profession depends not only on the mastery of a body of knowledge but on an ensemble of techniques for the discovery of new knowledge. Criticism becomes eligible for separate membership within the academic community—like history, to which criticism was once subordinated. The "history" of art and literature gain autonomy; their temporal and causal sequences become increasingly isolated from traditional political, military, economic, and, eventually (since modernism is an internationalism), geographical history.

For the nineteenth-century German formalists (e.g., Hegel, Alois Riegl, Heinrich Wölfflin), a body of art and the age in which it appears are linked by structures of meaning common to both. The art says what the age says. Interpretation always includes the understanding that reality does not appear the same in every age: the formal devices used within any specific culture are those most suitable to expressing its outlooks, those relationships that comprise the world. Worldview can only be found in art by means of an analysis of the formal devices employed to yield that view, which makes the approach a formalism.[12] For the modernist formalists, the emphasis changes to formal and technical strategies conceived as independent from the historical context. While an age may use or even invent a specific strategy or device, the formalists treat the strategies and devices as if they were abstracted from an idealized permanent repertoire of devices. While various human beliefs and dispositions change over time, and while every artwork contains beliefs and dispositions, art concerns the human emotions. As a set of all possible human emotions, these have remained the same over time. Therefore, art always works in the same way. Specific beliefs and opinions are not the central concern of art; rather, the aesthetic organization of the emotions can occur in similar ways at all times, although some ages favor certain practices and ignore others. The modernist formalist can treat each artwork as if it were detached from the temporal or geographical contingencies of its production. Analyzing the art object employs universal criteria, based on the relationships of human emotions to the forms in which they best find coherent and orderly expression. This is what art is, in contrast to the often disordered or confused emotions of daily life for ordinary people. Biography and traditional history become irrelevant, although because of various qualifications (changes in the meanings of words, for example) not all formalist critics discard them completely.

When the work is finished by the artist, it is released as an object, complete in itself. The creator and the creation can be formally severed, in just the way the deists conceived the relationship of God and the cosmos. (A universe created as a mathematically perfect machine can run by itself.) Interpretation begins neither with the biography of the artist, nor with the social circumstances, nor by positioning the work within the historical sequence. These factors are subordinated to considerations internal to the specific artwork: the relationship of its structure and its semantic devices, its syntax and its rhetoric. This relationship is presumed permanent, like the basic relationships between structure and materials in a chemical or a plant. The relationship in the plant or chemical, however, include structure and materials but not meaning; the artwork must contain all three.

Formalism in art criticism is the belief that meaning can also be an objective property of an object. Meaning emerges from formal properties not themselves inherently meaningful; rather, their assemblage yields meaning. During the same years when formalism evolves, linguistics likewise describes the basic constituents of language as phonemes, which are the (arbitrary) components of meaning yet not themselves meaningful. Meaning is no longer that which is communicated, but that which incipiently resides inside the structure of communication. Meaning is always a construction, not a discovery. Facts can be discovered—a fact is defined as what would be true in the world even if it were not or could not be spoken—but meaning must be an artifact. A meaningful system exists as a structure independent from its users, although it could not exist were there not users of it. Language and artworks achieve their formalist independence simultaneously. While there would be no artistic rhetoric without a history, the history of the rhetoric is not the history of the rhetoricians (artists), any more than the history of the spoken language is the aggregated biographies of its individual users.

The artwork is object-ified, and the critic is dissuaded from conjecturing about the empathetic affiliation between the subjectivity of the artist and the subjectivity of the viewer or reader. In high modernism, artists themselves become obliged to enumerate their formal procedures, minimizing their personalities (at least in the theory) in imposingly serious essays. To each body of work a formalist theory is appended, which the work is both to ratify and exemplify. Even if motivated by subjective considerations (one likes some works and not others), formalist criticism aspires to exercise the faculty of objective analysis on a stable physical object. For the formalists, the relation of art to its rules resembles the relation of nonorganic material objects to physical laws. The laws are logically prior to events, although the laws are also derived from the summation of events (regularities). However, because the aesthetic object must be describable with a unique vocabulary, in order to give the discipline an autonomy not subordinated to history, properties presumed independent of the observer are enumerated by terms that once referred primarily to states of mind. *Irony* and *paradox* are relentlessly employed by the New Critics, together with *ambiguity, resolution, complexity, dissociation, harmony, symmetry, tension,* and *balance,* which become used as structural terms to objectively describe the qualities of the artwork, not simply the qualities of its reception.

For formalist criticism, an artistic method—the relations between rhetoric, syntax, and materials—is independent of its practitioner. Artistic methods have a history distinct from those who employ them, although the historical situation of the artist makes specific methods available. *Method* is not personal; *style* is the personalization of method. A method is a small set of techniques, exhaustively characterizing a large body of works by numerous hands. No one technique is sufficient to identify the particular work of a particular artist. Style is a subset of techniques drawn from the method, characterized by limited individual variations on their application. A method can become a movement; people can join and even lead it, yet in an important sense they neither control nor own it. For example, while nineteenth-century artists viewed Japanese art as displaying the attainments and insights of individual artists, the modernists view African art as a formalism and the individuality of the artists is irrelevant. The modernists admire African art, not African artists. From imagism and cubism forward, method is considered external to the practitioner.

In formalism, then, aesthetic movements are identified by practices rather than by the beliefs that stimulate those practices, which it had previously been the function of the modernist manifestos to disclose. Cubism, for example, is considered profoundly important not because it necessarily leads to superior innovation or insight but because the formal qualities of the method are so obviously distinct from particular users of them. Cubism illustrates how a transpersonal technique can be invented. The modernist production of various transpersonal techniques eventually overwhelms the major example of such a technique inherited from the past, namely, Renaissance perspective.

In formalism, art is reified as Art and presumed to have a historical life of its own. This is quite different from Renaissance classicism, for which the Roman artists of antiquity had mastered the forms invented by the Greeks to be thereafter permanently venerated and imitated. From a Renaissance view, the history of art contains (a few) episodes, but instead of being causally sequenced they are attributed to the unique characteristics (ethical, civic, martial, religious) of special times and places. For the romantics, alternatively, the history of art is the story of successive autonomous contributors. Modern formalism occurs after causal evolutionary theory had already permeated all disciplines, from the eighteenth-century notion of advancing stages of history to *The Origin of Species* (1859). The history of art, too, becomes a causal sequence of unidirectional motion over time. The histories of the arts then need to be rewritten, based on how the formal relations embodied in any method advance the evolution of methodology itself.

The artist and the critic both comply: the content and purpose of certain principal artworks are the method of their production. Personal style is repeatedly put forth as if it were transpersonal method. Meaning and method are fused; so are content and form. They have become more than bonded; they have become unified. As modernism advances, the form and structure of the work become possible modes of meaning. Method may be the end as well as the means. Formal criteria become the focus of both artist and critic. Even the early modernists talked about "experiments" and "researches," terms that always refer to formalist method. The experiment is to have technique determine meaning, even be meaning, rather than to have one's intended meaning determine the choice of technique—otherwise it would be not an experiment, but simply what one has to say. (Wordsworth used *experiment* in the 1802 preface to *Lyrical Ballads* to mean his use of the language of common people: not, at least ostensibly, his style but their method.) Since meaning corresponds to method, no subject matter is excluded in any modernist theory, since no method is excluded. Style is judged as if it were innovation in method; the important work advances Art, aside from whatever it might mean.

Since an advance of method is an advance of meaning, the best artists are not only skilled but also wise. The wisdom granted to artists by the romantics because of their potential for transcendence now becomes a matter internal to the history of art. The test is a performance, not a state of being. Of course, since the meanings of artworks become inseparable from their methods, and as such experimentation becomes more complex, modern art is further and further removed from those kinds of meanings that the public considers appealing. The public looks for meanings presumed to exist independent of method, believing that (with concessions to the scientists) there are plain truths that can be plainly stated.

Validating criticism as an independent object of study encourages specially trained arbitrators and evaluators. Art can no longer be appraised principally by the feeling created in the beholder; feeling may evidence nothing more than sentiment, shock, novelty, or loveliness. Nor can art be appraised by an avowed correspondence to truth, nature, or reality that the personal sensibility of the critic responds to or recognizes because of a refinement of taste. The "man of letters" is replaced by academics, curators, editors, columnists, producers. The work must not only say and do something, but it must be a certain something, evaluated technically. Judgments require criteria for assessing not only the use of method but the advancement of method, without which the meaning of the work will be a repetition of the meaning of other works. Ingenuity or dexterity is demanded; so is innovation that is more than novelty: the work must be not only new, but important.

The rise of an aesthetic professional class creates and perpetuates formalism as well as responds to it. Only formalism can give criticism the status of legitimate academic disciplines, which require formally defined objects of study. In some cases, to be sure, the artwork and formalist criticism draw apart. Surrealism remained relatively insusceptible to formalism, since the term *surrealism* applies not to certain properties of the work but to the ideas behind it. (There is no surrealist method, although a remarkable abundance of its styles are drawn from almost every method.) Cubism, on the other hand, becomes the formalists' favorite. (Cubism is surely a method.) Picasso becomes identified as the greatest genius of modern art. The novels of Joyce and the cantos of Pound also reside on the summit of literary modernism. As formalist critics gain authority, the artist must provide the critic with work that lends itself to formalist criticism, or else be denied the certification of importance.

Judgment solely by responsive feeling is increasingly assigned to the middle class, who are presumed to lack the credentials necessary for an appropriate level of aesthetic appreciation. It is the business of the critic to inform the public what it ought to admire. The public is a reluctant audience. It craves sensation rather than meaning, gratification rather than instruction, entertainment rather than art; furthermore, the formal devices and technical innovations of modern art often appear confusing, obscure, or ridiculous. For the formalist, art becomes radically distinct from entertainment. To appreciate entertainment requires minimal training; one's responses are rapidly sequenced emotional changes, not evaluations of the formal properties of the technical craft, which are customarily masked by the performance. To marvel at the display of skill is not equivalent to understanding the practices that are its origin.

Previously, the academies had trained artists in the techniques of producing pleasure and truthfulness that simultaneously institutionalized and celebrated the official public morality, the values of church and either royal or civil authority. In modernism, the public morality is the antagonist of art. The commercial media reinforce this stance. Modernist works are often declared immoral, disreputable, or harmful; scandal verifies the work's significance to the initiated and its perniciousness to the uninitiated. At the same time, a superior university education involves passing through the canonized works of mid- and high modernism, usually up to a point about twenty or thirty years in the past. (Late modernism is still a specialized field of study.) The student learns how to pay them homage, or at least some respect. Although usually stripped of any insistent meaning, the artifacts of modernism will decorate the work settings of the educated (the better the job, the more modern the environment) and will often distinguish that setting from the home.[13]

The triumph of modernist artistic form in the capitalist work setting parallels the history of capitalism itself. The successful capitalist masters the forms and procedures of economic transactions; the (non-monetary) value of the product is irrelevant. Ethical, social, familial, and religious meanings are no longer criteria for assessing successful capitalists' entrepreneurial value—whether they are "good," rather than "good at." The product's nonmonetary value mattered once, and specialized guilds validated the merit and necessity of certain products arrayed in a limited number of permanently necessary categories. Unions, however, protect the worker rather than the product. Capitalism concerns itself with the means of production, not with the outcomes of production.[14] In capitalism, then, mastering the principles of capital growth and earning is distinct from any meaning inherent in the product. Surplus meanings are often assigned by producers and distributors as factors determining a product's price and status, although such surplus meaning is then disingenuously presented to the public as if it resided inherently in the ownership or design of the product. As in formalism the meaning in art is also the meaning of Art, so the surplus meaning in products is actually the meaning of Products—namely, capitalism itself. The meaning of a product emerges as one more product of the system of producing products. Modern capitalism, then, consists of mastering the how but not the why of things, the production of meaning but not the meaning of production. Capitalism is economic formalism.

In most modernist theories, it cannot be assumed that the average person has any insight into truth. Truth is precisely what has been suppressed or distorted in the public consciousness. Public consensus is error. The Freudian psychoanalytic theory of repression and the Marxist theory of ideology (the former more in the United States, the latter more in Europe) provide ample theoretical ammunition that the uppermost contents of consciousness are deceptions. Furthermore, for two hundred years science has repeatedly discovered that what lies hidden inside publicly observable phenomena is a surprisingly different truth of the matter. Yet while consensual agreements about innovation in science become rapidly popularized in the media as newly discovered truths, artistic innovation becomes increasingly removed from public view (architecture aside). The proverbial 99 percent of the public has no idea what constitutes contemporary art, aside from the random *cause célèbre*.[15] While modernism is founded on objections to middle-class values, presumptions, and behaviors, science collaborates with all of these, as governmental and corporate funding awards verify. Like psychoanalysis and Marxism, modernism was not only supposed to be a set of new methods; it was also supposed to be a set of new truths made available (only) by those methods. Yet while a scientific consensus about the bizarre (black holes, for example) becomes a new truth, in art there is usually little distinction, outside the art world, between the innovative and the preposterous. Yet artists and critics still insist upon their prerogatives to assess society from a position of lofty privilege, inherited by early modernism from romanticism.

Modernism first attempts to cast off the past, freeing the individual. But when formalism dominates in high modernism, the past is not a burden but "tradition," which the artist embraces, contributes to, and modifies. The histories of the arts cannot be rewritten by formalism unless the history of art actually exists—unless, that is, art history is not subordinated to political, social, or economic history. The writers and artists of high modernism eagerly reenter the stream of time, although modernism (as we shall see in a later chapter) arose as a movement striving to relinquish the historical stream of time. The legitimating procedure for this reversal is to forfeit history proper—to leave its texts in the possession of the middle class in exchange for control over the now autonomous history of art.

One result of this exchange is that formalism's focus on technique rather than conviction, on the internal dynamics of the artwork rather than any necessary external import, makes formalism ideally compliant in a politically conservative environment. It was the ideal approach throughout the "McCarthy era" in the United States during the 1950s. Formalism and political activism are readily detached by assigning the former but not the latter to the universities, as the more recent formalist movements (structuralism, post-structuralism, postmodernism) confirm.[16]

Formalism protects the territory of later modernism, a territory in danger of being forfeited because early modernism had likely already failed. Modern art and literature would not spiritually transform the world; they would not become the source of value and transcendence that religion had once been. The modernist attempt to combine empiricism and romanticism had been unsuccessful—or extremely successful, but not in the way originally envisioned. This is not to belittle the actual achievement of modernism: its visual transformation of the world, its opening up of new fields for the intellect and the emotions, its successive generations of indisputable genius. Formalism recuperates modernism by substituting aesthetic structures for social purposes, the "principles" of art (the word *principles* is often found in the title of formalist treatises) substituting for ethical and social "principles." Devotion to one's art can be a fully adequate and commendatory moral commitment, regardless of one's behavior or one's position on any particular subject.

Modernists do, of course, subscribe to ethical and social positions, but these positions are extraneous to the criteria for the advancement of an autonomous history of art. The ethical and social positions are not based on enduring truths (for truth is now internal to the aesthetics) but on dilemmas (traceable to the dilemmas of empiricism). The modernists preceding World War I looked favorably on science and technology (which they did not equate with capitalism) and on its potential to improve the world. Postwar modernists viewed science and technology as antagonists, for science had become subsidiary to the values it might once have been expected to change. The Great Depression and World War II confirmed the flaw in empiricist modernity, which nevertheless prevailed. The high modernists attempt to reconfigure modernism by bringing empiricism inside their aesthetics, through formalism, as if by that means to subordinate empiricism, while claiming to leave romanticism outside. They thought that formalism (now called "classicism" to signify the purported turning away from romanticism) as a system of criticism rather than a system of beliefs might propel the continuation of modern art as a movement. They were correct.

Psychology substitutes for the earlier belief systems. Because psychology presumes to make consciousness and selfhood objects of study, it is the science most compatible with art. One learns not what to believe (there are no eternal truths) but only why beliefs are believed. Again, while facts are both real and discoverable, meaning is always a construction of the formal system that both creates and communicates the meaning. Meaning is no less real because meaning is not fact. The post-structuralism of the seventies, incidentally, is the assertion that this distinction (the basis of dual-truth theory) is arbitrary: that "facts" are actually meanings, too. But such a qualification had never occurred to the modernists, and that the idea gains notoriety in the seventies is one indication that modernism is concluding.

Before the transition to formalism, the romantic features that characterized modernism were ideas about aesthetic transcendence, passion, commitment, frenzy, guilt, mysticism, elation, compassion, anguish, longing, neuroses, and isolation, combined with hopes for the emergence of a spiritually reconstituted society. The formalists take a different approach, naming themselves "classicists" in a purported repudiation of the elements of romanticism in early and midmodernism.

Surrealism rests on fundamentally literary presumptions and practices: for example, that the symbolic contents of the unconscious are ideas as well as images. It does retain the romanticism that the literary high modernists reject, which is why the surrealists find, by default, their most rewarding work and their most enduring reputation in painting. (Although Breton's *Surrealist Manifesto* is not about painting.) The painters to whom the high modernists and literary formalists are most attracted are, again, the cubists, who are viewed as rejecting any literary allusions or narrative symbols and whose work therefore can be discussed technically without having to decide its meaning.[17] The American abstract expressionists will be the last modernists to attempt to unite the formalist integrities of Picasso (the Picasso of cubism through the *Three Musicians*) with the idealism of spirit found in Kandinsky, Mondrian, and Malevich. But since idealism in philosophy and "spirituality" in art have already been depleted by the midtwentieth century, how can sublime art be created without any sublime myth? Through formal structural considerations alone, the formalists argue. The formalists immediately make abstract expressionism their foremost personal critical domain. In painting, this marks the triumph of formalism (and the consequent demise of surrealism).[18] Abstract expressionism provides the formalists with the critical test cases—Pollock's "dripped" paintings, for example—just as Joyce's *Ulysses* and *Finnegans Wake*, Eliot's *The Waste Land*, and Pound's *Cantos* had for the literary formalists.

Although it calls itself a classicism,[19] modernist literary formalism is not synonymous with the literary neoclassicism of the seventeenth and eighteenth centuries. In neoclassicism, meaning is considered to precede its expression. The truth contained in art can be stated as propositions outside of art. It confirms the accustomed social verities; it is prescriptive (the three unities in drama, for example); its ultimate criterion is artistic propriety, balance, and beauty, evidenced by a harmony in the beholder between elevation, decorum, equilibrium, and insight. Accustomed verities are not conventions but truths, which is why neoclassicism is useful not only at royal courts but to Jacobins and, in the twentieth century, to fascists. In modernist formalism, however, that art and literature concern the coherent organization of emotional states releases them from propositional (factual) verification. Art is about how this organization can be accomplished, not about the facts upon which the organization is performed. For modernist formalism, art is detached from and elevated above society, as a commentary, judgment, or feeling. In later formalism this comes to be called a "truth" unique to and internal to art, the unison of meaning and the form that has created it. Modernist formalism, at this point, professes to transcendence in a specialized way alternative to romantic transcendence: the dual-truth theory evolves, arising out of formalism as the principle underlying the distinction between fact and meaning. By the late forties, the later high literary modernists recognize that if formal analysis can only produce meanings that, while meaningful, are not in some objective sense truth-full, then poetry will not be allowed a very influential role in the world. (They will be proven right.) Art will become solely emotional territory, not about anything but feelings. In dual-truth theory the residue of romanticism is gradually imported back inside formalist aesthetic theory: science is true but so is art, in some other way. The coherent organization of emotion is an access to truth, since by discovering that organization criticism discovers truths about human emotional life.

It should by now be clear that the dual truths in this theory are actually the customary empiricism on the one hand and romanticism on the other, allegedly now reconciled. The "unity" of the poem is retrieved through paradox and irony, which reconcile opposites. It is as if the modernist poet has inherited the power of Hegel's conflictual dialectic and empirically tamed it. An underlying ideational (conceptual) disunity and conflict, which in neoclassicism would have been a structural flaw (inconsistency), becomes the chief basis for the aesthetic unity of the whole.

Unlike neoclassicism, modernist formalism is not prescriptive. Formal experimentation is itself a modernist formalist principle as well as a value, as long as self-conscious control and artisanry remain. Outside of a single body of work, repetition in art is unacceptable: repetition is best consigned to manufacturing, entertainment, and sports. The codes of genre do not dictate the work, for every important work is itself a new genre. In addition, for the formalists, art need not be beautiful, but it must be significant. The ultimate commendation is to call the work "important" ("beautiful" is today an offhand compliment, and sometimes a polite dismissal). That a work is important can be proved. Exegesis replaces emoting; "close reading" replaces impassioned appreciation.

The themes explicated by the modern formalist are not those of neoclassicism—the eternal verities, "human nature," the stability of political and religious institutions grounded in permanent truths. The young modernists believed they had been promised the best of all possible worlds. During the next thirty years, there will be two world wars bracketing a deep economic depression. The predicaments identified during high modernism by the modern formalist are alienation (whether as courage or despair), trial, urban anonymity, sexuality (as passion, obsession, delusion, and disease), the search for value (no less ardent for being hopeless), and emotional upheaval, often linked to the earlier romantic themes (usually to the darker side of these themes: not Wordsworth but Byron, not Rousseau but De Sade). The predicaments are reworked by the modernists' unique binding of elation and self-doubt, optimism and hopelessness, the fear of mortality and the impetus toward self-destruction. The most conspicuous themes, then, involve the same binding of opposites found in the work's structure. And, art aside, the psychic binding of opposites is precisely the formula for anxiety.

Late Modernism

In its fourth phase, which follows abstract expressionism ("American" art, as Greenberg called it) and literary high modernism, the original project of modernism must be admitted to have failed. Modernism has not, will not, transform the world spiritually. It has succeeded to the extent that the cultural environment of the Western world—its au courant ideas, homes, furnishings, shops, commercial buildings, museums, clothes, curricula—is now modern-ized. The emotional repertoire has been greatly enhanced. Modern life now knows how to talk about itself, and that life has been embodied in unprecedented forms. Formalism has allowed the arts to flourish as a discipline of practice, rather than a system of values. The criteria for good art no longer resemble or are attached to (or confused with) the criteria for "good" people or a good society. Experimentation becomes institutionalized. When it is not surprising that the new is shocking, the shock no longer surprises. Art does not require mastering the rules nor, as for early modernism, mastering the creation of the rules. Art now requires a rule breaking that is itself rule-governed. The outrageous is another convention. The novelty of technique surpasses the novelty of thought: although there are more things to think about, there are no more thoughts to think about these things. The earlier modernist manifestos have become historical documents, without recent successors. Aesthetic theory is no longer artistic manifesto but critical exegesis.

In T. S. Eliot's notion of "tradition" (which the original modernists would not have worried about considering), present artworks retroactively reshape the past. Tradition is not irrevocably behind us but must reorient itself to us. For the Anglo-Americans, the military victory over Germany confirms the authenticity and value of the English tradition. The past becomes malleable and acquiescent to the triumphant. Only for the defeated had the past culminated in apocalypse. (Recall how for the dadaists, the fall of German culture would leave Europe destitute of meaning.) But by late modernism, around the late fifties and into the sixties, it becomes clear that modernism, too, will have a history. (The Museum of Modern Art was already distinguished.) Modernism will be a narrative and an episode inside history, not superior to it. Young artists sense that they have arrived toward the end of the celebration. Modernism can no longer be created, it can only be joined.

The dilemma of late modernism is not, obviously, what the dilemma was for the early modernists. The early modernists were well aware that the techniques of representation, ornamentation, and profundity of theme had been thoroughly explored for centuries, and these techniques had been codified. How to improve upon, or rival, the consummate technical skills of past poets, painters, architects, and sculptors? In response, the technical virtuosity specifically associated both with the skills of realistic representation, classical architecture, and ornate decoration had been demoted as aesthetic values. These skills eventually became commonplace tricks of commercial trade; to master them is not to cultivate art but to look for work. Creative inventiveness and traditional skillfulness became distinct; so did creativity and the old forms of artisanry.

The late modernists cannot, of course, use this same tactic of countermanding the achievements of the past, for to do this would include rejecting what gives their own work importance. That is, the late modernists cannot reject early, mid-, and high modernism. They can, however, undertake the project of closing modernism, finishing it. By the midsixties, the late modernists turn early, mid-, and high modernism into museum masterpieces, into the past. Photography helps; all the paintings can be put in a book on the shelf. Pop art, conceptual art, minimalism, and photorealism discover forms that are at once new and simultaneously the apparently terminating consequences of the modernism that preceded them. They come as surprises when the surprise is the most expected event of all.

Afterward, things still can be modern, which has for centuries meant new and intriguing. (*Modernus* was used in the fifth century to distinguish the Christian from the Roman past; cognate words were used in the days of Charlemagne, in the Renaissance, and in the seventeenth century.) That they are modern does not continue to make them modernism. By the early eighties, everyone is eager to learn what is supposed to happen after modernism, impatient to move on.

Once formalism finishes setting its standards for art and certifying the official modernist canon, formal and technical skills become widely absorbed, taught, and mastered, especially as American universities expand their art history, studio, and creative writing programs. The virtuosity in all the arts is astonishing. All major cities have active arts communities and numerous outlets for display, from restaurants to museums. This enormous proliferation of art is accomplished by intensifying, not expanding, modernism. The sphere of modernism becomes denser rather than bigger. Modernism is filled up, tightly packed with the continually innovative outcomes of its own potential. Experimentation is now what art is, not something on the frontier. The frontier is around every corner. Modernism originally enlarged the capacities of the various literary, visual, and musical genres by competing with tradition for aesthetic space. When the old guards that defended the borders of the genres become superannuated, the prerequisite for critical attention is an originality in competition not with any traditionalism but with the other original works of the modernism in which the new work participates. Artists are no longer a contemporaneous peer group competing with preceding tradition (like the impressionists or the fauves or the high modernist writers) but a collection of separate individuals competing with one another. Having something new to show is taken as if it were equivalent to having something new to say.

In late modernism in the visual arts, the meaning expressed by the artist has been transferred back to the formal properties of the artwork, where it had been firmly situated before high modernism gradually drifted into confessional modes. Meaning is a property directly in the work, a property of the system, not an external referent for the system. For high modernism, human meaning, even if delegated to the world, is nevertheless real, complete, and potentially satisfactory. It is naturally constituted in, through, or out of the natural organizational capabilities of mentality (contemporaneous empiricist theories generally argue that the child is born into sensory chaos, which the mind organizes) or the reservoir of the unconscious. But for visual late modernism, which extends through pop, op, minimalism, conceptual art, hyperrealism, neo-expressionism, and so on, until today, meaning is always undermined by self-awareness of the unavoidable artifice in the construction of meaning. No meaning is innate to the structure of mind; any meaning is a provisional, tentative, and even implausible fabrication of mind. Better, in most cases, to construct things, not meanings, which the critics will in any case supply, even if arbitrarily. Many visual artifacts rely on geometrical construction, but with the spirit and the aspirations of their geometrical forebears (De Stijl, the Bauhaus, suprematism, constructivism) discarded. Instead, momentary, though nonetheless stunning, visual experiences offer modern life fragments of ephemeral meanings that also insist upon their own unavoidable momentariness, whether through formal severity or abandon, the repetitious or the unrepeatable (like "happenings"), shock or comedy, confession or mockery, the idealization of the object or its deprecation.

In literature, too, meaning is contrivance, always temporary, preventing the world from falling apart (notably in mental breakdown, suicide, or alcoholism). Wallace Stevens's theory of "necessary fictions," offered before the Great Depression and World War II subverted the roaring twenties' optimism in England, France, and the United States, does not bear the same temperament as Sartre's insistence that this is humankind's "absurd" dilemma, not its solace.[20] Being committed to a "fiction" yielding happiness is not the same as consciously knowing one is doing this, or intending to do it.[21] Although a commitment qualified in this way can be made with dignity, without optimism such commitment is simply self-deception, even if humankind has no other choice. The sense of contingency accompanies every step; and every achievement is beleaguered by the finitude surrounding it. Sartre's idea that humans are not born with a preexisting essence, but define their own essence during their lives, corresponds precisely to the high modernist definition of an art object, which does not manifest preexistent meaning but creates a meaning inseparable from its own created form. Existentialism's solution to the human dilemma was the answer high modernism had given to the aesthetic dilemma when transcendent truth had deteriorated, but now that answer is charged with human finitude and anxiety.

For authors who bridge mid- and late modernism—Hemingway or Fellini, Pirandello or Camus, Gunther Grass or Ingmar Bergman, Garcia Marquez or Milas Kundera—having to contrive meaning is the chief evidence that the world has already fallen apart. The work need not even be perceived as a bridge to private meaning located in the artist's mind. In fact, the meaning in the work is often no more the

artist's than the observer's or the reader's, although the talent to simulate it is the artist's.

In late modernism's reaction to the confessional personalization of
expression, artworks are created on the basis of formal principles allegedly separated from personality—as in the "new" novel, op art, or
minimalism. One can now quite easily tell the dancer from the dance.
The modern ego itself becomes unable to avoid or deflect the knowledge of its own fundamental superfluousness. This motivates asser-
tions that personality ought to be removed from art, as if to do this
voluntarily mitigates the irremediable loss. Afterward, modernism will
have nowhere left to go.

This fourth and last phase of modernism is, again, extraordinarily
productive. Works that can compete with, or at least not be embar-
rassed by, the work of mid- and high modernism regularly appear, in
abundance. Some question arises about whether masterpieces are still
possible in an era that exploits rather than invents a worldview, but
masterpieces do still seem possible through the forties and fifties,
when the United States reaches its modernist height in abstract expressionism, the novels of Faulkner, Hemingway, and Wolfe, the plays
of O'Neill. The novel had become the only literary genre where an
audience still anticipated a masterpiece. (Nowadays only film seems
to meet that demand.) Eventually even the most ephemeral or transient worldview is subordinated to technique. The various styles of
late modernism in the sixties and seventies—op, pop, conceptualism,
minimalism; the theater of the absurd, black comedy, the inauthentic
confessional, language poetry; the experimental film; electronic music; the "new" novel; the high-speed photograph taken with a small
hand-held camera—emerge from the increasing implausibility of
modernism's original projects, doctrines, and commitments, combined
with the still abundant productivity and invigorating ingenuity of its
multifarious techniques. Invention becomes standard practice: the
brand new is generated by the need of the culture to satisfy its inquis-
itiveness. Such art is drawn, like air into a vacuum, into fissures
opened in the modern psyche, which apparently only news and entertainment can momentarily plug. Despite themselves, artists become
one means of fulfilling this end. This does not, of course, make these
artists any less talented than previous modernists. Artworks burgeon
with the growth of the publishing industry and the art world, and in
the years following World War II (that economic cure for the Great

Depression), with the wealth that pulls down cities and then reconstructs them. New York becomes the headquarters of modernism and of the United Nations, too. (The UN building is itself a lavish tribute to modernism.) Modernist buildings are decorated with the artifacts of modernism, usually in replica, for the prolific replication of its own work is modernism's exuberant finale. The employees who work in these buildings symbolically depend on modernism to advance their lives, their status.

Modernism's critique of itself becomes institutionalized in the universities, the official source of cultural accreditation as increasing numbers of people attend college. The professor replaces the "man of letters," as in the sciences the university facility replaces the amateur's laboratory. Becoming an artist is accredited as an authentic mode of university education, and many artists, writers, and critics are employed as faculty. A substantial portion of the liberal arts curriculum is modernism clad in textbooks. The fourth phase of modernism is, accordingly, a period of strength and influence for modernist institutions, a time of great prestige, especially in America. The wealthy and the powerful affix their names to the letterheads of these institutions, on whose boards they serve.

Nevertheless, the artist's position oddly weakens. Now that there is a modernist establishment and an official history, the new artist is always the latecomer, arriving after all the geniuses have completed their work. ("Belatedness" has recently become a quasi-psychological theory of art generally.[22]) To be proclaimed a new genius by the media or by some critics seems nothing more than ordinary publicity. The steadfast lament the proliferation of fads and ephemera. Institutions do agree to accept new members into the pantheon, or at least into the antechamber, even while they are still alive (Warhol, say, or Stella or Johns; Bellow or Vonnegut; Cocteau or Woody Allen; Borges or Beckett; Ionesco or Fuentes), but while numerous artists receive favorable, if often fleeting, notice, the overwhelming number of quite serious and talented artists are ignored or disparaged, without "contacts" or prospects. The population of artists and writers grows enormously larger than the demands of even the most insatiable society can support. In painting and sculpture, the gatekeepers of modernism—the universities, the critics, the gallery owners—replace the Academy. They are no less prescriptive: not about technique any longer, but about context, about how the work fits the criteria that authorize it to sell at the high price that signifies art is taking still one more step forward. They insist a work should technically advance Art as a whole and the business of art, too, while avowing that the essential qualities of the aesthetic experience (beauty, awe, knowledge, rapture, etc.) remain the same as always.

As "transcendental" becomes, on the one hand, no more than an antique technical term in philosophy and, on the other, an adjective referring generally to any elevating experience, there is the understanding that modernism's substitution of the aesthetic experience for all the preceding varieties of transcendence has been inadequate. There remains inside art an experience of what seems like transcendence, but which is actually an effect that occurs through the devices of art, evidencing nothing else. This simulation of transcendence offers no access to a truth outside art—except, of course, to the truth about what art can do. Allied with an increasing ethical and political relativism, this circumstance may appear cause for optimism. One is free to choose a philosophy or a life-style. Experimentation in art resembles the individual search for personal values: everyone is "creative," and everyone is instructed to learn values by discovery, not instruction. Humans define, shape, and implement their individual destinies. This unlimited diversity confirms that life can be given meaning. Long ago, of course, this would have meant just the opposite.

Between the late sixties and the midseventies—when we enter what is called postmodernism, a phenomenon without its own name yet (as early visual modernism was at first called post-impressionism)—neither the romantic nor the phenomenological outlook, neither the psychological nor the scientific, neither the empiricist nor the transcendentalist, nor the aesthetic, nor the fictional perspective can support the modernists' optimism. The high modernist's self-consciousness of one's own self-consciousness had provided some justification, and even some salvation, in a world from which the sacrosanct had disappeared. But now that modernism has already decorated the world, new works are not triumphs but repetitions. Modernism—once oppositional, then the official opposition—is now finally the status quo. Any legitimate avant-garde must denounce modernism, just as postmodernism does; yet to be part of a denunciatory avant-garde is itself the typifying feature of the modernism that is being rejected.

The cities are stuffed full already, and they cannot now expand into the village or countryside (no new Montmartres, no new Greenwich Villages) as they could when modernism was young. Where will new works go unless the old ones are torn down or put in a vault? Modernism is being archived. No one has the power to do this but the powerful, to whom postmodernism dedicates its work. So many alternative propositions have conceptualized human existence and its meaning (or lack of it) that they can all now be seen as limited and shortsighted, even if for a time exciting. There may be truth, but we will never know it. Besides, what would we do differently tomorrow if we did know it? Our truths are, as we well know, temporary enthusiasms. Only the scientist is obliged to guess at truth; for anyone else, simply to act is sufficient. Where once everyone had a theory, now everyone has a story. The important thing is to experience sporadic joy and to avoid fatigue.

Modernism and Empiricism

4

The Strategies of Empiricism and the Alternatives

Since modernism is principally a set of practices, manifestos, and public positions rather than a coherent conceptual system, it is not obliged to submit to supervening logical demands. The aesthetic transcendentalism of what has been called (in chapter 1) modernism's oxymoronic "transcendental realism" is often used interchangeably with the idea of transcendentalism in philosophical idealism. While the modernists continually move away from idealism, and eventually break from it altogether, idealism retains an indirect influence because of the modernist's romantic predispositions. The modernists gradually disconnect romanticism from its roots in idealism in order to transport it inside empiricism. Empiricism will provide the knowledge of what humans are; romanticism will provide the knowledge of what they should value and do. Through art, romanticism can presumably function as a critique internal to empiricism, rather than as a critique external to empiricism, where romanticism stood when it began. (The importation of romanticism into empiricism is, to anticipate a later chapter, the strategy allowing Marx to employ Hegel.)

The modernists themselves often treat their position inside empiricism as if it were somehow also equivalent to a vantage point outside empiricism. Indeed, the general dilemma of modern art is that artists are in fact inside what they believe they are critiquing from the outside.

Modernity at first conceives of the natural law as God's means. "Law" as a command of deity and "law" as the inherent natural order are intermingled. When a potentially full mathematical description of nature becomes increasingly plausible, the creative imperatives of Nature's God are considered mathematical edicts. Eventually the natural order alone supersedes the edicts. The laws of nature are no longer considered to resemble the laws given by God in Deuteronomy, for the latter ordain free moral compliance with a directive, while the former designate invariable causal relationships. A theological theory of duty is replaced by a theory of inherent "rights." "Law" as legislative or judicial decision is linked to universally valid natural principles, as formerly the Greek word *nomos* had come to include custom, judicial decision, and the ordered cosmic structure.[1]

Originally in Judeo-Christianity, the orderly universe was the residential setting for humans, who themselves were not fully contained ontologically within the natural system they physically inhabited. Physical nature remains conceptually subordinated, even negligible. The biblical religions had distinguished themselves from the heathen worship of immanent nature gods by opening a permanent space between heaven and earth. This emptiness is quite different from a geographical remoteness. Geography is contiguous and can be traversed: the gods live on Olympus; Odysseus visits the land of the dead. In Judeo-Christianity, nature is a convenient asset, whose merit does not extend beyond its practical employment as a collection of resources granted by God for human sustenance. And most of nature is only useless wilderness. Since nature has not yet attained the autonomy that science will attribute to it, it can be neither awesome, sublime, nor beautiful.

Assuming their spiritual constitution and capacities, and allowing for the necessary bodily exigencies, humans are customarily exempted from the principles to which the rest of the universe is subjugated. Humans have free volition—not only desire (which animals also possess) but the powers to assess, manage, and even contravene nature. In contrast, the physical universe runs off the energy of God's persistent volition, which acts upon inert substances by setting and keeping them in motion or appears in plant and animal organisms as an activating vitality ("life"). In addition to a vital animation, and as a result of being endowed with spirit, human life has mental content. (Whether this originally implies an isolable "soul" or not is another matter.) Language allows humankind to possess knowledge of its own origin— the most important knowledge of all, and the content of the holiest texts, since the origin of human life and the ground of meaning are both presumed in (from) God.

During the Reformation there was an attempt to reinforce the unique and always present relationship between the deity and all human beings (not only certain privileged ones) through the direct mediation of a power of mind or intellect. The existence of this capacity limits the range of events that can be ceded to the sciences. In the second version of the creation in Genesis, the heavenly lights are established once and for all; the earth, once isolated from the "waters," brings forth plants when God showers it with rain; and birds and beasts are formed "out of the ground." Into Adam, however, God's breath is introduced.[2] This breath serves as the biblical basis of the inherent human potential for a communion that eludes physical naturalism. But when communion with God is possible for everyone, not only for priests or prophets or mystics, then the failure to experience communion can be taken as evidence against its possibility. For whatever reasons, most people will not experience communion with the Divine. Democratizing transcendence ultimately undermines it.

Empiricism provides alternative tests for the legitimacy of knowledge, in response to the failure of religious transcendence to substantiate its claims. Those who do not experience communion can demand evidence for it from those who say they do, while in fact the development of empiricism assures that nothing in regard to transcendence can legitimately count as evidence.[3] Empiricist knowledge becomes the general cognitive capacity. Public consensus, based on an epistemology of the senses, eventually replaces the privacy of communion. For the empiricists, even a knowledge of God need not result from any special theocentric experience. It can be deduced, as in deism. This gradual abating of communion will eventually result in its replacement by the "intuition" of an idealist aesthetics. Art will reauthenticate and redemocratize transcendence. Unlike communion, art can provide the public physical evidence for its transcendent authenticity: namely, the artwork itself.

It is difficult to believe in a deity that usually provides no direct evidence of its existence. The unavailability of God is the finding of a long experiment, named the Reformation, once intended to demonstrate the contrary. The scientific method is a consequence of, not a cause of, this dilemma of an unavailable deity.

A century into the Reformation, Descartes had allowed human mentality the power to deduce the existence of God. This is different from achieving communication, in either direction, with God. Descartes's most unique deduction is not performed through appeal to logical dilemmas (like the argument for a first cause or a prime mover in Aquinas) or to the basis of the necessary structure of logical thought (as Anselm's ontological argument). Rather, a psychological proof is produced—having to do not with the primordial functions of God or with the necessary ontological qualities of God, but with the thinking personality of God, a personality based on the natural psychological tendencies of humans, including an inherent trustworthiness. Descartes's argument is that God would not deceive us.[4] Because God's psychology can be logically deduced, psychological assessment is included in the purview of philosophical science. Feelings, emotions, and passions, even if among them are the baser aspects of humanity, are incorporated in a naturalistic ethics. God's ethical feelings and beliefs are also natural, like those of humans at their best. The chivalric code becomes applicable even to the deity. Honor, honesty, and reliability are natural aspects of human society, which are also shared by, since nature is itself derived from, the divinity. Faith, honor, and justice come to describe not only action or thought in accord with external principles (authorized codes), but also mental capacities based on internal principles (human "nature"). Accordingly, emotions need not be linked to transcendent communion any more than need rationality—which had always been recognized as a structure (logic) fully internal to mentality. In both cases, conclusions are reached by humans, not communicated to them.

When Descartes severs immaterial mind from physical matter, he nevertheless assures that the two realms of heaven and earth are not alienated by introducing the mediating efficacy of a God who has created both mind and matter, yet remains external to both. To remedy this Cartesian contrivance, Spinoza makes mentality and materiality two "aspects" of a unified, irreducible, and uncaused "Substance," at once both nature and God. This maintains the inherent unity between mind and matter, but without the need for an external mediator, a superfluous third term. Materiality and mentality are what God is, not what God does. As a result of the necessary concordance through time of materiality and mentality, neither God, nature, nor humans are free from the operations of strict and inviolable causal necessity.[5] Since, for Spinoza, God and nature are two names for the same thing, his position can be interpreted both as pantheistic and as compatible with the causality of science. Spinoza, therefore, is extremely attractive to the romantics,[6] for whom physical nature is sanctified, unlike for most idealist philosophers. As artists, the romantics demand that objects be fundamentally real in themselves, as Kant did. Via this route arises the indebtedness to Spinoza of the modernists, for whom object and meaning (materiality and thought) are congruent—although, as transcendence wanes, this bonding of object and meaning is detached from physical nature by the urbanite modernists and shifted entirely into the cosmopolitan artwork.

Spinoza's idea of inviolable necessity fits the scientific model. Likewise, the inherent union of mind and matter contributes to empiricism's expansion of the sciences into the study of humankind. A scientific psychology or economics or sociology, each relying on cause and effect, customarily assumes that the physiological and the psychological directly correspond, with no mediating third term. Yet the human sciences are also prone to maintain freedom or latitude of human will, contrary to Spinoza, as if scientific validity can be bestowed upon free will, too. It is the empiricists who once thought Spinoza went too far. The fully deterministic approach, a strong determinism, is compatible with a mechanistic epistemology, with structuralism in sociology, and with psychological behaviorism or (later) computer-based theories of intelligence. However, a weak determinism, allowing more latitude for human freedom, encourages an optimistic humanist view of humanity. Some human essence or human nature (if not the soul) can thereby be enhanced, advanced, or fulfilled, while also resting, although always uneasily, on presumably scientific ground.

Empiricism, then, advocates both strong and weak determinisms. Modernism associates itself with the latter, since the idealistic roots of its romanticism can then conveniently (even if not always consistently) be compromised with empiricism. Yet the conflict between a strong and weak determinism that occurs inside empiricism is taken by modernism as if it were actually a conflict between empiricism and an alternative to it. This is a singularly important and attractive factor in the growth of modernism's influence. The definition of modernism is assembled by artists and writers who attempt to reconcile inside empiricism two divergent patterns of thought, empiricism and idealism (and Platonism and Aristotelianism, theism and materialism, science and art), at a time when events in Europe and America are confirming, and even celebrating, the overwhelming success of empiricism. The attempted reconciliation is not considered a dilemma.

Although it is impossible to reconcile empiricism and idealism inside the boundaries of empiricism, the modernists undertake the project enthusiastically. Their aesthetic theory proclaims the union of irreconcilables as a precept.

An empiricist maxim states that structure (organized material) and process (motion) correspond. The two are inseparable: their conceptual connection is force or energy, which names both their relationship and what drives that relationship. A "psychology" could not be possible before mentality was placed fully inside physical nature. For the empiricists, structure (the brain, for example) and motion (mentality, conceived of as internal "motions" since Hobbes[7]) exhaustively correspond, which in the Judeo-Christian theology would be a blasphemy. Only in empiricism could natural and inherent propensities or tendencies of human thought be predicated as causal processes and mind be given structure, instead of only a content. The processes of thought are assumed to correspond to the physical dynamics of that structure, even if these dynamics are not yet known.

An empiricist psychology requires autonomous psyches, like machines whose internal mechanisms fully account for their motions. These autonomous minds need not be connected through a common subsuming source, God or some Absolute. Idealism can never ground a psychology—although Kantianism can because Kant places the categories separately in each individual mind. (Idealism does ground the modern alternative to psychology, namely phenomenology.) In empiricism, isolated minds link themselves externally through language, by communication with one another.

In empiricist modernity, free will loses its long-standing status as an axiom and instead requires logical demonstration. This proves impossible. First, there is an internal contradiction: the logic used to generate the proof is itself assumed to work because its own order corresponds to the order of nature, yet the proof is supposed to release human volition from this extrinsic order. Second, biological studies increasingly reveal the extraordinary interior complexity of the body; the body is nearly as much a wonder as the mind, yet its internal workings appear lawful and mechanistic. Furthermore, the intricate material components of the human organism resemble those of other mammals. (Linnaeus's taxonomy appears in the eighteenth century.[8]) If the human body is subject to the same laws of nature as the animal's body, the mind cannot be exempted.

By the seventeenth century, humans had become partially integrated into nature. "Human nature" is both natural yet different from the nature of everything else; for creation was believed to consist of the genesis of perpetually distinct categories arranged in a hierarchy, the "great chain of being."[9] The unique workings of the mind separated humans from the encompassing deterministic laws of nature by granting the mind laws of its own. Part of the mind's uniqueness is its affiliation with what transcends the nature in which mind is engendered and embedded: this provides the vantage point from which the mind can know itself. For some, this distinction entails an immaterial mind that can influence matter, although the mechanisms are obscure (the mind/body problem). For others, like Spinoza and like Leibniz, who provides Spinoza's metaphysics with a mechanics,[10] the distinction suggests an immaterial mind that can know but not influence matter, although mind and matter operate in perfect harmony. Still others assert that the mind is simply a product of matter—but even this does not solve all the problems, for if this product of matter is free to control the matter that produces it (the body), then the original question of its apparent powers reappears. And if it is *not* free to control the matter that produces it, then it is fully determined, which undermines any "objective" knowledge of it. If the mind is a by-product of matter, and a materialism can fully account for mental content, the ground of ethics disintegrates—because ethics has always been based on a special valuative procedure of mind presumed superior to (elevated above) all other specific content of mind (its knowledge). Ethics can never *be* knowledge in the empiricist sense. Relativistic or evolutionary ethics eventually respond to this dilemma, but a question then arises: Are such ethics ethical? That this question makes sense is itself the dilemma.

Since the empiricist theory of mind rests on mechanistic principles of mental "associations," it cannot account for creativity beyond positing unique combinations of fixed elements linked together (a Lucretian chemistry). It cannot account for how humans actually "create" (assuming, as the romantics assumed, that they do), and certainly not for why they do so. The empiricist aggregational concept of mind corresponds to the capitalist notion of wealth. Money accumulates to riches one coin at a time, as atoms are combined into bulky matter, as discrete ideas are accumulated in the mind. The entirety is the sum of its assembled parts (its assets), and one's personal definition is a calculation of these aggregations, whether money or ideas.

No empiricist theory is privileged to explain the most significant perplexity: How do self, and its consciousness of itself, and its consciousness of the consciousness of itself—an infinite regress—first issue into being? The basic problem is not about mind, but about consciousness. Although the mind is known only through consciousness, the mind is not synonymous with consciousness. Even if the brain is thought to produce consciousness, the operations of mind are not explained, even if they can be said to be accounted for. Empiricism eventually steps into a materialist's monism, by having mentality emerge as an evolutionary property of organized matter, although why mind should have emerged cannot be explained. The problem of consciousness is, however, left unresolved in empiricism: for an empiricist the problem of mind, but not of consciousness, allows an empirical solution. In empiricism, consciousness itself cannot be addressed as a problem. No practical consequences would arise from problematizing it. Consciousness, oddly, becomes a description, but not a description of any*thing*. Those unhappy with this empiricist strategy frequently reinstate a body-mind dualism (and are soundly berated for it[11]) in the midst of what, in every other area of study, is a pervasive monistic empiricism.

Empiricists, having systematized a mechanistic theory of cognition and emotion, attempt to determine whether the belief that mind can be an independent influence on the body is still tenable. When they discover that rationality refuses to yield a positive answer to this question, romanticism emerges. No scientifically rational hypothesis ever refutes an encompassing materialistic naturalism. Nevertheless, speculative metaphysics and theological conclusions are still actively defended. Sacred texts remain essential to the orthodox. Many champion the idea of a revelation sustained in purported balance with reason. (This claim had been made as early as the twelfth century). For example, much speculation had appeared in the seventeenth century concerning the possibility of a universal wisdom, acquired through intuition and feeling but also confirmed by reason. Those seeking to prove that religious beliefs were also rational beliefs had proposed that religious and moral precepts had universal resemblance, under the supposition that the most ancient wisdom in all cultures is mutually confirming. (Confucianism was of particular interest.) This approach had not succeeded in the long run. (Not only is it inaccurate, as freethinkers of the time quickly demonstrated; besides, it might be error that is universal.[12]) Even in the eighteenth century, however, the clergy in France were among the most eager purchasers of the encyclopedia—despite its condemnation by Clement XIII in 1759—as if it might be employed to unify science and religion.

In the nineteenth century, the romantics take a related approach, only they universalize not the rationality of belief but the emotional intuitiveness of belief. Ancient spiritual insights had presumably spread with the expansion of human settlement. Spiritual wisdom shared a common ground, although expressed in diverse systems of religious myth. Its source was likely in the Caucasus or thereabouts, whence the Aryan invaders of India had come, from ca. 2000 B.C. (The discovery of the Indo-European language system enhanced these speculations.[13]) Indian abstract thought, believed to have been preserved quite close to its original inspiration, was studied throughout Europe in the few texts available, particularly the Upanishads. The Indian concepts of *atman*, the ultimate human essence or true self, and *brahman*, the ultimate reality behind the disparateness of appearances, and the idea (most convincingly described by Sankara in the eighth century) that these two are the same, undoubtedly contribute to shaping the idealist's relation of human soul and cosmic oversoul.[14]

Romanticism accepts the universalization of spiritual intuition and the ubiquitousness of spiritual wisdom, together with the Kantian tactic of psychologizing the mind in a way that, via the idealists, also can be employed to respiritualize the mind. An idealist phenomenology circumvents the materialistic and deterministic consequences of an empiricist psychology. Romanticism means to force a retreat of empiricism. Idealism assumes Kant to have originated what could serve as a rational foundation for counteracting empiricism (i.e., a rational foundation for the supra-rational), based on the presumed validity of attributing to mentality not simply physical correlates (sensation and perception) but also an inherent conceptual structure (innate ideas). This conceptual structure includes itself as a category: mentality can know its own organization and can, eventually, validate a nonempiricist psychology (a phenomenology). This philosophy uses, or perhaps invents, an extraordinary power of reason to transcend its limitations, by making those limitations not the margin of knowledge but an object of knowledge. Reason concludes by paradoxically subordinating itself to its own powers, overcoming the empiricist conundrums that entertained Hume. The mind can again comfortably be thought to be allied with the metaphysical—ultimately, in idealism, with an Absolute. For the romantics, Kant's purported rebuttal of metaphysics is ultimately an exotic plant in the garden of metaphysics.

Empiricism had eliminated the need for a god who intervenes in world management. The Old Testament deity had been promoted, "kicked upstairs." The romantics revitalize the presence of the spiritual to elude an entrapment in physical causality; this they accomplish not by reattesting to Christianity, but by discarding the literalness of the testaments and transforming the theological narrative into a branch of aesthetics. The Bible is testimony of the poetic kind, rather than the legal kind. Mythology becomes an aesthetic discipline well beyond the old Renaissance narrative pictorial symbolism. For the romantics, the Renaissance symbol can only represent the idea that the myth itself embodies, illuminates, and confirms. All mythic systems substantiate the shared underlying poetic inspiration.

In romanticism, as for Plato, truth is "vision." On the other hand, the classicism of the Enlightenment is verbal (aural): all truths can be stated as propositions. Even paintings are narratives. In romanticism, theistic revelation is reworked into a theory of poetic metaphor, imagery. Deity and artistry become affiliated in the context of "sight" rather than hearing, a distinction that also marks the transition from the Middle Ages to the Renaissance.[15]

In empiricism, creativity is an intensification of capabilities everyone possesses to some extent. In romanticism, creative poetic power can produce the entirely new, the original (that which is its own origin), only through genius. While the term commonly applied to the visual and written arts by the neoclassicists was *imitation*—a praiseworthy compliment indicating the artist's essential relationship to nature (holding up a mirror to nature)—for the romantics this term comes to suggest mere copying. The term *imagination* for the neoclassicists suggested fantasy or novelty, hardly the highest form of art. (In the Renaissance *fantasia* meant free invention, detached from the religious and historical narratives; for Turgot and Condorcet, imagination instigated error and superstition.) In romanticism, *imagination* names the supreme creative faculty. Creative power emulates the deity, who is also an artist. (Both Vitruvius and Plotinus compare God to a creative architect, and the idea that the human artist emulates the deity is apparent in the Renaissance, in Leon Alberti, for example.[16]) As Schopenhauer would show in regard to an epistemology based on

the primacy of will, and as Kant had shown in regard to an epistemology based on the primacy of intellect, the artist (like God) can escape, through creativity, the causative chain of materiality.

In romanticism, the aesthetic emotion is unqualifiedly positive,
both in the artwork's creator and in its recipient. An abiding conscious
orderliness assures that subjectivity is not lost in the emotion (as in
bliss or ecstasy), but clarified by it. As for Plato, beauty is a signification of goodness. All other human emotions can potentially overwhelm when their intensity becomes disproportional to their cause.

Furthermore, the passions are not what leads one astray, the intem-
perate urges of the flesh. "Passion" (not equivalent to "emotion") is
instead admirable, recollecting the Platonic union of religious fervor
and physical longing celebrated by the eleventh- and twelfth-century
troubadour poets. Emotion and sensibility substantiate spiritual and
moral purity. Romantic passion is linked to the "passion" that names
the suffering of Jesus, a passion that warrants transcendence.[17] Yet in
romanticism the passion needs no external theistic revelation or confirmation. It is an inherent self-substantiating element of artistic genius that involves its own particular form of suffering, also with transcendent rewards. Such passion is above desire: one yearns for what
one already is, yet one also needs to discover what one is, since to
discover it is to complete it.

For the transcendentalist, beauty has its source in the immaterial.
The artist has rapport with the immaterial; the evidence for this (cir-
cularly) is the beauty of artworks. The perception of beauty, then, contains more than the mechanics of perception can account for. Nor is it
a matter of rationality, since feeling and emotions are considered valid primary access to knowledge.

The word *beautiful* is applied to nature as well as to art. By the end
of the eighteenth century, the fact that the beauty of nature may not
have been formerly acknowledged is attributed to an error of judgment. The recognition of the beauty *of* nature is believed to be a perception of the beauty *in* nature, just as in a work of art. In both cases,
beauty derives from the same transcendental source. God is never
called beautiful, however: the Platonic idea of beauty has been situated in the intellect of a Hebraic God who has no body and who in the
Old Testament shows no interest in beauty. The Hebrews' biblical sacred ark had only given a volume to the location of spirit. According-

ly, nature for the Hebrews was neither beautiful nor, in itself (sacrifice is different), sacred. In Christianity's most significant distinction from Judaism, God acquired a body. The ability of God to become physically beautiful had been advantageous in the competition with Greek and Roman religions, and eventually Renaissance artists appropriated the classical aesthetic forms to visualize the beauty of the embodied Christian God.

In transcendentalism, the beauty of art receives conceptual priority over the beauty of nature, and the universe itself is then imagined as if it were an artwork. God is an artist. (For millennia God would rather have been a moral worker.) The universe is inherently beautiful, like the best art. Since art has been present from the beginning of human history, the recognition of beauty must be an essential part of what it means to be human.

For the empiricist, beauty is a result of design, and design is an intellectual conception. The beauty in a work manifests the beauty of its plan, the criteria for which are rational and also natural. What is found beautiful results in part from natural physiological dispositions of the organism, a response to certain colors or forms (like the golden mean) whose attraction can be rational-ized using concepts like symmetry, simplicity, harmony, proportion, propriety, and balance. Rational criteria are assumed to be timeless, ahistorical. God is a mathematical engineer. For the empiricist, beauty is naturally contained in the interactions of the mechanisms of sensation (especially seeing and hearing) and rationality. Feelings and emotions are a response to this interaction—approval, disapproval; pleasure, pain; attraction, repulsion. They are not direct access to truth, although they can accompany truth to enhance the ease of its reception. The universe is beautiful because the planner made it so—or because its stupendous intricacy and harmony are such that humans can recognize what it would mean for it to have been intentional.

The relationship of art to beauty, then, may result from nature, from that which is materially and biologically fundamental existing beneath and prior to any specific civilization. Beauty would be the universally natural aspect of art. Any specific historical manifestation of it (method/style) is not natural but a result of specific social circumstances. For the romantic, beauty is timeless, but evaluative criteria change, and one of the functions of great artists is to change them. For the empiricist, what specifically is beautiful retains a formal consistency over time; hence the reliance on classical models. The evaluative criteria are universal, and one of the functions of great artists is to exemplify them. (The eventual turning of modernism into formalism, it should be reemphasized here, is modernism's most significant concession to empiricism.)

In transcendentalism, beauty may result from the supernatural. The supernatural is beautiful because spirit in itself is beautiful, with the beauty not of a multiplicity but of a metaphysical unity, which underlies the aesthetic criterion of the same name. The recognition that behind the world's multiplicity is a creative metaphysical unity brings to the perception of beauty the feeling of *awe*.

Within the empiricist setting that encompasses it, modernism will both integrate and redirect romanticism.

Early modernists use the word *spiritual* to indicate a connection to the source of the creative power underlying the material universe: the traditional God, or personified Nature, or not quite definable forces suggested by a dwindling idealism. A reliance on biology—which, after Darwin, must be a component of any worldview—aids the reshaping of the romantic roles of God and Nature. The "science of life" is no longer an oxymoron in the nineteenth century. It yields organic models, at once scientifically "natural" yet creative without the intervention of a deity who makes daily decisions.

Evolution suffices; nature is itself creative. Organicity can then be retained as the metaphor for creativity. Yet the modernists' idea of organicity is not exactly the organicity of the romantics, for whom the metaphor of the plant is opposed to the Enlightenment's metaphor of the machine or clock. The modernists believe that scientific advances will confirm and elaborate universal organicity, not refute or undermine it. The world, its inhabitants, and the surrounding universe relate organically (as in Whitehead's philosophy), and organic creativity becomes an alleged property of things in general.[18] Biology then seems a reconciling science that allows for quasi-scientific, quasi-metaphysical "vital" forces propelling and inhabiting the human race. In the long run, however, such forces prove to have much greater aesthetic appeal than scientific appeal.

When modernism begins, some discern that Judeo-Christianity and its anthropomorphic God cannot be sustained except by generalizing them as "myth," as the romantics had done. The modernists define "myth" by means of a more anthropological conception of the function of poetry. Poetry conveys and substantiates a coherent worldview. Studies in comparative religion and languages strengthened this aesthetic anthropology of poetry. The Greek religious myths, for example, had since the days of Winckelmann[19] been taken to demonstrate that narrative, if received literally, might mistakenly suggest religious immaturity; if received poetically, it could instead express the highest ideals of beauty, morality, and human passion. A central tenet of all aesthetics emerges: A phenomenon can be aestheticized so that it yields a meaning superior to its ostensible content.

While myth may offer a pathway to spiritual truths for some early modernists, as modernism evolves it more frequently corroborates general conceptions of human psychic need and functioning. Modernism shifts the debate from philosophy to psychology. Spirituality can be a function of mentality, not an abstract truth discovered by mentality: the mind produces or achieves spirit, rather than the spirit producing or achieving mind. That spirit resides in us is no longer equivalent to our residing in the spirit. "Spirituality" takes on a meaning quite distinct from religion. Whereas spiritual truth surrounds the romantics, the modernists surround spiritual truth. Myths bear meaning, but they are not quite "true" in the same way as for the romantics. Early modernism can therefore ignore Christian myth as a genre outmoded and exhausted—like the epic, like history painting. As modernism advances and idealism yields to psychologism, art is itself granted the primary organizational function. Myth appears to be a special form of early poetry. Myth and art are no longer mutually distinct; rather, myth is a genre of art.

For nearly two thousand years Christianity had provided a communal warehouse of artistic content: metaphor, allegory, character, narrative, poetic and visual form, a binding of the ethical and the aesthetic. The religious symbols functioned as an inherited symbolic code for artists, an aesthetic vocabulary even when not necessarily a religious one. But modernism quickly learns one of its most essential lessons, that modern life is itself an adequate myth. Entire compendiums of myth can be created and proliferated by the media, bringing shared texts to entire populations nearly overnight. Inventors, scientists, authors, artists, and entertainers (everyone but gods, saints, and conquering kings, who were once almost the only figures in this category) become known to the public through mythological narrative. The film industry easily proliferates ready-made mythologies.

Theories evolve alleging that myth and symbol are the basic forces of social cohesion, truth value aside (and indeed irrelevant).[20] Myth is a form of commitment. History as progress gains mythological stature, and volumes that stride boldly and familiarly through the immensity of world history are great commercial successes.[21] The American way of life becomes mythologized in the roaring twenties. International socialism, too, recognizes that it cannot succeed without creating new myths and symbols in addition to programs.

As for Eastern concepts: the eighteenth-century West had looked toward China with admiration for its practical Confucianism. In the nineteenth century it looked toward Indian culture and philosophy, thanks to England's occupation. Eastern ideas are imported to bolster the reliability of Western metaphysics, since Indian thought seemed compatible both with modern science and with a Hegelianized religiosity. Modernism investigates Eastern thought as a metaphysical science of mind and spirituality (like modernism itself, a transcendental realism). Asian thought is viewed as neither an alternative form of religion nor a confirmation of universalized religious truths. (The more that was known about Indian religion, with its innumerable local gods, the more would it seem preposterous to the West.) Particularly in England and Germany in the first quarter of the twentieth century, modernism can regard this Eastern science of mind (generally called "yoga") as a refinement of "spirituality," released from superstitions derived from the literal interpretation of sacred texts. Religion is imposed from the outside; spirituality radiates, even spontaneously, from the inside.

Nevertheless, while Christianity may have been weakening under the onslaught of Darwinism and biblical textual studies, and although theosophy was becoming a substantial movement[22] (as would Zen Buddhism over half a century later), the majority of Westerners felt intimidated by Eastern thought: by its stupendous time schemes, immensely longer than even geological time; by its intimidating surrender of selfhood and personality to a unified undifferentiated consciousness; by its intellectual density and proliferation of philosophical terms; and by its demand for an absolute social compliance with caste structures, together with an unrelenting regimen of meditation and the eventual forsaking of secular pursuits, including sexuality, if transcendence is to be achieved. Some other source of creativity needed to be found, one more hospitable than *brahman* and the void.

The Unconscious

For modernism, the psychology of the unconscious offers that new source of creativity. Creativity is still assumed to be innate in humans, as the romantics had come to believe. (In the Renaissance talent was bestowed, a divine gift.) But whether creativity has been placed inside humans by God or by any metaphysical source comes into dispute, or is thought beside the point. The search for an immaterial ground to account for matter wanes; now the search occurs in the opposite direction, for the organization of matter that will account for what is only an apparent immateriality (mind). Any psychology reinforces materialistic empiricism because the mind is treated as an *object*, distinct in each head. This recognition had caused phenomenology to separate itself from psychology. Phenomenology will presume to supersede empiricist psychology, claiming that psychology is subsumed by phenomenology, that psychology can be a source of information but not of any theory that gives the information meaning.

While a psychology of the unconscious legitimates creativity, it revokes the transcendence that once made creativity sacred. (Is not the slow bringing into self-awareness of the long-buried unconscious in one's personal history a substitute for Hegel's Absolute slowly coming to an awareness of itself in world history?) Yet a theory of the unconscious preserves awe by transferring it from the mysteries of the sacred to the mysteries of the mind. The artistic process of symbolic transformation is considered the work of the unconscious. This is a new universal-in-the-particular, operative to some degree in all minds. (Within empiricism, creativity is always a quantitative measurement of a generalized capacity.) Whereas the romantics had hoped to ascend to the heavens, employing a Judeo-Christian geography, the modernists instead propose a geography of descent. The unconscious replaces both the Greek underworld and the region of hell and the devil. The devil's name is id (what else had Satan been ever since the Middle Ages learned to be terrified of forfeiting salvation?) and the domineering god is superego ("above"-ego). In between, the creative ego (humanity, as always, between two realms) quests for its autonomy. Admittedly, the modernists frequently ally psychological depths and aesthetic elevation quite indiscriminately, as if one can descend to the transcendent.

Early on, before the mechanisms of the newly discovered neural synapse were widely discussed,[23] the psychology of the unconscious lent itself to mystification. By the twenties, behaviorism would presume to remedy this, although hardly to the satisfaction of artists and writers, who were generally repelled by behaviorism's mechanistic determinism. Just as the confrontation between empiricism and idealism yields the opposition of psychology and phenomenology, so does that same confrontation, brought inside empiricism, yield the rivalry between behaviorism and psychoanalysis. Freudian psychology—a psychological modernism—proposes to supply a science of the unscientific, an empiricism of the symbol, a science of art.

A psychology of the unconscious prolongs the feasibility of artistic elevation and spirituality, however suspicious their source might be. Mind is given a third dimension. Its unconscious depths can be used to counteract the empiricist's two-dimensional tabula rasa. (The perspectival dimension of depth that disappears from painting reappears in psychoanalysis: the depth in the artist replaces the depth in the canvas.) The mystery of a mind structured in levels, the deepest and most hidden being the most profound (an empiricist apostasy), appears awe inspiring, no less so than what was previously imagined to be the preternatural source of mind. Nor are Aristotelian logic and the world order synonymous at these depths. Even in the last half of the nineteenth century, before psychoanalysis, the art and literature of dream and hallucination had flourished. (It appeared much earlier if one returns to Johann Fussli's *Nightmare* [1781] and Goya's *Sleep of Reason* [1798].) The predecessors of modernism had invited phantoms and angels to swim to the surface from below, half from inspiration and half, we might now think (after experiments with cortical electrostimulation), from neuronal activity.[24] The symbolists often disengaged poetry from commonplace reality, withdrawing to the dream, to the suggestive mystery of imagery, to the hidden recesses of the mind. The German expressionists produced an art of vision surging from deep regions within the psyche, with all the pain and distortion of a knowledge one seeks yet cannot bear to find. Freudian psychoanalytic theory includes a mechanics of metaphor-based creativity, through which the genuinely new erupts from a deep creative reservoir into the configuration that is the artwork.

Nevertheless, psychoanalysis purports to be an empiricist theory. From the view of philosophical idealism, psychoanalysis is a blatant and offensive reductionism. Yet modern artists are not dissuaded from using psychoanalysis as a mediating theory. It is especially compelling as the spirituality once derived from idealism and romanticism declines and theories of the autonomous and isolated modern personality intensify. Even though Freud attributes art to neuroses, the modernists find psychoanalysis appealing as a critical method. While psychoanalysis claims to be the science of *willing*, the unconscious is actually reified in a metaphysics of prioritized and reified organic *Will* (id). Schopenhauer and Bergson had shown how a reified will can be linked to a universal force in which the individual mind participates, sustaining a metaphysics. An aestheticized and reified will serves early modernism as a reconfiguration of the Gnostic demiurge, more the God of the romantics than the demanding and moralizing Jehovah.[25] In the long run, however, this must be discarded—for although psychoanalysis originally emerges from Schopenhaurian metaphysics, the reification proves implausible. The verb "to will" need not substantiate any entity named "Will" (the verb "to run" substantiates no entity of "Run"). Id eventually is taken as a new kind of energy, a scientific "force," not a thing.

In the twenties, during high modernism, some writers (especially those writing in English) take what they imagine to be an antiromantic turn in favor of classicism, following T. E. Hulme and T. S. Eliot. This will be a classicism not of universal truths, like neoclassicism, but of formalist method. These postwar Anglo-American classicists reject any reliance on Germanic sources. They are tempted neither by Freud nor by phenomenology but (guided by I. A. Richards) by a modified behavioral science.[26] Afterwards, a reliance on Freud will characterize the aesthetic and political left, while the new classicism will characterize the aesthetic and political right.

In this ostensible classicism, truth is knowing the process by which one's own truths, shared or not, come to be fixed in the psyche. This occurs through a fully empiricist dynamic, allied with Locke and behaviorism; the psychoanalytic unconscious does not pertain. Conviction is not only the conscious assent of rationality to sound logic but also a matter of individual personal psychic integration. In fiction, people are presented not as character (stereo) types with easily classifiable unvarying predipositions (like the ancient theory of humors or the neoclassical theory of human nature), but as unique personalities with egos that must reveal their own stressful dynamics, since modern behavior arises from anxiety. While the integrative procedures are shared, each psyche is unique; integration requires assigning objects simultaneous symbolic and emotional values, which depend on local and personal circumstances. Rationality and emotion are therefore interwoven in unique and multifarious ways, and transferring these into art by formal procedures qualifies as "creativity."

At first the Anglo-American New Critics argue that what satisfies the emotions may not satisfy rationality, and vice versa. By the forties they will propose, for reasons identified in the preceding chapter, that poetic truth is an alternative to scientific propositional truth. Both are "true": a dual-truth theory that essentially readmits romanticism into the empiricist stronghold.

Humanism and Modernism

In an empiricist epistemology, the truth about reality is discovered by setting will aside and momentarily relinquishing individual desire. A natural harmony can then arise between the internal and external, the objective and subjective. Empiricism allows for an inventiveness associated not with unconscious will but with consciousness and rational intellect. Will is the means of rational implementation: not urge, but volition. This is humanism. Unlike Renaissance humanism, modernity's humanism is a fully empiricist secularism. Ideally addressed to rational, educated, temperate, democratic citizens, it is freed by science and, more specifically, by the scientific logic of analysis from the superstitions of the past, when the not-known erroneously suggested a mystery at hand. Political and social freedom and equality, the unconstrained ability to make rational decisions, become inseparable from humanism's aesthetic values.

Humanism intensifies at the end of the nineteenth century as an alternative to evolving modernism. It takes pragmatism (John Dewey's, although the approach was named by Charles Peirce in the 1870s) as its philosophy. Humanism rejects the romantic aesthetic—together with the entire history of metaphysics, including Husserl's contemporaneous phenomenology—in favor of a theory of artistic moral use value. Insight and "perception" (as a term of commendation) and a judicious employment of the text, not a succumbing to it, is more reliable than a susceptibility to inspiration or emotion. The aesthetic experience is a psychic dynamic involving knowledge also attainable by other means.[27]

For humanism, truth is always a proposition. Any truth marks a consensus at one point in the evolution of truths, which like biological organisms undergo radical species changes as time progresses. Any truth is an organism in the evolutionary chain. (This is also the best way to understand Kuhn's "paradigm" shifts.[28]) Although values in the widest sense need not change—humanism intends itself to be a permanent ethics—*what* is valued changes. Art serves as an intermediary between the permanency of value and the changing specificities of its application. Art is a form of evidence and trial for values and actions, the setting where (as Dewey argues) emotions and decisions can be tested and observed before one makes an irreversible commitment to personal action. What is unique to art is its use and its beauty, not its truth: art is conceptually subordinated. Genius is not creativity in the romantic sense, but intellectual synthesis. These syntheses can be hierarchically ordered, genius being at the highest level. Intellect, not will, has precedence. Rationality is sufficient to discover and define (in pragmatism the two are fused) what the human naturally and freely (these are assumed compatible) ought to be like.[29] In humanism, while humans have the potential for persuasive moral insight, the status of this insight remains uncertain. If it is natural—since humans both have a nature and are part of nature—it may be biologically determined. Morality would rest not on a theory of ethics but on a natural propensity. Humanism, therefore, always relies on the presumed intrinsic attractiveness of altruism, the permanent ethical value in the midst of otherwise modifiable truths. Humanism repeatedly attempts to incorporate altruism both as a beneficial biological adaption in the theory of evolution and as an intuitional good.

In humanism, rationality can discover the *means* for satisfying moral aims. Happiness can be planned. Altogether, these means, if enacted, would compose civilization in its most admirable form. That rationality can also devise means for satisfying immoral aims is to be counteracted by rationality's recognition that moral cooperation naturalizes public and private satisfaction. In humanism, immorality can be defined by negative social consequences, leaving anything without such consequences entirely to free individual choice. There is no private sin. However, as both a logical qualification and a social restraint, the notion of an indisputably free choice is made to depend on the notion of "mental health," defined as the absence of self-destructive or other-destructive tendencies, the first unnatural in the human animal and the second unnatural to the human citizen. Because the mentally ill are not truly free, coercion can be exercised in their case. Since an authorized professional class adjudicates what qualifies as mental health, humanism originates therapy.

Because the conscientious consent to the social contract takes precedence over the beneficent "invisible hand" of self-centered economics, humanism, like modernism, can propose itself as an alternative to unconstrained capitalism. An unconstrained capitalism is not considered rational, according to twentieth-century political liberalism. Human nature is comprehensible because of its order. Law involves both naturalism's universal scientific lawfulness and the rule of civil law. Legality is comprised of statutes mutually agreed to. The consent of the governed is taken to align legal structure with psychic structure. Social institutions become analogs of rational mentality.

The modern artist is not a humanist. Individuality is paramount, and consent to the social contract is often purposely withheld. While humanism would collaboratively humanize capitalism, modernism would detach itself from capitalism. The artist's individuality is not an economic self-interest but a free personality. A system of economic self-interest has actually suppressed this freedom in the masses of people consigned to inferior economic functions. (That the capitalist is the exact *opposite* of the artist is a modernist axiom.) In capitalism, as in humanism, the mind supervises the body; will is a form of control. In modernism, the mind conspires with the body; will is a form of expression.

Modernism bases its expectations for the future on what human nature might become, not on what human nature currently is. Modernism's project for humankind is not only the empiricist goal of freeing a fundamental rational human nature, afterward to be educated through rational knowledge and planning; it is the forging of human nature from emotional raw material still being created. Not only is human nature composed of natural animal endowments, to which certain mental capabilities have been added as a result of increased skull volume; it is also a potential, still unrealized. Yet the artist can envision its realization.

Artists make order out of chaos. (This was formerly God's assignment when chaos was a state of matter instead of a state of mind.) The unconscious mechanisms are not irrational in any negative sense; only when they malfunction do illness and loss of control occur. The unconscious functions as a poetic language. This is reminiscent of the romantic belief of Herder, and of Rousseau before him, that all language derives from primeval poetry and metaphor.[30] Humankind's origins remain intact in the unconscious, unsullied by millennia of civilization. The workings of primeval metaphor are inseparable from the workings of creativity, through which the artist transcends the apparently normal appearance of the world. Here, too, descent is ascent; one goes forward to the beginning.

In psychoanalysis, the contents of the unconscious result from the repression of passion; humans need to recover what has been repressed. To Freud, art was a manipulation of the unconscious made palatable to consciousness, a strategy of the neuroses. To the artist, however, neuroses are not illnesses (at least not in artists). If mastered, neuroses can serve as creative energies. The artist confidently releases the passion that others advise us to prudently subordinate to rationality. The empiricist method of scientific inquiry is based on the repression of passion: all its truths are passion-less. Is not the repression of a potentially cognitive passion the Enlightenment itself? In modernism, the world must be made metaphorical again.

Art would perform this simultaneous reversal and advance, the irrepression. What has been repressed is "nature" itself. Humans are now living in an unnatural state. In modernism, we return to nature by creating that nature. Art is at once cognition and creation. Paradoxically, while the theory of evolution had outmoded Rousseau, evolution is heading toward our origins, which lie in the future. All the arts produce work to rehabilitate humankind. Although the sciences can train reason, art shapes the emotional content that forms the values toward which reason aims. Science provides the methods for social progress; art supplies the meanings for social progress. The modernist artists, these romantic empiricists, propose both to advance the Enlightenment and to disrupt it. Modernist knowledge and modernist ethics come from different heritages. Empiricism provides the knowledge of where humans have come from; romanticism provides the knowledge of who humans are to be.

For modernism, the artistic elite significantly differs from other humans in at least one qualitative way (artistic creativity). For the artist, aesthetic passion is not the same as, nor does it lead to, unrestricted detrimental emotion. The artist's emotions do not trespass over the creative, moral, or social borders; they define those borders. In the humanistic model, to the contrary, *all* humans share the same fundamental qualities (differences being quantitative); as for Montaigne, they are capable of rationally recognizing and acceding to the fundamentally good.[31] Humanist morality is grounded in seventeenth-century deism, where the laws of human nature both participate in and correspond to the laws of nature—which are morally good because their source (God) is good. But in humanism, God has disappeared. The human moral sense itself becomes both good and the criterion for the good. Emotion and passion are often humanist synonyms. Except when used in moderation, they may lead to social pathologies.

The modernists expect the population at large to be receptive to artistic genius. Not to do so signifies one's philistine insensitivity. The revision of society will be accomplished not through the exercise of innate capabilities already fully present in all humans but through artistic works that create both the receptivity (as a brand new capability) as well as the object to be received. For the humanist and the classicist, wisdom discovers the truth, which is propositional; art is only one way of stating, embodying, or transmitting it. For the romantic and the modernist, wisdom makes truth take a specific and singular form, from which the truth is indistinguishable. For the classicist, saying the truth is beautiful; for the romantic, making the beautiful is truth. Art at once creates and speaks the truth, for speaking it is not repeating it but fashioning it.[32]

From the modernist view, artworks both express and verify the genius of the artist. Artistic genius is simultaneously a doing (a skill) and a knowing (a wisdom). Artworks awaken people who lack artistic experience but nevertheless can achieve an intense and sometimes transforming experience corresponding to it. Of course, the aesthetic experience of the reader or viewer cannot be identical to the creative experience: the artist's uniqueness cannot be vicariously invaded.

Artists must resign themselves to being a misunderstood vanguard, at least until public sensibilities are appropriately trained. For the rationalist philosophers, like Descartes and Spinoza, and for the empiricists, truth is attested to by an absolute rational clarity and conviction;

if its attention were properly focused, any human mind could experience this. But in modernism, the mind must be modified in order to be receptive to the truth. Truth is contained in art, which also performs the modification. The container is equivalent to its contents. Some of the avant-garde are resigned to permanent misunderstanding by the general public. The talented few educate the rest, through small galleries and small presses—not, significantly, in classrooms or in museums, at least not for a few decades. As they experience art, some people will undergo a transformation; others will gain momentary insight; still others will achieve not so much a knowing as a believing in something—or in someone, since artists and writers are made seers and saints and gather disciples. And some people simply follow the latest fads, occasionally bumping into truth in the guise of trend.

Essence

Art cannot be justified solely on the merits of its formal properties, even if art might be primarily (perhaps even exhaustively) analyzed in terms of these properties. Art also requires a content—otherwise there is only design. Nor is an artwork simply a "picture" of an object (so photographers were cautioned) but a revelation about it, a truth concerning it. How, then, the modernists ask, can a visual artwork portray or elucidate the "essence" of thing? Let us here assume the validity of the question. Not all modernists, especially as modernism turns toward formalism, do assume it.

For the Renaissance, the essence of an artwork's subject emerged through the use of narrative and iconography. Essence was equated with meaning; what a thing essentially *was* as a material object corresponded precisely to what it essentially *meant* as a concept. Insofar as all things inherently bore meanings, everything in the world functioned the way symbols and metaphors would begin to function in the artwork some centuries later, once things themselves lost their inherent meanings.[33] Art continually augments its sanctity only as the world continually loses it. In the Renaissance, the world was, in fact, God's visual artwork. Material things were incarnations of the immaterial meanings residing in God. In paintings, meaning was signified through a shared code of narrative icons primarily derived from a religious textual tradition. The icon denoted both the object and the meaning held inherently (not simply contextually) by the object. The object, in that sense, can be called an emblem, of which the icon is a stylized representation. As representations, icons were not themselves sacred (both the Reformation and the Counter-Reformation knew it was sacrilegious to think they were) although they might indirectly manifest the sacred. The biblical religions never consent to the sanctity of art; no artists are ever made saints, whatever their miracles. Art develops a sanctity only when these religions become incapable of maintaining the sanctity of the world.

This visual congruence of object and meaning gradually expanded to include the notion of the correspondence between human physiology and psyche. Physiology can then be considered not only as an external encoding (as when a beard is intentionally grown as a signifier) but an externalization of the psyche, as if the physiology and the psyche exactly correspond, like object and meaning. The body is a symbol not only of humankind generally but of the individual inhabiting it. Psyches and faces are increasingly individualized. The psyche becomes more self-conscious as social and economic roles modify ego development and adaptions, particularly in republicanism and capitalism. The visage reflects one's beliefs, status, and even moral worth, whether one wishes it to or not. (The business of facial cosmetics subsequently prospers.) Rembrandt's stature, for example, grows as European individuality itself grows, so that viewers can appreciated how the "consciousness" of his human figures seems to emanate from their faces, especially from their eyes. (One can, mysteriously, best see the psyche by looking at the organs of sight.) A psyche individuated in ego is a concept different from the vaguer concept of soul. For the Middle Ages, the soul was the meaning of the body but did not correspond to it. The soul might be discrete in each human, but this discreteness is not the personality. The envisioning of a future bliss in heaven or torment in hell had, to be sure, always encouraged the person-alizing of the otherwise nebulous soul. (Souls are represented in paintings no differently than the persons whose souls they are.) Assigning specific rewards and punishments to individual souls requires not only a discrete substance but a discrete consciousness to experience them.

By the eighteenth century, when it might have been anticipated that nature would soon be well understood, empiricist science had removed any inherent meaning from physical nature. Meaning and order are distinguished from one another; empiricism can claim the latter, but not the former. Descartes and his successors had insisted that human consciousness, as the source of meaning (even if derived from God), is completely separated from all other phenomena. This distinction remains enforced. Human gesture, posture, and expression become consonant with the essence of the person, even while human mentality and human physicality are kept conceptually distinct. Only in humans (since God has no body and everything else has no soul) can essence, meaning, body, and psyche be integrated and unified, even while metaphysically severed into two distinct realms. (Otherwise God and things, creator and creation, could not be different.) Despite a perpetual puzzle of the actual mechanisms of the unification, the integration, in humans, is never denied.

For things, essence is a categorical placement—the essence of a thing is that without which it could not keep its present name. For humans, that level of essence (species identification) is inadequate. The important level of human essence is individualized (personalized). The personal name of a thing (my cat Aristede, Mt. Olympus) is a convenient singling out, an identification of an object distinct from any specific features it has. But in modernity the name of a person stands for the essence of the person. (In the largest sense, this is the fundamental message of the modern novel.) The newborn is assigned a name so that, as its essence as a human gradually develops, it can be unambiguously signified. Of course, the giving of the name also commences that development. As egos are increasingly differentiated, names become increasingly unique, until each person (at least theoretically: through ethnic blending, unusual names, middle names, nicknames, stage names, etc.) can bear a singular name, a singular essence.

Before empiricism, human essence was not considered to develop over time. The theory of humors, for example, like subsequent psychological theories, classified human personality into a few categories, attempting to connect the notion of permanent essence in things with the notion of permanent essence in the human psyche—to simultaneously categorize and individualize.[34] But in modernity such general theories of classification, from morphological ones to psychological ones, have never for long successfully displaced essentialized individuality.

The separation of the individualized psychologized personality from the generalized soul (all essence but no content) also becomes central to the urbanization of capitalism, which relies on each individual presuming absolute uniqueness. For the modern personality, the soul has become completely contentless; all content has been transferred to ego. The body becomes a possession, intentionally modifiable, like any other object.

In empiricism, the physical universe becomes the environment where human meaning and action occur. Physical nature does not correspond to human meaning, as it did when all of physical nature (the stars, the rainbow) inherently signified meaning via emblematic incarnation. The physical universe is quite indifferent to human meaning. After empiricism arrives, the term *nature* refers to the principles of intrinsic orderliness in phenomena and to what occurs naturally (appropriately to something's nature). "Nature," meaning everything organic and inorganic other than humans and their creations (cities, farms, culture), becomes a much reduced concept. Things are inert—they move because of forces or (in animals) impulses, not intentions. In painting after empiricism, physical surroundings appear as setting, formal structure (elements of balance and harmony), ornamentation, or sign. A sign indicates the relevance of a certain external narrative to be introduced by the viewer into the painting. This differs from iconography, where the image acknowledges that the thing it represents not only can be assigned a meaning but also bears or embodies that meaning as part of its own essence. In literature, too, until well into the eighteenth century, little attention is given to nature as meaning. Nature is the out-of-doors, employed in the common conventions of establishing location, assisting plot transitions, and getting people lost, discomforted, or cast out. Nature no longer has any essence beyond its natural laws.

In romanticism, the idea that nature is pervaded with a meaning equivalent to its essence (re)appears. Nature as well as humanity can now unite essence, meaning, body, and psyche. Symbol and metaphor acquire an enhanced profundity: they are not signs for meaning, they resonate with meaning. The portrayal of the landscape can evoke this essence, which is manifested by the landscape's beauty, its solace, and the suggestion of world order, beneficence, or the sublime. Special techniques for piercing the veil characterize the painting of Caspar David Friedrich, Joseph Turner, and John Constable. The essence of nature is replicated with softness of color and of focus, in contrast with meticulous neoclassic detail; by elusive permeation of one structure by another (clouds and mountaintops); by establishing psychic grandeur through physical remoteness, through capacious scenic prospects or expanses of sky; by contrasting forms so that significant objects seem to loom (blighted trees against the sky, stone ruins against the trees); and by profuse organic lushness or natural tempestuousness.

In a romantic aesthetic, any technique for revealing essence through artistic form, visual or literary, requires the "imagination" of the artist. This imagination is not simply inventive fancifulness (what in the Renaissance was called "fantasia" and what Coleridge called "fancy") but a sacrosanct creative power. The Renaissance had uncovered the compelling manuscripts of one Hermes Trismegistos (the name is actually a Greek designation of the Egyptian god Thoth), purportedly a contemporary of Moses, who contended that since humans were made in God's image, they shared God's creative powers. Fabricating exceptional artwork requires more than skill, talent, knowledge, or dedication. God did not create the universe by crafting an object to illustrate a meaning; rather, the universe emanates from the intrinsic creative power that in God is inseparable from meaning. So, too, with the artist: the sanctification of genius as both a consummate skill and a consummate knowing becomes fully integrated into aesthetic theory by the time of romanticism. "Creativity" encompasses both skill and knowledge. Genius becomes more than an incomparable gift of craft bestowed on its recipient, as it was in the Renaissance, when talent was not at all the same as wisdom. Creativity becomes instead explicable through a metaphysics of higher knowledge. After empiricism, any power of mind requires the identification of a faculty—which names not the process but the psychic mechanism that performs it. Imagination becomes that faculty. The exercise of imagination is both an intuitive knowing and a transmission of that knowing into the artwork. The mystery of creativity is the mystery not of an inexplicable gift of doing but of a transcendent power of knowing. There cannot be an inept poet or artist who is nevertheless surpassingly wise, even if there might be a stupid poet or artist with elegant skills.

The creative artistic imagination works by both inclusion and exclusion, not by copying but by eliminating the inconsequential and emphasizing, modifying, and even recreating features in order to manifest essence. Whereas God can create absolutely new things from nothing, the artist creates new relationships between things, relationships that are themselves then new things of a unique order (art) where difference and identity are fused. God's power is a fission; the artist's power is a fusion. Through this artistic imagination the narrative sign becomes more than an indicative rhetorical message. By the beginning of the nineteenth century, metaphor and symbol coalesce, moving beyond the Renaissance icon and the empirical sign. The iconographic image denotes the correspondence of material objects and meaning, although that image is not itself such a material object. It is Plato's once-removed (hence inferior) copy of the object and its meaning. The metaphor, however, is both a trope of comparison, of fusion, and, as symbol, a divulgence of an essential truth and relation otherwise inexpressible. The act of creativity simultaneously reveals truth and literally makes (crafts) it. Metaphor as symbol creates the meaning it confirms; at the same time, that special act of creation makes the symbol *real* in its own right. The symbol is not subordinate to "real" objects but superior to them: it creates meanings that objects do not inherently possess, drawing upon the meaning that, for the romantics, the universe as a whole possesses.

After the rise of empiricism, meanings were no longer inherent inside things. The science of modernity concerns itself not with the essence of things (the major emphasis of Aristotelian thought) but with the law-governed relationships between things. In romanticism, too, the relationships between things are paramount; but now, through visual and poetic metaphor, the relations reassume profound meaning. The world regains meaning-full essence.

The Renaissance use of perspective had already begun moving metaphysical essence behind (distanced in back of) the outward appearance of the object. The physically real, aside from manifesting the essentially real (the ultimate source of reality), is eventually valued for its own sake by both Florentine and Dutch painters. The reality of flesh becomes as imposing in the south as the reality of clothing becomes in the north. Prolific detail is used gratuitously in Flemish realism and in Italian painting (Rogier van der Weyden and Fra Filippo Lippi can serve as examples) and not only for purposes of iconography. One looks *at* the image, not *through* it. Surfeiting the eye is frequently sufficient. In Italy, splendor is the aggregation of opulent detail; at the same time, wealth becomes the aggregation of opulent objects. The artwork *as a whole* does not completely yield to a secular narrative meaning: since the image not only invokes a meaning but represents the incarnation of meaning in things, the image remains an acknowledgment that meaning pervades what the image represents.

As mercantile economics advances, things dominate meaning. While these things lack intrinsic meanings, they are given meanings as components of the purchase. (By the time of empiricism, God the creator will in fact be a manufacturer.) Artworks, too, eventually assume autonomous object-ivity. Not only do they become transportable commodities, but even their spiritual function achieves autonomy. By the "high" Renaissance (the twenty years under Popes Julius II and Leo X), artistic representation itself takes on the meanings that it formerly had only been able to acknowledge. The artwork becomes autonomously meaningful, almost as sanctified as that which God has created. The Protestants will object to this; and the Counter-Reformation will unhappily agree in 1564, condemning elegance in painting and sensuality in music.[35]

In high Renaissance painting and sculpture, to show meaning is to announce meaning. Visual display takes precedence over speech. The visual challenges the auditory for preeminence. Platonism, based on the metaphor of vision, successfully competes, as visual art, with its predecessor, a philosophical and theological Aristotelianism still retained in Renaissance humanism. This requires visual techniques that enhance the sense of detail, accuracy, order, intention, and clarity: as if these might be fundamental characteristics of eyesight. (Eyeglasses, incidentally, were invented in the thirteenth century.) As already mentioned, ordinary eyesight is actually characterized by blur at the periphery, by the limited range of sharp focus (depth of field), and by a constant retinal motion. Nevertheless, the Renaissance intention is to make the ocular processes resemble accurate verbal thinking—clear, steady, and precise ("in-sight" and "vision"). Revelation then can be a visual perception, the very opposite of the auditory reliance of medieval theology—truth as the Word, as hearing or reading. This is, to remphasize the point, the fundamental demarcation and severance of the Renaissance from the Middle Ages.

From the time of Cézanne, Van Gogh, and Gauguin, painters recognize that the degree to which the "essence" of a subject is captured need not be proportional to the degree to which its features are represented. The thing itself as pure physical presence is its meaning. The meaning (essence) is not some interior substance or form like an immaterial soul or a principal. Being is in itself essence. To know the essence of things is to know what they are, which is no different from how they are, how they appear or can be made to appear, a phenomenological principal. Things are animated by energies, which are physical, like objects themselves. The energies and their embodiments are not two different orders or levels of being. Insofar as the physicality of the object is its meaning, and consequently its essence, meaning is accessible to vision (eyesight), as it was for the Renaissance artist. For the modernist, meaning is, as the visual metaphor suggests, bringing things to light, into the light. Physical light is taken to reveal essence, as spiritual "light" had once done. Meaning is literal illumination,[36] and what is illuminated by light is color and form. Meaning has floated up from deep in the interior of the object to its surface, where sunlight can shine on it.

Early modernism includes this intuition that meaning adheres to the physicality of things. Sensing such meaning is often taken to be transcendence, although such meaning (which coincides with physical being) is actually a substitute for transcendence. In early modernism, the union of essence and meaning in aesthetic discourse substitutes for the union of essence and meaning that was once the basis for theological discourse. A thing may, of course, be given a meaning—such is interpretation; but for the early modernists more than interpretation is meant. To endow a thing with a new meaning in an artwork is, astonishingly, equivalent to discovering an essential meaning that the object already had possessed. Even the inherent meaning of a manufactured object may not be what its makers intended if it is stood alone as an artwork, as an *objet trouvé*.

As modernism progresses, there is a persistent weakening of the intuition that meaning adheres to the physicality of things—whether of each thing in particular or of all things (the world). There is a weakening of confidence in the phenomenological principal that existence itself stipulates there must be meaning. In phenomenology, human existence and the existence of the world are inextricable, so that existence demands that meaning emerge. This fundamental meaning is more than an interpretation: it is an emergence rather than a construction. But meaning and interpretation eventually become synonymous in the arts. The artist projects meaning, rather than receives it; meaning is an imposition on the world, which itself fails to provide it or sanction it. Existence does not stipulate meaning, an empiricist conclusion. Essence vanishes.

While early modernism retained a sufficient infusion of romanticism so that essence, spirituality, and transcendence could be combined, the modern industrialized, capitalized, and technological setting eroded this union. Formalism arises to shift modernism on to some base other than romanticism. In painting and sculpture, once realism and duplication have been assigned to photography, meaning is no longer narrative: meaning is not what one can say about the subject in the work, but a revelation of its form.

While essences could once (long ago, it now seems) be considered special immaterial substances, in modernism form can be produced by what is at once ideal yet not immaterial, neither an object nor a spirit, just as energy is for the scientist (electricity, for example). Energy can be transmuted into objects, and objects can be transmuted into energy. Einstein's equation $E=mc^2$ is notorious for showing that energy and mass can be placed together in the same equation. Modernity has discovered an alchemy that works. In modernism, similar transmutations occur between the imagination and the artwork, mediated by form.

The painter, unlike the photographer, can produce a work positioned in between the form and its usual embodiment, severing them. By mid-modernism, the visual artist "situates," as it were, the canvas and the imagination so that the energy of an object is interrupted from being embodied in its own customary container. The intrinsic physical energies turn not into the ordinary object but into the painting. The form is captured in the painting, although this need not closely resemble the exterior look of any customarily visible object. This new incarnation of form occurs through the three techniques described earlier: through color, through form itself (spatial geometric structure), and through using customarily realistic techniques for producing fantastic images. Painting then can define a territory to which photography has no deed. The camera is customarily situated outside its intended content, viewing it, while the painting is inside its content.

Part Two

The Dilemmas of Empiricism

Science and Modernity

5

Empiricism as Dilemma

Neither Cartesianism nor seventeenth-century rational Protestantism intended to undermine religious belief by their assertion that nothing true could be found unreasonable.[1] In contrast, empiricism is a fully materialistic rationalism that eventually boasts it is sufficient to generate not only an epistemology but also an ethics and an aesthetics. Kant's response to empiricism's claim to autonomy was to subordinate Enlightenment rationality by calling its reason "understanding" and then subordinating this to a "pure reason" transcending empiricist rationality, but despite Kant's logical qualifications, this strategy reinforced all the commonplace assumptions about transcendent realms. In the late nineteenth century empiricism will claim that it can now finally institute an ethics on its own. Following advances in biological theory, this empiricist ethic is fully compatible with the capitalist outlook: the animal world, like the economic world, is based on competitive survival, even if somehow tempered by an unavoidably contradictory moralizing altruism.

Modernism participates in the attempt to reconstruct a surer footing for those who find the dominance of the empiricist-capitalist narrative unacceptable, even repulsive. Not that the modernists despise science (even telepathy, hypnotism, somnambulism, and automism were scientific pursuits); on the contrary, most varieties of modernism share a scientific optimism. Factories or railroad terminals might be like cathedrals. For modernism, the dominance, not the usefulness, of the empiricist worldview is the issue. Yet the modernists maintain that an ultimate and permanent source of value exists outside of empiricism—by exempting from empiricism either a portion of the world order or of the mind. They also endorse the socialists' premise that empiricism need not be necessarily combined with capitalism.

Judeo-Christian religion once informed humans that the earth and the heavens were fabricated for them. In Christianity, the transcendent God assures the enduring importance of the commonest human soul, which can aspire to salvation and perpetual bliss. Pre-Christian classical art ennobles humans by elevating only certain of them to the stature of gods in cultural artifacts, by idealizing their mental or physical proportions in statuary or drama. (The Romans, of course, literally make their emperors gods.) In relation to the Greek and Roman gods, ordinary humans are fundamentally inconsequential. In contrast, the often pious or at least compliant forerunners of the Enlightenment had firmly believed that all humans might be not only secure but even comfortable on this earth, although this was not an original Christian goal. For the early empiricists, the inherent inviolable order of the world could confirm—as some Enlightenment *philosophes* would conclude—the grandeur of the Creator, for whose intellect the world was evidence.

For the Renaissance, however, as discussed in the preceding chapter, the world was not simply evidential but emblematic. All natural objects were emblems, symbols literally embodying the truth, manifesting it rather than only representing it. (The stylized representation of an emblem in an artwork is an icon.[2]) The conversion of the world and its individual parts from emblem into evidence defines empiricism as a historical event. When empiricism begins, the earth can still be considered the "center" of the universe. Even if, according to Copernicus, the sun is spatially positioned at the center of the solar system, this is quite compatible with the solar system itself having been created with humans in mind. But this earth-centeredness becomes increasingly implausible. How can human purposes be served by the millions of galaxies in the preposterous enormity of space? Since empiricism's mechanistic epistemology must lead to a theologically ungrounded moral relativism, the astronomical insecurity erupts hand in hand with ethical insecurity. Together these shape the quandary of modernity: *Where Do We Come From? What Are We? Where Are We Going?* is the intriguing title of a Gauguin painting. No empiricist solution has been found other than to proliferate economic activity.

Modernism is one adaption to these insecurities, part of the attempt of humankind to feel at home again not only on earth (where science will make consumers tranquil enough) but in the universe as a whole, as if it might pertain to us. In the Renaissance, art reflected the theology that legitimated the place of humanity in the cosmos. The grandeur of the Creator, the dignity of humankind, and the beauty of art were interrelated. Modernism proposes that art substantiate the latter two, omitting the obsolete Creator.

Events in the nineteenth century outmoded the old teleological narratives, the stupendous Hegelianisms. As modernism intensifies, a weakened Judeo-Christian theology is excised from the Kantian foundation of romanticism; the aesthetics of transcendence detach from theology. The modernists assume that the aesthetics, standing alone, will be sufficient: art can discard the theology against whose side the aesthetics once leaned. The art-for-art's-sake movement that preceded modernism, without its social consciousness; Continental symbolism rooted in Mallarmé and his contemporaries; impressionism in painting; the writings of Matthew Arnold and Walter Pater; German expressionism—each takes part in this displacement of theology by aesthetics. Each is an effort to counterbalance the domination of the empiricist narrative that had successfully hounded religion since the days of Hobbes and had finally emerged victorious.

Meaning and Modernism

The empiricist narrative provides explanation, which is not the same as meaning. While an explanation must be given a meaning before it can work as an explanation, a meaning need not be given an explanation to work as a meaning. In the empiricist narrative, the meaning given to explanation is that the universe is causally ordered and knowable only through the senses. And, the Enlightenment adds, such knowledge will serve as the basis of human well-being and progress. But this is the meaning of empiricism as a whole, not the meaning of anything discovered by empiricism. Empiricism can assign meaning to what it is, but not to what it finds. Accordingly, it must be motivated by values that come from elsewhere. Although the empiricist method can be employed as if it confirms these values (by confusing values with hypotheses), it cannot generate them. One value brought to empiricist explanation, for example, is that a certain kind of knowledge improves humankind, either by having it or using it; but that humankind can improve or ought to improve, and what it is that defines "improves," requires still another sort of encompassing narrative.

Moral, ethical, and aesthetic beliefs and propositions cannot be generated or justified solely by the method of empiricism, whose narrative cannot legitimate any notions of ethical valuation. The method is defined to exclude Aristotelian final cause (teleology) in favor of efficient cause; yet value is inseparable from teleological considerations—every value predicates an outcome that is the aim or consequence of an action or event. In empiricism, the criteria for assessing outcomes, including those reached through the scientific method, are used in what is now called "e-valuation," no longer a question of determining value and meaning but of corroborating the application of method to agreed-upon goals. Empiricist value still customarily derives from some external teleological narrative concerning the goals and aims either "natural" to human intellectual needs (physical needs, unlike intellectual needs, can be quantifiably determined) or inherent in the history of humanity. Where empiricism dominates, there is always this dilemma: while there can be a morality, there can be no ultimate ground for it. The tendency is always toward ethical relativism, with the related insecurities that effect both the anomie of Weber's theory and the alienation of Marx's.[3]

By the late nineteenth century, the biological theory of evolution is used in empiricism as an explanation; the apparent *direction* of evolution (toward "higher" forms) is used as a value. Empiricist explanation provides the immediate causal predecessors of an event; those predecessors are explained by their own predecessors, ad infinitum. Time can have no beginning in this narrative. (The theological narrative provided a "first cause" or "prime mover," retroactively limiting the causal chain.) Empiricist causality comes to be widely accepted as the only valid causality. Cause and effect universally applies, based on the movement of particles that impact one another and accept, lose, and convey force. The characteristics of an object's "being" are then defined to be precisely those characteristics subsumable in the causal narrative. Aristotle's "final" cause—the purpose to be served by, or the use to be made of, or the state to be reached by, or the effect to be achieved by the object—disappears from science (certain aspects of biology aside), since this, unacceptably, puts the cause of the object ahead of it in time. Final causes are afterward assigned either to a disreputable metaphysics defended only by Hegelians, intuitional ethicists, and the religiously orthodox or to a scientifically suspicious "intentionality" in human ethics and animal biology. Psychology will define desire in a way that has desire (*a* desire, as if it were a thing) precede the behavior, which nevertheless aims at an outcome that is the object of the desire. Achieving this special causative status for desire is the function of much psychology and now its major claim, weak as it may be (as the behaviorists knew), for admission into the sciences.

Aesthetic modernism arises when the empiricist's materialistic notion of cause has disqualified all other such notions. Darwinian evolutionary theory moves toward a mechanistic genetics in order to remove intention: the gene and its "mutation" replaces any reliance on the inheritance of traits acquired during the animal's lifetime.[4] Special and general relativity theory, modern atomic theory, and quantum physics emerge by 1920, following upon nineteenth-century discoveries in electricity and chemistry. Every event now has a branch of science for which it is an object. Whether in biology or in the physical theories of the extremely large, the amazingly small, and even the invisible, scientific investigation becomes more meticulous and more encompassing. Science gets better: theories of phlogiston and the ether disappear; precise optical and electrical instruments measure time, the speed of light, astronomical distances, small emissions of energy; minute particles once unknown and unthinkable are discovered, classified; unprecedented cosmologies evolve. When science finds itself in conflict with other forms of reasoning, it proves more convincing, because empiricism cultivates, trains, and disciplines its own audience. That audience is defined to include everyone not deluded, deranged, mischievous, or irremediably stubborn. Other varieties of explanation appear cumbersome or implausible, since their "facts" can no longer be equated with evidence, even in areas that science had once avoided, like religious or artistic matters.

From the empiricist perspective, beliefs unsubstantiated by acceptable methods become tolerable only as personal eccentricities. *Opinion* becomes a personality trait. As one result, the novel becomes modernity's principle literary genre. The novel is structured as an aesthetic unity, a unity arising from assuming a certain relationship between plot and character. The plot is not simply what happens *to* a character, as an anthology of events; rather, the plot unfolds *for* a character, for a specific unique interior psyche. The older fictional "types" were derived from a limited set of readily classifiable psychic traits, one of which dominates; in contrast, character in the novel derives from assortments of many traits, some of which vie for dominance in a single person. The potentially unlimited assortments allow for individuals. The novelists do not invent the uniqueness of individuated personality; it had emerged during the Renaissance in places where the advance of mercantilism was strongest, as Rembrandt's paintings and Shakespeare's plays attest. But the novel eventually becomes modernity's chief aesthetic promoter of individuality. From the rise of the novel—from around the time of Daniel Defoe and extending through the time of Henry Fielding and Diderot's *Rameau's Nephew*—fiction isolates personal eccentricities as the core of personality.

That beliefs become opinions and opinions become features of the personality reflect how the individual's interior world has become a purely personal matter. Beliefs are the psychic channels into which desire flows; and belief, like desire, relates to actions inside a causal narrative, centering on character, in which "truth" need no longer figure. The dilemma is that empiricist truth, by definition, is impersonal; consequently, what is personal is no longer true. One's existence is no longer primarily situated in the world but in the head: what one does is an effect, which shifts the meaning of "choice" and "determination" into a causal explanation of the psychological kind. Events inside the mind become open to scientific method and language, like events outside the mind. Knowing, thinking, believing, feeling, and willing are no longer simply the "givens" of experience. (Since the mideighteenth century, retaining these as irreducible "givens" has been symptomatic of a reaction against science.) The mind is to know itself as an object through the same procedures by which it knows other things, even though it knows those other things by means of the mind. The mind is granted an empiricist self-reflexivity (Locke's definition of *reflexion*). The instrument does the measuring and is measured: the ruler measures its own length for accuracy.

Classifying the mind as an object of science entails that all its operations, including artistic and religious capacities, must be attributed to physical causation. Not only depression, elation, fear, anxiety, and infatuation, but also the most elevated human accomplishments result from chemical-electrical forces, from neuronal activity influenced by physiological predispositions, blood sugar, fatigue, stress, temperature, disease, and atmospheric contaminants (toxins, electromagnetic waves). The physical organ of this activity, the brain, is both the material and the efficient cause of consciousness and selfhood, which emerge in an intricate organization of a certain large number of neuronal clusters. This is why humans have conscious selves but simpler organisms apparently do not, although they too have neurons.

Consciousness is, in this view, an effect of complex material organization. Crossing the line into self-consciousness is taken not as a mystery but as a biological fact (self-evident since, obviously, it has happened), rather than a fact inside some other order of explanation. Metaphysics, theology, ethics, and aesthetics stagger under such an assumption. Each had depended on the assumption that some source of value subsumes the empiricist narrative. But when the operations of physical nature can be accounted for by laws, nature becomes completely inanimate. Even organic matter is basically an advanced chemical organization. With teleology removed from the "natural" philosophy, one can ask, What reason might God have had for setting the whole system in motion? (Would God derive pleasure from this wind-up toy?) Even to posit that there may be divinely destined outcomes built into the causal process (Leibniz's solution) is quite different from having an immanent and ever-present God whose daily acts of will, based on judgments and intentions, drive the cosmos.

More and more the individual ego is forced into its own uniqueness, domiciled in the head. How far apart the universe and the personal ego become: one expands into unlimited inert space, cold and mostly vacant and dead; the other retreats into the haven somewhere deep inside the head.

Scientific Method

The methods of observation characterizing astronomy in classical Greek culture reappear in modernity as the rudimentary procedure for gathering the information upon which rationality is to be exercised. Astronomy had always been of substantial importance. The discipline was from the beginning of the medieval curriculum included among the seven liberal arts: the trivium (grammar, dialectic, rhetoric) and the more advanced quadrivium of sciences (arithmatic, geometry, music, and astronomy). These methods provide modernity with an alternative to scholastic theological rationalism, which is primarily the study and validation of what happens only once (the creation, the incarnation, individual salvation). In scholasticism, meaning, not observation, is the measure of theoretical plausibility. Numerous explanations, including the medieval cosmology and epistemology bequeathed to the Renaissance, depend on necessarily unobservable phenomena—under the assumption, which once seemed incontrovertible, that the ground of what is observable cannot itself be observable, since the cause cannot *be* the effect. In modernity, however, the purpose of theory is to account for an observation, not to give meaning to it. Every observation tests a theory, and a theory not leading to observations is useless. The process of deduction becomes verifiable; logic can be tested, must be testable even to qualify for being logical. Verification through arranged novel observations (experiments) becomes a criterion for the definitions of truth and error. Ethics and epistemology part company.

The astronomical measurements of the Greeks serve (with a little manipulation) the astronomy of Copernicus; the more accurate measurements of Tycho Brahe serve Kepler, whose calculations are accepted by Newton. The specific method of analysis is the logic of geometry expanded, after Galilean mechanics, to include motion. The fundamental characteristic of the science of modernity is that motion is the subject under discussion. Certain of the conic sections described statically by Euclid are thought or found to be the natural paths along which planets and ordinary objects travel: the circle (for Copernicus, as earlier for Ptolemy), the ellipse (for Kepler and Newton), and the parabola (the path followed by an object thrown forward and up into the air). As earlier, the form of a thing is static—a thing is the sum of its parts, and knowing the aggregation is to define the thing. But when motion becomes the subject of science, change is given greater prominence than form. The essential concerns are not the things themselves, but the relations between them. Laws describe these relationships in equations, with each thing subordinated to a large category, any member of which can serve to substitute for the generalized notation (the x). Form, albeit permanent, is what enters into motion; and the empiricists' scientific laws are not about the form, but about the motion.

Copernican astronomy demonstrates convincingly that geometrical reasoning produces conclusions unavailable to or controverting the unaided senses or ordinary reasoning. Truth is the disclosure of what has been hidden. A geometry of motion calls things into question, then answers the question. This geometrical analysis changes the conception of what it means to know the universe: before science, humans were ignorant about the universe, despite theology. The method is abstracted for use in various areas of science. The hidden truths to be made evident are principles of inviolable order, mathematical in form. These principles require neither the daily volitional actions and intentions of the deity nor (living matter excepted) the workings of intangible active immaterial essences. The geometrical method is increasingly enhanced by advances in algebra. Descartes graphs algebraic equations on a geometrical grid, linking the two mathematical disciplines; Leibniz and Newton later invent calculus.[5] The deductive chain of philosophical reasoning increasingly takes a geometrical format, stating axioms as near to the self-evident as possible and deriving theorems.[6] Philosophy and mathematics intermingle in modernity. From Descartes, Newton, and Leibniz through Bertrand Russell and Alfred North Whitehead, both disciplines are often the specialty of a single thinker.

It was understood in the late 1500s that since the cosmos is itself beyond manipulation, situations yielding observations might be locally contrived or prearranged. This method goes beyond the observation of naturally occurring phenomena. Aristotle, for example, knew something about observation but not about manipulation. The experimental method suggested by Roger Bacon is applied by Galileo to the mechanics of all uniformly moving bodies, meaning nonliving matter.[7] ("Life" can move itself.) Insofar as local manipulation is assumed to display the same rules that solid bodies (including the heavenly bodies, now all considered weighty masses) everywhere obey, all visible or potentially visible phenomena are placed in one category. The real is uniformly constituted; nature is a coherent and continuous ensemble. This is the premise of "natural philosophy," as Newton and other scientists call it—a name retained until the nineteenth century when, under the influence of idealism, the natural sciences and speculative philosophy appeal to different interests.

The scientific method is extended throughout the entire range of nonliving matter by an empiricist principle of cause and effect: change is explicable by properties known as forces inherent within the collection of objects undergoing change. A force is a causative principle of an object's motion, rather than a formative principle of an object's structure. The concept of force, whose power is in its quantity rather than (like essence) in its quality, allows the removal of will, including divine will, from the causal chain as a necessary explanatory ingredient. "Necessity" as an autonomous concept replaces intention; law replaces will.

The double meanings of law involve proscription and necessity. The first remains the basis of civic and religious ordinances, while the second becomes the basis for the scientific determination of the action of matter. There is no longer a valid method for connecting these two realms. Neither the will nor the intellect of the deity can effectively serve that function any longer, and the Renaissance theory that all things, living and inert, inherently bear meaning has also disappeared.[8] For modernity, the inviolable in nature is not an instruction or demand, as civic law is, but a matter of the collective properties, propensities, and principles of matter. Proscriptive law, human or divine, can be violated, even if it should not be. The laws of nature are inviolable. Meaning is not an issue. Order is not *an* order (a command). Matter can be described without reference to the properties of anything external to matter. Causation is kept internal to materiality.

Animal life is eventually included within nature as well. Beyond Descartes's belief that animals are automatons, this comes to include human life, too, insofar as humans have "natural" tendencies, physical needs, carnal desires, and anatomical capacities. Including humans inside the idea of empiricist nature is not at first meant to place human behavior in the category of those motions of objects describable by mathematics. "Behavior" is considered more than "motion" because it is performed volitionally. From the time of the Enlightenment, however, techniques of empiricist reasoning and deduction are applied to a brand-new form of information: society, as an entity, itself becomes a phenomenon. Social institutions can, then, presumably be created and modified, just as machines are conceived, invented, and repaired. Society can also be an experiment. Over time, various social behaviors are demonstrated to be hospitable to mathematics: economics (in particular) and population dynamics. Behaviors are not only quantifiable, but their cause-and-effect relationships can be stated in the aggregate as mathematical formulas. The behaviors are functions, dependent variables; humans, too, can serve as x's in the equations. Eventually, even behaviors apparently motivated by individual and perhaps transient human emotions (like marriage and suicide) can be understood in this way, as descriptions of a collectivity. Even language undergoes autonomous changes (loss of grammatical inflection, for example) not in the control of the speakers. By the midtwentieth century, any human behaviors not yet scientifically explicable (which is to say, not yet made motion), like feeling, intention, or contemplation, seem only temporary exclusions, problems whose solutions are impending.[9]

Accounting for Reality

In empiricism, all knowledge relies on initial sensations. The evidence for underlying causes—as properties within objects, not external impositions upon objects—becomes detectable through the senses rather than through any direct powers of intellect, inspiration, or revelation. Inside the real and the visible are forces and potentials that both are the object and are manifested by the object. Although the forces that underlie the universal order of nature are invisible, their effects always are visible or can be made so, so that they can be known, which is to know the universal underlying order of nature. The operations of human mentality on sensation yield a coherent understanding of the external world that theoretically will have no missing pieces, no spaces that need to be artificially filled by metaphysical suppositions or entities.

The forces residing in matter are invisible because they are potentials, rather than "qualities" available to any of the senses (as shape, color, and weight are). Explanation is an accounting for the visible by explicating the effect of the invisible.

Originally, the experimental method reproduces, on a small and local basis, occurrences otherwise observed in unmanipulable situations. But eventually the experiment is arranged so that ideal observations are intentionally contrived. (Such as a near-perfect sphere rolling on a near-perfect inclined plane.) Categories of phenomena can now be created. When science becomes creative, in this specialized way, it can rival art in offering access to truth. Art is also the demonstration of truth through the manipulation of ideal appearances: in the Renaissance, the principle method of science was drawing.

That a chain of mental manipulations can lead to a conclusion verifiable by contriving previously unobservable phenomena is surprising: the structure of mathematical logic and the structure of the world must somehow coincide. The absence of observational verification becomes evidence either of error (in the premises, reasoning, or observation) or irrelevance (since there is little point in theorizing about what has no observable consequences). Once the experimental method devises situations where unprecedented and even unanticipated or inexplicable observations can be made (and only then can the sciences of chemistry and electromagnetism evolve[10]), the experiment, not "nature," can verify the theory or undermine it. Which of these it will do is unpredictable by the theory itself, since the theory accounts for an event being produced as an experiment only because the theory demands it as a test. Instruments signify the occurrence of previously unobserved events; that an instrument is required to detect certain events explains their previous unobservableness. To test the existence of what it has been designed to observe, an instrument is placed between the invisible and the senses, so that the invisible may affect the instrument in a way that the senses can detect.

In the scientific method, objects correspond to sensory perceptions, which are described in language. From the ordering of these perceptions can be deduced the underlying invisible order, which cannot itself be a perception. The underlying order is both the essence of orderliness (law) and the cause of orderliness (the operations of the law). These operations of the intellect include the expansion and the refinement of language through a mathematics whose function is to describe the order manifested in matter by corresponding to it. Mathematics is a language based on the complete transfer of speaking and hearing to reading and writing: the extended strings of notation cannot be understood apart from the page. In empiricism, ordinary language is best suited for describing the visible world but not its underlying order. Because the common languages serve art better than science, the scientifically minded will exercise special care in using the vernacular with clarity and exactitude. (So Thomas Sprat advised the Royal Society in the seventeenth century.[11]) Mathematics is to be a language (or, more precisely, is to be used as a language) with no errors of correspondence to real relations, errors with which ordinary language is replete. Ordinary language is infested with metaphor. The errors arise and deduction often fails because sensory, emotional, and volitional content—for all of which there must, obviously, be words (how else know them?)—become mixed together in the deductive process. Grammatical structure is such that, at a space where a particular part of speech (noun, adjective, etc.) is called for, any member of the set can be inserted. This is why it is possible to say what is false. Mathematics presumably can eliminate this confusion between the lexicon of things and the lexicon of desires. This is the confusion that makes art and literature possible.

Linear Causation

Many observations are still logically classified by static relationships of similarity and subordination, as they were for Aristotle. But for modernity the linear sequence of logical deduction comes to correspond to linear causal processes. The order of deductive logic corresponds to the order of the universe. In the traditional logic, later propositions follow necessarily from earlier ones, like the statements in a syllogism. This does not require the efficacy of time, since the later propositions are already inherently contained in the earlier ones. (Euclidian geometry is the paradigm.) Cause and effect, however, require the notion of time. The deductive linear sequence of logic is allied with the directionality of time. This means more than simply that events reoccur over time, as astronomical bodies return to where they have been before. (Those events that were not known to reoccur, like comets, were for that very reason perplexing exclusions, perhaps unnatural omens.) In an astronomical sense, although repetition takes time the process is cyclical: closed curves continually reengrave themselves. Time itself, by analogy, is circular, just like the Greek theory of cyclical history, in which events revolve, presumably on the pattern of the sun returning every day. But when logic and linear time are conflated, nothing ever returns to an origin. Eden is irrevocably lost. The sequence, whether of argument or of history, acquires a unidirectionality.

The linear procedures of deduction presumably correspond to the procedures by which the physical processes are themselves generated. Consequently, events are necessarily logically consistent. Natural phenomena become themselves rational—a different matter than assigning rationality to their creator. Logic is generative and generativity is logical, requiring that time be included in the explanation. The term *t* appears in equations, which become what scientific theory is. In a static syllogism, logic does not go beyond a configuration of internally subordinated propositions describing the state of things. Nothing new can enter a syllogism, although something new can always enter time. In an equation, the older static balance is represented by the equals sign: the stability that makes the law a "law" is in the equals sign. Simultaneously on either side of the equation are time, force, and motion.

In medieval astronomy, based on Ptolemy, bodies move because they are pushed by an external force continually emanating directly from God. Otherwise, they would stop, since it is assumed that the natural state of bodies is at rest. In the Newtonian version of Copernican heliocentricity, the flow of time itself yields movement, since inertia is a property of the body.[12] Movement prolongs itself, at a constant velocity and in a straight line, as long as time flows and no counteracting force impedes motion. (Is this not the underlying rationale for the Enlightenment's idea of progress?) The linear movements of time and of things correspond.

But also in Newtonian physics, matter itself contains a force of attraction. Gravity is an odd kind of force, since it does not work by the pushing of one body directly against another to transmit or retard motion. At one stroke, since all objects attract one another, gravity connects every physical thing in a single field of cause and effect. Space is completely filled by this field: there is no longer a vast empty region where nothing exists but God.

The concept of gravity allows normal motion to be conceived of as always linear, exactly like the movement of time. The circular motion of astronomical bodies, considered primary by Ptolemy and Copernicus, is not primary; neither is the planetary elliptical motion described by Kepler. In both Ptolemy's theory and Copernicus's, the planets are required to have innately circular motions,[13] since no force provides connection between the planets and the body around which they revolve. In Newtonian physics, the straight line of ordinary unimpeded motion is bent by gravitational effect. The moon, for example, would move away in a straight line if the earth suddenly vanished; yet the linear gravitational pull of the earth causes it to fall, at a rate, fortunately, that exactly balances the impetus to go straight ahead. Two linear forces in contention generate a smooth (and, most notably, a predictable) curve.

Even the history of the cosmos will someday be included within the narrative of two conflicting linear forces. All matter attracts, yet an alleged explosion has conveniently propelled all matter apart; this presumably accounts for why the universe has a structure and therefore a history, why it is neither coagulated into one mass nor randomly dispersed and moving aimlessly.

Aristotelian "cause" circumvented the efficacy of time by positing—in addition to material, efficient, and formal causes—final causes, a telos. This is eventually bequeathed to Christianity by Aristotle: there is no teleology in the Old Testament. By having the future somehow contained as a cause in the present moment, present and future are conceptually unified. That events occur in time does not make time causally influential. In a teleology, time fulfills, not creates. Modernity's limitation of causation to a position always prior to the effect grants time an irrevocable priority, with "before" and "after" becoming fundamental to the definition of causation. Linear motion in linear time becomes the primary characteristic of all activity.

Previously satisfactory metaphysical notions become outmoded because they cannot be employed in the equations. The concept of force replaces them all. The physical forces do not themselves demand a subsequent metaphysical explanation for complete knowledge about motion to be achieved. (Newton asserts that there is no need to "hypothesize."[14]) An initial cause of the movement of matter may, of course, be posited, because even if linear motion at a constant velocity is fundamental, the ultimate origination of motion is not contained in the physics. Because time can be extended infinitely backward, this problem need never be directly confronted in the sciences. Even assuming a creator of matter and force, knowledge about the visible creation can still be derived from matter alone. The ordered structure of the universe is internally complete. (In 1864, Pope Pius IX would be compelled to argue in *Quanta cura* not only that God exists, but also that he has some effect on the world.)

Allying sequential logic and sequential time eventually means even more than this in modernity. A unidirectional time can bring about what has never occurred before, the absolutely new. Judaism and Christianity had introduced a notion of linearity in history—the idea that, at specific points along the line of an unrepeatable history, God had chosen his people and God's son had descended, events that for the Hebrews and the Christians are, respectively, the demarcation between a Before and an After. In the Judeo-Christian view, the absolutely new is always introduced by God's volition. In empiricism, originally, there is a permanent inviolable order in the world: the physical universe is stable, perhaps eternally. Novelty is merely rearrangement, unique combinations of unvarying elements. Even the basic patterns of human nature and of society were believed to be already known and classified. The ethical goal is to understand the permanent order of the world and to conduct oneself in a harmonious relation to it. Such is the basis of a natural morality. In choosing between the good and the bad, the options are knowable in advance, not because a list has been provided by divine guidance but because history has continued long enough for all the alternatives already to have been manifested.

But when empiricism is transformed into the project of the Enlightenment, true novelty becomes logically comprehensible in a different way. There was a time when any phenomenon occurred for the first time, and so will there be such times in the future. While the enactment of the new requires the rearrangement of already existing matter (there is only so much stuff in the world), the conceptual world has not generated all alternatives. The Enlightenment is not a summation but a new beginning. The idea of progress summarizes this belief. Since Enlightenment historiography is based not on a cyclical theory, but rather on this idea of progress, scientific method must become, unlike the strict experimental method, applicable to unrepeatable sequences. What occurs only once cannot be accounted for by attributing the singularity to divine intervention (no more miracles) or by citing a fate or destiny. Instead, processes are characterized as evolution-ary. This direction is not equivalent to a teleological aim; direction is inherent in events as a force pushing events forward, not as an aim pulling events toward it. With this notion, an encompassing unidirectional history, geology, biology (evolution), and cosmology (the current big bang theory) can be promoted and legitimated. The behavior of individual humans and societies can be classified as unique events in an ordered and gradual linear singularity. For early empiricism, the forms of objects remained stable even though the objects were in motion—hence objects, and humans too, could have essences. But an evolutionary theory both posits and accounts for changes in form. No longer can things have permanent essences. Heraclitus had been correct. Plato, Aristotle, and the Old Testament—their long supervision of Western thought now rapidly declines.

Empiricism originally anticipated that discovery would continually lead to refinements and expansions of theory. Discovery would expand, but not call into question, the entire structure of knowledge within which the discovery was made. It was assumed that each discipline could be carefully built from the ground up. Lacking procedural errors, knowledge would be indefinitely and smoothly cumulative. Newtonian cosmology was the paradigmatic example. At the end of the eighteenth century it was generally believed that the workings of the celestial universe had been sufficiently described. By the midnineteenth century, discoveries in geology (that the earth, too, has a narrative history, of extraordinary length) and biology (both evolution and cellular biology) necessitated massive theoretical revisions. Mathematical models alternative to the common suppositions were also put forth; non-Euclidean geometry, relativity theory, and (later) quantum physics undermined deductive sequences based on what were once presumed obvious propositions.

By the nineteenth century, whole disciplines of thought once external to the physical sciences are assigned principles of linear developmental order. The procedure even reaches into art, as aesthetic formalisms and structuralisms give art, too, an evolutionary history that encompasses as much as it is caused by its practitioners. By the third decade of the twentieth century, formalism decrees the standard assumptions of art history.

The scientific concept of force similarly affects that particular structure of language which is logic. When the concept of natural forces is introduced into logic, argument can be described as proceeding forward in a straight line unless opposed by a force that alters its course. The Hegelian dialectical logic purported to provide these oppositional forces with an idealist metaphysical basis. That empiricism cannot account for why there should be motion (or anything else) in the first place is not a dilemma for empiricism. Idealism, however, always requires the origin of things, meaning, and value to coincide. The Hegelian dialectic provides the logic of opposition with a mechanics of conflict: by amalgamating logic and force, the relationship between logical propositions becomes generative. The Aristotelian syllogism contains no internal generative conflict; the purpose of the syllogism—a permanent and necessary relationship between propositions—is to eliminate conflict. In the Hegelian dialectic, there is an oppositional contention both sides of which must arise from the same ultimate source. History is the motion of the Absolute, based on the idea that the ground of being generates its own resistance to itself (the idea found in Boehme and Fichte) in order that a universe be possible. There is no possible explanation for why anything should generate opposition to itself, unless this is attributed to the metaphysical nature of things.

Empiricism is not compelled to account for ultimate origins. Any existing dualism (gravity and inertia) can be extended back in time indefinitely. But idealism must answer this question: Why has any disturbance at all occurred throughout eternity? Even in Eastern philosophy, the emergence of the world from the original void is admittedly inexplicable. By conceiving of conflict as deriving from unity, to conceptually reconcile the unreconcilable, idealism insinuates perpetual conflict into Enlightenment reason as if that were reason's driving force. The conflicting forces inherent in material nature (like gravity and inertia) are given metaphysical origins with counterparts in logic. Logic is also the origin of matter insofar as dialectic generates the world, which is continually in process. Like empiricism, dialectical logic introduces time into the static schema of Aristotelian logic; but to say that reason is constant motion is not to say (as empiricism says) that motion is constantly reasonable. Reason must feed upon itself because in a Hegelian monism both sides of conflict must derive from the same metaphysical source. No proposition is without its antithesis, so no proposition can permanently endure as truth.

Various nineteenth-century theories can be construed from either the empiricist or idealist perspective. For example, in empiricist social theory, desire is described like uniform forward impetus, always aiming in a straight line toward its object; reason (logic, law, and custom) acts like gravity, attracting desire away from its course. The empiricist prefers to think that conflict can stabilize eventually, through consensual harmony, while those influenced by the idealist environment (Georg Simmel, for example) assert that conflict is perpetual and the only way history can be generated. Marx's class warfare unites both theories: a perpetual conflict, modeled on Hegel, is simultaneously envisioned as being someday reconciled. (So time and Eden are reunited.) This juxtaposition is the central ingenuity of Marx's theory. Similarly, in psychoanalytic theory, ego and id are linear forces in contention, yet the oppositional force of ego must be naturally generated out of the id. One might ask, what reason could the id have for contravening itself, for generating its (Hegelian) antithesis? Freud posits an empiricist answer involving the dualism of the organism and the environment, again two forces in opposition. Ego is produced as an adaption, with the organism protecting its own survival by compromising pleasure. The dualistic opposition of organism and environment provides an empiricist explanation for a theory originally grounded in a Schopenhaurian metaphysics of monistic will. This alliance of idealism and empiricism is precisely what makes psychoanalysis not simply attractive to modernism, but an aspect of modernism's intermixture of romanticism and empiricism.

The theory of evolution likewise inserts the logical structure of conflict over time into biology. Organisms are produced gradually through the perpetual conflict of two linear forces: the physiology of an organism striving for nutrition and copulation (not necessarily in that order) and the impeding environment it inhabits. Linguistics, too, is discussed in dynamic terms of movement and conflict. (This conflict marks the distinction between linguistics and the earlier etymological "philology.") Language has a history; linguistic change can be caused by historical processes, like invasion and migration. Language change also depends on what appears to be language acting somehow on itself, such as in large shifts in vowels or consonants (Grimm's law). Language, too, is given autonomous generative energies. Encompassing structural changes in language cannot be attributed directly to the intention of individual users; nor can social, political, or economic history be identified as a cause. There is a science of language, linguistics. Like other objects investigated by science, language also must have a form that can be set in motion, the relationship, in Saussurean terms, between the synchronic and the diachronic.[15]

The more the transience of the large components of the universe becomes acceptable—the solar system will someday be gone—the more does instability become a principle of every aspect of human study. Logic no longer entails generating unchangeable truths; logic is the conflictual process of truth changing over time. Premises are generated and refuted. No premise is immune. The negation (a minus, a "false," a "no") is the only absolutely pure signifier, unable to correspond to anything outside language, but capable of being applied to anything inside language. Since the negation of any statement is an intrinsic part of the system of language within which the statement acquires its meaning, the process of premising and refuting appears not only as the method and technique of logical procedure but its ultimate aim and purpose.

Modernism Evolving

Modernism, too, is structured on a dialectic of conflicting forces, and the modernists frequently describe themselves in that way. The fundamental conflicting forces, they contend, are bourgeois society and the avant-garde (modernism itself). The more encompassing conflict, however, is the attempt to further Enlightenment modernity without losing the romantic reaction to it. For the modernist, the artwork arises as the result of a conflict between the artist and society. Modern art is generated by the act of standing in opposition to the forces that would impede its production. Nevertheless, this social conflict is conceived as an aesthetic unity. In the modernist aesthetic theory, the union of opposites is the shape of artistic unity.

In science, the law is presumed to preexist its discovery. The law is known and shared as language: although the phenomena it accounts for are for the most part visual, the accounting for those phenomena is aural (written). The aesthetic experience also includes the sense that general aesthetic principles are manifested in the individual work. These principles, in turn, may seem to offer access to universal "laws," as if knowledge (different from opinion) is gained not only about the work but also about the world generally. In art, according to the aesthetic derived from Kant, the "law" cannot be disentangled from its embodiment. In science, events are demonstrations of the law; but artworks are incarnations of the law. In physics, the law can exist without any event having to exemplify it. (That hydrogen and oxygen can yield water was true before there was water.) In art, the law exists only through and following each exemplification.

Since each aesthetic exemplification occurs only once, art has a history—a narration of a continuous, irreversible, linear sequence, occurring only once, of causally related events. For a universe considered stable, as in early empiricism, science simply describes changes (rearrangements), which is not equivalent to a history. But during the time when modern art flourishes, the notion of unidirectional evolution enters all disciplines. The subjects of the various sciences can then each have a history and not merely experience changes. Modern art, correspondingly, becomes about the transient in motion. Evolution in motion—not harmony, balance, tranquility, or the eternal—becomes the essentially permanent: the permanent is impermanency.

The empiricist's scientific forces have their counterpart in modern art, especially visual art. As matter is filled with force, so art is filled with energy. Energy has created the work, is contained in the work, and is exhibited by the work. Modern art is the first art for which the establishment of harmony is replaced by the radiation of energy as an aesthetic and a conceptual purpose. Art has always been taken to radiate emotional energy, but the energy in modern art is also a purely physical energy, emanating from the materials composing the work. The materials are distinct from the content; the content can no longer subordinate the materials. Only in modern art is no subject whatsoever excluded, since the work is no longer quite about its subject. That such artistic work, based on the organization of the energies of the shaped materials, can be profound art, meaning-full art, and not merely decorative art (like the disparaged rococo) is unique to modernism. No longer is the work constructed around symbols of the timeless and the enduring. It exists in the world of continual motion—which in literature is the world of the novel—that is now the only world there is. Meaning is not behind motion, but about motion. The work arouses and does not calm. Art is incarcerated motion. Every artwork captures a fleeting moment in its motion, just as every event in physics is an intentionally bounded incident abstracted from continuous time. Everything called an event—and this can include the modernist artwork—is one immediate solution to a permanent equation.

Empiricist reasoning eventually controverts the autonomy of the reasoner. The idea of human freedom had traditionally been based on the existence of humanity's faculty of reason, which presumably allows actions to result from considered choice. But when reason is freely undertaken in an empiricist environment, it leads, paradoxically, to the discovery of ubiquitous causal determinism. Modern art and aesthetics are to form the basis of a reconciliation between free will and determinism. (Calvinism had earlier proposed this reconciliation on religious grounds.) The social structure is to be given an aesthetic core to serve as the source of value. The shapes of historical structures are conceived to resemble the shapes of artistic ones, an alliance meant to displace, or at least to supplement, the Enlightenment bonding of linear historical structure with the linear structures of time and determinism posited by natural science. For modernism, art, not science, is to become the discipline of pure form wherever a structure derives from human mentality. Social structures, machinery, mathematical theories, cities—all become amenable to aesthetic criteria, including the criterion of beauty, for although everything that is pleasing is not of high value, the forms that are most valuable are always aesthetically pleasing.

Narratives about the "stages" of history had been an Enlightenment preoccupation. (Saint-Simon employs three stages; so does Comte; Fourier had sixteen.) While historical novelty on the largest scale (era, epoch) erupts necessarily as part of the historical causal sequence, it can and must be assisted in emerging—so argues the Enlightenment. Even revolution becomes justifiable, for the first time in history. (In geology and evolutionary biology, too, catastrophic theories are advanced, preceding the more common gradualist theories.[16]) The most recent part of the historical sequence is characterized by the self-consciousness of the human assistance that brings history into being. Human subjectivity has not been constant: it has emerged over time into its present form. The development of the ego has a chronology. Paradoxically, history—conceived as a single structured event, rather than as an aggregation of individual transient events—generates the self-consciousness by which that history is itself to be controlled. While laws define what is necessary, they can be used by humans to institute change. Paradoxically, freedom occurs within and contributes to historical mechanisms that are themselves determined. The necessary is, oddly, contingent. This unusual position is taken to define a boundary between human history and natural history, protecting humanity from classifying itself as simply one more part of the animal kingdom.[17]

Nonhuman realms gain histories only after humanity's discovery of its own fundamental historical structures. Evolutionary natural science follows Enlightenment theories of evolutionary human history. The animal, geological, and cosmological realms can be destabilized and can be discovered to have histories only after human history has already come to be described as a sequence of structures (biological, governmental, cultural) rather than a sequence of individual human actions.

Oddly enough, while the apparently free exercise of reason allows for the progress of science, that very procedure must also turn on itself to disprove and countermand the free efficacy of the reasoner. This is modernity's dilemma: empiricist reason, having once subverted the immortal soul in favor of an autonomous selfhood (and what other compensation is there for the loss of immortality?) for which reasoning itself has been presumed incontrovertible evidence, then subverts the autonomous self by that very same power of reason. The self's exercise of its autonomy (freedom) leads to a denial of that autonomy (ubiquitous causality). The nineteenth century searches to remedy the discomfort by allowing for some form of human efficacy in specially developed social and economic theories, notably within capitalism and socialism. By accepting Spinoza's assertion that free will is a compliance with necessity in a Hegelian framework (where freedom has been reified as a metaphysical force or aim), Marxist socialism introduces a looseness or tolerance in a basically determined system. Hence Marxism always considers itself a science. Democracy, on the contrary, always sees itself as using science, not being science; it retains the Cartesian duality of mind and matter, the coexistence of free will and determinism, even though accepting this illogicality means that the pursuit of metaphysics must be permanently abandoned. (Forsaking metaphysics is not everywhere lamented as too steep a price to pay.) Democracy relies on the eighteenth-century theory of natural "rights," immersing liberty and freedom in an encompassing permanent and inalienable moral "law." But using the term *law* here is derived from the Greek *nomos,* not from any empiricist principles. Again, empiricism must import its system of moral valuation from other narratives. The moral law is legitimated by confusing the legislated absence of social constraints ("rights" are not what one can do, but potential constraints that cannot be imposed) with freedom of the will, as if an extensive variety of possible and admissible behaviors can serve as evidence for the freedom of behavior.

The increasing sophistication of mathematical probability theory and statistical analysis precipitated a most important change. Although the discipline is traceable back to Jacob Bernoulli's *Ars Conjectandi* (1713) and Condorcet's work in the 1780s, it is in the nineteenth century, as one long-standing truth after another is called into question, that chance and probability gain their potency. When a genetic theory based on probability—the arbitrary mutation of genes, the random selection of either member of a pair of genes—replaces the idea that traits acquired during the lifetime of the individual animal can be directly passed on to offspring, evolution need no longer be assigned a necessary direction. The acceptance of a completed mathematics of probability allows outcomes to be orderly but not predictable. The order is the overall summation of a sequence, not the specific progression of the sequence, and an occurrence can be lawful without being anticipated. Humans may exist by chance. In the 1890s Henri Poincaré suggested that the laws of nature might all be statistical laws; this insight matures during the modernist era. The likely contingency and arbitrariness of human existence is the most significant blow ever given to the status of the human ego. It is far more extreme than the relocations of Copernican astronomy. Wherever the earth is located an argument can be made that God has made it just so and for good reason; in contrast, the linking of evolution and probability theory raises insurmountable problems.

Many modernists refuse to allow this discovery to undermine optimism, just as the humanists find alternative reasons for their own optimism. Since progress is caused by the self-reflection of the species, whether in art for the modernists or science for the humanists (for whom aesthetics is a component of psychology), the cosmic isolation may even increase ambition. In contrast, an often brooding pessimism permeates the offspring of idealism, namely phenomenology and, in particular, existentialism.

Modernism intends to demonstrate that in human affairs novelty and even genius is unpredictable. It cannot be fully accounted for by science, which fills up time and leaves no room for that variety of the unique and unprecedented called (following romanticism) "creativity." Although humans are natural creatures and natural laws are inviolable, the permutations permitted by these laws are perhaps infinitely varied. Just as evolutionary theory in biology had made nature intrinsically creative despite its absolute lawfulness, so are the same dynamics transferred to the mind, binding it to scientific law (psychology), which is simultaneously a liberation. At every moment creativity can be inserted, as if the present is a small interstice of free will between the past and the future. The moment of genius is in this present. The possibility of the unprecedented exists not only according to probability theory, which is a matter of materialistic redistribution, but according to the new aesthetic theory as well. In art, the unique arises from inspiration. While the workings of the mind might in theory be fully known (although the modernists do not really believe this is possible), they are not now known. Inspiration and mathematical probability can be united to reinforce the notion of a will capable of the new and the unpredictable—even if it is not free in the older sense (of a soul exercising free volition).

But modernism's response is more extensive than this. Into the midst of the causal sequence, at the present, is inserted not only personal freedom of will, newly defined, but an entire tradition alien to empiricism: the romanticism issuing from a philosophic transcendentalism and idealism. Kantian subjectivity, the ideas of Schelling and Friedrich Schlegel, Coleridge and Shelley, Rousseau and Bergson, Hegel's freedom and Croce's intuition, the Platonic ideas of beauty as spiritual transcendence—all these are combined to balance, surround, or dominate the modernity that modernism cannot reject but strives to correct. The form that history will take is embodied in the work artists will create. All history is art history. The lives of artists, as well as their works, become examples: artists embody the form they transmit to their materials. The relation between the life of the artist and the form of the artwork corresponds to the relation between the present, where free artistic will resides, and history as a whole, in which the artwork is physically created. Only in retrospect will the historical chain seem to have had a direction, although the apparent direction is not equivalent to a determination (as, when we look back, biological evolution only appears to have had a predetermined direction). The foremost exemplar of this free will newly defined is the artist, who for that reason is said to live, unlike other persons (the insane excepted), always in the present.

After Classical Physics

The premises about the "givens" premised in the physics of modernity—atomistic "matter" that is solid, with a constant mass; the universally invariable flow of time; the paradigm of cause and effect; the homogeneity of empty space—will be called into question by scientists while modernism is evolving. In atomic theory, while the universe is composed of dozens of basic elements, each characterized by an atom uniquely organized, the constituents of all these atoms (protons, electrons, etc.) are identical. Since the transient visible world rests on these absolutely identical constituents, where do phenomena originate? What might begin the causal process of differentiation if divine intervention is excluded? Quantum physics can yield (only) a theory about the interactions of these small particles, a theory that leads to the search for ever more basic constituents.

In quantum physics, scientific predominance is gained by thinkers whose intellectual influences derive less from the classic empiricist tradition than from the Kantian one, especially from the late nineteenth-century German neo-Kantianism that had influential groups of adherents in five or six German universities. But the scientific theorists rely on a basically idealist interpretation of Kant, not quite in keeping with Enlightenment goals; in this sense quantum physics can be seen as a reassertion of idealism within the empiricist scientific environment. Specifically, classical physics, including the earliest nuclear physics, contains the belief that it is possible to know what for Kant was the unknowable thing-in-itself underlying what to the senses are phenomena. Empiricist science can discover the basic physical structures on which the world is founded. Beyond this, no additional underlying numinous level of things-in-themselves need be posited. The subordination, the refutation, of such thinking motivates Kant. As empiricist science had put all causal forces inside objects and their relations, so Kant, in retaliation, moves *all* of science inside mental relations. Observation of the physical forfeits its priority to the structure of mind. This allows the recuperation of notions of causal immateriality (God and the soul), which the ensuing idealists find most attractive and useful.

Unlike classical physics, quantum physics rests on Kant's incipient idealism. In quantum physics the fundamental particles, like the electron, are as unknowable as the thing-in-itself is for Kant. Even beyond this, the constituent particle is conceived of not as a discrete entity but as some hypothetical thing represented by a mathematical description of a set of possibilities (a probability matrix or a wave function: the two are mathematically congruent). One of the possibilities is found to materialize whenever a measurement is made (the particle appears), because the technique of measurement yields results that characterize not the underlying phenomenon but the act of measurement itself. As in idealism, the fundamentally real cannot be known to be anything else than the mental construct that constitutes knowing it. New instruments become the conditions for and, in a profound sense, the cause of new observations. The formulas that comprise the theory predict experimental results; but since such results cannot include *direct* observation of the phenomena posited by the theory (the wave functions are not entities), the validity of the theory and the actual existence of the particles in the form proposed by the theory cannot be known to correspond.[18] And since no direct observation of the ultimately grounding phenomena is possible, the quantum physicists eventually ask, why call the ultimate object of investigation an entity?

What modernism is to aesthetics, quantum physics is to science: an attempted reconciliation between empiricism and idealism inside an empiricist-dominated environment. The subordination of idealism to victorious empiricism following World War I will be partly recuperated in a science that, like modernism, tries to unify realism and idealism inside empiricism. The strongest influence is in the German tradition: quantum physicists are temperamentally idealists.[19] (A recent example is the idea that the origin of time itself can be placed at the moment of the big bang, making time, as all transcendentalists argue, a subsidiary and derivative occurrence.) But because quantum physics develops in a German context while modernism is moving into formalism in an Anglo-American context, the quantum physicists retain a greater degree of idealist influence than the high modernists can find themselves in sympathy with. (It is the same kind of influence that the high modernist classicists reject as the "romanticism" of the early and midmodernists.)

In the Anglo-American setting, it is Einstein who comes for decades to represent, for the general public, physics in its most advanced form, although Einstein would not accept a quantum physics fully based on probability theory even when the idea was standard thinking in the field. Einstein attempted to recontextualize or deflect a Kantian/idealist quantum physics inside the invigorated Anglo-American empiricism that had welcomed and esteemed him after Germany had politically rejected him, despising his religious origins and denigrating his science. In the United States, Einstein was portrayed like the modernist genius-artist (his hair disheveled, his sweater rumpled, his profound gaze enigmatic), just at the time when the centers of both modernism and science were being simultaneously shifted across the Atlantic.

But the quantum physicists certainly experience a success equal to what the aesthetic modernists achieve. (Einstein's opposition is generally attributed to shortsightedness; although when American universities dominate theoretical physics, his theory of general relativity experiences a rejuvenation.) In the long run, so it now seems, the alternative to the traditional empiricist science of Newton and other members of the English Royal Society (through, say, the time of Rutherford's cloud chamber experiments) will not prove to be art, as the modernist artists and writers advocated, but an alternative science— that of Planck, Bohr, Schrodinger, and Heisenberg. In quantum physics, Kantian idealism experiences a recuperative victory after World War I[20] that the politicians in Germany were unable to achieve during the war or its aftermath. To be sure, the politicians do not relinquish their battle for an idealism unattached to empiricism. But their method is hardly (like the scientists') to attempt reconciliation between idealism and empiricism. On the contrary: fascism is the politician's response. Empiricism and idealism wage war once again in the late thirties.

A Matter of Time

```
┌──────────────┐
│              │
│              │
│  6           │
│              │
└──────┘
```

Time and Determinism

With the continued empiricist naturalization of humankind, which soon becomes a temptation even to the idealist, the passing of time becomes the fundamentally irreducible feature of human mentality, as Bergson argues.[1] A discussion of temporality and related issues will, consequently, benefit the elaboration of the concept of modernism.

By the early twentieth century, Einstein concludes that the speed of light will be measured at exactly the same speed by any observer in uniform motion, whatever the orientation of that motion to the light's source. The observed speed of light becomes a universal "constant." Moreover, not only is the speed of light always *observed* to be the same, but the speed of light *is* actually that value. This is the oddity in Einstein's theory: light has an actual speed, and observers moving in various directions will measure that speed identically. (In contrast, if a car is moving at a particular speed, its apparent speed will depend on one's movement relative to it.) Without light having this actual velocity, the theory would simply be a statement about the observation of light, not about light itself.

That light in fact has a velocity, that it does not travel instantaneously, had been confirmed in the century when modernity commenced. (The finite velocity was demonstrated in 1676.[2]) What was once thought to be instantaneous transmission takes on a finite velocity. No known aspect of natural reality is afterwards exempted from a formulaic description of motion in time. Nothing the senses can observe is outside the measurable dimension of time. Even the traditional metaphor of light can no longer be used to represent the timeless.

Even worse, we now know the sun, our source of light, will someday burn out. This awareness contributes to, even completes, the irretrievable submergence of modern humanity in time.

Modernity eliminates the daily exercise of divine power by substituting for it the causal sufficiency of time in motion. Miracles had been the primary evidence for God's superiority over determinism, because direct intervention evidenced the overflowing of the timeless (God's will and providence) into time. Modernity displaces a usually unpredictable (and often angry) God with cosmic inviolable reason, corresponding to the logic that structures human reason.[3] Logic and world order are analogs. The formulas that account for the physical universe do not absolutely demand an inventor. The behavior of the universe is like human behavior at its best—consistent, orderly, controlled, and predictable. Subservience to God's capricious will can, then, be remedied through logic and rationality. God's personality, which Descartes had counted on to assure that his senses were not being deceived, becomes a deficiency—especially once psychology becomes a science and mentality becomes inseverable from its biological mechanisms.

The eternality of time is partitioned; time can be conveniently handled as an episodic collection. Formulas segment the universe into distinct phenomena, each lasting a certain necessary (calculable) time. The formulas are narratives with Aristotelian beginnings, middles, and ends. Segments of the past are constructed like completed narratives, like novels. Unlike earlier lengthy prose narratives, the novel art form matures, coincident with the rise of modernity, by quickly developing formalist criteria for its structure; novels are encompassing, coherent, and internally complete, also with Aristotelian beginnings, middles, and ends.[4] As published books become numerous, the historical past is also partitioned into separate volumes, according to the idea of unique, cohesive, and even logically successive "periods" or ages. The power of history becomes domesticated, attesting (like experiments in magnetism and, later, electricity and the theory of gases) that invisible and once incomprehensible forces are susceptible to causal understanding, gathering, and manipulation. (Harnessing the invisible in the wireless communication of the radio was indisputably a momentous moment.) Time is conceived of as a "thing," a useful commodity.

No longer corrosive and wasting, time is the fuel consumed in the engine of advancement. Human progress and initiative somehow compensate for individual mortality.

Geological studies demonstrate that the vastness of time is neither the prerogative nor the domain of the deity alone. Previously unimaginable stretches of time become familiar, perhaps unintimidating; by the twentieth century, even Kelvin's respected reestimation of the age of the earth, a hundred million years or so, becomes a stupendous underestimation.[5] Geological ages and eons are given names, convenient and manageable units whose textbook familiarity belies their deepest impact. Astronomers eventually discuss years by the billions and distances by the light year (approximately six trillion miles), reducing the once perplexing infinities to comprehensible immensities, just as Aristotle had concocted a rudimentary notation for counting numbers as huge as all the grains of sand. The age of the universe is presently estimated at fifteen billion years: 1.5×10^{10}. In mathematics, the theory of "limits" in the calculus of infinitesimals and the definition of certain numbers, like pi, as the sum of an infinite series brings order even to infinity. Cantor devises the mathematics of an entire sequence of infinities, each of which has different magnitudes, although each is in itself infinite.[6] More and more is time segmented, in large units, in minuscule ones.[7] A nanosecond is a billionth of a second. The order of succession, of linear measurement, is a minutely divided line rather than an encompassing fluid. The line has been growing narrower as it grows longer, like something spun into thread. The earth has also narrowed to a mere speck in its own galaxy.

While modernity has made time a manageable natural resource in the context of empiricist science, such time remains fully implicated in deterministic causality. For modernism, this is too high a price to pay. Modernists prefer to sever themselves from the causality of the past, however amiable science has made it seem. Of course, the Enlightenment theory of progress also included human free will, albeit qualified; but by the end of the nineteenth century it was clear that this was a theoretical inconsistency. Besides, one could look at modern industrialized society: if things continued as they were, most humans would become subsidiary manufacturing machines. The modernists prefer the future to remain in principle undetermined, a completely open possibility. There need not be direction, only opportunity. Producing the widest variety of artworks—no matter how surprising, bizarre, offensive, humorous, or maniacal—is itself an aesthetic proof that free will is unconstrained.

Modernism is, then, the aesthetic form (there are also political forms) of the reaction to scientific modernity's logical implication that determinism in linear time must reign supreme. At the same time, scientific modernity also maintains that some notion of freedom as a historical force can be preserved. This is the empiricist paradox, from Spinoza to Hegel to Marx. Modernism circumvents the paradox by isolating the past on the far side of a temporal moat. Modernism considers itself alone to be the cause of the future.

The Hebrews and the Christians had exercised, in turn, the same prerogatives—but not through art. Romanticism taught modernism how creative artists might assume the perquisites of God. And modernism situates the past not only behind itself in time but also below itself in value. (It is also during modernism that organizational diagrams signify value by placement at the top—in biological evolution, for example, or in corporate business charts.) The present is superior to the past, which no longer requires adulation; the future can be better still—the very opposite of Golden Age mythologies.

Yet this is not exactly the same kind of progress exhorted by the Enlightenment. For the late eighteenth- and early nineteenth-century utopians, a stable, permanently gratifying epoch could be reached in a relatively short time. For these utopians there is a predictable conclusion and fulfillment, an elaborate plan that includes even the smallest details of how everyone will live, work, love, celebrate, and even die.[8] Modernism foresees more of an expansion than a linear advancement to a set goal—an explosion, rather than a path. The metaphor is spatial, not temporal. The straight and narrow, which characterizes the linear uniformities of all Enlightenment social and moral theory, is repugnant to the modernist.

Transcending Empiricist Time

While the Judeo-Christian sense of unidirectional time had created a purposeful, directed, and unrepeatable history, the Old Testament self it defined eventually became released as the New Testament soul. Moses is converted from the outside, Paul from the inside. The Old Testament begins with a historically contingent self that comes into being and disappears. Later theories of the soul give humans an eternal component. This component is different from the breath of God in Adam, for the soul is a unique and enduring entity, more than just "life": it retains distinctiveness, individuality, and perhaps even personality, originally denied to Adam. The forbidden tree gives a knowledge of ethics, which entails the action of agency; but self-knowledge is knowledge *of* the self, not *about* the self. Adam and Eve become self-conscious—but there is no indication that they become intelligent. Only when selfhood can be detached from the body, yet still affixed to the (once impersonal) concept of the breath of God in Adam, can the self of the Old Testament become the soul of the New.

This soul can be eternal because the immaterial deity has eternal existence. God lives in everlasting time. The new kingdom will arrive and then permanently endure. Contemporary history (of the heavens and earth, of humanity) is subordinated to a transcendent history, a history that happens primarily for and to the deity. If the deity thinks, then such thought must occur in time, since thinking requires sequence. That God can think and act posits the infinite linear sequence of time, the everlasting. The segment of eternal history that is secular history is part of a larger whole, comprehensible only by a consideration of its original cause, a will-ing mind. In theological naturalism, history emanates from and reflects this. History and eternity (which, here, is infinite time) commingle: because thought is linear, time is linear, and history is the enactment of their combination.

The eternal can also be envisioned not as time infinitely extended but as timelessness. The supposition that the timeless is not the indefinite extension of time but outside of time finds its way into Christianity through neo-Platonism. (Reconciling the paradox of how the timeless can relate to time had not been a problem in the Old and New Testaments, although it had early been the basic dilemma in Indian thought.) How can there be sequential time, thought, bodily existence, and ego if what is fundamental exists outside time? Professing a singular, unchallengeable, and anthropomorphic God, Christianity relocates the (neo-)Platonic eternal Ideas into that God's mind; later, Kant and the idealists transfer them to the human mind. In both cases, thought and timeless eternality are ostensibly bonded.

Theologians had long recognized that sin must enter at a certain point in time, even if at the beginning. Because time emerges from an eternity that knows no sin, humans must therefore be the culprits.

Perhaps the first sin starts time. In both testaments, such philosophical intricacy would have seemed a superfluous ornamentation of the upper classes, the Egyptianizing to which the Greeks were attracted. But even after timelessness can be conceptualized in Christianity, the paradox of the relation between time and the timeless remains unreconciled. The idea of a heaven that is timeless and the idea of a resurrection that is everlasting are left to exist side by side. Over the centuries, the idea of heaven became increasingly liberated from time; eternal time is hell, since pain is always accompanied by (might it not even be the same as?) intense time consciousness. Time is pain; the timeless is bliss.

Once such philosophical intricacy had come to characterize scholasticism, perplexity was put forth as an opportunity for an exercise of faith. "Faith" cannot exist until it is needed to confirm the apparently incongruous, and the incongruous cannot exist without a prior commitment to a structure of logic. The greater this commitment, the greater the need for a faith to circumvent it. As their strength must grow proportionately to one another, so must their conflict irreversibly intensify. The ultimate meaning of the purportedly rational life can only be grounded in the apparently absurd.

In a philosophy of transcendence, time is a corruption of eternality, a falling or (when allied with theology) a condescension of God, a fundamental reality only for mortal creatures who live in time, which makes them possible. Time corrupts and is itself corruption, since it does not exist in the eternal. For the early Greeks, the afterlife is inseparable from everlasting duration, a different matter than timelessness. Even the philosophers who consider all that exists as a unified, immutable, and eternal Oneness (Parmenides and his pupil Zeno, Melissos, the Stoics) believe that oneness, which is materiality, exists throughout everlasting time, rather than transcending it. Transcendentalism first severs the realm of spirit from the realm of earth and then connects them again by positioning humans between them; the "beyond" is not eternal duration, but something outside duration. The eternal and the everlasting are not identical: it takes over four hundred years, between Plato and Plotinus, for this idea to install itself fully in Western civilization. In Christianity both ideas are incorporated side by side. Resurrection yields an eternal duration, but in heaven there is no time.

In empiricism, time incessantly progresses. That consciousness can be oblivious to time—like a person in deep sleep—is of psychological, but not ontological, interest. Encouraged by the Copernican cosmology, the turn to nature that begins in the Renaissance (for reasons reviewed in the next chapter) and that will ultimately yield empiricism spreads rapidly in the seventeenth century. Two empiricist concepts of time appear: time as the medium in which truth emerges (time as truth's father, a common symbol in baroque art[9]) and time as the medium in which the necessary natural changes described by the formulas occur. For most empiricists, change yields improvement, or can be made to do so through conscientious application. The saddening aspect of change—mortality and unavoidable corruption—is, accordingly, found much less frequently in the sciences than in the arts.

In empiricism, time is known, real, and "natural" to the universe. Time is detached from its relation to God, whose existence is imagined not simply as long endurance through time but as a state of existence exterior to time. Because Kant recognizes that fully detaching God from time threatens to leave an exhaustive description of the universe in the care of the empiricists, he situates time internal to human subjectivity to counteract that threat. He posits time as a property of the mentality of humans, who are themselves the creations of God (although Kant admits he cannot prove this). It follows that what humans know as time is created simultaneously with the humans who live in time. Kant thus subordinates time in a way quite compatible with Christianity, by making time a condition of human knowledge rather than the object of human knowledge. The human is born with time, not in time. This presumably repairs the severance between God and the universe instituted by empiricism.

But it will be scientific empiricism, not Kantianism or idealism, that will predominate by the twentieth century. As the political underpinnings of the Austro-Hungarian Empire, of Prussia, and of Russia are contemporaneously subordinated to systems of representative parliamentary government and civil law, the concept of a god who rules omnipotently and perpetually is replaced by the concept of rule by law. The operation of a political system is to be determined by the configuration of collective human will (the system's "energy"), rather than by an enforced hierarchy of dominant and submissive wills.

But dethroning God in favor of a system of dependable impersonal law has this consequence: that neither God nor humans can do anything about time. Time is more fundamental even than space, since space endures in time but time endures without space. No power can be exercised over time. Artists and writers endeavor to produce work that will last indefinitely throughout the very time that assures that it cannot last indefinitely—a compelling and anxiety-ridden project. When all is said and done (and painted and carved), the "immortality" of the art can hardly compensate for relinquishing the immortality of the soul: better for fame to accompany salvation than to serve as compensation for its loss.

The faculty of reason requires time in which to operate. Rational thought is ordered sequentially, like time, with "results" achieved by advancing through the sequence in the singular direction defined by logic. As a result, the Enlightenment elevation of reason subordinates humans to unidirectional time, without remedy. As compensation, there is "progress": while the human succumbs to time, humanity as a whole progresses toward the good. The time that destroys us individually advances the species generally. Time allows and is the condition for the perpetual extension of the rational sequence (called the advancement of knowledge), which is then assigned a foremost value.

To escape the consequence of modernity's most abhorrent theorem, that the inextricably time-bound creature is inescapably mortal, Kant and the ensuing idealists must subordinate the faculty of linear deductive reason, which shares the sequential structure of time, to some transcendentally defined realm. Contriving to have logic surpass itself by resorting to purportedly unavoidable postulates and presumptions (Kant) or to "intuition" (the idealists) is exactly what makes their argument transcendental. A transcendentalism overcomes and subordinates the grounding conditions of its arguments during the process of constructing those arguments. The logical deduction of an atemporal realm cannot, however, be logical because logic itself has the linear structure of time. Relying on this conundrum as if it were itself a logical strategy allows the repeated alliance of idealism and an orthodox theology.

(Midtwentieth-century post-structuralism, incidentally, admits that to allow logic to produce its own technique for surpassing itself cannot be justified by, or issue in, any transcendence. Yet this cannot be avoided, since the ostensible surpassing of itself, toward reality, is an absolute condition of language. Language itself continually performs the necessary though illegitimate move.[10])

The transcendence of time had once been tenaciously held as a motivating intention even by the most rationalistic philosophers, who believed that immortality could be defended as a philosophical proposition. This is a defining condition of all seventeenth-century Cartesian rationalism. Ultimately, however, the very faculty of reason that authorized such projects yielded all the techniques of logical scrutiny necessary to vitiate them. To subordinate time, Descartes introduced a deity to ground the temporal in the eternal, to guarantee the legitimacy of a rational epistemology. The axiomatically self-evident becomes external to time, because such truth cannot change with time. The human mind is considered immaterial, as if removing the contingency of one category of statements is equivalent to eliminating the contingency, the mortality, of the maker of statements. "Modern" philosophy achieves a release from history; consequently (immaterial, ahistorical) mentality can be severed from the material, historical body. This is not the same as the separation of body and soul achieved by Christianity; in Christianity truth can only be disclosed through a revelation within history. The Cartesian method, however, absolves truth from its historical obligation, whatever pieties Descartes avows, as Pascal easily recognized and deplored. Kant presents a more complex variation of the Cartesian tactic: the deity becomes a formal necessity of logic, although undemonstrable by and beyond logic. The ontological argument for the deity is inadequate; nevertheless, ontology itself demands the idea of deity. For Kant, knowledge of these higher truths is substantiated by the power of a reason that paradoxically justifies the transcendental leap that leaves logic behind in the very act of using it.

For Hegel, subsequently, the spirit evolves in time. Yet, since this is a cosmic teleology, neither the origin nor the aim is contingent. Spirit is given a history, spirit is given motion. The movement of spirit provides the metaphysical counterpart of steady velocity (Newton's first law, that a body will continue in motion unless impeded) in the scientific equations for force. History is aimed toward an ultimate achievement, freedom, which unfolds in time but whose source is timeless. Time is an elaboration of the timeless. The accompanying principle of acceleration is placed in humans, who can assist or retard (accelerate or decelerate) but not change the predestined direction. The direction of time is again subordinated to the transcendental, by having the movement of time adhere intrinsically to the essence of a spirit that must itself evolve both from itself and into itself. For Kant, this would have been preposterous.

Freedom from History

The avant-garde is modernism's most advanced experiment in artistic creativity. The avant-garde inaugurates modernism and can be defined as modernism once artistic inspiration is accompanied by the vigorously asserted belief that artistic creativity can be exercised free from the constraints of the historical past. (The focus at this point is on modernism's beginnings, well before the onset of literary formalism.) The recognition that the artwork has broken free from the causal chain of history through the inherent creative power of the individual artist causes an initial disorientation, shock, or dismay. Empowered by genius, the artwork transcends the historical setting, which nevertheless has brought that genius into being, as if in order to be addressed by it. The past may arguably be a resource, but it is certainly not an obligation. The imposition of the past is rejected. The past cannot be totally incapacitated as influence, because the modernist achievement requires the past for comparison: the genius of the past defines what genius still means. But the causal efficacy of the past, the burdensome immediacy of its coercion, is relinquished.

Visual artists reject the obligations handed down from an art world controlled both aesthetically and commercially by the academies. (Writers had long been developing independent commercial markets, where the buyer is the only significant critic.) That older world of the church and the court had been weakening in Europe throughout the nineteenth century. The alliances and aristocratic leadership formed at the Congress of Vienna in 1815—the Hapsburgs, Hohenzollerns, Bourbons, Romanoffs—gradually yielded to the constitutional reform for which England had provided the model. Modernism arises as part of this liberalization, which World War I would nearly (although very imperfectly) complete.

When dynasties fall, the courts and clerics are replaced not by artists (or by the working class) but by capitalist industrialists and the bourgeoisie. Modernism is in part the admonition that this substitution is an inappropriate way to advance universal well-being. Most Europeans were still stifled in tedious, repetitive, and economically insecure lives, whether in the politically conservative rural areas, in the more impatient liberal urban environments of the major capitals, or in the growing factory towns. The entire system required rehabilitation. The late nineteenth-century solutions were proving to have effects as deleterious as the original problems. Even if life might be made easier—and there had been social innovations like limiting the working day, for example, or providing disability coverage or old-age pensions[11]—it might not for that reason alone prove better. The project of the Enlightenment could not be completed by the guidance of empiricist reason alone, just as the romantics or Saint-Simon (eventually) and Fourier had contended.

The modern artist is provoked, not determined, by the past. Exactly the opposite conclusion is being reached contemporaneously by sociologists and psychologists, who are expanding unbroken causality into all aspects of human behavior. One special and controversial form of psychology proposes that the essential early drama of human life (at least for males) is the incipient rejection of the tyranny of the past, the hostility toward the father. Time and the father are symbolically equivalent. Although the deep suppression of this rejection is the foundation of ego, artists are granted an important (albeit partial) exception, because they can transform (sublimate) repression into artwork. Rejection of the past, of the progenitor, is the source of art. For the avant-garde, the present is in the hands of the artist, rather than the artist being caught in the grip of Father Time.

The artist envisions the future, then makes it "appear." The form and content of artworks are to be congruent with the shape of the future. The future (time) will be an aesthetic work, just as the romantics had imagined the entire universe (space) to be. This breaking loose of free will and creativity from the tightening bonds of an empiricist causality applied to human behavior is fundamental to modernism and psychoanalysis.[12] It also characterizes Marxism, in which free will becomes, enigmatically, an independent ingredient in the causal chain of history. The proposed effect of therapy on the psyche is precisely the same effect that revolution is to have on society: the revelation of hidden truth empowers the will, releasing it from its own causality through knowledge of that causality. Modernism, psychoanalysis, and Marxism are all allied on the issue of time.

The disabling of time as modernism arises is not, however, a destruction of the past. The past cannot be destroyed. For decades the work of modernism was accomplished by filling cultural spaces still empty, just as modernist buildings were at first constructed on vacant land, their presence ostentatiously asserting the new in the presence of the old. (Such was the purpose of the Eiffel Tower. During the days of Louis XIV, another great architectural age, all the palaces and chateaus were built out in the countryside.) The artworks and writings of modernism are displayed, distributed, and sold by developing new sites and advocates in the spaces uninhabited by established authority. The Salon des Refusés provided the earliest model. But as modernism disseminates, the artists find themselves actually surrounding the past. Furthermore, since modernism is the individual work of people of modest economic means who are uncomfortable with imposed civil authority, monumentality is not, at first, their prerogative. Only after World War II will modernism literally knock down the nineteenth century to build its own new buildings, and at the same time large outdoor modernist sculpture will be accepted by the general public.

In painting, extensive instruction in a traditional school where the minute details of portrayal are codified, accompanied by a discipleship (paintings were often exhibited in the Salon with the words "Student of . . .") diminishes as a requirement for the artist. In instruction, tolerance becomes a pedagogical principle.[13] The individuality of the visual artist comes to resemble that of the writer, for whom the success of the work had lately not depended on any academic (or aristocratic) authentication. Both are equally free and uncommitted except to their own work. Being an artist is one of the few ways a middle-class person can have a "destiny." The modernists wish to discard any subordination to a history already so full it might have seemed that their nineteenth-century predecessors had already brought it to completion. History becomes an archive for the modernists, just as today it is modernism's turn to be stored in the archive. History has occurred, but its influence can be managed, even evaded; it is like the difference between a bequeathed financial inheritance with no strings attached and one carrying an entailment—exactly what distinguishes capitalist from feudal inheritance. The power of the past can be negated by free will.

The modernists appear toward the end of decades of relative quiescence and peace only sporadically interrupted (the Crimean War, the Franco-Prussian War). For them, history appears in some sense concluded. The writing of multivolumed histories occurs regularly between Gibbon's day and Toynbee's—volumes meant to be as stately and permanent as the libraries built to house them. (In his lectures on history, Hegel mentions Johannes von Muller's twenty-four-volume history of Switzerland, written over thirty years.) By 1900 it seemed as if one were not so much in history as following at the end of it. If the last volume in the set of "history proper" had closed, the twentieth century, the last in the millennium, would begin another, fundamentally unlike all those that had preceded—"Greece and Rome," "The Middle Ages," "The Renaissance."

This anticipated rejuvenation is provoked by the need to remedy the fatigue of nineteenth-century history. Its relative tranquillity after Waterloo had been attended by perpetual political maneuvering, backroom trade-offs, disputes over territorial boundaries based on nationalist indignity, alliances of major powers shifting yearly, with more conniving than planning. And to what purpose? The really important problems were internal to nations, not between nations. The traditional politics of rulers, ministers, wars, and treaties seemed outmoded. Nations ought to be defined by the aggregations of the people who composed them, not simply by their geographical boundaries and by those who ruled, often ineptly. Social history seemed vital, a transfer of attention from the politically privileged few to the many. People had been learning for four hundred years, in a movement advancing from the neighborhood of Holland and eventually reaching distant Russia, that selfhood and personality were sufficient qualifications for social esteem, economic advancement, and a measure of independence.[14]

Empiricist modernity itself—those conceptions of the physical universe and human society that arose in Europe toward the end of the seventeenth century—had already, of course, been participating in this severance from the past. Superstition, dogma, and the authority of the ancients were banished. And modernity had provided the most important criterion for the discovery of the new: science. The empiricist method of resisting the impositions of past authority is to separate time from history by making time a contentless even flow, a medium, which is why it can be used in equations. Time is causally simultaneous with events, a condition for them, yet separate from them. As long as time moves, things move. Time is like an empty room, which is why experiments can be made. An experiment can be defined as artificially attaching a contrived circumstance to a portion of time where it would not have occurred naturally. Only when time is an independent entity can this be considered. In empiricism, although time and events occur simultaneously, they are nevertheless discrete; one can initiate an event but not change the rate at which it occurs. Time is somewhat like a fuel. Nevertheless, the modernists will understand, quite correctly, that the scientists' time ultimately proves synonymous with determinism and complicitous with capitalism. If time was a fuel, it had come to resemble the coal and oil that stoked the industrial machines. The modernists would rather view time as a power, not a chemical fuel but an immaterial potency. Like the romantics, they were attracted not by the fire but by the light.

Does intellect empower will, or does will empower intellect? Modernity bases its distinction from the past on the exercise of intellect. The modernists, however, favor a theory of will ratified by "creativity." While modernism emerges within modernity, it is also an appropriation, sometimes hostile, sometimes patronizing, sometimes confrontational, sometimes hidden and subversive. At times it displays good humor, at other times invective and disgust. The avant-garde, as the aesthetic project of modernism, is permeated with romantic notions of will and vital powers, whether from English, French, or German sources, combined with Renaissance definitions of the artist and artistry. Rational intellect may be an impediment to will. (So Hamlet becomes the most renowned protagonist,[15] and Nietzsche attains his notoriety.) Hegel had proposed an especially attractive paradox that would allow for Marx to reconcile freedom and determinism in the specific economic details of history (hardly Hegel's concern). What was determined in history, Hegel asserted, was the emergence of freedom itself. Freedom is the necessity.

Throughout the nineteenth century there had been a succession of goings back in time, always an aesthetic reaction to growing empiricism. By the midnineteenth century the Enlightenment could be seen as a failure, having led not to liberation but to Napoleon. The English romantics and later the neo-Raphaelites looked back to the Middle Ages or the later Renaissance. In France, some looked back to the days of St. Louis in the thirteenth century. The romantics, particularly the literary romantics, had been attracted to the medieval Gothic, for they admired the Middle Ages as a time of spiritual unity and coherence emerging just when Roman civilization had reached its most pessimistic stage (an interpretation earlier proposed by De Maistre); there are literary discoveries and revivals of archaic forms, including the fraudulent.[16] The romantic painters most commonly make political, social, and moral statements through allegorical history painting. Also, the romantics always reverence Greek antiquity (the Greeks are to romantics what the Romans are to classicists). In contrast, the modernists never go back in time. Even high literary modernism, which does display renewed interest in the continuity of history (in "tradition"), exercises a control over the past, not a yielding to it. The official canon is revaluated: John Donne and the other seventeenth-century English "metaphysical" poets, for example, gain prominence. The past is malleable. High modernism's attraction to tradition does offer a modified view of the past, but only because a modernist stipulation for so doing has been met: the history of art and literature are granted autonomy. Artists and writers gain ownership of a past all their own.

Writing and Painting

Whatever the medium, "artists" engage in a similar task: such was a proposition of the Renaissance humanists concerning the unity of the arts,[17] although they well knew that distinctions between poets and painters/sculptors had been asserted by the Romans and much earlier by Plato. The concerns and practices of modernist visual artists and of writers are not uniformly the same.

Writing is primarily linear, as time is customarily imagined to be. That writing has the linearity of time suggests why the growth of capitalism and literacy occur concurrently and collaboratively. In capitalism, the growth of money can be calculated as a function of time alone—the interest rate. (Because time is irretrievably secular, interest has periodically been considered sinful.[18]) The twentieth-century writer cannot overcome time but is infected and haunted by it. At the beginning of the century, time's passing is more threatening than ever, since the discovery of the earth's enormous age makes any individual's allotted portion of it inconsequential. (The enormity of space is never a threat; mortality is temporal, not spatial.) No religion, theology, or philosophy offers a remedy or a consolation—at least not to the educated urbanite.

Because the linearity of language reproduces the linearity of time, modernist literary techniques are frequently employed in a quasi-spatial way, as if by this means the bonds of time might be overcome. For lyric poetry, which increases in importance as narrative poetry declines (the epic vanishes altogether), theories of image, symbol, and metaphor pictorialize meaning. Words build images, whose meanings suddenly spring forth, as if the words had been painting as well as talking. A poetic image is not a sequence but a juxtaposition. Even in the novel, which cannot relinquish the "story," the use of the stream of consciousness and also of sharp breaks in the chronological narrative sequence correspond to a traveling about in time. It is as if novelistic time spatially fills the world, instead of flowing (and Einsteinean science was arguing that time was another spacelike dimension, a fourth dimension[19]), and also fills the head, through which reflection can freely wander. In the modern novel, time is constituted by abstracting the spatial qualities of memory. The reader is sent back and forth in time chapter by chapter, lacking the whole "picture" until the conclusion. No part of the modern novel is complete until the whole is complete. Reading such novels resembles viewing a single complex painting: the viewer achieves satisfactory completion by having moved, sometimes in a seemingly haphazard way, over the entire surface.

The drama cannot easily adopt such techniques because of the demands of staging. Ibsen, Chekhov, and Shaw, for example, modify subject matter, not form: they are modern, but not modernists. Drama does not become a prominent modernist genre until the audience has been trained to make the necessary adaptions. This training is provided by films, which incorporate all the novelistic strategies easily, from overdubbed interior voices to dreams and hallucination to instantaneous change of time or place or (most importantly) viewpoint. In the staged drama, however, one cannot see through any character's eyes; the camera, like the novel, makes this possible.

In the traditional nineteenth-century novel, time apparently moves forward at about the same pace as in the world. The omniscient narrator structures breaks in the narrative sequence by announcing how much time has passed. As modernism progresses, breaks in the sequence signify spatial shifts. Location changes, although time need not move forward; it may either stand still or move backward. (Here, too, one recalls Einstein: two events that appear simultaneous for one observer may be sequenced, either way, for another observer.) The writer's emulation of the freedom to travel through time as if it were space—as the painter is free to daub the pigment on any spot on the canvas—is a strategic literary duplication of memory. Nevertheless, this cannot revoke time. Memory actually intensifies the real irrevocability of time, since memory is the only mode of thought where the consciousness of past time is intrinsic.

In the traditional novel, when the tale concludes, the time in which it has occurred, presumed to be ordinary time, continues—there is a next day. In modernist fiction, when the narrative concludes, the time in which it is contained is closed and sealed. The narrative occurs within a literary time sealed within a literary space. Modern alienated consciousness also exists as an awareness of being bound to an isolated and detached segment of time (called one's life) sealed in a spatial cavity or dimension (called one's mind). Modern humankind is a collection of lives structured like literary fictions.

While writing inherently has the shape of time, painting has the shape of space. The writer striates the white surface with lines of black ink, darkness configured into alphabet. The most threatening thing of all is speechlessness: silence. But the modern artist completely covers a white surface with contoured color: color masses replace line, the field replaces the linear grid that is the basis of Renaissance perspective. The most threatening thing of all is darkness: blindness. (Some impressionists actually forbade the use of black.[20]) Modern visual art abruptly pulls us out of time. In abstraction, the linear sequence of narrative is circumvented: the story disappears. History painting, which began to dominate the Salon as early as the 1770s and was the most popular nineteenth-century genre, becomes obsolete. Or a sequence occurs as a simultaneity, as when the object is seen from a variety of perspectives that would ordinarily necessitate walking around it or watching it move, a strategy often attributed to cubism.[21] The diminution of the third perspectival dimension (depth) is a revocation of narrative time. Much of the prevalent optimism of visual artists reflects the happy circumstance that memory, and consequently time, is not their concern. Novels, in contrast, are usually written in the past tense, and even fiction written in the present tense is understood to relate what already has happened; the reader comes to the events after they are over. Modernist painting, sculpture, and architecture are always in the present; the events in the visual artwork have not already happened, they are now happening.

Modernist visual artists are generally optimists, while modernist writers are pessimists. The former are enlivened by the possibility of social rejuvenation; the latter despair because of the likelihood of further social debilitation. Writers give more attention to the thermodynamic theory of entropy—to the idea that the universe will degrade to a homogeneous mass of dissipated heat[22]—then to any utopian enthusiasm; science fiction is for that very reason classified as an inferior form. (The science fiction of social degradation is a recent phenom-enon.) For modernist visual artists the world is still young, blossom-ing; for modernist writers the world is old, decaying. Freed from time by color and the flat field (space), the artist escapes time and tradi-tion; bound to time by the necessary linearity of prose, the writer tries to control time and tradition.

Modern visual art does away with myths; modern writing strives, against the odds, to create new ones. The artist looks for aesthetic sal-vation; the writer looks for esthetic reconciliation. The profoundest meaning of modernist visual art primarily concerns life; the profound-est meaning of modernist literature primarily concerns death.

Time Concerns

7

Time, Art, and Nature

In other times, in other cultures, the potency of and obligation to the past are not only recognized but honored. Nor has it always seemed plausible that the past is an ordered collection of "packets" of time, fractured into units and stored like wine in the cellar, labeled by year. To view the past in this empiricist way, to inherit its contents but not its obligations, to make our relationship temporal rather than ethical, requires two ideas. First, a separate entity of time must be conceivable: the even-paced succession of identical moments, time counted by the clock. But more than this is required, since mechanical clocks were invented three hundred years before empiricism. Time and events must also be connected. Events are given a necessary orderliness and progression resembling and inextricably linked to the order of time, which allows for physical "laws" and consequently for scientific determinism. Such an idea was foreign to earlier times, when the order of events was presumed to be caused by the persistent application of external forces, willed by the deity or deities, rather than by forces internal to the relations of matter. Even Robert Grosseteste and Roger Bacon, who early (in the thirteenth century) believed nature to have consistent and perhaps even invariable laws, understood these laws to be imposed by an external source. Empiricist notions of time and determinism bind us to the past in a new way: time and objects move uniformly and are coordinated simultaneously in the equations, which both describe and verify the connection.

There was an era when time could be understood as an external unit of measurement, but before time was implicated in irrevocable historical causality. Between the sixteenth and mideighteenth centuries, one can trace the change by following the decline of the assumed efficacy of magic and, later, prayer. History, in that era, then appeared to be a narrative of episodic succession, like strung beads rather than a flowing stream. From each story in the sequence could be derived a meaning and a lesson; attending to these properly was wisdom. The present used the past by knowing it, a different notion than a present that is caused by the past. The Renaissance humanist literarians had looked to Rome (Greece, in the hands of the Turks, was relatively unfamiliar) and to the pristine Christianity of the early church in order to circumvent the centuries that constituted the Middle Ages. The possibility of circumventing time, of a return to the past, allowed for the Reformation.

Renaissance painters and sculptors also had shown (or by the first quarter of the sixteenth century believed they had shown) how obligations to that same expanse of time could be revoked. This revocation characterizes all aesthetic classicisms and neoclassicisms: principles of ethics and sensibility are considered above temporal contingency, valid everywhere. The stability of principle, which protects against relativism, is lost when the romantics have inspiration, as the exercise of a special aesthetic faculty, replace principle as a source of art. For the romantics, beauty and truth are not the same as the neoclassicists' principles of beauty and truth. Feeling and intuition correspond to truth for the romantic; for the neoclassicist they are means by which to be led toward the principles of beauty and truth.

The Renaissance attitude toward time contradicts the orthodox Christian outlook. While the Renaissance looks admiringly back to a time when things were glorious, for Christianity the unbroken positive sequence of linear time is essential to the ultimate meaning of biblical history and for future salvation. The notion of history as a progressive, irreversible, and errorless movement toward foreordained designs and goals, toward that which has been promised (for some in Deuteronomy, for others in the Gospels) derives from Judeo-Christianity. Human will is exercised on behalf of a movement toward the preordained.

In Christianity and (in some sects of) Judaism, time will come to an end. Itself a destructive force overturning old religions and conquering the old guards/gods, Judeo-Christianity provides the weapons of warfare for secular modernity generally: unremitting law, undeviating purpose, unlimited arrogance. These weapons are eventually turned back upon religion when the external cause of history is replaced by causes internal to history, so that law and purpose are not equivalent. In pre-Reformation Christianity there is no going backward, nor any reason to want to do so. As empiricism replaces theology, this lesson is not lost but refashioned, with causality replacing teleology.

For the Renaissance to break the preordained sequence of Christian time required reconsidering the concept of the future and salvation. Movement in both directions in time requires new choices. As time is severed from the preordained (although hardly completely), the Renaissance turns its attention to daily life—to the use of time. One must decide how to spend one's time properly and successfully.[1] The question of how time is spent becomes more compelling than questions about the eternal, the time-less. Even salvation depends on seeing time as capital to be spent according to one's best insights, an investment. (Pascal would later see it as a quite capitalistic wager.[2]) For capitalism, emerging in the Renaissance, money and time become interrelated substances. (For the vast majority in the Middle Ages, money had been irrelevant.) That money grows in time according to principles of investment is an idea antecedent to the empiricist idea of events unfolding lawfully in time.

The Renaissance artist instructs the modernists that time need not be a burden; time is neither seamless nor recalcitrant. What the freedom of going backward is for the Renaissance, the freedom (not only the necessity) of going forward is for the modernists. The science fiction of time travel in both directions is a characteristically modernist discretion.

Unlike the modernists, the Renaissance humanists and artists gazed back to classical times with devotion, compliance, and obligation. This attentiveness to classical form, technique, and what the Renaissance understood to be the spirit pervading the work could be most comprehensively addressed in architecture, the highest art in the Renaissance. (Roman buildings still existed, and the writings of Vitruvius gave ample instruction.) And while the sculptors could actually view Roman sculpture, the painters were largely guessing what the form, technique, and spirit of Rome might have been, some of this based on the legendary reputations of the Greek masters Zeuxis, Polygnotus, and Apelles, none of whose paintings survived.[3]

Unlike architectural work, sculpture and especially painting need to incorporate a narrative, they need to be about something. That architecture and music do not is why they have usually been the primary candidates for the "highest" art. (Contrapuntal music, as linear as both writing and time, approaches its culmination as empiricism gains prestige; the romantics, accordingly, will prefer the nonlinear harmonics of chords.) But Christianity had outmoded the classical myths; the only major narratives whose majesty could fully challenge the new techniques of representation were the Christian ones. Classical subject matter was subordinated, or perhaps used allegorically, as are Botticelli's Venuses.

The painters derived from the past presumed models, attitudes, and inspiration, rather than a creed or spiritual guidance. Even though a major purpose of perspective was to display Roman architectural forms in a realistic manner, Renaissance painting was not a recreation of the past but a reawakening of its methods. Renaissance artists knew Christianity would allow them to surpass what the Roman artists could achieve. While the Romans may have reached the heights of intellectual and aesthetic achievement, they had not been granted the ultimate spiritual disclosures and were not eligible for Christian salvation. The exquisite classical forms were arrogated for the Old Testament legends (often also used allegorically—David, for example, was a favorite figure for Florentine sculpture, representing their success at not succumbing to conquest) and for the revelatory narratives of Christianity. There always remains a tension between the two, since classical works inspired reflections on the dignity, grandeur, and capacities of the human spirit. The Christian spirit or the immortal soul, in contrast, was strengthened by humility, unworldliness, unworthiness, and acquiescence.

The Renaissance recognition that the most accomplished artists had been heathens, a lesson so graphically depicted by Dante, causes the development of the concept of "nature" to explain how the heights of artistry and human nobility were attained without the appropriate revelation. Roman religion was heathen and immature, even if picturesque and useful for allegory. But since God had made nature at the beginning, before either the disclosures to Abraham or Moses or the assured salvation warranted by the coming of Jesus, nature had always been observable. Aristotle's work had sufficiently proved this to the scholastics. Nature and humans had not been fundamentally restructured by revelation; rather, a new knowledge had been imparted, revealed. The classical artists had observed nature and humanity with the clearest of eyes. Lacking the mediation of the revelatory knowledge that yields Christians the key to interpretive meaning, they would have been observing nature and humanity directly. The direct observation of nature had become replaced, following revelation, by texts and commentary. (And for the ancient Hebrews pictorial art had been forbidden altogether, an abhorrent Egyptian practice.) The world was now understood indirectly, with an explanation inserted between it and the observer.

While these explanations based on revelation were true (they were the ultimate truth), the direct observation of nature had diminished. The reliance on sound, on hearing and reading, had replaced sight. By the late Middle Ages, the Platonic (which for Aquinas was the enemy) had yielded to the Aristotelian. The Renaissance combination of classical vision and Christian revelation is a recuperation of the purity of an originally unclouded "vision," which Christian meaning can inform without obscuring as (for the Renaissance) the Middle Ages had done. It would be possible to see the truths of revelation through the clearest forms of visual perception, and thereby to remain close to nature as well as to God. Humans were a part of nature and had a nature, yet they also transcended nature. The genius of antiquity had captured natural beauty, harmony, grace, and dignity, even if not the true meaning behind it. On the other hand, numerous generations that had known true meaning (Christianity) had obscured nature and human nature, including the human body, inside texts, inside language. The reasoning and disputation that marked the Middle Ages were not conducted with any attentiveness to vision: revelation itself was a message, a speaking. But for the Renaissance artists, the alliance of the classic and the Christian should be based not on Aristotle but on Plato, not on abstruse aural philosophy but on visual art.

Even the humanist writers, themselves perpetuating writing, looked back to their oldest predecessors, to the Romans for rhetorical forms and to the early church leaders (not the medievalists) for spirit. They sought to coalesce and unify rhetorical models (from Cicero, from Quintilian) of direct, clear (*clarus* is also the visually "bright"), and unencumbered language with Christian belief. The humanists revered Christian beginnings and devoted much attention to restoring

early texts, uncovering corruptions or misconstrued usage and etymology, projects whose practical consequences would be church reformation. The purest texts were the oldest ones, the ones written clos-
est to the days when the truth had been visible on earth.

Insofar as God's creation is beautiful, complex, harmonious, and
sublime, and had been so even before revelation, these qualities in art
can become both formal aesthetic criteria and a reflection of the "natural." Visual beauty can signify both the holy and the natural, both
the mental capacity to translate aural truth into visual objects and an
accurate representation of nature. Vasari relates that the formal dimensions of classical architectural structures are proportioned to correspond to the human body. For the Renaissance, beauty can be discovered directly and then reproduced, while meaning can be inherited
indirectly and then represented. To unify beauty and meaning, nature
and revelation, the Renaissance finds the technique of perspective in-
comparably perfect—not only because of its apparent realism, once
one knows how to look, but because it symbolically combines solidity
with a "vanishing point": the point in the distance toward which all
lines perpendicular to the surface of the painting converge. It is extraordinary that everything earthly and natural can be convincingly
displayed by using the point at which they disappear. In perspective,
things in space and time converge upon what is without space and
without time.

Once mastered, the artistic techniques of the Renaissance, perspective in particular, no longer require direct religious devotion or intent
for their execution. That technical practice can be craft alone is not
new, but talent or genius becomes a unique kind of human capacity,
a gift (a Platonic notion) separate either from revelation or from training. The techniques, now a set of skills detached from any particular
use of them, can be widely applied by the artistically gift-ed to portraits, classical myths, fantasies, ornamentation, even trivia. The latitude continually expands, and Renaissance art becomes a mannerism
in the midsixteenth century: the free virtuosity of technique is detached from its correspondence to a commensurate meaning. A man-
nerist style begins with all the inherited meaning it will ever need and
exquisitely perfects technique. Mannerism yields to the baroque,
which is to transfer the technique to a new meaning for which it had
not been originally intended. A baroque style begins with all the inherited skills it will ever need but must evolve its own meaning. Visu-

al technical skill and inspiration become conceptually distinct, even unrelated. (The separation had previously occurred between literary skill and revelation, once presumed allied in the language of biblical prophecy and, the church contended, also in medieval philosophy, so that medieval philosophers could be made saints.[4]) That artistic skills can be mastered does not, by the midseventeenth century, necessarily authenticate either inspiration or revelation. In the most imposing works of baroque art, like the sculpture of Bernini, technical skills and inspiration appear to be unified. Nevertheless, such an appearance can be taken as one of the effects of art, rather than one of its causes. Artistry seems incontrovertibly a skill of fabrication, of appearances; that is why artists are the only humans whose work depends on inspiration who are never made saints—although some surely have done more than three miracles for Christianity. The notion of a specifically artistic inspiration separates from the more generalized concept of revelation: while inspiration involves intuitive *meaning*, revelation demands the much less secure and verifiable intuitive *knowing*. While the presence of meaning can be validated by understanding alone, knowing cannot be validated without confirmation. The act of meaning cannot be in error, but the act of knowing surely can be. Meaning and truth begin to sever.

In the North, too, artistic skill and religious devotion, or commitment, or at least acquiescence, had been separating, especially since small artworks could be purchased for the home even by those with modest incomes.[5] Woodcuts and engravings in the fifteenth and sixteenth centuries—Dürer's, for example—illustrate how the imagination can be secularly indulged, since these were not commissioned as public works. More and more buildings without primary, or even secondary, religious functions (private houses and civic buildings) offer walls on which to hang paintings, which yields a different art then when the walls themselves are painted. (The hung painting is *in* the building, not part of it.) Working in private at an easel on small paintings also permits an uninhibited variety of imaginative possibilities, since these paintings can be easily moved, carried around to customers, used in various settings, sold, stored, or obliterated.

Private patrons pay for the stimulation of their senses, regardless of any accompanying meaning. The Renaissance had quickly discovered what, besides piety, can be aroused by visual art—the sensual for example. Over the course of two centuries the stimulation of the senses increases so much that meaning, temporarily, becomes aesthetically inconsequential. Art will then have reached, beyond mannerism and the baroque, the panache of the rococo.

For the Renaissance humanists, nature is good, since God made it. Human nature is also good, since it is defined not by animal instincts and passions but by higher emotions: love, honor, loyalty, sympathy, and most significantly, the potential predominance of reason and intelligence. Human ignorance and folly are not natural tendencies. Rather, folly, greed, selfishness, civil disobedience, and tyranny are unnatural, resulting from the inadequacies of education and social institutions. Human nature does not change; although it is inseparable from time, it is not changed by time—which is why the ancients could know human passions and behaviors thoroughly.

The Italians inhabited the same land as the Romans, whose descendants they were. Like human nature, the bond of the land (also part of nature) was unchanged by although inseparable from time. The land—and the language, too, since Italian is a derivative of Latin—could provide a connection over time, through time. Christianity disavowed such connections, intending itself as a universalized religion, not dependent on transient temporal contingencies like land or language or even human nature. Looking at land and language in the Renaissance way will, incidentally, eventually characterize the leading competitors to Christianity: the spatial and temporal phenomena of nation and ethnicity.

For Renaissance humanists and artists, human nature and the immortal Christian soul are good and conceptually unchanged by time, although for quite different reasons: human nature because it is uniform throughout time, the human soul because it can exist external to time. Society, which is human life over time, functions to unite the two in time. (The Incarnation provides the historical juncture.) Human nature and the soul coinhabit society, bound inside the individual; society is both the fulfillment of the former (human nature), insofar as social structures are reasonable and lead to peace, harmony, justice, and prosperity, and the salvation of the latter (the soul), insofar as the church superintends one's moral, domestic, and social lives and codes. This unification of nature and Christianity permits both the admiration of the heathen ancients (obviously discouraged by Christianity) and the achievement of salvation within a Christian society whose visible forms (churches, statues, paintings, artifacts, fabrics) are derived from sources originally antipathetic to Christianity. Society as a whole, then, is to unify nature and revelation, just as artistic genius is presumed to do by the early Renaissance.

By the late Renaissance, however, inspiration and revelation are already in the process of separating. Inspiration, once thought to resemble revelation, becomes a separate aesthetic faculty—of skill and meaning, not truth and knowing. An artist can have one without the other. An artist can be skilled, but not wise. (Romanticism will see to their reunification.) Nevertheless, the concept of human nature does not change for the late Renaissance, and society's function remains the unification of the qualities of humanity defined by both nature and Christianity.[6]

Eventually, unifying the qualities of humanity defined by nature with those defined by religion proves difficult. The two diverge, despite the efforts that extend from Descartes through deism. This divergence yields five different movements, some that widen the breach, others that attempt to close it.

First (beginning in the sixteenth century), for the Reformation a correction of the church's errors, of its accumulated distortions of biblical authority, would obviate the discrepancies between nature and religion. The latter would subordinate the former, making the nature of human nature nothing but temporal contingencies ultimately irrelevant to salvation. A reliance on faith rather than deeds transfers the essence of humanness away from nature. Consequently, for the Reformation the proposed unification of religion and nature is unnecessary. Art, most particularly visual art, is fundamentally useless. Even when art is beautiful or inspiring, it offers deficient alternatives to, even diversions from, authentic knowledge.

Second, religion itself, in its entirety, can be called unnatural and challenged, since what is unnatural is not a counterpart to nature but error. While the scholastics had tried to make Aristotle and Christianity compatible, a tendency arises to use Aristotle contentiously. Although homage is paid to religion—those standard expressions at the end of philosophical texts insisting no heresy is intended—nature appears to subordinate religion. Texts like those of Pompanazzi contend that the soul cannot be proven immortal or that revelation and the exploration of nature lead to irreconcilable conclusions.

Third (beginning in the seventeenth century, in response to the second approach), a school of Protestant thought emerges, especially in Holland, where Protestant expatriates from Catholic countries are welcomed. It holds that there is nothing natural reason discovers in nature that can be incompatible with God's exercise of will. The Socinian declaration (from Faustus Socinus, around 1600) asserts that while truth surely resides in the Bible, the truth will be found absolutely reasonable by the intelligent conscience; Spinoza would argue that the Bible could be studied objectively, like nature, as a text; and John Toland's *Christianity Not Mysterious* was published in 1696. Incompatibilities result not from unresolvable mysteries but from misunderstandings and dogmatic manipulations. Religion and rational intelligence (science) can never be at odds; they are mutually confirming. God does not act in violation of nature.[7]

Materialistic rationalism and rationalistic Protestantism are both consistent with the scientific method, which can be equally conducted by the rationally pious (no longer an oxymoron), the atheistically rational, the deist, or the humanist. Materialistic rationalism, however, is often more hospitable to art and poetry than rationalistic Protestantism, which accuses those arts, as Plato had accused them, of illusion and deceit.

A fourth approach (beginning in the mideighteenth century) is to argue that traditional religion can be discarded in favor of nature, but then to attribute to nature the spiritual qualities once attributed to religion. Nature itself provides the unification previously thought to have been the source of nature, uniting both what exists in time and what exists beyond time. "Nature" is itself now the name for this duality that is also a unity. Spirituality is not forsaken by discarding institutionalized religion; spirituality is rediscovered, revitalized. This approach distinguishes romanticism. The romantics believed that some of the ancients, notably Plato and his followers, advocated this kind of spirituality, as did Spinoza. In its rudimentary stage, such spirituality pervades pantheism generally, for example in hunter-gatherer cultures (the idea of the noble savage). The romantics make an abstraction of the land as both "nature" and a symbol of nature: the fertility of organic growth, the seasons, the beauty of the countryside, the ability of natural phenomena to provoke elevated and spiritual thoughts. Nature, in the guise of the symbolic earth itself, is the particular portion of the cosmos inhabited by humanity, the globe envisioned as a single place, as if Eden might be everywhere. Assuredly, for many romantics race (ethnicity), land, temperament, and culture are conjoined. Nevertheless, these are always variations within the more encompassing concept of nature as a whole, since the One can exist in the multifarious.

A fifth approach to the failure of the Renaissance to bond nature and Christianity, or to unify the wisdom of the ancients and the revelations of Christianity, is a consequence of the Enlightenment and is enthusiastically pursued by the time modernism arises. By 1900, empiricist science will have discarded all romantic notions, and even the few accommodations with idealism (like Bergson's) would soon prove superfluous to further research. Nature is the mechanistic assemblage of materiality in motion, the unfabricated (unmanufactured) things in the world and their order. "Life" is not a thing, a unity or a substance, but a category of complexity. Human mentality is nonetheless unique in nature, for human mentality includes not only consciousness but self-consciousness, hence the personalized ego. Each individual has a separate "nature"—a unique mental organization. Fulfilling this individual nature is a personal mission, a new earthly purpose. Humans once sought to discover how they were all like one another, which was wisdom; now humans must discover how they are unlike one another.

This individualized human nature is not identical to Kantian subjectivity, which connotes a set of impersonal processes that everyone shares in the same way. (Kant and modernity had long ago, despite the neo-Kantians, parted company.) The discipline of psychology develops to substantiate individualized human nature as its subject matter. This individualized human nature can then be regarded as good or bad, free or determined. If society is primarily an aggregation of individuals, each acting for his or her own purposes, then these purposes can be considered either ethically positive (mutually enhancing, cooperative, or even altruistic) or ethically negative (selfish). The purpose of society would be to encourage the first or discourage the second. Conversely, if society is viewed as a unified entity that generates individuals as its subordinate parts, then individuals can be considered either free to detach from their origins (to autonomize the self) or not free to do so (determinism). In any of these cases, such an individualization would not be possible without both the Reformation and capitalism.

Modernism rejects what, for the Renaissance, would have been nature and the natural; nor does it accept the Enlightenment and scientific versions of nature. The romantic approach is also outdated. For the early modernists, the classical past, the Christian past, their Renaissance amalgamation, and their neoclassical revival are all traditions that have been fully exploited, used up. The "natural" would be accounted for by natural law; even the study of humankind could be divided into allegedly scientific realms (anthropology, sociology, psychology). The modernists' resolution is to import the romantic theory of creativity as a power and to place it inside mentality at a special place, where mechanistic psychology cannot get at it. Romanticism is detached from nature (the earth) and relocated in the mind. The romantic philosophy becomes a modernist psychology, yet it is kept outside the range of empiricist psychology by retaining the romantic transcendence of art. The artwork continues to inspire romantic awe; each artist personally arrogates the mystery. But how can one continue to remain (like Croce) so indebted to idealism while idealism is being discarded? Modernism itself will come to appreciate this incongruity when it converts to formalism.

The evidence for the success of modern art cannot, therefore, involve (as it must for the Renaissance) the representation of nature or being "true to nature," formerly art's most important motto. Instead, modernism generates artworks completely unlike nature. "Nature" is now the name for precisely what science explains, whether physical nature (earth or cosmos) or individual human nature (personality). Artistic creativity is the least "natural" of anything on earth; art and nature are opposites. For the modernists, meanings once found in nature or given in revelation are created directly from the mind. The opposite of one truth may be another truth. Truth is equivalent to the form that produces rather than contains it. Even if one grants a spiritual realm that the artist perceives or senses, mentality communes with this unnaturally, since nature itself can know nothing of that realm. And from the modernist viewpoint, life at its best is art, not natural but inspired.

In reaction against nature, then, the Greek ideal of clarity is made obsolete. The accurate observation of nature is replaced by interpretive complexity, oddity, uniqueness—by the completely unnatural. The vocabulary and syntax of art become simpler (vernacularlike speech, simple shape and color), while meaning becomes extremely complex, available only via an advanced interpretive method. Science holds precisely the opposite: the clarity of vocabulary and syntax is believed to equal clarity of meaning, or else one is misusing the language.

When modernism begins, the subject matter of art is being increasingly confined to the cities, from which nature is steadily expelled. (Urban parks are planned as substitutes for nature.) Modernism is a cosmopolitanism. Nature is a farm or a recreational place, some troublesome distance away, or the useless or as yet unused wilderness. As abstraction becomes predominant, representation ("picturing") becomes inconsequential for aesthetic appreciation and criticism. It is not "nature" to which one must be true. Complexity, obscurity, distance, irony, loss of boundaries between the internal and the external, between the artwork and the world—all are ways of casting aside "nature," in the name of the imagination. After four hundred years or so, nature can no longer serve artistic purposes.

Rebirth

While the vocabulary and syntax of the modern arts became stylistically simplified, meaning became more complex, requiring an indoctrination into interpretive methods. In painting, the intent is to create an immediacy of sensation, a pure sensation that supersedes, even revokes, the passing of time. Yet time is canceled not by the formal representation of the timeless—the classical artistic forms of the enduring, the harmonious, and the "beautiful," in which the senses rest momentarily—but by the suspension of time that occurs whenever the emotions are suddenly and unpredictably stimulated, as in moments of shock or surprise. Modern art captivates as it disorients—so briefly that one holds it and loses it simultaneously. In an age where the irremediable passing of time is the only certainty and the idea of the eternal appears an anachronism, nothing beyond this brief and anxious escape from time is possible.

This suspension of time returns us to the purity of sensation that the infant is imagined to experience. Artists recreate the experience in which the infant first composes its knowledge of the world, before spontaneity of sensation is subordinated to culturally ideological concepts and before the child learns about the inevitable passing of time. The richness of saturated colors applied in bold wide strokes or dominating the canvas as a field, or the geometrical patterning that competes with or entirely replaces representational content: these recreate the pristine sensation one would imagine Adam to have had on the first day.

The immediacy of childhood sensation had often been related to the perceptions of humankind at its beginnings. (Anthropological field study was becoming a formidable university science.) Precivilized humans, in this view, would not yet have evolved discrete selfhood.[8] The borders between the self and the external world would have been weak. African art, and afterward Oceanic art, illustrated how the world would appear to the artist before civilized mentality fortified the severance between mind and world certified by Cartesian philosophy. (This is not, by the way, a return to Rousseau. To believe that uncivilized people are good or naturally moral is another matter.)

Not until the middle of the nineteenth century had Michelet applied the term *Renaissance* to the quattrocento.[9] The idea of "Renaissance," arises, then, four hundred years after the event and names a nineteenth-century value. (By the 1870s the word can be used in English to mean any revival of learning. The names of the artistic movements following the Renaissance, specifically *mannerism* and *baroque*, were used contemporaneously as derogatory terms.) Visual modernism is meant to be or to effect a "re-naissance," a rebirth. Modernism assumes the task of becoming the re-naissance. Romanticism had been fundamentally a literary movement: late eighteenth- and early nineteenth-century painting could not inspire modernist painting (with some exceptions, like Delacroix) as the literature could still inspire the poets, since so much of that painting was technically conventional. Except for the precursors of modernism itself (Turner, Corot, Degas, Manet, Monet) customary nineteenth-century painting had disappointingly failed. The modernist painters identify the quality of their own inspiration with the epic exaltation of the painters of Florence, Venice, and Rome. Not coerced to emulate or to adulate, the modernists feel an affinity, not an obligation. The modernists reject Renaissance method in the name of Renaissance inspiration; they sever that inspiration from the religious implications of Renaissance painting in Italy, turning instead to Rembrandt, who had demonstrated that surpassing inspiration and secularism were quite compatible. As Shakespeare had been refashioned into their ancestor by the romantic poets, so the Renaissance visual artists, together with Rembrandt, are refashioned into modernist precursors (half empiricist, half romantic). Every early modernist in Paris knows quite well the contents of the Louvre, even if some would claim, like Pissaro and Duranty, that it should be burned down.[10] Even impressionism had, after all, claimed to be an optical realism. Modernists claim a spiritual authorization from the Renaissance.

Italy around 1500 was retroactively remodeled into an earlier form of romanticism; even now the popular media describe it so, as if Michelangelo's life was much in the spirit of Byron's. The connection centers on the notion of inspiration accompanied by pure and accurate vision. Leonardo's advice to copy nature directly, unimpeded by convention (as if this were possible), is transformed by the modernists into an injunction to free eyesight from cultural predispositions. Eyes will then see the pure qualities of things: not their "nature" but their "essence." Extension and mass evanesce. (The early modernists are Platonists here. Essence can be seen; the visual is not merely evidence, as in Christianity, for what cannot be seen.) In the Renaissance, architecture, the art form of mass and extension, had been the highest art. (They did not know that the Greeks had painted the stone.) The neoclassicists had claimed to follow in the footsteps of the Renaissance, especially in their insistence on the authority of classical forms. Modernism would release the Renaissance from that co-optation by empiricism. Modernism would accomplish this not by inheriting the outward forms of the Renaissance (perspective, the architecture of column and arch, the drama of Roman proportions, or formulaic poetic meter), but by looking to the spirit or essence of things. Modernism intends to return to the sources of spiritual inspiration, before they had been buried under the debris that is the history of civilization.

"Renaissance" involves a literal waking up; it is used as a historical term and a psychological one—as "enlightenment" often is used. The modernist's "re-naissance" contains the ideas of rebirth both as a social metaphor and as a description of the aesthetic experience, in the artist and in the viewer. To become like a child and be born again is also the exhortation of the Gospels. In an age when religious commitment is faltering and aesthetic commitment increasing, modernism arrogates the biblical rebirth, too.

Although their romantic predecessors had hoped art would confirm the spiritual truths at the heart of religion, the modernists had no such hope. Unable to remain Christian believers, the modernists found the romantics' admiration of the Middle Ages—of its social unities and spiritual coherence, whatever its superstitions—self-deceptive and naive. While the romantics had disdained dogma, they nevertheless respected, even venerated, the religious narratives as sacred art forms.

The criteria for spirituality could be aesthetic, as Chateaubriand advocated,[11] not dogmatic. The hypothesis resulting from researches in the Indo-European languages—that all religions had arisen from one primal religion, from archetypal experiences translated into archetypal myths—eventually encouraged the presumption of a universalized "religion." But in modernism religion, which art will replace, has depleted spirituality, which art will augment. Color and form themselves provide immediate sensory access to the spiritual, without subordination to obsolete myths.

(The conservative literary high modernists will later resanctify the concept of "myth" by fully poeticizing the term: the poem becomes the only sacramental object. The political resanctification of myth occurs in fascism, where the state becomes the only sacramental object.)

Religion and urbanity had parted company in late nineteenth-century Paris, London, and Berlin. Rural folk were not considered pure at heart but the backward and unredeemed, even if innocent. Modernism is a cosmopolitanism that, by its very definition, repudiates the mythic superstitions of the pious. For the artist, the entertainer, and the entrepreneur with a foot in the door, urbanization is an escapade—this, despite the destitution of the unemployed and the entrapment of the employed. (Few modernists are regular employees, as most of the German and French romantics were at one time or another.) The city promises sophistication, excitement, freedom, possibly fame and fortune. Nevertheless, for the many artists who had inherited spiritual craving, but no adequate means for satisfying or appeasing it, only an aesthetic re-naissance can fulfill the biblical injunction to be born again, since the strategies of city life reinforce only an economic ethics.

The late romantic religious resurgence had been, after all, a conservative reaction, occurring after the Congress of Vienna: the Restoration, Louis Philippe, the Second Empire, and the German Confederation. The eighteenth-century Spinozan pantheism or Rousseauean neopastoralism was subordinated to more conformist outlooks, and those who were hostile to the Enlightenment felt at last revenged. Besides, the romantics had been guilty of what now appears much nebulous and foggy thinking in spiritual matters (does all of romanticism yield one great spiritual leader?); and in late romanticism the spirit had been besieged by a sometimes pathological doubt and an at times ecstatic sense of betrayal. Of course, many English and American thinkers advanced unabashedly unromantic, liberal democratic, scientifically enlightened freethinking, but England and America did not produce great painters (Turner, Constable, perhaps a neo-Raphaelite or two excepted).[12] How valuable was their advice for artists? Modern art could begin again entirely on its own terms; the rebirth would return society to the purity of primary sensation. The most sophisticated modes of perception and thought are also the primary unencumbered modes, a Christian paradox: to become like a child is to go not backward, but forward. While the modernist rebirth recovers the intensity of infant sensation—children's "art" shortly came to look like modern art[13]—it also marks the furthest advances of the avant-garde. One advances back to the beginning. Being born again requires an aesthetic baptism, a submergence in artworks, a rejuvenative cure for the spiritual debilitation and impotence so often described by the world-weary poets.[14]

The empiricists also begin with pure sensation. The positivist philosophy begins by identifying the smallest units of unquestionable sensation (color perception or pain, for example), as if such knowledge might serve as philosophy's apodictic foundation. The truth of any complex thought can be verified only insofar as the components of that thought can be shown ultimately to rest on rudimentary physical sensation.[15] That the arts provide a different route back to pure sensation is a most significant connection of modern art to empiricism. Of course, the connection is also part of the conflict between them, since modernism strives to achieve a unifying aesthetic, not an atomistic psychology. The same means—a return to primary sensation— lead to different ends. For the artist, the immediacy of the contact between mind and world is itself a higher order of truth; for the positivist, it is the lowest order of truth.

What, fundamentally, are we born with? What is fundamentally in us and outside us before we are instructed how to know these things? The empiricists proposed a mechanistic and materialistic theory of perception: the mind is a physical organ with the capacity to receive motions resulting from external objects, which are in that way directly known. Kant proposed a "subjectivity" by presuming that the known world is not equivalent to the rudimentary nature of things but an effect of the exercise of innate mental structures; things-in-themselves cannot be known. Reducing the world and the mind to primary components and qualities in the pursuit of knowledge, freeing the inquiring intellect from misapprehensions and cultural conventions, has, then, two distinct traditions. Empiricism rests on the trustworthiness of the senses, based on the belief that the world is atomistic. Both physical and mental aggregations can be disassembled through experiment and thought so that the original components can be known. On the other hand, the transcendental idealism evolving from Kant presumes that the world is an encompassing union originating in a source not made up of components. The fundamentally real is the unity from which they are derived—usually God, spirit, or being, depending on whether the vocabulary is theological, idealistic, or phenomenological. Empiricism seeks the unit; idealism seeks the unity.

In its attempt to replicate purity of sensation, modernism will at first prolong the romantic idealist predisposition and reassert belief in the ability of artistic genius to reach the truth behind appearances. Early modernist comments on the meaning of color and form have a compelling mystical quality, sometimes derived from the poetics of symbolism. But philosophical idealism ultimately proves unsuitable in the empiricist environment. The further decline of an already weakening idealism precipitates the conversion of modernism to formalism, which might be called "critical positivism."

In his phenomenology Edmund Husserl had also asked what might fundamentally be known about the "essences" of things before any distorting conceptual biases affect human perception. Husserl's notion of phenomenological "bracketing" appears around 1900. The phenomenologist intends to determine exactly how the rudimentary contents of consciousness are used in the construction of "knowing." What consciousness (and consciousness of consciousness) is in itself cannot be known, since consciousness is the condition for knowing and cannot be a content of knowledge. (One cannot be aware of contentless awareness.) To know the how of consciousness is not to know the why of it. Nor is the phenomenologist a psychologist, since the mind can never be made fully external to itself: the fundamental ground of epistemology cannot be included inside the science of epistemology. While psychological investigation can disclose mental or physiological mechanisms that correspond to or accompany the process of knowing, finding such mechanisms does not explain the ground of knowing. That the mechanisms and thought-in-consciousness can be correlated establishes a relationship between two sets of incompatible terms: the causal empirical description of the mechanisms must itself be enclosed inside the consciousness from which it is subsequently granted its independence, as if it were actually consciousness that was contained inside the mechanisms.

Although most artists find the abstruse rationalism and textual complexity of the phenomenological method unappealing, they are attuned to its conclusions. Phenomenology is modernism in philosophy; it proceeds through stages associated with modernism, from Husserl to Heidegger to existentialism (these are early and midphenomenology—the break occurs in Husserl's later writings) to structuralism (high phenomenology) to post-structuralism (late phenomenology). Phenomenology does not separate mind and world as if these can be known and analyzed separately. One is an effect of the other: the world can appear only in subjectivity, and subjectivity can exist only in and by virtue of its situation in a world that is at once subjectivity's object and its form. Subjectivity does not live in history; rather, it is the history it lives and the history that lives it. The literary technique of following the "stream of consciousness," for example, is derived from the phenomenological method of objectively observing the formal and sequential relationships of the mind, where Eastern meditation also begins; and modernist writers favor fictional characters whose persistent awareness of their own inescapable mental processes is often the only powerful event in their daily lives.

Concurrently, artists and writers usually find Anglo-American philosophical positivism repugnant or insipid, a trivializing of matters in the name of a meticulous precision that yields perfectly rational knowledge of the tediously inconsequential.

The two philosophical approaches for reducing mentality to its fundamental content become antagonists. The English and the Americans commit themselves to positivism; Germany and France, outside their scientific circles, to phenomenology. After the acceptability of German thought declines following World War I, the Anglo-Americans and the French construct a history of modern art that excludes the Germans, except for certain expatriates and a few whose reputations were established well before the war. As a result, the names of many French modernist artists and writers are readily familiar to Americans, but the names of most German expressionist painters or writers are obscure. The rejection of German thought means that the official history of art and literature will be detached from the history of philosophy in England and the United States, still another underlying cause of the emergence of critical formalism. Where the arts and philosophy are not separated, where the Germanic philosophical tradition remains appealing, we have the subdiscipline of philosophy usually named "aesthetics."

In the United States, when German thought falls into disfavor, William James will inherit a certain amount of the credit for phenomenological discoveries. But only in such a detached context can pragmatism appear original. Pragmatism is, after all, phenomenology with every originally important transcendental question persistently removed. (One grants the extensive metaphysical speculation of Peirce in his later years.) And in places where pragmatism successfully asserts itself, modern visual artists (and writers too) will abandon the remnants of spiritualized metaphysics. By the time modern art becomes notorious in the United States, around the 1917 Armory show, World War I is occurring; afterward, the early modernist spiritualized aesthetic will rapidly erode. (Alfred Stieglitz, whose parents were born in Germany and who was educated in Berlin, continued to typify that aesthetic outlook for many years; one finds accounts of visitors going to his New York gallery as if they were making a trip to Lourdes.) In France, too, an empiricist and scientific temperament will prevail, although what can be included as "science" is wider than what would today be permitted, in part as an attempt to replace the metaphysical concepts of idealism with corresponding scientific concepts, like Bergson's *élan vital.* Art becomes immersed in the scrutiny of its methods; method is access to insight. And if artistic method is justified by any broader theoretical concepts, these concepts are imported from a growing psychology, most powerfully expressed in surrealist painting and in the novel.

Fascism in the 1930s and World War II intensifies this circumstance. Continental phenomenology is generally removed from the Anglo-American curriculum. (The Bauhaus style loses its German name and becomes the "international" style.) In literature, the New Criticism comes to dominate. French thinkers develop existentialism, their own branch of phenomenology on the political Left; and by this circuitous route phenomenology, through the work of Sartre and others (Merleau-Ponty, Maritain), will eventually be welcomed again in the United States when the McCarthy era subsides and the Left reasserts itself. Yet such existentialism has far more effect in the arts and in revisionist theology than in Anglo-American philosophy, which summarily discredits it. After World War II, two or three more decades must pass before German intellectual affiliations can again be acknowledged in some philosophical quarters. The history of European thought coalesces again, even while Europe itself remains politically divided by an "iron curtain." By the late seventies, Husserlian phenomenology infiltrates the curricula of philosophy departments in the United States, although not without calling forth the opposition of the dominant Wittgensteinians. By the eighties even the work and reputation of Heidegger, who was complaisant toward the Nazis, can be rehabilitated.

Modernism, too, eventually finds ingenious means of accommodating both sides of its ancestry. That modernism arises inside an expanding empiricism, while striving to retain the romanticism that aesthetically had inspired it, led to the esthetic theories contending that paradoxes and oppositions are held unified in ironic tension in the artwork. As philosophical positivism and experimental psychology expand, modernism discovers a newer juxtaposition of the idealism that inspires it and the empiricism that subsumes it: the idealism is placed in the artist, and the empiricism is placed in the artwork. The artist's personality retains the romanticism; the criticism of the artwork becomes a quasi-scientific formalism. Biography and criticism part company. This separation between the artist and the artwork then becomes a fundamental tenet of formalist criticism. To the formalist, biography is critically superfluous. This division assures a perpetual supply of romantic artists and formalist critics, who are often temperamentally incompatible. The universities even develop separate curricula for them.

The Unconscious

Arising alongside aesthetic modernism, Freudian psychoanalytic theory postulates the need to conquer the father and be liberated from his dominance—the need (at least in males, and both modernism and modernity are surely masculine) to be the self-sufficient cause of one's own behavior. Self emerges from the reaction to the external suppression of independent self: ego is an adaption to and triumph over subservience. It is shaped in the contours of the resistance to it, in the spaces the omnipotent paternal resistance neglects to fill. Modernism has been described here in a similar way: its freedoms are obtained through rebellion against what would subsume its autonomy. Modernism itself is an ego adaption, an ego fortification.

The descent into the unconscious, where creativity finds its sources and its truths, is a descent into the timeless. The infant does not know time, and the unconscious is permanently infantile.[16] Time does not inhabit that unconscious mixture of symbolic association and pure willing. The content of the unconscious is visual, which is why it appears in dreams. The unconscious is also prelinguistic, preempting the temporal sequence intrinsic to both grammar and logic and substituting for it the fortuitous and coincidental aural resemblances (puns, homonyms) in that pattern of sounds called language. Puns and homonyms exist only inside the phonetic repertoire of language; since they preempt the semantic (the juxtapositions occur outside the structure of grammar), they are prelinguistic.[17]

Modernist writers attempt through strategies of "vision" (image-ry) to escape entrapment in linear time. Painters forsake narrative and the traditional technique for portraying it (perspective). Modernism allies itself with a psychology of the unconscious, encouraged by the psychoanalytic postulate that time does not exist there. In psychoanalysis the attempted conquest over the father is allegorically the attempted victory over time, over both personal history and mortality. The psychological consequence is the familiar rebellion, described as if it were directed against the physical or sexual domination of the father. But it is the Cronos myth, not the Oedipus legend, that best recapitulates psychoanalytic theory. The founding psychoanalytic myth of opposing the father rests on the escape of the Olympian gods from the belly of Father Time, from Cronos/Chronos,[18] who has devoured them. In the modernist reaction, the new gods, who are artists, emerge from the old by escaping prior history, just as Zeus and his siblings liberated themselves from patriarchal Time, who had swallowed them.

Contemporaneously, the dynastic regimes in Eastern Europe from Germany to Russia are also authoritarians soon to be overthrown. The clerical orders undergo a similar demotion. God as Father, King as Father, Time as Father, even one's father as Father—each is deposed.

For Freud, only varieties of repression, distortion, and subversive hostility are available as "defenses" against omnipotence, but these prove inadequate to effect a complete severance from the past. So the ego adapts: the ego is adaption. The artist is no exception, concludes Freud (who inhabits the same Vienna as Musil, Schnitzler, Klimt, and Schoenberg, and the same Europe as all the others). Art is produced through the same psychic mechanisms as are neuroses—through the diverting of energies into channels unoccupied by established authority. For Freud, that diversion is the sublimation that makes art a permissible rebellion, insofar as it releases the unconscious but controls its potential damage by incarcerating rebellion inside an aesthetic structure that society can then integrate into "culture" generally.[19] Both art and ego evolve, then, under authoritarian psychic constraints during the act of rebelling against these constraints.

For Freud, art is a special exercise of the mechanisms of repression and neurosis: art is public dreaming. For psychoanalysis, creativity is a transformation, empirically explained. While the artist may master the forms and materials of art, the true content of art has not and could not have been mastered, because until psychoanalysis it had been repressed. The modernists' romantic inheritance does not allow them to accept the subordination that psychoanalysis imposes on art because the formative influences on art are unconscious mechanisms. For the modernist, the unconscious itself, now exposed, can be mastered; being an artist displays that mastery. Exposing the unconscious gives the artist even more prerogatives than the analyst, for while the analyst tries to reconcile the unconscious with the reality that opposes it (the ego adapts), the artist uses the unconscious to modify reality (reality adapts).

Freud concedes, pessimistically, that the escape of the ego from determinism is in principle impermissible. Understanding this is the psychoanalytic achievement, the therapeutic resolution. The psychological bonds can be loosened, not cast off. In psychoanalytic theory, freedom is adaption and reconciliation. The ego breaks out of the psyche according to the principles of its mechanistic construction, but this breaking out is not a breaking free. Freud here replicates Spinoza's point that true freedom is not an autonomous freedom of the will but a harmonious reconciliation with how things are, a reconciliation that releases one from coercion, even if not from causation. (Americans, being natural optimists, confuse autonomous freedom and harmonious reconciliation; hence their optimistic post-Freudian you-are-what-you-want-to-be psychologies.[20]) Overcoming the burden of the past requires a resignation to it. The ego obtains release from the past by a consenting to it, which outmodes the past by making it "the past." The past becomes an object by naming it the unconscious. Understanding determining forces is a form of control, insofar as agreement to the necessary is an escape from its duress. Reason becomes the key to power, although that power is a reconciliation of reason to its own irremediable subordination to will, a reconciliation that, amazingly, reverses the subordination. The neurotic symptoms disappear. The capacity of the genius, as described by Schopenhauer, to escape the demands of the primal universal will whose urgings generally constitute all human motivation and desire is made a therapeutic outcome, available to the middle class. (Even if only partially: psychoanalysis does not make the patient a genius.) In psychoanalysis, the predicament comes from Schopenhauer and its solution comes from Spinoza.

Since romanticism, the achievements of art are the chief examples of genius. Modern art is the content of the unconscious bursting through the boundaries of the ego, overrunning mechanisms that normally contain it but remaining within the organized constraints of aesthetic form, which the artist controls. In an important sense, knowing that this is happening is also the content of the artwork. The self (ego) gives shape to the content of its origin (the unconscious, the id), which although it cannot change, it can nevertheless master, by imposing form.

Artists, at least the geniuses, can manipulate the contents of the unconscious by mastering the symbolic forms in which the self was once an embryo. There is a descent to the nether regions: the journey of Odysseus to the land of the dead or a visit to Christianity's hell, which is likewise the psychoanalytic descent to the dark and mysterious womb, to sexuality. The id is Satan; the superego is God; the ego is humanity caught between them. The unconscious, as unbounded by time as are God and Satan, is the anti-heaven established by the fallen angel, the eternal abode of the unredeemed fallen human. (In psychoanalysis, there is hell but no heaven, exactly the opposite of a liberalized Christianity.) The artistic ego descends into the maze of the unconscious and brings that timeless realm to the surface. Just as a sunken boat can be raised by filling its hull with a huge balloon, so the artist fills the content of the unconscious with aesthetic form. The timeless is raised into the normal world of time, ascending through the crevice that modernism has split in the present to separate it from the past. The unconscious becomes subordinated to creativity. Psychoanalytic theory is structured like, and comes to be used as, an aesthetic theory. Although living, immense and unfathomable, the unconscious can nevertheless be conquered, like all fabled monsters. Structure is control. Aesthetic structure turns the source of ego (the unconscious) into the product of ego (the artwork). Transforming psyche into the material artwork is both to know it and to control it.

The rejection of the progenitor also appears in modernity through capitalism. While fifteenth- and sixteenth-century mercantilist theory concerned the wealth of nations, capitalist theory addresses the wealth of individuals. Political boundaries only designate the extent of a specifically protected marketplace. As individual communion with God supersedes church membership for Protestantism, so in capitalism, wider clan memberships and nationality become reduced in importance, not only as economic determinants, but also as the ground of ego formation. The ego is predominantly formed in the immediate family, and the "family drama" is generalized into the site of human nature. (Oedipal relations are one specific form of this capitalist model.) The family unit becomes increasingly important for the formation of selfhood as the family's productive financial impact becomes less important.[21] The only cottage industry remaining is ego production.

The economic system in which this ego participates is based on competition, just like the Oedipal dynamic. One's possessions are, by definition, those to which everyone else is denied possession. Darwin was correct: nature is not an edenic harmony but a struggle for limited resources by numerous contenders, among them parents and progeny, old entrepreneurs and new ones, owners and workers, the supervisor and the supervised.[22] (Freud's speculation that there actually had been a primal historical rebellion of the sons against the father[23] corresponds to the history of labor unions. Freud and Samuel Gompers are nearly exact contemporaries.) Capitalist theory quickly accommodates the Darwinian model: "social" Darwinism[24] simply requires adding human will and competitive capitalistic intent as admirably adaptive biological mechanisms in the evolutionary model. What had been externalized as natural law in Darwin has been internalized as psychic law in Freud. Both depend on antagonistic competition, as does capitalism: on the slowly evolving strengths of subordinated lifeforms seeking power, on unrelenting anxiety (survival threats and the fear of retaliation), and on strategic repression (in biology, the latent potential of recessive genes).

In capitalism, the most admired figure is the "self-made man." To be born anew is also to determine the circumstances of one's birth, as essential in capitalism as for the modernist aesthetic and salvational Christianity. When rejection of the parents becomes a psychological developmental stage in modernity, adolescence—the years during which one learns to "make" oneself—emerges as a significant social phenomenon. There is the persistent attempt to find a preferable father in one's own self, an attempt to elude the inescapable causation that has brought us into being.[25] Sexual reproduction is the hidden truth: this is the disclosure of psychoanalysis. It accounts for Freud's finding that so many of his patients had seen, or (he concludes) fantasized, the parents engaged in the sexual act. To view that act is to view one's own conception. One strives to escape the inescapable sexual origin, which has situated each person's origin at one moment in historical time and has given us our physical, mental, and behavioral limitations and (still worse) our mortality. The presumed Oedipal desire to possess the mother is to reject one's origin in the parental sexual act, to claim one's origin for oneself.

The ultimate father was once God. But when God is sent into exile, the origin of the self in God must be abandoned. Yet the alternative is that the source of self is the parents, their physical act, their personal pleasure. The thought of this is preposterous or disgusting to the child first learning the facts of the matter. One is repelled by being no more than a natural physical product. The parents must also be rejected: they created the child in the "wrong way"—a way that simultaneously gives life and dooms it.

As the Enlightenment ethos with its emphasis on rationality and progress dominated nineteenth-century culture, there were those who foresaw a renewed spiritual awakening. Religion would not succumb; it too would evolve, leaving superstition behind. The industrialist and the scientist might find themselves side by side in a church based on new principles (those of the Saint-Simonians, for example) allowing for the collaboration of faith and rationality. Fantasy (quite distinct from the romantics' poetic imagination) and dream would be excluded as legitimate inspirations; they were irrational, spontaneous, and usually detri-mental, nearer to madness than insight. But a widely acceptable transformation of orthodox religion gradually appeared less plausible, and alternative proposals (like the various communal movements) convinced only small minorities. Dream and fantasy became a possible source of insight and inspiration for artists who were disillusioned with capitalism. Voting and merchandizing would not elevate the soul to heaven. Even before Freud called attention to the psychological implications of dream and fantasy, artists and writers had already turned toward both of them, especially in German expressionism; but the most important psychoanalytic innovation is to trace dream and fantasy to an unconscious defined as a mental location or entity, like a chamber. (The explorations of Africa and of the ocean's depths are related to the psychological descent.) The artists take this step toward territorializing the unconscious along with Freud, who legitimates this spatialized unconscious (where time does not pass, although it accumulates) for modernity by attaching it to scientific hypotheses.

The unconscious is, then, generated as part of the Enlightenment dialectic. The unconscious as a place, a location, is a reconfiguration of those specific aspects of consciousness that the Enlightenment presumed to be logically subjugated and subordinated. Logical subordination is transformed into a literal geographical submergence, creating a topology of the psyche with various levels, like an anthropological dig. The unconscious is furnished with the "irrational" materials that Enlightenment rationality rejects; the unconscious is the burial ground of these materials. Writers and artists of all modernist persuasions can turn to the unconscious—not because the unconscious is a permanent part of the human psyche now put to conscious artistic use but because the unconscious is first given a shape, a perimeter, and a spatialized location by the content of the nineteenth-century progress that surrounds and encapsulates it. Like unclaimed territory, the unconscious must be defined by the claims on the territory surrounding it.

Employing dream and fantasy also justifies the artist's breaking away from the rules of visual perspective established in the Renaissance. The violations of Renaissance norms and the later arrival of abstraction in art is congruent with the emergence of the unconscious psychological structures created in reaction to the empiricist Enlightenment. In literature, too, naturalism loses its power, which symbolism gains. If dream and fantasy reflect an unconsciousness that contains an underlying "reality," then the natural world is simply a surface effect—just as natural perspective is an effect lying entirely on the surface of the canvas. Customary reality is the illusion fostered by hundreds of years of artwork. By the time of surrealism, this notion will have become a manifesto. Two incompatible worlds, the interior and the exterior, depend on one another for their mutual definitions even as they draw farther apart in the first half of the twentieth century. The mind grows deeper and more secluded; the universe grows vaster and more inaccessible. In literature, the same effect is achieved through the widening dissociation of the interior mental narrative and the exterior descriptive narrative, which are then so thoroughly intermixed stylistically that the reader often cannot tell whether the narrative is situated inside or outside the character's mentality. This stylistic integration strives, always unsuccessfully, to resolve the incompatibilities that the meaning of the work is meant to disclose. The literary work appears to have as a purpose what it simultaneously discloses as an impossibility.

That appearances are not accurate replications of the underlying causal reality connects Freudian theory to the artistic imagination. It also relates to Marxism, for which the conduct and suppositions of everyday life conceal, rather than disclose, the underlying economic relationships. Similarly, quantum physics emerges contemporaneously: the fundamental processes and materials of nature are not what gross matter would suggest to the naive observer using the unaided senses. Earlier discoveries of things previously unseen (like Leeuwenhoek's observation of microscopic organisms) had not challenged the notion of what kinds of things basically constituted the world; it was simply that human senses were insufficiently refined to see or hear certain things, since the range of the senses was understandably confined to regions of maximum utility.[26] In classical physics, all phenomena, however large or small, are identical to phenomena ordinarily sensed; even atoms are simply the smallest bits of ordinary matter. But in quantum physics, the phenomena to be explained depend on other phenomena that must be posited but cannot be directly known. That observation can reduce them to momentary entities (a trace on the film) does not contradict the fundamental sensory unknowability of the world. Since, at the deepest level of analysis, the senses are ineffectual, quantum physics is not an empiricism. (One should realize by now that the search for primary particles generates a limitless number of them.) This same charge—of not being a true empiricism—is often leveled against psychoanalysis and Marxism by those who would, however, excuse physics from the charge.

The content of the unconscious according to Freud, the hidden economic reality according to Marx, and the unobservable subatomic world according to quantum physics—each can be brought into consciousness, just like the content of art in modernism. This process involves not by knowing truth and then describing it but by saying it and doing it (praxis). The expression of the truth is not a description of the truth; the content is equivalent to the expression of it. Modernism in art—like the methods of psychology, political theory, and the physical sciences with which it is most compatible—rejects the reality of preceding generations as misleading surface phenomena. Modernism seeks reality elsewhere, where finding it, knowing it, and describing it are all one act.

Part Three

Politics and Modernism

Modernism Left and Right

8

Considering Capitalism

The English proved the most adroit at combining commerce and territorial expansion. Economic colonization, or imperialism, occurred simultaneously with the successes of the other intellectual products of empiricist modernity. The system of government established by the former British colonies in America was influenced by Locke's writings on government; those writings are also a major source of empiricism. Empiricism, democracy, and capitalism became collaborators. The mechanistic epistemology of empiricism suits capitalism quite well: the mind manufactures thoughts, like a machine with hidden parts. In capitalism, financial transactions depend upon the hiddenness of mentality, because of the need to conduct business in secret, no longer out in the street (the public market), and because each party contrives to disclose as little as possible.

The scientific concept that motion is caused by the transfer of physical forces (energy) from one body to another corresponds to the idea that human action is also motivated by the exchange of a physical substance, money. (In recent quantum physics theory, all interactions whatsoever are transactions involving the exchange of particles.[1]) The relationship of money to the external world is no less mysterious than the relationship of mathematics to it: an economic depression can occur even when the amount of physical resources in the ground and the amount of people available to exploit them are the same as the year before. Like gravity or "potential" energy, money takes on invisible but causal powers. The causal power of human energy is stored in money, like energy in a battery.

The dominance of empiricist modernity becomes quantitatively measurable on a most interesting scale: the increase of technology. Capitalism's growth is measured by the increase of urban industrial manufacturing, by the large-scale trading and monopolizing of the materials of consumer products (cloth, wood, steel, rubber, etc.) and by the large quantity of foods shipped in from a distance and processed in factorylike settings (slaughterhouses, for example) to feed urban dwellers. A capitalism of industrial manufacturing replaces a capitalism of mercantilist commercial trade: raw materials become increasingly useless to the ultimate consumer because they can be transformed into products only in factories. Workers need to live near the machines to which their personal labor is now subordinated. The means of production is not in itself considered an evil—technology might help free humanity from tedious and arduous labor. But either the inevitable economic conditions of work (according to the Malthusians) or the distribution of the ownership of those means (according to the Marxists) is a source of social evil. Urbanization is accompanied by crowding and lack of sanitation—conditions not considered social problems until the nineteenth century—as well as by poverty, crime, deplorable working conditions, alienation, and spiritual vacuity. Those whose lives are most diminished by the system work for those whose lives are most enhanced by it.

Although the larger European cities had always been characterized by squalor, capitalism had promised a cure as part of the Enlightenment dream. Instead, as the modernists well knew, capitalism had become the major perpetrator. When it appeared obvious in the nineteenth century that poverty would not vanish, capitalist economic theory conveniently asserted that a permanent impoverishment of the lowest class of workers is an economic necessity: the "iron law of wages" will keep wages at a minimal subsistence level because there are always more willing workers than jobs.[2] That the field of economics develops "laws" allies capitalist economics and empiricist science: the functions of the capitalist marketplace are made to appear not simply as a series of contingencies but as the results of operative natural law. As nature is productive because of the laws regulating its motions, so society is driven by laws of economic motion. The hardships are not a flaw in the system but a necessary feature of it.

But to whom, exactly, does the advantage accrue? The attraction of Marxism was its promise of a remedy for the unpredicted ills resulting from a system in which the riches of one class can apparently only be maintained through the continued poverty and ignorance of another, as if this disparity resulted from natural economic law. The pre-Marxist socialism was based on voluntaristic ethics and shared moral values. Marxism offered, instead, a new kind of scientific economic lawfulness: a transformative progressive model based upon an evolutionary lawfulness. Capitalism can then be seen as but one economic phase in a determined history. Marx proposes this dynamic just when evolutionary theory in biology can provide an empiricist analogy. Throughout nature, conflict yields advancement as a natural law. For Marx, the energy for change is class conflict. Marx's dialectical model of economics propelled by this conflict provides an alternative to the static classical model—the supply-and-demand curves emulating the geometrical mathematics of classical physics. At the same time, the Marxist model ostensibly remains consistent with the methodological demands of empiricism, which has itself been expanded specifically to include evolution.

Some assert that evolutionary theory and the static supply-and-demand curves can be integrated by making supply and demand the testing ground for survival of the fittest: economic competition and biological competition are correlated. For Marx, however, the least successful at acquisition are not the least fit to survive. Indeed, the oppressed proletariate must be the source of evolutionary change. In this regard, capitalism identifies Darwin as a discoverer of the kinds of ethically impartial laws for biology that Newton discovered for cosmology. Marx, however, remains allegiant to the Hegelian compromise between empiricism and idealism so that the direction of history can be not only economically progressive but also moral, a discrimination rare in empiricism. That the oppressed are destined for victory is the narrative of the Hebrew slaves in Egypt and of the Christians as well; in this sense Marx preserves (as did Hegel before him) the biblical narrative of a predestined liberation from bondage for a chosen people.[3] The union of capitalism and Darwinism yields exactly the opposite result: power and dominance is freedom, and deservedly so. Liberation comes not from having been chosen, but from having the power to choose.

Many early modernists believe that inexpensive manufactured products (capitalism's specialty) will widely disseminate aesthetic values. Engineering, manufacturing, and art will achieve a harmony of purpose and form. Modernistic products designed for mass consumption (kitchen goods, inexpensive furniture and clothing, greeting cards) do indeed elicit new cultural practices; nevertheless, the production and consumption of consumer products gradually becomes a business separate from art, even when its forms derive from art. First, the economy of the visual art marketplace is based (quite unlike manufacturing) on the single unreproducible and hence costly work. Many people may be able to view the artwork, but very few, perhaps only one, can use it. Second, the commercial products are all style and no meaning—the very opposite of what artistry intends. For consumer products, style can be assigned only transient meanings by designers, manufacturers, and distributors. Meanings are made and confirmed by purchases, rather than by insights. Such meanings cannot embody enduring truths.

Mass consumption eventually represents superficiality and banality to the modernist. The art produced for mass consumption becomes a distinct social institution, incorporated in the media, supported by advertising. The advertiser's message will insist that traditional values can remain stable, yet the advertising itself is one of the chief causes of their destabilization. In response, modernist artists intentionally make their works unlike any (other) consumer item, rejecting commercially sentimental values. Yet modernism can never relinquish its affiliation with the middle class, which, after all, supports these artists, even if meagerly. Modernism would be impossible without such patronage. The modernists are striving to convert those who see art not as a source of spiritual conversion but as pleasure. (It is hardly poor workers who find modern art to their liking.) But only a fraction of the middle-class public can be convinced to redefine itself by accepting modernism's hostile critique of their own well being. Modernism will augment capitalism, not undermine it, as the Marxist socialists soon surmise.

Modernism is capitalism's bad conscience. Modernism's doubt about capitalism is also the reflexive self-doubt of capitalism, since modernism evolves inside the capitalist setting. Capitalism's self-doubt is provoked by the inability to control cyclical economic depression or to eliminate poverty, illiteracy, or disease. Further, wealth cannot fill spiritual vacancy if wealth is what promotes that very vacancy. Art can be requisitioned both to explain the spiritual vacancy and to fill it, although those who turn to art for such explanation and support are relatively small in number and generally from the middle class.[4]

Art further offers therapeutic diversion from the tensions of the business day. Aesthetics and relaxation become combined as entertainment. Intended to critique economic modernity, art becomes integrated into the economic system, which has already appropriated the Enlightenment humanism it cannot satisfy. (A recent example: humanism as public television.) Artistic innovation becomes another exciting aspect of the daily commercial life artists profess to abjure. (Art Nouveau provided an early paradigm.) Modernism, once meant to unify value, meaning, work, and style, yields to modern life, which is propelled precisely by the implausibility of that integration, whose possibility the media nevertheless assures us is near at hand. This results in guilt and self-doubt. "Stress" and "tension" accompany the social and economic behaviors questing to satisfy the dissatisfaction the behaviors themselves cause. The guilt and self-doubt are brought to the surface in art as themes. But the meaning of the work is sabotaged by its conversion into one more product. The artistic object is taken to object-ify its content, making guilt and self-doubt objects rather than dilemmas. At first this does not prevent modernism from doing valuable critical work, but eventually the obvious appropriation of art by entertainment becomes a permanent exasperation. Artists become angry, then cynical, then nasty. By the third quarter of the century, they become entrepreneurial.

The psychotherapeutic procedure that raises repressed guilt into consciousness also comes to function as solace for the repression. For those who can afford it, the id is to the patient what inspiration is to the artist: creative energy. Psychoanalytic theory becomes the shape the problem takes. The psychotherapeutic profession assures that insight yields adaption and conformity in the name of liberation: one cures the illness by contracting for lessons in how not to feel it. Modern art has come to do likewise, since in late aesthetic modernism the externalization of the problem (as if the subject can become its own object) is often presumed to be the cure.

Like the unconscious, art became identified as the specific realm of the emotions. In psychoanalysis, as in most therapies, the source of guilt is assigned not to the social system but to the family system. The family becomes severed from working relationships, a site for the emotions that work discourages. Products are produced in settings presumed ideally rational, while the family setting, where the products are consumed, becomes ideally irrational, the fulfillment of desire. Like the modern family, art provides still another repository for the emotions. The artist is imagined to be an observer of the system, rather than a by-product of it, as if to confirm that such detachment is really possible. The socioeconomic system as a whole (both the idealized work setting and the idealized political setting) is then seen as emotionally neutral, rational.

The advocates for modernism are a small portion of the middle class (although a small portion of a very large population is still a sizable number). The schism between high and low culture opens. Modernism offers a form of aesthetic nobility to a portion of the public for whom the appreciation of art, which requires no capital, can become a criterion more important than the ownership of art. Birth and funds are, in principle, secondary. In the United States, innumerable children or grandchildren of immigrants will attend college and major in the liberal arts. The production and discussion of artworks are usually the occupations of those without significant financial resources or patrimonial inheritances. (Even in wealthy families it is usually the younger children who incline toward the arts.) Culture, creativity, and education become criteria for the evaluation of character distinct from one's origins. Paradoxically, elitism in modern art serves a democratizing function, despite itself: it allows for a type of middle-class aristocracy.

The schism between high art and low will not close again until the seventies, as modernism wanes. Even then the closing occurs in limited areas (in fiction but not in poetry, in architecture but not in painting). By then the distribution of products finally does become, ironically, the distribution of aesthetic values—but only because the aesthetic values are no longer the criteria for evaluating products. Rather, aesthetic values become a special type of consumable product. "Culture" is no longer the encompassing societal structures from which production emerges, but the content of production. While culture might have been considered the source of the ideas and values that rationalize modes of production and ways of life for the citizenry, now these ideas and values are themselves economic products.

The conflict between science and art also involves capitalism. Capitalism rests on inviolable property rights. Locke argued that although the earth was originally given by God equally to all humankind, the current unequal distribution of private property has resulted from exertions of individual labor and is therefore legitimate.[5] Locke affiliates constitutional government and private property; and since Locke also founds philosophical empiricism, empiricism can afterward be attacked as an ideological accomplice of capitalism. Modern artists can then put forth as an alternative the remnants of philosophical idealism inherited from the romantics, much removed and simplified from its original philosophical sources. But this idealism and romanticism increasingly become matters of personal temperament and inclination. The artistic pronouncements and manifestos of the early modernists are a mixture of personal confession, illumination, and prescription. They do not proclaim impersonal norms and policies that had characterized the academies, especially the French Academy since the days of Charles Le Brun, under Louis XIV.[6] (The high literary modernists do return to the assertion of impersonal norms.) Even the visual art of the French Revolution—David's is the best example—had been a conservative extension of classicism. The behavior, speech patterns, dress, and living arrangements of the modernist artist become consciously oppositional to business owners, managers, merchants, or investors—although even when such opposition is strongest, it remains more an antagonism than a subversion. The capitalists never regard it, as they must regard socialism, seriously.

The Left and the Right

The dominant figures of modernism have conflicting perspectives. Some discard tradition (in the avant-garde generally) and, later, others venerate tradition (in formalism generally). Some search for permanent and enduring values, while others reject the possibility of such values. Some advocate stable, harmonious social structures, while others believe in the necessity of constant upheaval in the arts and in society. Modernists are both optimistic and pessimistic about the potential of modern times.

These dualities are often related to the writer's country of origin (whether in a militarily victorious or vanquished country), place of residence (between the wars the artist or writer is frequently an expatriate), genre (poem, painting, novel, drama), and individual temperament. The ideological combat between socialism and capitalism after the Russian Revolution influences much of the writing, as does the rise of fascism. Modernism, in its broadest outlines, is always twofold: every work, action, and belief premises a confrontation with a political or social opponent. Yet every work is also an adaption to and compromise with that opponent.

Modernism has a "right" and a "left," although these terms must be qualified. The aesthetic right (traditionalism, formalism, elitism) and the aesthetic left (rebellion, bohemianism, popularism) do not invariably coincide with the political Right and Left. Modern visual artists are generally unwilling to subordinate themselves to a conformist political agenda, and visual modernism remained on the Left even as literary modernism moved to the Right in high modernism. After all, innovations in nineteenth-century painting necessarily incorporated opposition to the state, namely the government-supported academy—whether in Paris or, as for the Sezession, in Berlin. And certain of the immediate precursors of modernism had been on the political Left: Courbet was a socialist; Monet left Paris for London in 1870 to avoid perhaps having to fight on behalf of Louis Napoleon; so did Pissarro, a proclaimed anarchist. Later, Breton's socialism would be a controversial issue among the surrealists. Throughout the 1930s, many critics associated the attacks of visual artists on tradition with Bolshevik communism or anarchy, condemning modern visual art on political grounds. But even as these accusations were occurring, literary modernism in the Anglo-American environment was evolving on the Right, encouraged by fears and apprehensions provoked by the Russian Revolution. Various activities of the Left were proscribed, by legal or other means.

As the political situation further unfolds, modernism remains a movement only inside the capitalist democracies. Since modernism is embedded in empiricism, and the roots of philosophical empiricism are the same as those of the theory of constitutional private property rights (in Locke especially), modern art comes to be rejected elsewhere. Russian socialists view it as an ineffective instrument of revolution, and fascists consider it capitalist decadence.

To assign the history of art the name of "tradition," as formalism does, will be most appealing to the political Right. During the transition to formalism in the twenties, high modernists, including Eliot and Pound, had (to put it mildly) sentiments compatible with the political Right.[7] The search for aesthetic structures whose formal internal relationships are permanent and noncontingent (and therefore superior to the flow of history) enhances the appeal of religious or political institutions that proclaim ahistorical truths. Institutions like an established church, for example, or a constitution (given a fundamentalist definition) or a monarchy or, for a few (like Pound and Wyndham

Lewis), even fascism, are often compelling to formalist critics and writers. The rituals of politics based on universal inviolable principles—on visual symbolism, canonized texts, and discipline rather than cogitation, customarily take on a recognizable aesthetic structure.

After World War II, modernist literary formalism allies with the democratic Right, now called conservatism in the United States. By the midthirties the fascist Right repudiated modernism as much as did orthodox Marxist-Leninism, although when fascism had meant Mussolini and not (yet) Hitler, it had been easier for modernists to find some merits in the movement. The case of Futurism is best known.[8] (Interestingly, the Nazis granted German expressionism some appreciation.[9]) Visual modernism stands almost unanimously on the political Left; hence formalism comes to be fully established in visual criticism well after it is dominant in literature. (In literary modernism, to be sure, the major domains of the novel and film always remained on the Left, at least for the writers.) The reception of formalism and consequently of academic and political legitimation in the visual arts is detained because that formalism issues from the socialist Left and must be gradually separated from it. In literary formalism—in poetry especially—the New Critic's methodology dominates English departments (politically neutralizing them) well before the essays of Clement Greenberg achieve their full impact, mainly because his essays came from the political Left. The initiators of visual modernism had transformed painting early, before World War I and the Russian Revolution had intensified political antagonisms. (The fauves exhibited in 1905 and Picasso's *Demoiselles d'Avignon* was finished in 1907.) Their aesthetic maturity occurred in a different political environment than did the writers'. High modernism does not coalesce in literature until the twenties: Eliot's *The Waste Land* and Joyce's *Ulysses* are published in 1922. Also, politicians worry less about visual artists than about writers: the pen is mightier than the sword, not the brush or the chisel.

Representative figures on the aesthetic right in Anglo-American high modernism maintain that a unified tradition in Western civilization exists from the Greeks to the present day. Institutions embody enduring truths and values. Truths about the physical world, unaccompanied by values, are discovered by impartial and objective science; but literature and art, with the humanities generally, address the truths of human nature and both reveal and create the enduring and permanent human values around which the future should be organized. Society is improved by amelioration rather than by cataclysm and evolves within a stable framework that incorporates the best of political, philosophical, aesthetic, and (for some) religious traditions.

Those on the aesthetic left assert that while enduring human values have emerged and are still to emerge (humankind is unfinished), political and social history has reached a point where society is impeding human liberation. Increasing frustration, injustice, and self-deception mask true happiness with inferior substitutes (creature comforts), which serve only the interests of the prosperous few. The remedy can come only from radical and fundamental changes, not from the programs for gradual improvement and refinement offered by the right. As high modernism progresses in the Anglo-American setting, the left will watch the artistic and literary establishments become increasingly appropriated by the status quo. By the fifties literary figures on the right become the modernists who are granted respectability and academic legitimacy. The growing fear of communism further separates the right from a continuing albeit weakened avant-garde on the left. Only in the midsixties will the left regain substantial influence in Anglo-American universities. The left then becomes a "liberalism" no longer necessarily attached to, even when attracted to some of the positions of, political socialism as it has been advocated in France and Italy.

Those on the aesthetic left who believe themselves a small minority convey the sense of loss and alienation, often combined with self-doubt, anguish, the comic, the grotesque, and the ludicrous. The specific choice is, again, often related to the artist's national and ethnic relation to military victors and vanquished. Fictional characters are often portrayed as emotionally beleaguered, misunderstood, sometimes incapacitated, and sometimes capable of grand although publicly ineffectual personal gestures. The artist, whose personality also becomes an artwork, is often portrayed in the same way. Death, despair, and disillusionment are often synonymous with profundity—even nowadays, to judge by college anthologies. Dostoevski's underground man becomes a hero of sorts, as does Melville's Ahab. So do Baudelaire, Rimbaud, and the "bohemian" artists. Even Laurence Sterne's *Tristram Shandy* becomes a precursor. Certain philosophical writings, from Kierkegaard through (what later becomes) existentialism, which is a phenomenology on the political Left, serve as inspiration. While there are those who optimistically believe in a personal fulfillment or even an aesthetic salvation, this too comes at the expense of disaffection with society.

On the other hand, some who ally with the political Left have more confidence in social revolution. The Russian Revolution and the increasing prestige of Marxist socialism influences their work. When the Russian communists reject modern art, "socialist realism" emerges, an unambiguous rejection of the methods of modernism proper (abstraction, fantasy, metaphor, stream of consciousness). Yet this rejection of modernism continues to fulfill the modernist avant-garde project of undermining middle-class capitalist values in nonsocialist countries like the United States, while also reaching out to the working class through a readily accessible style and content—often addressing injustice, poverty, and the callousness of the wealthy. Revelations about Stalinist Russia after World War II will eventually cause the democratic liberal Left (including the aesthetic left) to separate from Marxist-Leninism, although in some places not completely. But by then we are in late modernism, and New York City has become its center.

Still others reject the Marxist Left, declaring totalitarian communism repugnant while fearing its power. Yet these same writers have an equal distaste for the greed and corruption of democratic capitalism, in the midst of which they must live. Consequently, their writings take two directions: either they are political critiques (exposing social and moral corruption, and sometimes creating allegorical or alternative fictional societies), or they are intensely introspective, often displaying a complete absorption in personal artistic expression as if this were a virtue.

Some on the Left place their hopes in democratic institutions, celebrating the possibilities of personal liberation. The freedoms of the imagination, sex, travel, prosperity, and hedonistic experimentation generally are celebrated from the Roaring Twenties onward, although with a hiatus during the economic depression of the thirties. After World War II, having crossed the Atlantic, modernism and a thriving American economy will be mutually congratulatory.

Finally, still others on the Left attempt to reformulate the relationship between the two competing political systems, socialism and capitalism, to maintain the feasibility of a dialectical relation. This is customarily a systematic project in France and, after World War II, in Germany.

Those on the aesthetic right maintain that art has a position and mission superior to the social and economic setting in which it is produced. They grant an often sacrosanct autonomy to the artwork or text, placed in a tradition separate from social and political history. The history of art can be fully explained by a causation internal to that history. In every culture, enduring human values have been best expressed by artists, writers in particular; and since form is inseparable from content, the history of one (method) is the history of the other (ideas). This is formalism. The truths that art manifests can be values, rather than facts.

For the modernist on the aesthetic right, a command of artistic craft is a prerequisite for a command of truth. It is not clear that non-artists can know the truth other than through what has been derived from art. The Bible, for example, can be construed as having artistic rather than literal authenticity. The early Tolstoy is preferable to the later Dostoevski. This approach is taken to substantiate dual-truth theory, since it is both a defense against science and a collaboration with science, partitioning the field of truth in half, relinquishing one half in order to claim the other.[10] No virtue surpasses clarity; no fault surpasses obfuscation. Prose style becomes trim; poetry loses its filigree. The philosophical "intuitionists" (such intuitions being natural psychological mechanisms, rather than metaphysical derivatives) and even the logical positivists, whose (circumscribed) task is the clarification of language and logic, are preferable to the cryptic Hegelians or phenomenologists. Society may be flawed, confusing, and exasperating, but great art can display perfection. Society is the forum for art, not an impediment to it. The desire for lasting fame, for admission to the canon (perhaps burial in Westminster Abbey), is not only an ambition but a compulsion.

From the position on the right, the decline of a society need not be presumed to necessitate the decline of art. On the contrary, this decline is often modernism's subject: there would be no modernism without it. The artist is neither lost nor alienated, but derives great power from being present at an auspicious moment (the decline of the West). On the left, artistic power is always in direct confrontation with sociopolitical power. On the right, to the contrary, society's power is not so much to be opposed as co-opted or manipulated. (After all, the middle class provokes, funds, and institutionalizes modernism in the first place.)

Literary formalism can be placed, then, on both the aesthetic and political Right, even though formalists often insist their critical position transcends politics. Formalism's purported neutrality is actually compliance. The New Critics have already been mentioned. The method becomes most respectable when the political Right ascends in fear of communism, which accounts for much of formalism's success in the university. Even in the genres where social issues often preside—in the motion picture, the photograph, and the novel—formalism can be introduced as a critical method and the "message" can be subordinated to notions of worldview or point of view, ways of discussing beliefs without necessitating any commitments. Formalism on the right legitimates, by co-optation, the study of works coming from the left. The tone of such criticism is often aloof and cosmopolitan. Knowing how the artwork works is a discipline of knowledge requiring technical proficiency, a heightened sensitivity balanced by an alleged objective detachment. The politics of authors can be subsumed, excused, and finally incapacitated by aesthetic concerns, by meticulous critical scrutiny.

Elitism and Popularism

The distinctions between an aesthetic right and left in modernism also raises the distinction between a modernist elitism and a modernist popularism. The distinction particularly involves the relation of art to the middle and lower economic classes. Certain of the arts maintain a closer attachment to the public market: the motion picture, the novel, some drama, outdoor sculpture, and the architecture of commerce and the apartment complex. The nineteenth-century novelists (and a few poets, like Tennyson) provided the transition to an art exchanged in the industrialized marketplace. The novel becomes the narrative form through which readers can understand and configure the story of their own lives; one's biography is intentionally shaped as if it were a novel in progress. This inaugurates a mass culture that makes unprecedented commercial success possible for writers. Poetry, easel painting, music, and dance have a more tenuous affiliation with the public, although there is mediation through the museum exhibition, the public "reading," the experimental theater, the concert (a short modern piece between the Beethoven and the Mozart), and the university. Audiences are quite limited until late modernism, when prosperity and the expansion of higher education follow World War II.

In elitist modernism, art is set in contrast with customary experience and in some ways provides preferable alternatives to it. Technique is complex, and access to intricate aesthetic meaning is challenging. Without special training in formalist critical skills, the viewer or reader is dismayed, even offended or repulsed. A willingness to undertake such training is the sign of a conferred membership.

In popularist modernism, however, common experience is to be enhanced through art. Art is an instrument of change, to which the average person is susceptible if properly addressed. The readily decipherable language of everyday life is immediately accessible, even if it takes extraordinary training to produce it as art. In popularism, the skills of the artist are submerged in the impact of the work, and criticism addresses ideas rather than techniques. In elitism, the virtuosity of the artist is prominent and critically essential.

Elitist modernism restructures ordinary experience; populist modernism exposes ordinary experience. The artworks of elitist modernism appeal to personal and private sensitivities. Experiencing the artwork is a private affair, for in the midst of social institutions the individual is basically an isolated being, with a solitary destiny—which the lives of certain artists are presumed to exemplify. The artworks of populist modernism, on the contrary, appeal to the psyche as it functions in the collective structures of society, to public integration or the lack of it, to behavior rather than thoughts, to actions rather than concepts. For popularism, belonging is desirable. To be alienated is a loss rather than a distinction, even though the social and economic institutions of modern society promote more alienation than bonding. (The artist whose work communicates this theme may, incongruously, have to be alienated in order to do so.) The film and the play, for example, require crews of people and continual interaction, and even the writing of a novel may involve research, advice from friends, the editor, and the publisher. The populist modernist has a community; the elitist modernist has a coterie. The populist modernist has an audience; the elitist modernist has disciples.

The elitist modernist recognizes, and objects, that modernity has indoctrinated the middle classes so that technological novelty, the consumption of products, and momentary excitement has for them replaced insight and fulfillment. Information should serve, not substitute for, wisdom. Conformity has yielded mediocrity in the guise of comfort. Transitory opinions are mistaken for enduring values; easily replicated behaviors and goals are mistaken for shared communion.

The development of sociology has brought the idea of the "normal," and normality has become a morality. Politicians have made truisms out of claptrap, proclaiming the union of patriotism and prosperity that (in sequence) fascism, the economic depression, totalitarianism, communism, and world war belie. Art amply displays where alternatives are to be found, most importantly in art itself.

The increasing audience for high modernist literature is a cause for elitist optimism. The writers' audience expands beyond the "little" magazines and patron-supported presses. Nevertheless, the writers know they cultivate a small minority, while the visual artists are confined to small galleries yielding few sales at inadequate prices. Besides, the capacity for change in the urbanized middle class may be meager, even if their society has been decorated by modernism: to believe that the middle class is truly open to conversion by high modernist art would be to undermine precisely what makes that art elitist. The exclusivity of the audience for high modernism often enhances its attraction for its devotees: the few must serve as the aesthetic conscience of the many.

The popularist modernist agrees that modernity has corrupted the middle class through technology, consumption, and the emphasis on income; yet these are the very forces that can liberate humankind from the drudgeries of unsatisfying (even when easy) work. The cities may be corrupt, but they are also where resources are generated for an improved standard of living and the expansion of opportunities for legal and social equality that art will provoke. Art yields social remedies, not an alternative domain of sensibility. The popularist will create the public conscience rather than, like the elitist, serve as the public conscience.

Elitist modernism hopes for a new order; this is its classicism. Popularist modernism hopes for a new freedom; this is its romanticism. For the elitist modernist, tradition reflects order, in the arts as well as in society. Political stability is admirable. Although a psychological vocabulary increasingly replaces a metaphysical one, concepts of aesthetic transcendence remain associated with notions of genius and inspiration. This is the prevailing romanticism nestled in this classicism.

For the popularist modernist, however, to aggrandize tradition is to prolong its errors along with its achievements. Science depends little on past authority, since the truth is what one finds, not what one has been told; likewise with art. This is the prevailing empiricism nestled in this romanticism. For the popularist modernist, the uneducated working class has not been co-opted by the social and economic system, even if they have been subordinated by it. Because workers are not the ones who derive the benefits from the system, they serve as a reservoir of energy that can be directed toward reform. The elitist modernists do not address the working class, even when they commiserate. Since elitist modernism relies on the patronage of the well-to-do and since the readership must come from the highly educated, who may be (once more frequently than now) drawn from those who are economically comfortable, socialism is rejected, especially Marxist socialism. Consequently, elitist modernism customarily remains attractive to the political Right (which can always turn artistic attacks upon it into "culture") and popularist modernism to the political Left.

The widespread distribution of books and films depends on mainstream sources, so even those on the Left stimulate a lucrative business for the economy they are attempting to modify. Popularist modernism becomes integrated into the modes of distribution that serve the entertainment industry, and for a while a significant portion of the entertainment industry embraces the political Left. For the general public, art and entertainment will come to coincide—although this is not what the modernists originally had in mind. This stimulates the often acrimonious debate over the merits of "high" and "low" art, part of the now ongoing debate, which remains popularist, that also includes matters of the official canon, the media, race, ethnicity, gender, and non-Western culture.

The current controversies initiated by post-structuralism and postmodernism concerning critical theory and the relation between critical theory and political theory should not be confused with an extension of popularist modernism, even though the initiatives occur on the political Left. The formalist intricacy of the texts, and their consequent appeal to a highly specialized academic audience, opens the contentions to the charge of a new elitism—especially since modernism has for three decades now been ubiquitously disseminated. That the elitism shifted from the critical right to the critical left, even as (and perhaps because) political power shifted from the Left to the Right during a time of renewed conservatism, was a defining characteristic of art, of criticism, and of Anglo-American social and political life from the late seventies through the early nineties.

The Politics of Empiricism and Transcendentalism

9

In empiricist modernity, a substantial portion of individuality is identified with nationality. As its prosperity grows, England serves as the governmental paradigm and the economically assertive Englishman as the model individual.

Each citizen automatically acquires the privilege, upon maturity, of consent to governance. Each nation assumes this privilege will be exercised in its favor, either (depending on the political theory) as the rational expression of self-interest or as recognition of an allegiance imposed by birth (Latin *natio* is both *birth* and *race*). Moral obligation is also a necessity. While individuals, as self-interested units, remain in theory "naturally" free (ideally uncoerced, as in a free market), the ego must have a defining context of membership, because without such a context an ego could not have become individuated in the first place.

The concept of nationhood requires the concept of linear time, since the individual is defined as a "subject" (in both the psychological and political senses) existing at one point on the line that is the extension through time of the nation. Individuals are linked through time, as well as at any moment in time. Nationhood, as an idea distinct from either domains of rulership (the lands of the Bourbons, for example) or ethnicity, does not become the primary motivating factor in European history until the Enlightenment, with its concept of linear time, matures.

As European colonialism develops, a nation will be distinguished from an empire. Nationality is based on shared ethnicity, often itself used to explain or condone the need for the cohesive governmental structure. People in the dominated, conquered, or uncivilized ethnic groups are not considered individuals. They cannot form the structures of governance or of the marketplace by personal and rational effort: their minds, then, are not presumed superior to the systems that determine their actions, as European minds are presumed to be. To be sure, nationality and "race" are not equivalent concepts in empiricism: the former is usually accepted in empiricism and the latter usually discredited. In empiricism, nationality is primarily a social contextualizing of the individual, while the idea of race suggests, at least until recently, the bearing of innate properties. Empiricism currently uses "ethnicity" as a mediating concept: shared biological traits are accompanied by shared learned behaviors, not innate propensities. This avoids the fascist connotations of "race." For empiricism, "race" now names the largest human classifications sharing multiple physiological traits, including (as especially important) skin color. "Ethnicity" names subdivisions of race, usually coinciding with the boundaries between or within nations.

Human essence remains distinct from individuality in empiricist modernity and is manifested in a universalized rationality, understood to be the purest exercise of self-consciousness. Rationality is supranational. In empiricism, ethnic and social behaviors are learned habits, contingencies of birthplace, often extraneous or detrimental because they are irrational. "Human nature" and the faculty of reason are defined as invariants. Holland, the home of Spinoza and of many seventeenth-century Huguenot émigrés after Louis XIV revokes the Treaty of Nantes, establishes the model for basing intellectual tolerance and freedom of thought on this idea of the universality of rationality.

Older notions had placed the manifestation of personhood (not quite "individuality") not in an ethnicity conceived as a learned set of beliefs and behaviors but rather in "race"—the idea of a people, a folk, or a nation possessing inherited physical, behavioral, and temperamental traits. (Color frequently serves as an external signifier of membership.) While the origins of race or "a people" are left obscure or mythologized by the transcendentalists, they are believed real and permanent—or at least attached to a process (eventually Hegelian) that is permanent. Each person exemplifies the race. Once philosophical transcendentalism allies itself with nationalism in the German Federation, race serves the function that voluntary citizenship serves in empiricism. In this politicized transcendentalism, the race acting in unison—Fichte's and Herder's *Volkgeist*—bonds the community or the "country" through the expression of natural psycho-physiological elements. In empiricism, on the contrary, the political union that comprises the nation is contractual. A constitution creates the possibility of nationality for the individual who joins it. Birth offers automatic membership; yet, in a notable innovation, people can voluntarily become citizens of countries where they were not born.

While a politics of race relies on the intrinsic traits of a specific population, an empiricist politics of nations relies on a universal reason or universalized natural characteristics of mind: political structures are conceptual designs discovered by this human reason. Nature and reason are conjoined. The empiricist universalization of natural features that are mental structures and potentialities, not behavioral or temperamental determinants, creates humankind as a whole and therefore allows the universalization of "rights." Rights are legal boundaries believed to be logically necessitated by the basic characteristics of a universalized human mentality; to impede them would be unnatural, hence ethically mistaken. The origin of rights must be placed outside history; otherwise they would be mere conventions or opinions. Rights can then become the motivation for revolution.

Empiricism's secularized universality of reason replaces the religious universality of the Middle Ages. The universality of mind as essence competes with the universality of soul as essence. Natural rights and laws, legitimated by appeal to a universalized inviolable logic, nullify the daily intrusions of God's wishes and dictates or of his delegating authority through "divine right." The advancement of society consists of increasing the harmony between the essence of humans and their social structure, between nature (again, Locke and Newton's nature, not Rousseau's) and society. That the struggle between empiricism and its antagonists always involves elevating some specific form of universality clarifies why the Middle Ages again become compelling for those seeking an alternative to empiricism. Catholicism's universalizations (its catholicity) struggled to displace the earlier universalization of political structure: in the Roman system, human essence had been an assigned or inherited civic ranking. Christianity employs the empire's structures (subordination of the Celts; relatively safe mobility) as conduits for expansion and integrates certain political practices into religious forms, including the church hierarchy, the use of Latin, and ecclesiastical law. Whether the fundamental determinants of universality are to be placed inside or external to the individual is the underlying dispute between Christianity and Aristotelianism. In the former, essence is interior immortal soul; in the latter, essence is citizenship: the soul is as mortal as the body.

In the late seventeenth century, empiricism gained control over the universalization of humankind. This universalization is modernity. Capitalism and socialism, both claiming the legitimation of reason and natural law, were eventually to become modernity's chief economic means. Philosophical transcendentalism and idealism, in reaction to empiricism, originally tried to universalize subjectivity by universalizing certain contents of mentality (e.g., Kant's categories or idealist intuition) rather than only the structure (mechanisms) of mentality. The more politically influential form of transcendentalism, however, individuates the essences of national and ethnic groups—particularly in Germanic romanticism, which a century and a half later will be used to corroborate fascism both in Italy and Germany. In romanticism in England and France, the approach is to universalize emotional capacities (spirit, sentiment) in opposition to the neoclassicist's empiricist universalizing of logical deduction and good (not common) sense. When it comes to nations and races, the empiricist is (in medieval terminology) a nominalist; the idealist is a realist. The word *Reich*, for example, a realm or domain, cannot be used as equivalent to the term *nation*. For the idealist, political consent is a form of both voluntary and mandatory *obedience*. For the empiricist, political participation is a form of voluntary contractual *consent*.

Attempted compromises appear in the late nineteenth century. Darwinism and Hegelianism are quickly, even if impermanently, made compatible by placing a spiritual or at least mental force—*Geist* or *ésprit* or *élan vital*—inside mechanical (biochemical) causation. This union at first seems indebted to Schopenhauer's earlier reification of a universal Will and, within empiricism, justified by the assertion of Darwin and Lamarck that animal traits develop because intention or desire can be transmitted to offspring. The giraffe stretches its neck because it wants to get food, so the offspring inherit long necks: so went the argument preceding Mendelian genetic theory and the idea of "spontaneous" mutation. Evolution comes to have goals. Humans incorporate, summarize, and fulfill these goals. The history of "life" becomes a biological teleology, since it includes desire. Allowing desire to function as a motivation grants evolution mentality; this is used to affiliate the theory with the older theology, in which creation is the outcome of the exercise of God's will. God's will, external to the creation it causes, is transformed to a will interior to nature, just as science had earlier put physical forces inside inert matter.

The sustained popularity of Hegelian philosophy temporarily, albeit uncomfortably, allied the incompatible strains of naturalism and transcendentalism. This is also Bergson's strategy, although Bergson can claim an affiliation with naturalism that Hegel cannot pretend to. Bergson discards the metaphysics (although today the *élan vital* seems metaphysical) by turning Schopenhauer's reified Will into a natural empirical force. Quasi-physical evolutionary forces of movement (desire, need) are conceived both as the physical cause of nature, humanity, and society and as their logical structure, although in each case the possibility of voluntary commitments and decisions are admitted. Again, this permits some reconciliation between empiricism and transcendentalism. As transcendental *cause*, the evolutionary "force" is neither natural (since it is the cause of nature) nor material; as transcendental *structure*, it is dialectical, at once a logic and a movement. As empiricist *cause*, these evolutionary forces are the apparently natural propensity of inert matter to coagulate into organic molecules under specified atmospheric conditions; as empiricist *structure*, evolutionary force is the struggle for survival.

Freud's theory also contributes to empiricism in a mediating role. It provides a universalized psychology of urge (the mechanisms of the unconscious are presumed to operate identically everywhere), just as Darwin's and Bergson's theories had provided a universalized biology of urge.

From the seventeenth century onward, the word *instinct* had designated an inherent motivation in animals to perform actions benefiting them—a built-in unconscious rationality, as it were. Rousseau's "instinct" (which he called our surest guide) is the transformation of this idea into a human faculty comparable with, and a forerunner of, idealism's "intuition." But in modern genetic theory, based on chemical mechanisms, animals seem to act in their best interests only because their ancestors who have had certain behaviors survived to transmit the behavior. A mechanistic genetic theory circumvents the role of desire. The link to rationality or self-ishness can be broken, since behavior can be attributed to a purely mechanical origin in linear time. In earlier nonevolutionary theories, the origin of seemingly rational animal behavior had to coincide with the creation of the animal, presumably by God at the "beginning," and time was not an ingredient. Empiricism reasserts its proprietary claim on Darwin by universalizing the mechanistic nature of genetic instinct. Instinct serves the impulse toward survival—or more specifically, for reproduction (that the former becomes converted into the latter is an intriguing development)—that nature alone has created. Individual traits within species are empiricist means, not ends; they evidence nature acting, not God's having reached decisions. Furthermore, all humans are considered by empiricists to constitute a single species, since the criterion for species membership is breeding ability.

• • •

In both capitalism and socialism, human will is to operate under the guidance of universal truths discoverable by reason. They are both empiricisms. Nevertheless, there are conceptual distinctions between them.

In a Marxist socialist theory, secular history is the evolving of the necessary with the cooperation of free will. History is as law-determined as physical systems are. In capitalist theory, secular history is not determined but evolves under the leadership of free will. Human freedom harnesses physical laws, so that history can be fully determined by human decision. In Marxism, as in Hegel, history yields human freedom; in capitalism, human freedom yields history. In both systems, what ought to be is posited: but in socialism what ought to be is also what must be (as Spinoza had argued), and that human history includes the evolution of the awareness of historical lawfulness contributes to the enactment of necessity. Intention is also compliance. Such compliance, which is a reconciliation rather than a subservience, is inseparable from successful political activism. In capitalist democracy, what ought to be is not an eventual necessity but a conclusion reached through evolving rational assessment. For socialism, the truths about the historical process as a whole, necessary to advance history, have come to be recognized only recently; these new insights can now be transferred to the long-suppressed proletariat. For capitalism, the necessary truths were discovered quite some time ago by the intellectual community that the union of democracy and private property both generates and sustains. For socialism, that group is least likely to discover the truth.

In socialist politics generally, transcendent human freedom is paradoxically constrained and limited by scientific determinism. In a capitalist politics, scientific determinism is (equally paradoxically) escaped, through a liberation of the will by human freedom. Each of the two systems uses the theory least compatible with its underlying assumptions to constrain the extreme logical consequences of those assumptions. Each system has as its internal control a principle in conflict with its basic tenet. The productive energy in either system is transformed into stable social structures through this constraint. Socialism has human freedom somehow serve historical necessity; capitalism has scientific necessity somehow serve human freedom. Political equilibrium is achieved through this conceptual incongruence.

Modern political structure, accordingly, by its very nature always requires the imposition of constraints that must be illogically derived. This is how ideology works and how it differs from the ostensible rationality of, say, philosophy. In philosophy, illogicality is error in the argument; in ideology, illogicality is itself the structure of the argument, which serves to keep opposites in a stable, and hence socially productive, tension. The ideological illogicality provides both the impulsion and the constraint that allows a society to believe that it can remain in an orderly and stably evolving historical path (as the conflict of gravity and inertia yields the smooth elliptical paths of planetary bodies). At the same time, ideology places checks on both exploiting the system (selfishness) or escaping it (deviance or subversion). Laws forcibly check selfishness by punishment; social programs, from education to public welfare, check transcendence by making it a category of socialized behavior, as in the classroom, the secularized neighborhood church, or the clinic. In both capitalism and socialism, everyone has a foot in two camps, not without confusion. One fully accepts both the premises of the system and the limitations imposed on the enactment of those premises. The politics of modernity, then, rests on a conceptual incompatibility that motivates the system and keeps it within bounds; accepting this conceptual incongruence underlies citizenship. The free individuality of the modern ego is in constant encounter with the social and economic system that can only define individuality by setting limits inside which it must operate.

While both socialism and capitalism are presumed grounded in reason, Marxism claims to have the primary causal process of history on its side: the citizen participates in a process that has also caused that citizen's subjectivity. Capitalists, however, congratulate themselves as the cause of history: their subjectivity determines the causal process. For Marxism, knowing the origins of selfhood is considered a necessary ground for thought and belief. In capitalism, ego has been detached from selfhood—the me detached from the I; the subject has turned into object. In capitalism, ego does not care to know its origins, since it wants to be the source of itself. That source is not to be the body (the repugnance toward a purely sexual origin has been discussed earlier) but the mind, as if mentality were not a constructed subjectivity but an autonomous object that can reproduce itself like the body does.

"Scientific" democratic capitalism requires a continual alliance with religious belief, since only in that way can individuality and personality perceive (or deceive) itself as having overcome the materiality of "economic man." In American polls, for example, nearly everyone claims substantial religious beliefs, whatever their behavior. Religious structures preserve the sanctity of the self that would otherwise fall into irremediable depression. Marxist socialism is a forthright materialism that openly acknowledges the body as the source of mentality; religion is presumed irrelevant, a view truer to science but for that very reason immensely threatening to personality. As various communist governments have learned, such an attitude toward religion proves to be a tactical error, although certainly not a logical error.

Since most people find it uncomfortable to learn that the ego is ungrounded in any transcendental origins, that its origins are materialistically explicable, the ego distracts itself by a focus on productivity. Solitude—more specifically, being at economic rest—becomes intolerable. In both capitalism and socialism, making and consuming things becomes the most important social function. The work week has not been reduced from forty hours (an optimistic prediction forty years ago) because the individual could not psychologically endure it: and there is evidence that the hours committed to work in many settings has actually been increasing—in the United States and Japan, for example. Where substantial vacations are mandated by contract, as in some European countries, and often taken simultaneously (the factory closes), vacations remain subordinated to the planning schedule of the encompassing economy. "Vacation" only has a meaning in relation to the structure of work from which it is an authorized respite, and contemporary vacations entail sizable planned expenditures and detailed schedules.

In Enlightenment politics, history identifies with spatial and temporal internationality. All humans existing at any moment are connected across space with each other and with their predecessors and successors through time. The physical form of the connection is media: most significantly, in modernity, thought contained in books. Each generation is obliged not simply to continue the project (ordinary tradition) but to redefine and carry it forward in new and unexpected ways (progress). Continual advancement is essential: the idea of progress reflects modernity's scientific principle (Newton's law) that forward motion continues indefinitely unless impeded.

This vision Europe and the United States have exported to the rest of the world. Exporting a social and economic system, in addition to the goods produced by that system, marks one of the differences between mercantilism and capitalism. Progress in history is like productivity in manufacturing. The motivation for change (progress) is assumed to be a set of beliefs and strategies that have emerged at a specific moment in history; before that, history had been largely misguided and haphazard, its events like products from an inefficient cottage industry. History becomes subject to rational free will exactly at the point when all else is gathered inside scientific materialist causality. Freedom emerges for humanity just when everything else has lost it.

Human characteristics not directly relevant to the encompassing historical project of modernity become assigned to private life, to personal idiosyncrasy. Traditions and customs become quaint and sentimentalized; or else they embody superstition and ignorance. The distant past becomes texts in the archives and uninhabited monuments, placed in the hands of antiquarians. Destiny and the concept of God's (perhaps hidden) intention are replaced by determinations of human intellect. A "goal" is invented in the present and then thrown ahead into the future as an attracting force: a reified temporarily transferable intent. That we are "pulled" into the future, rather than pushed from behind, also reflects modernity's cosmology, specifically the discovery of gravity: creating a goal is like casting off a moon, which then draws the tides. Effort and will, motivated by reason (including Adam Smith's proposition that selfishness is reasonable), create the design of history. The concept of fate or fortune is overcome. Caesar had a destiny; we have a plan.

In both socialism and capitalism, the pliability of human character (beliefs, attitudes, behavioral tendencies) is unrestricted. Anyone may be taught to reason. However, in the aspect romanticism inherited from German idealism and later bequeathed to fascism, race and community membership are determining forms. In socialism and capitalism, reason uses will to implement its judgment; in fascism, will uses reason to implement its desire. For the empiricist, will fuels consciousness; for the idealist, will constitutes consciousness.

For the empiricist, society is to be the product of a subjectivity that through an awareness of the distinction between its content (facts, experiences, beliefs, desires) and its universalized essence (reason) can determine its response to its own origins. Freedom emerges from understanding this distinction. The modern ego is the entity that, in theory at least, understands this and exercises its will in accord with it.

For the transcendentalist, the content of subjectivity must take a form matching the structure of subjectivity. As fascism arises, this becomes the idea that the essence of a specific society and of the subjectivities that compose it are identical; this essence is not (as for the empiricists) reason, but the form given to reason by an innate psychic inheritance. From this view, therefore, the modern ego errs in distinguishing itself from its origins. The self does not construct society by applying its will; rather, the will of the self and the reified will of the society from which that self has emerged are two aspects of the same phenomenon. For the transcendentalist, empiricist individuality is the creation of an entity that, by seeking to master its own origins, falls into a deplorable disharmony with those origins. This disharmony is often manifested—as the expressionists in prewar Dresden and Munich also perceived—as social pathology, personal unhappiness, anxiety, greed, or despair.

• • •

Before its mechanization in biochemical genetics, evolutionary theory in biology is a theory of will, the will to survive. Life is defined by will. In empiricism, to act with a purpose requires knowing the purpose. But with will described as a quasi-scientific force, outcomes are the result of pressures. Unlike goals that pull, will pushes. Evolutionary theory comes to depend upon this concept: will causes behavior. The whole process of evolution is part of the natural order of things; all of animal nature is reified will in physical form. Nevertheless, an empiricist theory of reason continues to ask that humans subordinate this natural will to reason and escape the nature they come from. But since reason is also considered a natural endowment of humanity, humans are naturally unnatural.

Of course, even a theory of intellect requires motivations for the setting of goals, which themselves must be desire-able; and this seems to require some prior will. One can always trace mentality back to an act of will that logically precedes intellection (from where comes the will to deliberate?)—and this undermines any Enlightenment theory of reason. Freud makes this primal will an unconscious so it can then be raised into consciousness by reason; by means of a geography of mentality, the unconscious can then be dominated by reason. Imperial reason colonizes the "primitive" unconscious. Reason forces will to assume a direction the will would not of itself have assumed, although (paradoxically) reason has no power to exercise its coercion other than through the power of will itself. Reason inverts its subordination to the will through the process of knowing it, of exposing its secret schemes. Knowledge is power. Through natural reason humanity masters its own origins.

In contemporary evolutionary theory, "will" might be understood to have arisen from chance, an electrochemical process that began "life." Chance requires time, because chance is a distribution of possibilities over time. Any theory of probabilistic evolution makes time and a supply (an admittedly large supply) of material in motion sufficient cause for any phenomenon. "Life" is defined as the presence of behavior that can only be accounted for by reasons for it (behavior is motion produced by motivation), a reason being an internal striving toward survival or pleasure. Some level of consciousness is presumed necessary, but not self-consciousness: a being need not know itself. Humans are the ones who decide whether such a reason exists or not, whether the object under scrutiny should be called an organism or not. Human reason defines the difference between organisms and other objects by having the essence of an organism correspond to the logical structure of reason: the relation between purpose and behavior resembles the connection between premises and conclusions. This does not make any organism reasonable or rational; rather, it makes its structure correspond to the structure of reason. The cloud moves, we conclude, for a different reason than the mole moves. The cloud moves not because of internal motivation. That there is a reason is not the same as something *having* a reason.

The faculty of reason requires self-consciousness. That consciousness of consciousness has developed in a specific organism (humans) is an inexplicable fact in any theory where mentality arises during evolution from materiality. Although the originating causal relations between mentality and materiality are baffling, it is assumed that at some point "life" gains a mental structure that parallels its physical behavior. Self-conscious reason is understood as the way "life" is able to come to know what it is. "Life" then can provide its own definition.

Humans could have recognized the existence of a nonliving material universe only subsequent to an original presumption (humankind's earliest presumption) that everything is living. That the lifeless exists is a deduction self-consciousness can make only when it reaches the point where it can assign criteria for what is unlike itself. The category of the lifeless begins with minuscule content, perhaps no content at all when human consciousness first emerges. The category steadily expands as reason progresses, until the vast universe, once permeated by life, is almost entirely empty of life. Science develops when this recognition proceeds far enough to isolate the lifeless as its object and to establish systematic (causal) relationships between objects. These relationships are determined by law-abiding forces, not by motivations, intentions, or impulses contained inside objects. (This distinction marks the difference between modern science and Aristotelian science. Recall that for Copernicus the planets traveled in circles because of internal compulsion, not because of a physical relationship to the sun, which gravity later adds.)

In capitalism and socialism, evolution is a process generating a creature who can subordinate will to reason. Reason displaces chance. The mathematical probabilities that underlie the evolutionary process become of decreasing importance, perhaps inoperative for humans. (Even genetic engineering becomes feasible.) Ideally, human intention can assure that of all possibilities only one (the best) emerges—the utopian future. In empiricism, the future can be planned because human nature can be objectively known, hence maximally satisfied. Unlike animals, humans not only can experience pleasure or the satisfaction of urge but they can also identify and create in abstract thought the structures of pleasure and satisfaction, which can then be transformed into political structures.

From the perspective of idealism, however, humans cannot use reason to know a world from which they are completely detached, as objective observers. Rather, humans know the world through the structures of subjectivity, including reason, that determine the form in which the world can be known. The structure of reason is not separable from its object. In empiricism, reason develops *in* consciousness; in idealism, reason develops *as* consciousness. In empiricism, will becomes dominated by the faculty of reason although, oddly, reason has no power over the will except by deploying the power of the will. In idealism, will becomes strengthened as natural reason provides the predetermined channels into which it will flow. That is, in empiricism, will is given "directions" (orders, commands), while in idealism will is given "directions" (order, routes). In both empiricism and idealism, political structures separate humanity from the rest of nature. In empiricism, this separation is explained by subordinating will to intellect; in idealism, or the political systems that depend on it, it is explained by infusing will with intellect. In empiricism, reason emerges as human self-reflexiveness. In idealism, will constitutes self-reflexiveness.

As empiricisms, both socialism and capitalism qualify or circumvent Darwinism by arguing that reasoned altruistic cooperation overcomes the unreasoned mechanisms of a purely selfish nature. "Reason" detaches humans from their biological will-dominated determinism, overcoming their very origins. For empiricism, reason allows the crossing over from all the rest of nature into humanity: what is externalized is a structure (logic), not a force (will). The externalization of a *structure* (universalized logic) establishes the logical positivists' response to Hegel's having externalized a *force* (reified will, freedom) as if externalizing that force might effect a permanent compromise between idealism and empiricism. Hegel's Absolute, evolving toward freedom, is reified will. Consequently, the "logic" of will is dialectical, the perpetual motion of its content (its ideas), while the empiricist logic of intellect, in contrast, is a set of permanent and contentless rules. The logic of intellect consists of rules of logic in the abstract; dialectical "logic" has no such abstract paradigms free of specific content. (To the analytic positivist, therefore, Continental philosophy is generally illogical or alogical.)

For the empiricist, organization of knowledge is imposed upon the facts by the exercise of discovering (which is the not the same as generating) congruence between the laws of reason (logic) and the laws of nature. The facts are ordered by a volitional act—although not an arbitrary act, since both facts and mind are inherently orderly in the same way because both have "natural" (material) origins. For the idealist, in contrast, knowledge is equivalent to the form of its organization. (This suggests that pragmatism is not quite the empiricism it proposes to be.) It is not that the natural order of external phenomena (the facts) and the natural order of the mind are inherently congruent, but that the world becomes knowable in an act of will. The "world" is equivalent to, not additional to, what appears in subjectivity. For the empiricists, humans are the most advanced creatures; human rationality has freed itself from will so that it can know the world objectively. The "desire" or "passion" to know then becomes absolutely distinct from all other desires and passions, which generally confuse and interfere with the gathering of objective knowledge. The transcendentalist, however, believes that humans are advanced creatures precisely because will and knowledge are interdependent. Unlike in lesser animals, the content of will (desires plus the conscious volition) and the content of the world can be made to match, and known to match. This matching is equivalent to subjectivity itself.

The empiricists admit the apparently incontrovertible evidence for biological evolution. Nevertheless, in order to have a systematic ethics, they must assume that altruism emerges from evolution near to the point when humans evolve, though such altruism at first seems contrary to the presuppositions of evolutionary theory. If the individual animal can protect its best interests by serving the local group as a whole, this capacity must have emerged sometime during evolution. To see this new capacity as arising spontaneously from random mutation seems to beg the question. Yet it seems equally odd to assume that such a capacity is exercised because the animal has figured out what it is doing when it yields its immediate interests to the interests of the group. (Some circumvent the dilemma by arguing that individuals are biologically compelled to protect gene pools by defending offspring and near relatives.) Whether as behavior or as a form of consciousness, altruism cannot be logically made to emerge from evolution. And if one posits that altruism first begins with humans, then do humans choose altruism because they must, driven by genetics? This would not yield an ethics of free will. If, to the contrary, humans can freely choose moral principles, what foundation for these principles can replace an evolutionary origin in the "nature" from which moral principles are simultaneously said to be the escape? Where could altruistic (or any other) moral principles have come from to present themselves as choices? For a short while an intuitive ethics, such as that of G. E. Moore, would be thought a possible solution to this dilemma.[1]

One way of overcoming the dilemma of accounting for altruism is to link the economics of Adam Smith with evolutionary theory. One could argue that the exercise of individual self-interest works at a higher organizational level to advance the society or the species. If in fact evolution has been advancing life toward higher forms, and if this has been based on the exercise of survival mechanisms, then evolution is itself evidence that Smith's principle is a universal natural law beyond human economics. The validity of the economic law is confirmed by the biological law. But by the end of the nineteenth century, it was difficult to sustain the belief that this optimistic interpretation could be applied even in the advanced "civilized" nations. As the modernists recognized, selfish interests yield unhappy social outcomes. The cities were not havens of happy and fulfilled people under capitalism; and those who were happy were happy because they disregarded the fact that material prosperity had been accompanied by spiritual suffocation. It became more frequently reasoned (albeit not by the wealthiest) that the preferable human task would be to replace evolutionary ethics ("social Darwinism") with humanitarianism.

It was also possible to link romanticism and evolution. The aspect of romanticism inherited from idealism that immerses human subjectivity in notions of race, soil, blood, myth, power, and will also provides an alternative to the dilemma of altruism. Human behavior is cooperative within bonded societies because those societies are the original source of individual psyche. The bonding is not so much exercised by unique individuals (the discrete Cartesian selves of contractual democratic capitalism) as it is an inherent mental energy of the society that flows through its members. Nietzsche could identify the energy as a power (an energy whose outcome can be described in terms of domination and subordination), but he could not identify its source. For him, the energy was irreducible. Marx's innovation is that this energy is determined by and reducible to economic relations. Fascism will later attribute the energy to place relations, the interaction of blood (race) and land.

In Marxist socialist theory, intermediary between capitalism and romanticism (though nonetheless an empiricism), the psyche is constructed by the social and economic environment. In Marxism, as in capitalism, the beneficence or harm of a set of relations, or even its possibility, is irrelevant to place. But for Marxism the contents of consciousness do not emerge (as for fascism) from the stream of history, as if the self incarnates all that preceding history as an entirety. Rather, the contents of consciousness are constructed at the time of the organism's specific location in history. Individual selfhood is a construction, not an incarnation. While Marxist socialism is an empiricism like capitalism, it is not a Cartesian empiricism. Socialism denies the belief in a selfhood that is an autonomous entity resembling the egos of employers or employees as they are imagined by capitalism. Socialism rejects the necessity of that relationship, just as it also rejects a selfhood resembling the soul in Protestant thought. The self does not have a historical past; rather, it is given a historical past during the assembly of consciousness. The past—to the chagrin of those outside the socialist system—can be revised. High modernism's notion of a malleable artistic "tradition" is the co-optation by the political Right of this insight of the political Left. If it led to totalitarianism in socialist politics, it equally has led to totalitarianism in art.

The autonomous entity of selfhood that is the Cartesian ego, motivated by forces internal to that selfhood (for the self and the mind are one) and to the body (physical desire and need), corresponds to the objects in an Aristotelian science rather than modernity's science. The self's impulses to motion (action) are internally driven. For Aristotle, similarly, things fall because they have an internal "urge" to proceed to the center of the earth, just as the planets for Copernicus must go in circles. But in science after Newton, the laws concern the relationships between things, not the incipient impulsions within things. Capitalism relies upon an autonomous ego, with free will releasing it from nature's causality, based on a model of objects preceding modern science. Since the self for Marx is constituted in consciousness through relationships, specifically economic ones, the socialist self is fully compatible with modernity's idea of causality. The socialist self is not free in the same way that the capitalist self is presumed free. The socialist self can attain the freedom praised by Spinoza (for Marxist socialism is as much Spinoza as Hegel), a harmonious concord with necessity. The capitalist self imagines itself not as being caused by relations but as freely entering into them. Whether a happy society needs to include knowledge of the real origin of the self is, of course, another matter: it could convincingly be argued that happiness may be *not* knowing this.

The Politics of Fascism

10

Fascism arises during the years when it becomes indisputably apparent that aesthetic modernism will not remedy the problems of capitalism, at least not the spiritual problems. Fascism cannot simply be thought of as a conscious response to the incapacities of modernism. Nevertheless, it is as if modernism had been given the first opportunity to reconfigure European sensibilities. It failed (just as romanticism had failed) because it could not generate a politics equivalent to its aesthetics. German fascism is firmly tied to a specific theory of classical art, in avowed opposition not, significantly, to romantic art but to modern art, which fascism finds repugnant. From one perspective, then, fascism is an alternative to modernism.

Fascism deforms socialism by displacing socialism's empiricism; it also deforms modernism by intensifying modernism's original transcendentalism, modernism's romanticism, of which fascism is a specific kind of pathology. The idea of the artist and artistic inspiration is transferred to the area of political leadership. Fascism presumes the need for a single political party headed by a leader whose genius and inspiration make representative democratic government superfluous. Interestingly, when Hitler joined the German Worker's party in 1919, he listed himself as a "painter." (Hitler had been twice refused admission to the Vienna Academy of Art and for a time sold his work to support himself, barely, in Munich.[1])

Fascism endeavors to remedy the failures of both modernism and socialism to curtail or meliorate capitalism, and it employs a military nationalism to promote a self that defines as its essence the culture that germinated it. Personality is believed to be a configuration of this innate essence, a transcendental notion. Freedom is the voluntary exercise of loyalty, neither to the members nor to the structure of the sociopolitical system but to the *essence* of that system, which corresponds to the essence of those individuals whose genealogies have occurred, over numerous generations, in the same place. Individuals are bound to one another by way of the shared essence that precedes any specific personal ties, even at times those of the immediate family. Consequently, individuals are psychologically isolated, even if metaphysically connected, and exceptional measures must be taken to have them perceive themselves as integrated. (While individuals under capitalism are isolated economic entities, they negotiate directly with one another; this is considered a strengthening of political bonds, which are voluntary, not a threat to them.) Political cohesion can only be maintained in fascism by provoking a constant military exuberance, by displaying persistently visible legal mechanisms (the ubiquitous presence of uniforms), and by treating national, ethnic, and racial ties as essential metaphysical qualities and values, expressed in public rituals. (A government does not, of course, have to call itself fascist to control its population in this way.) Freedom in fascism is the determination (the will-ingness) to subdue individualistic self-expression or self-knowledge, since the contingent should not subdue the essential.

True, the affiliation of romanticism and leftist politics reoccurs—whether during the French Revolution or the events of 1848 or the 1960s counterculture—and even today abides. But it was the political and military might of the alliance of the sources of romanticism and the Right that threatened to overwhelm Europe in the 1930s and the 1940s. In fascism, the philosophical source of romanticism is resurrected as the force of will incarnate not in the artwork—as, for example, when much contemporary German discussion of German expressionism concerned its Gothicness[2]—but in the people. The aesthetic rituals of the fascists are their political rituals. For them, modern art is capitalist and bourgeois; its ironies, its tolerance of opposites in suspension so essential to the modernist aesthetic, are weaknesses, degeneracies.

While fascism is not simply a transmuted romanticism, this (once common) charge does have merit, if understood correctly. Romanticism was originally inspired by philosophical idealism, although it could abandon almost all of that idealism except for the aesthetics in order to make art and literature the sole ground of creativity and value: this autonomous aesthetics is what modernism inherits. The romantic movement aside, the history of philosophic idealism itself takes the form of a conservative politics (tradition, monarchy) allied with religious orthodoxy, as in Hegelianism: this is what fascism inherits. These distinctions are not clear-cut in all cases, for certain figures remain affiliated both with the romantic aesthetic and with what eventually became an idealist antidemocratic politics. These figures comprise what might be called a "late" romanticism, a reactionary romanticism that can be regarded as a source of support for fascism, even if most late romantics would not have anticipated fascism. (The use of Nietzsche by the fascists, as well as his rehabilitation by those who defeated the fascists, shows the complexities here.) A conservative "late" romanticism is retrogressive, drawing romanticism away from its attachment to French and English progressive social thought back toward German political thought. The fear of this variety of German romanticism led to to the banning of Madame de Staël's *De l'Allemagne* in Napoleonic France in 1810; the book had earlier introduced France to the work of the German idealist romantics, which is not equivalent to the romanticism of Rousseau. Nevertheless, romanticism has been primarily subversive, supportive of revolution; while idealism, although it provoked romanticism in the first place, has commonly been the ally of the political reactionary. Even the German romantics were sympathetic toward the French Revolution before Napolean attacked Germany and confirmed the reactionary belief that the Enlightenment, which had never been pervasive in Germany, had been misguided. (Of course, the English also supported the French until the war with Napoleon, but this did not make the English and the Germans ideological allies.)

In fascism, the romantic aesthetic experience, or at least the romantic temperament, is arrogated by the politicians—but only by once again compelling the course of romanticism back toward the orthodox political and religious elements of the idealism from which romanticism had been once again separating itself, for the second time, as modernism progressed. Fascism also converts religious transcendentalism, the indigenous Christianity, into a nationalistic political transcendentalism. (Romanticism, in contrast, had converted Christian transcendence into a poetics.) Modernism continues the separation of aesthetics from idealism, eventually completing this separation by moving into formalism, avowing its repudiation of romantic influences in the name of a new classicism. (This happens in formalist aesthetic theory and criticism; the romantic personality of the artist was never forfeited.) Of course, modernist formalism would incur the cost of losing the romantics' transcendental idealist aesthetic.

The romantic theory of the *Volk*, attributing different innate "spirits" to different peoples, was of particular interest in late eighteenth-century Germany, since many German thinkers desired to unburden themselves of the long-dominant influence of French culture. (Frederick II had spoken French at court, the native German being too harsh a tongue.) Fascism directs the theory of the folk primarily toward political self-concept, urge, power, and military might, rather than to the summation of cultural achievements in art, literature, music, and language, the interests of romanticism. An art transferred to a politics becomes the doing, not the product; results are actions, not objects. As capitalism must expand by making more things, so fascism must expand by doing more things. Insofar as philosophical transcendentalism originated to overcome the epistemological limitations set on humanity by empiricism, fascism also overcomes these limitations. Idealism does this by a theory of intuition; fascism by a theory of action. While action has limits, they are not epistemological limits—hence action can be full or pure in a way that reasoning never can be. (As Nietzsche argued.[3]) Kant and Fichte tried to overcome the empiricist limitations of knowing by making certain kinds of thought a doing rather than a deducing, a willing as well as a thinking, a need as well as a goal. Romanticism converts these into aesthetic acts, the making of artworks; fascism converts them into political acts, the making of a national identity. Violence, for example, becomes a form of dramatic beauty, accompanied by spectacle, dress, and rhetoric. There are the romantic notions of the hero and the common people; the dominance of a will exercised in the counteracting of insecurity; the elevation of intuition and diffuse emotion; the glorification of passion in commitment. To these, fascism adds the use of inequity as justice, of evil to produce good, of chaos to generate order, and of catastrophe to generate triumph. Intense desperation can be seen as a variety of hope, control as exhilaration, inviolable order as incontrovertible meaning.

In Germany in the twenties and thirties, the romantic aesthetic could not have fully evolved into or been superseded by the modernist aesthetic because romanticism in Germany had been trapped (stuck, as it were) behind World War I. Fascism in Germany results from this confinement of the idealist's transcendentalism, and consequently of German romanticism, inside loss and humiliation, just as high modernism results from the reconfiguration of romanticism in empiricist strongholds prompted by victory. The better days of the past are idealized in politically insecure countries (Germany, Italy, Spain), and romanticism serves, through fascism, as a promise to recuperate them. In France, on the contrary, political liberals and socialists could place behind them the nineteenth-century disillusionments that followed the Revolution, the July monarchy, the failure of 1848, the usurpation of Louis Napoleon, the defeat in the Franco-Prussian War, the failed Communard of 1871. The twentieth century was a new beginning. And England and the United States had experienced decades of only sporadically interrupted prosperity and even tranquility. For the victors, World War I had confirmed not simply their military strength or nationalistic determination but their ideological superiority. As a dialectical conflict of concepts (and war has been viewed in that way since), the war evidenced, by its outcome, some universal moral judgment.

For the English and the Americans, victory was the triumph of empiricism (democracy and capitalism), while for the Germans loss was the humiliation of the conservative politics of idealism that had proven so successful for nineteenth-century Germans that the Hegelians had argued the future of all human civilization depended on it. (An inability to imagine any alternative to a defeated German culture was argued in an earlier chapter to be the source of dada's intended preposterousness.) For the English, Americans, and French, time was advancing as it should, given a theory of evolution based on the survival of the fittest. But from the German fascist viewpoint that same period of time is experienced as having debased place, as if time (the structure of history) were a plague upon place, evidenced by the economic crises of the twenties. And while the Italians were on the winning side, they could not claim to have won anything, since what one "won" was not simply the ethical debate, but land (place). Feeling betrayed by the denial of the land they claimed by right (Fiume, Dalmatia), the Italians turned to fascism even before Germany did.[4] In both countries, fascist place-consciousness overwhelms modernity's time-consciousness.

Fascism, then, inherits those aspects of romanticism grounded in race, ethnocentricity, and geography. As a hostile reaction against empiricist universalizations, fascism opposes both capitalism and socialism (communism) because they posit a universalized equivalence of human nature. In both Italy and Germany, fascism deforms socialism. (Socialism was not legal in Germany at the time of unification; the first socialist march occurred in Vienna in 1890.) Mussolini early broke with socialist colleagues to advocate what he proposed would be an even better socialism; and the twenty-five-point program of the German Worker's party proposed by Hitler in 1920 rested on socialist economic and land reform. In neither place were socialist premises implemented. Fascism is what happens to socialism when the empiricist underpinnings of socialism are replaced by assumptions derived from romanticism, itself based on idealism. More specifically, whereas idealism and romanticism had posited a universal metaphysics that also allowed for theories of race, blood, and land (these latter being unique incarnations of the metaphysics), the basic allegiances in romanticism were to the metaphysics of a universalized subjectivity rather than to the politics of race. The fascists reverse this: their metaphysics can only be derived from the politics, since they refuse to universalize subjectivity, although they retain a romantic metaphysics of will, power, and intuition. Fascism proposes itself as a "national" socialism, to counteract (1) the universalizing principle of empiricism, namely reason; (2) the universalizing principles of capitalism, identified with democratic representative government (disdained because of the inadequacy and docility of the governments at Weimar and Rome); and (3) the universalizing principles of Marxist socialism (the Comintern was founded in Russia in 1919), which had successfully proved its power in the Russian Revolution. Following World War I, fascism promptly disregards the socialist objectives that originally inspired that war because the bond of a racialized nationalism—the idea that a political nation can be defined and made equivalent to the inherent characteristics of the ethnic "people" who dominate it—can be made the essential goal, replacing the universalizations.

In Germany and Austria, the Jews are identified as the worst representatives of all three major universalizations: the worst empiricists because of their increased entry into the intellectual disciplines that challenge common assumptions about what the world is like (as Einstein and the many other German-Jewish scientists would evidence); the worst capitalists because of their growing business prominence;

and the worst socialists since so many socialists, Marx included, were born Jewish. Moreover, since Jews have no country of their own, they purportedly seek to appropriate the countries and resources that belong to others. Finally, by characterizing all Jews as members of a single physiological clan or biological "race," religious practices (which many Jews had already discarded) could be obviated as a criteria of identification.

In fascism, transcendental religious sentiments become cultivated as a political force, as the myth of racial destiny. Fascism neither denies religion nor outmodes it but converts it into a geographical politics. Here, too, a proposed universalizing inter-nationalism (Catholicism) is transformed into a fascist nationalism. Again the universal is disregarded in favor of the particular. Hitler becomes a political force first in Bavaria, a Catholic area.[5] (In Italy, Catholicism and nationalism could be equated: the papacy is there.) Protestantism is disparaged by fascism for the same reasons it was disparaged in the days of Louis XIV—as the ally of bourgeois representative government and liberal freethinking.

• • •

An important aspect of modernism, then, has its roots in the same tradition as fascism: namely, transcendentalism and romanticism. However, the relationship between modernism and fascism is here drawn inversely, to show them as conflicting manifestations of shared underlying structures. For the most part modernism quite readily forsook its transcendental inclination as fascism expanded. Between fascism and modernism there is, then, an important relationship of inverse proportions: modernism gradually relinquishes the transcendentalist tendencies that fascism increasingly appropriates for itself. The politics of idealism co-opts, by replacing, the aesthetics of idealism. By the midthirties, as fascism flourishes, literary high modernism has become fully a formalist discipline—a "classicism" that it believes (not quite accurately) to be in opposition to romanticism. The use of terms like *spiritual*, once commonplaces reflecting modernism's residual romanticism, slowly lapses. In the visual arts as well, the movement to formalism is advancing, even if more slowly than in literature because of its affiliation (in contrast to high literary modernism) with the socialist Left.

Modernism's romanticism never entirely disappears, of course. As the twentieth century progresses, what can possibly substitute for romanticism as the authorization for the aesthetic experience within modern art in capitalist nations? Empiricism cannot provide so appealing a setting or rationale for artists and artworks. Through the thirties Marxist socialism (in communist guise) seemed to provide a suitable alternative for many people in literature and the other arts seeking an internal modification of empiricism (modernism's basic role, after all). This alternative becomes infeasible, or at least imprudent, in the conservative fifties, following disclosures about Stalinist Russia. High modernist formalism intensifies its suasion over literary studies; and the visual arts detach formalism from the political Left, which allows formalism to flourish there, too.

Because empiricism can suggest no alternative foundation for an aesthetic, romanticism was surprisingly rehabilitated and revitalized once fascism was defeated. Romanticism, at least of the English if not of the German kind, has steadily been regaining acceptance and prestige. From the sixties onward, literature in particular, as a critical and academic field, moves from either political neutrality (uninvolvement) or the political Right (anti-Marxism, not fascism) back toward the Left, where romanticism began. The union of romanticism and modernism has sustained, and still sustains, the belief that capitalism might still be spiritually reawakened from within.

• • •

In modernism, the idealism behind romanticism underlies the notion of who the artist is, even after the empiricism behind critical formalism has come to describe what the artwork is. In modernism, idealism comes to reside in the artist, while empiricism comes to reside in the artwork. Artistic self-concept is sheltered inside the modernist mind as a mode of alienation. This alienation is often linked to the Marxist concept of the same name, as it is in philosophical existentialism, which is phenomenological midmodernism; but the alienation Marx ascribed to the working class is a variety of consciousness, not of self-consciousness. Under capitalism, the alienation cannot be recognized as such by the participant. For the modernist artist, on the contrary, alienation is the most prominent level of self-consciousness, a principal feature of a personality surcharged with talent (or the supposition of talent) but politically powerless. For the socialist, alienation is a suppressed disability; for the modernist, alienation signifies insight, awareness, and even potential talent. For the socialist, alienation characterizes the masses; for the modernist, alienation characterizes the elite.

Both modernism and fascism create prophet-leaders. Fascism is part of the transference of theocratic power into the mind: the Kantian categories and the idealists' intuition are situated neither in the isolated entity of a single mind (the Cartesian *cogito*), nor in the Absolute of all mind, but somewhere intermediate, in the racial mind, or *Volkgeist*. In modernism, as in romanticism, artists and writers become a distinct stratum of society—an ennobled and elevated *Kraftgeist*, as it were—for similar reasons. Only the geniuses can fully exercise certain forces and powers; the belief in a hierarchy of humans ordered according to their inherent value follows. (That outlook is firmly embedded in the obvious elitism of high modernism.) Since romanticism is part of the reaction against inherited aristocratic privilege, the presence of the innate aesthetic faculty does not depend on the social circumstances of birth: artistic capabilities appear in unexpected places. For fascism, the romantic concept of a specialized innateness takes a political instead of an aesthetic form. Like modernism, fascism does away with parentally determined qualifications for leadership but applies criteria to classify the inferior, the ordinary, and the superior. This is likewise true of literary high modernism: the purported antagonism toward romanticism, seemingly based on aesthetic and emotional criteria that will produce more unified and perfect artworks, is also the elitist formation of an aesthetic aristocracy. Fascism assigns various degrees of innate value to different races, as modernism generally does not; being an artist or not is the primary modernist distinction. Yet the anti-Semitism of prominent high modernists cannot be explained away.

Race is the primary fascist human classification. The person is born into the race. The family is a unit of race. In contrast, in democratic capitalism and socialism, the person is born into humanity rather than into the faith. As in Protestantism baptism comes later on, with consent, so in democracy "baptism" involves reaching the age of maturity (the vote). The family is a unit of enlightened governance. The person relies upon the universalized power of reason. One can personally create one's primary memberships—by education rather than inspiration or talent rather than faith. Membership often extends worldwide. One becomes a "scientist," a "writer," a "teacher," and all other categories are subordinated.

While the socialist finds the cure for alienation in equity, the fascist argues that the presumptions of democratic equity are the cause of social enervation. The cure is the assumption of one's place within an ordered social stratification. (Human essence was similarly defined in the Roman Empire before Christianity internalized essence as soul.) For the socialist, equality is the bond; for the fascist, the hierarchy is the bond. In Marxist communism, the self is a nexus of mental forces at a point in time and space (if two strings are tied together, the knot is not a separate entity). But in fascism the self is the physical embodiment of forces that assume the discreteness of entities (humans) as these forces move through time and space—a Hegelianized, nationalized, spiritualized individuality. Fascism can be seen as a return to those aspects of Hegel from which Marx had freed himself. As a philosophical debate, the combat between fascism and communism can be understood as the struggle for control over Hegel. Fascism would then be a transcendental socialism, in contrast to Marx's empiricist socialism. In Marxism, the self is a mental construction, an environmental product; in fascism, the self is a bodily incarnation, a manifestation of the metaphysical.

In socialism, the sharing of a self-definition is the insight that forms the community, an insight conditioned by education. In fascism, members of the community are bound by inherited essences. Socialism cultivates voluntary commitment; fascism promotes innate obligation. The fascist self is not controlled but confirmed; every self is a recuperation by incarnation of the reified racial will, striving for its own fulfillment. In Marxism, however, an autonomous reason—the logic of the society's socioeconomic relations—precedes individualized selfhood. The shape of the self is determined by history, which is not (as for the fascists) will infused into time, but a lawful causal chain. Will has not caused history, although now that selfhood has reached a certain point, reason can change history by employing will. For socialism, the ideal self has yet to emerge; humanity is incomplete. The ideal self of fascism is the re-strengthening of an entity already long completed, which modern history has debilitated. (On this issue, socialism is to fascism as evolutionary theory is to fundamentalist creationism.)

Both fascism and socialism oppose capitalism. But while the conflict between socialism and capitalism occurs inside empiricism, the conflict between fascism and capitalism occurs between transcendentalism and empiricism. Before World War I, and before fascism was given its name, a number of movements in France and Germany combined aspects of militarism, racial and national pride, royalism, antiparliamentarianism (a disgust with the government of France as well as with England's 1832 Reform Bill), anticapitalism, and anti-Semitism (as in the Dreyfus affair). To these reactionaries—whether the followers of General Boulanger, Edouard Drumont, or Charles Maurras—as to the later fascists, internationalist socialism was, like capitalism, a project of the misguided Enlightenment.[6] From the viewpoint of these activists in France, modernity is the modern counterpart of hubris in the Greek tragedies. They perceive European history from the French Revolution forward as a tragic narrative—the central episode being the defeat of Napoleon in 1815, reenacted, or reinvoked, in the defeat of France under Louis Napoleon by the Prussians in 1870, which had been followed by the bourgeois Third Republic. What had happened to the glory of seventeenth-century France?

From the German perspective, not only had humiliation and economic ruin followed World War I, but their antagonists represented the most deplorable of human values: the predominance of economic values, configuring civilization into a bustling marketplace. Unconstrained capitalist competition was not a happy thought for many of those whose ancestors had lived for centuries with the prerogatives of the guilds, whose major concern had been to divide the work among a peer group and to minimize internal competition. Like romanticism, inchoate fascist nationalisms are inclined to look backward with nostalgia. The Italians looked to the days of the Roman Empire, the Germans to the victorious days of the Holy Roman Empire, and the Spanish to the time of Ferdinand and Isabella.

For the nationalist or later fascist parties, the socialists had correctly identified the problems of the modern world: the failure of Enlightenment modernity and the domination of avaricious capitalism. These themes permeate both socialist literature and protofascist literature (in Paul de Lagarde, Julius Langbehn, and Moeller van den Bruck[7])—so much so that as far as the attacks on capitalist money, greed, exploitation, selfishness, depravity, and corruption, the two literatures appeal to the same "facts" and emotions. The opposition to unconstrained capitalism was often expressed even by those not seeking to abolish it (the literary high modernists, for example). Fascism asks a political version of the question raised philosophically by Kantian idealism and aesthetically by both romanticism and modernism: Since empiricism

cannot generate meaning and value but only understanding (a knowledge of cause and effect), where are values to come from? Empiricism,
capitalism, and democracy provide only utilitarian answers; to the
transcendentalist, these seem a matter of momentary convenience,
lacking any ultimate grounding. The socialists, as empiricists, based a
solution to the evils of capitalism on universal equality, rationality,
fully representational government, and science. Socialism shared
these premises with capitalism, not with fascism, since for fascism
these premises seemed to lead only to weak and lethargic governments. Although socialism and fascism at first identify the same enemy (which leads to their political pacts[8]), the communists become the
fascists' bitter enemies. (The ideological grounds become military ones
in the Spanish Civil War.) The major issues are, of course, private
ownership and the proposed universalization of human nature, together with a consequent internationalism in politics. While capitalism opposes socialism on the private property issue, it concurs with
socialism on the universalization; this latter agreement allowed socialism and capitalism to collaborate in World War II to defeat Germany.
Only afterward would the USSR and the United States belligerently
contend for world dominance based on differences concerning the
ownership of land and industrial wealth, a dispute internal to their
shared empiricism, but not with fascism.

In a "nationalist socialism" (Nazism), the worker is recruited
through the "socialism" and the entrepreneur through the "nationalism." This process is not altogether logical, but logic need not be a criterion for political success. All political ideologies, whether beneficent
or abhorrent, are founded on the internal contradictions discussed
earlier. The freedoms yielded by the basic premises are checked against
their full indulgence by controls derived from opposing premises. For
example, "democratic capitalism" recruits the mass of employees
through the sanctity of the ballot (the "democracy") and then recruits
the entrepreneur through the promise of free enterprise (the "capitalism"), which is defined as being business unburdened, to the greatest
extent possible, by any demands imposed by the ballot.

• • •

Following World War I, and during the economic depressions of the
twenties in Germany and the early thirties almost everywhere, fascism
is also a response to other, more encompassing issues of empiricist

modernity. Fascism attempts to escape the shackles of deterministic materialism and the inescapable causality of the smoothly flowing contentless time of the empiricists by binding human nature to place, not duration. Theories of race, earth, blood, and geographical place obliterate the power of time. With its classically columned buildings, built to endure as long as their Roman predecessors, the Reich can be envisioned as relatively unchanged for a thousand years.

In contrast, empiricism obviates place, for the fundamental truths of nature, including human nature, are universalized. Place is contingent; its effects are contingencies, and therefore secondary. Empiricism envisions internationalism and worldwide unification. Truth is everywhere identical; truths are testable propositions. In fascism, truths are not discovered but forged; they are not empiricist propositions but the outcomes of situations demanding action and requiring principles. But principles, even absolutist principles, are different from truths: a principle is a volition in the form of thought, while a truth is a fact in the form of thought. Fascism denounces whoever presumes to have truths free of territorial affiliation whether communists, Jews, capitalists, or aesthetic modernists.

Empiricism made linear time ubiquitous, undermining religious transcendence, which is the relation of time to the timeless. The fascists subordinate linear time not to the timeless but to place. Geography becomes the origin of value; human will, growing like a plant in and from and because of its soil, is the means of the transmission of value. Geography assumes political transcendence. As the romantics had converted the traditional theology (that had once been amalgamated with idealism) into an aesthetics, so the fascists convert this same theology into a politics. Led by fascism, transcendence again becomes society's organizing principle, as it presumably had been in the Middle Ages. Although romanticism and modernism had sought this transcendence in art and literature, they had both lacked the ability to transfer it as a politics into the modern world: their aesthetics was derived from an idealism of the political Left, while after Napoleon idealist politics moved quickly to the political Right. Fascism will accept the politics of the Right and replace the aesthetics of the Left with a revived neoclassicism, the striving for monumentality that always characterizes grandeur on the political Right.

Fascism ennobles place consciousness and abhors its violation by internationalism. Time is transcended by sanctifying place, by combining the Christian idea of a holy land with the Roman idea of an empire. Since the concept of human reason is a universalization (of Aristotelian logic), reason itself must be subordinated by fascism, just as it had been by the medieval scholastics. For fascism, the alliance of time and reason, causation and empiricism, has undermined the values that an atemporal transcendentalism holds in most esteem. Rationality is structured like time because deduction, unlike inspiration, is necessarily sequential. And capitalism is structured on the principle that capital grows by itself by earning interest over time. Money needs only time in order to grow—not in the organic sense, as if money were the plant and time the soil, but in the sense of Newton's first law: all that unimpeded matter requires to continue moving is for time to continue flowing. A number of early twentieth-century German books attack interest on money.[9]

In fascism, time is not the ultimate reality that it is for empiricist physics. Any transcendentalism seeks to discover the conditions for a world in which things exist in time, while these conditions are themselves thought to be independent of time. But what lacks the structure of time, for fascism, is not the transcendentally timeless; rather, it is place, which exists all at once, continuously and permanently. The Reich is not its history, but an inviolable place that conceptually transcends history. For fascism, the Enlightenment is an error, the perversion of conceiving that the essence of history is the efficacious use of time, an efficacious use called "progress." Whether in capitalism or socialism, empiricism releases reason from the very time that structures it, in order that reason can be interjected at will into history. Reason can be transported from place to place, like a movable asset, certainly not like land—as the large movements of immigrants into capitalist strongholds demonstrates. Immigration is repugnant to the fascists.

For fascism, history is to be embodied: the will is manifested in history and the manifestation of the will is equivalent to history. The will is not subordinated to intellect; while the will acts over time, the will cannot control or use time. In fascism, accordingly, political action is not the sum of "free" rational individual consent in a community, as it is in a democracy. Rather, political action is the community's "free" expression (not freedom of choice, but the removal of constraints from necessary action), of which the individual is itself an expression or example. In empiricism, the will moves through time; in fascism, time moves through the will. In empiricism, humans live in time as if it were a medium; in fascism, time lives in humans.

• • •

Fascism's view of time can be contrasted with Darwinian theory, with which fascism might speculatively be linked. Both are theories of the survival of stronger (therefore more suitable) life-forms through the imposition of power on the weaker (therefore less suitable) forms. For both fascists and evolutionary biologists, specific beneficial traits have been precipitated out of innumerable early possibilities; these differences, refined and cultivated, can then serve the fascists as the main categories of value (higher, better), approval, and admiration. Darwinism, however, in contrast to fascism, proposes that the human being is everywhere the result of identical materialistic processes. Differences between races are a matter of secondary adaptive physiological traits, certainly not the development of spiritual substance, idea, or essence. Fascism circumvents the universalizing humanist implications of evolutionary materialism by arrogating a quasi-religious orientation, sometimes in the form of semipantheism. Religious transcendence not only makes the body the manifestation or container of spirit but also permits overcoming time and sanctifying holy places.

Darwinism accounts for the changing physiology of organisms by having change serve favorable (adaptive) accommodations of behavior. Although the modified physiology helps make behavior increasingly adept, the physiology does not directly *cause* the behavior. Rather, the physiological change, randomly induced, *permits* the behavior. The physiological change will be preserved if it increases the chances of the carrier's survival. In Darwinian theory, the actual cause of behavior must be posited as a willing, as desire for an outcome—for food, for mating, for safety. An atemporal, universalized teleology based on will and desire remains necessary, since in all organisms the fundamental needs have always been and will always be survival. Time becomes the medium in which desire moves toward its fulfillment, just as the biological animal moves through space.

Evolution, then, requires time to manifest its adaptions, but the motivations for those manifestations are not themselves determined by time. "Willing" is ubiquitous and undeviating. Empiricism is powerless to explain where such will and desire originate. With its universalist epistemology, empiricism takes biological "drive" for granted. As empiricist psychology develops, "drive" is incorporated as an organic necessity (breathing, eating, mating) causing, not caused by, conscious volition. We cannot will a drive, but the drive makes us will to fulfill it. While these drives are necessary conditions of life, they cannot provide any insight into the purpose or meaning of life. Once theological explanations become less convincing, purpose and meaning must be derived from some inner intuitional source, as Kant, the subsequent idealists, the romantics, and Hegel also perceived. Each believed that the aesthetic experience might be used as a validation. What other possibility was there?

In fascism, however, meaning and purpose become inherent in the basic "drives." These drives are made to include ethnic and political needs and directions, not simply to fulfill biological needs. They are also directed toward manifesting and disclosing inherent human meanings. In such a political theory, ethnicity is treated like a permanent species adaption, geneticized, as it were, in the various "races." The German fascists take an extraordinary and repulsive interest in biological experimentation, seeking the linkage between the body and a racial ethos, which modern Darwinian biology firmly rejects as an object of biological investigation. In fascism, human races are fundamentally and irrevocably distinct. In the Western democracies, however, biological (physiological) features are attributed to genetic make-up (the phenotype is produced by the genotype), a rejection of the idea that political, familial, social, ethnic, or other specific cultural manifestations of specific peoples can be geneticized. (One notes the antagonistic rejections of sociobiology.[10]) Human races have physiological differences in empiricism, since "race" is defined by physiology (specifically skin color). But from the point of view of humanity in general, these differences are superficial. Empiricism denies species differentiation in humans, defining organic species only by the criterion of mating possibilities—obviously the most offensive criterion for those holding a sociopolitical theory of distinct human races.

From an empiricist biological view, cultural expression in art or in politics must therefore be ultimately fortuitous, contingent upon some other "level" of cause and effect whose vocabulary is not that of the biologist. This approach (that there are "levels" of cause and effect) is subsequently used to validate both psychology and sociology as sciences. The truth, for empiricists, becomes the sum total of the facts produced collectively by various autonomous disciplines—a fragmentation of knowledge that is ludicrous to any transcendentalist, whether theological, philosophical, or political. Empiricism then blithely predicts that the theoretical integration of the various disciplines can be anticipated in the not too distant future.

• • •

The modernists were exasperated by much of what they saw, although what they saw, as they well knew, were the conditions that were making modernism possible. The Enlightenment had become entrenched in a capitalist economy where greed, chaos, disruption, human homogenization, and spiritual stultification seemed the price of prosperity, progress, knowledge, and freedom, each of which seemed capable of growing only at the expense of what would make them meaningful. The cost of the Enlightenment seemed to be that it would gain its benefits only by forsaking the meaning that once was the purpose of pursuing them.

Although this ensemble of Enlightenment defects would be rejected by modernists, socialists, and fascists, they do so with differing intentions and by differing means. Modernism endeavors to use the aesthetic experience to enhance the kind of freedom that functions as an essential component of an individualized personality or self-sufficient ego with (ideally absolute) political and economic independence. "Freedom" applies to the individual; the person is free. Modernism serves capitalism, and modern art only flourishes in a capitalist market economy. In a modern capitalist democracy, freedom is institutionalized in the political system: as a structure of human nature, freedom in the individual precedes the political system. Socialism, on the other hand, endeavors to use social and economic relations to create a self for which freedom is a structure of selfhood: freedom inside the social and political system precedes individuality. Individual personhood is a specific configuration of citizenship, not what precedes and consents to citizenship. In capitalism, the members of the social system consent to the system because of the belief that the well-being of society can be calculated as the sum total of the well-being of individuals; in socialism, the well-being of the individual is an example of the general social well-being. In capitalism, the system is the sum of its parts; political morality is a quantitative assessment—if the members are happy, the society is good. In socialism, the parts are derivatives of the system; political morality is a qualitative judgment—if the society is good, the people will be happy.

The Enlightenment vision was to bring determinism into nature even as it brought freedom into humanity. That nature was a fully ordered deterministic system made it available to be manipulated by humans, who were somehow within the natural system yet superior to it by virtue of reasoning mentality, defined for modernity by Descartes as immaterial substance. Selfhood displaces soul as essence. Atemporal reason is the essence of humankind, an essence that excludes the body although it needs a body.

For the modernist avant-garde, the Enlightenment is itself a historical past that must be rejected. Modernism turns modernity against itself. For the avant-garde, the Enlightenment concept of reason seemed no longer a release from time but a shackle to it. The early modernists reasserted a spiritual aesthetic. It might be argued, consequently, that the avant-garde returned to a romantic irrationality and, despite itself, later contributed to the work of fascism. And it is quite true that modernism from the beginning sought to overcome empiricism's limitation on human knowledge by extracting the aesthetics of idealism from romanticism and then discarding the rest of idealism in favor of a generally empiricist worldview. But this is the dilemma, not the solution. In this sense, I have called modernism *transcendental realism*, an oxymoron. The same name I have also given to phenomenology; for phenomenology is to modernism what Kantian idealism is to romanticism.

While fascism shares the early modernist's transcendentalism, it does so not as an internationalized aesthetics but as a nationalized politics. Modernism is one of the glories of modern civilization, and fascism is one of its horrors. The universalization of spirit in art is not the same as the nationalization of the spirit in culture, but the romantics themselves, at least in Germany, failed to make this discrimination. That oversight has contributed to stupendous havoc in the twentieth century, although the romantics hardly can be blamed for all that followed—nor can the modernists, who themselves did not clearly perceive this distinction before World War II taught everyone how essential it was.

Part Four

Concerning the Self

The Sources of
the Modernist Self

11

The original impetus of modernism, under the influence of Comte, the romantics, Hegel, and, later, Marx and Bergson had inclined toward the belief that history contains a stable principle of its own evolving order: historical laws correspond to scientific laws, although room is left for human volition, either to pilot the course of history or to assist or augment it. This outlook is sustained into the twentieth century in both linear (e.g., Marx) and cyclical (e.g., Toynbee) forms. The capability to judge and affect history emerges at some specific point inside human history.

The idea that knowing, studying, and evaluating history can itself be a primary causal factor influencing the future of history, that history can be judged and that such judgment brings freedom, is relatively new (the French Revolution had been meant to test it). Historical study becomes a means to transcend the causal limitations of history. By the 1920s—partially in reaction to the Russian Revolution and the strengthening of socialism, which claims that history progresses in a necessary direction—the pervading ideology wherever socialism is considered a threat is that even if history might, looking back, be seen to have had a direction, it can no longer be believed that history *inherently* has a direction. History is granted a sequencing imagined to be different from the early model of the empiricist causal chain. Theories of fully deterministic causal historical change become modified in other disciplines, too. By the second quarter of the twentieth century, an extensive mathematics of chance and probability has evolved. Notions of the random and the unpredictable increase simultaneously in theories of history, biological mutation, quantum physics, art. What appears to be a logical sequence of events when perceived retroactively is not inherent in the causal process itself. Any sequence is influenced by external, random, unpredictable, and (so quantum physics reveals) theoretically uncalculable influences. Cause becomes a procedural constraint, an epistemological strategy instead of a fixed destiny.

In art and literature, unanticipated artistic genius—for which Shakespeare and Rembrandt serve as proof, just as Picasso will—"causes" histories detached from political and social history. The histories of art and literature have, of course, also caused the works of Rembrandt and Shakespeare, insofar as the methods available to them arose through a process the artists did not cause. Or, as dada and surrealism advocated, the unpredictable and the unconscious (where there is no time) precipitate into history the unexpected, the unexpectable.

The reaction of modernism against capitalism included the presumption that history not only can be but ought to be given a direction and that capitalism had appropriated historical instrumentality through a misunderstanding. As the nineteenth century turns into the twentieth, modernism shares with socialism the belief that unrestrained capitalism requires correction. The original romantic confrontation of capitalism's errors, which lingers in the manifestos of aesthetic modernism, had been to subordinate the social control of governing institutions—whether the aristocracy, the parliament, or the business community—to spiritual and aesthetic influences, especially since one of the charges against capitalism is that it cannot generate culture but instead always debases it. Romanticism was the first purely aesthetically motivated movement not to be dependent on the direct subsidy of any specific social class or group. The romantics supported representative governance yet wished to separate it from the domination of science, of which capitalism claims to be a surrogate. Early non-Marxist socialism, therefore, can also be classified as one of the romantic responses to capitalism.

Modernism looks to this kind of early French and English romanticism that supported the French Revolution. Yet while this romanticism was originally indebted to idealism, all romanticism needed from idealism was its aesthetics. The mid- to late nineteenth-century idealist confrontation with the errors of capitalism should not be confused with modernism's use of early romanticism to confront capitalism: idealism generally favored absolutism in government and the privileging of religious orthodoxy over aesthetics, even when art and the aesthetic faculty were considered essential warrantees of the transcendental. Also, idealism prioritizes pure subjectivity rather than the ego-personality that characterizes the romantic and the modern artist. In its political guise, this idealist (late romantic) outlook later yielded fascism.

The empiricist confrontation of the errors of capitalism is later socialism (the Marxism of *Das Capital*) and a new liberalism (legislative liberalism). The former identifies capitalist error as its theory of property rights but retains the belief that a scientific economics will liberate humankind through technology. (Following the Russian Revolution, portraits of Lenin and Ford were sometimes placed side by side in factories.) The latter retains the belief in capitalist property rights as long as abuses can be limited or eradicated through regulation. (In the United States these two views are, respectively, radicalism and progressivism.)

Social conflicts repeatedly occur from the 1860s forward, usually described by the ideologists as truth versus error and by the politicians as good versus evil. In the twentieth century, liberalism will look to legislative regulation: anti-trust, labor laws, the regulation of commerce. Fascism will look to "blood" (race), trying to forge a scientific idealism; it will take thirty years to demonstrate that this is an oxymoron, at least as far as Western culture is concerned so far. Marxism addresses these conflicts by postulating that the advancement of history toward harmony necessarily requires opposition within the social system as it struggles forward, just as birth is accompanied by pain. Truth emerges from the conflict of propositions enacted as history. History is, as for Hegel, argument; social animosity is the counterpart of propositional logic. (Modern symbolic logic began around the 1840s.[1]) Here liberalism and Marxism part company: Marxism attributes the conflict to the irreconcilable disharmony between the capitalist market economy and fundamental human needs, whether defined spiritually or naturally. Marx's insight is precisely to combine spirit and nature, by maintaining the Hegelian teleological *Geist* while also projecting into the future a human-made, human-dependent utopia. The dialectical materialism (which is from the Hegelian view an oxymoron) demonstrates how an idealism can be converted to an empiricism. Still other movements derive from pre-Marxist socialism, where social conflict results, as in Genesis, from having been ousted from an earlier Eden. Citing Rousseau, some look to early barter and agricultural economies. In the United States, one can look back to Thoreau or the experiments in living like Brook Farm or the evangelical communities in upstate New York.[2]

In each of these cases, an uncontrolled free market economy is identified as needing a partial or total transformation. Wealth itself is the only access to the machinery for producing wealth and to the raw materials on which the machine is to work. Since the only two applicable economic categories are the means of production and the owners of those means, hired human labor is classified as means, like machinery, and human functions become machinelike. The assembly line is not only a practice but also a theory. These manufacturing functions are tediously repetitive and minimally paid; equally important, they are unfulfilling in ways new to human society. Lack of fulfillment can be a technological innovation. The daily labor of being hired to make things becomes detached from one's "life," from that which gratifies selfhood or sustains it. It occurs in a place not included in the definition of where one lives (the factory setting is distinguished from the town, even if it is in the town, from the home, and from the neighborhood). It consists of specific behaviors performed only at work; and workers cannot keep the products they are paid to make (to keep them, they would have to buy them), since the means of production is detached from the ends of production.

Unlike manufacturing tasks, farming tasks change with the seasons and even by the week or time of day. A society with an agrarian economy is based on nature's invariable repetition (the foundation of Greek historical cyclicalism). But progress, modernity's historicism, is based on linear improvement. The distinction between the stable historical cycle, or circle, and temporal linear progression is the same as the distinction between the Euclidian principles of motionless geometry on a flat surface—which is imagined as the ideal surface both geometrically and economically (the flat tillable field: *plane* and *plain* are both Latin *planus*)—and the Galilean and Newtonian principles of inertia and acceleration along a straight line, "bodies" in forward motion (progress, and people on the move). In manufacturing, small operations can be done at any time, at all times. When time is measured by the seasons, work varies according to the transformations internal to this "clock"; but when the clock is a machine that undergoes no transformations (the difference between a machine and an organism), and when each minute is identical to every other, work becomes a set of identical operations repeatable indefinitely. Farming and manufacturing have antagonistic meanings in capitalism.

In agriculture, furthermore, the same products issue from the same resource in the same way every year. In manufacturing, technological advancement allows customary products to emerge more rapidly and cheaply from once nonexistent resources (new machines) and, more significantly, eventually yields altogether new products. From the beginning of human history up until the late nineteenth century, the total number of human inventions of products had been quite small.

Modernists infrequently consider the circumstances of the laboring worker. They frequently assess the rich, the bourgeoisie, the cosmopolitan citizen, the politician, the business owner, and the merchant, finding them complaisant, self-satisfied, greedy, insensitive, philistine, provincial, and having interests limited to the preservation of their mediocre (even when opulent) comfort. Workers are caught in a dilemma not of their own making. Those who intentionally prolong the situation—those with most conscious control and influence—are morally corrupt: they preserve and value what has distorted their humanity. For modernism, those who have the most and those who have the least are both without freedom, although the former are either too selfish or ignorant (equating diversity of economic possibility with freedom) to recognize this. The bourgeoisie can be despised, but not without pity that makes waking them up from their ignorance a justifiable project. One must surmise, however, that they will refuse to be awakened. This refusal then becomes exactly the point of the modernist attack, which has its continued justification only insofar as it proves its point by failing. In modernism, the representatives of aesthetic culture (artists, writers, intellectuals, critics) are permanently in the minority: to join the majority is to sell out. They fight a battle they cannot win, although since not winning it is intrinsic to the project, neither can they really lose.

In the mid- to late nineteenth century, when novelists can trace it, economists analyze it, and sociologists conceptualize it, the claim begins to be made that capitalism can now be seen in its entirety. (Marx identifies such awareness as itself a stage of capitalism.) The idea of progress, it is argued, had become attached to and was thought (erroneously) to be dependent upon a single economic system that could fulfill optimistic social expectations. This reaction to capitalism occurs just when capitalism had advanced far enough to subordinate science, once thought free of social coercions. (Presumably scientific truth ought to be the same in any political or economic system.) In the nineteenth century, capitalism appeared the younger sibling of science: the enactment of the scientific laws of economics. By the twentieth century, the reverse is the case: science is itself a product of the economic system. The subordination of science to the economic system is named "technology." The value of products resulting from scientific experimentation are measured on the same monetary scale as other merchandise. Even the advancement of "theoretical" science becomes a public obligation, a mandatory expenditure anticipating returns. Ideas are a category of financial investment. The discussion of the capitalist system is an active economic component of the system. Science (including the social sciences), formerly the province of amateurs, becomes employment, a profession. One's career can consist of producing ideas.

"Career" defines an area of employment in which the satisfaction of doing the work is one of the criteria stimulating its performance: the work enhances the self, instead of just using the body. Hence status becomes an obsessive concern. Careers also function to generate increased consumer products through ideas, a new type of metaproduct. Thought becomes a commodity not only in the professions, for which law and the lawyer (the secular clergy) very early provide the general model, but also in copyrighted (an eighteenth-century development) books, academic courses, radio programs, films, and the widening field of social and cultural "criticism." That ideas and their transmission can be commodified and controlled by the distribution mechanisms of the marketplace is the nineteenth century's own commercial revelation. And what else is the famous "Communications Revolution" of the twentieth century?

• • •

Empiricist modernity accepts that time flows in a single direction, as if in measured units, although there are no units of measurement except time itself. This premise provides empirical science with time that can be used in physical equations as a consistent linear independent variable. But when the notion of time is released from any religious underpinnings, time becomes a fundamental, a given, uncaused. No longer is time conceptually superseded by a realm of the timeless.

Speculations about whether the soul has an infinite extension in time or whether the soul enters the realm of the timeless are inseparable from the consideration of whether individuality might endure. An enduring individuality seems inextricably bound to ego (I-ness) or, not quite the same, personality. What could individuality be without characteristics? No more than a ladleful of ocean in a glass. Insofar as individuality involves thoughts and feelings, the linearity of time through eternity is a necessity, since thought requires sequence. Thought has the structure of time.

Admittedly, if individuality does not endure, then a realm of timelessness can be posited. But while this was perhaps acceptable in Old Testament Judaism, it is unacceptable in Christianity, the purpose of which is to serve as a belief in a fundamental irreversible individuality that (who) can be punished and rewarded indefinitely.

Both capitalism and the Reformation share in promoting individuality by designating the individual, not the community, as central. The bonds between autonomous individuals establish the community. The Christian soul has been redefined psychologically (by its states, aptitudes, and capabilities) instead of solely ontologically (by the nature of its constituting essence), in a reorientation that had produced the Reformation. The resulting tension between the (new) self and the (old) soul generates the dilemma of modern individuality.

In the "Protestant ethic" the means (the secular achievements of the self) and the end (salvation of the soul), once believed to be in different and irreconcilable ontological realms, must now somehow correspond. But before the full emergence of modernity, correspondence need not entail causality. At the Reformation, protestantism, which needs to subordinate nature, used salvation by faith instead of deeds as a release from the causal power of nature over humans. Faith is a state, but deeds require a causal sequence. Salvation cannot be earned, even though it can be deserved.

Capitalism looks backward to the day Adam and Eve were expelled from the Garden of Eden and told they must labor. The capitalist then looks ahead to Judgment Day, when it will be determined how well this command was fulfilled. Despite the fact that salvation comes through faith, not works, the latter is the paradoxical evidence for the former. In reward for labor there will be a return to Paradise, the blessed state in which work of the laborious kind is irrelevant—even though those with the strongest propensity for laborious work will be the ones most welcomed. The business world is where Christian knights go to prove themselves before returning to court. As population density grows in Europe (the plague disappears around 1660, after a little more than three hundred years[3]), the urban business world provides the field for the tests and challenges once undertaken in or represented by uninhabited or sparsely inhabited regions. The techniques of multiplying money inside wealthy cities allows financial achievement to be substituted for the fabled travels of knightly legends. Exploration is the search for treasure rather than for honor: treasure is a new kind of honor. The legendary dangers once encountered by knights in the outlying regions (now the space for the commercial travel routes linking the towns and cities) become, instead, legal trespasses and violations (as Robin Hood understood), crimes against the entrepreneur.

God's chosen need no longer be tested in the wilderness; in Protestantism, the cities provide sufficient trials. But as the economic system and piety become increasingly separated, economic secularity soon becomes the very opposite of piety. The secularized capitalist can no longer optimistically look ahead to Judgment Day: What capitalist will prosper then? So one surmises instead that the secular future will extend indefinitely, an endless continuation and expansion of technological and economic growth. Society has not lapsed from the Golden Age or Eden but is voyaging toward it. Landing on the shore of North America had represented that return which is simultaneously an advancement, not only to be recovered, but at the same time to be exploited. As capitalism matures, progress is considered a permanent voyage for humankind. This is quite the opposite of looking ahead to the Second Coming, which would abruptly bring to a close a history that has fallen into disorder, as if obeying the principle of entropy. Death, for the person of commerce, has become a secular liability, not a spiritual culmination, an unscheduled interruption; wills and other documents are prepared in order to do business from beyond the grave. The goal is not forgiveness but continued prudence and equity, not salvation but respectability in the eyes of posterity. One agrees to being judged as a contributor to the future of humankind.

Protestantism exchanges the politically inert concept of early Christian community for the politically vital concept of Old Testament Hebraic theologic nationality. This acquires political efficacy in the various Protestant Germanic principalities left unthreatened after the Peace of Augsburg, someday to merge into Germany. But in Protestantism an autonomous individuality substitutes for the Hebraic tribal structure that had defined religious nationality in biblical times. Members of tribes are bound by their bodies; citizens of nations are bound by their mentalities. In early Christianity, joining the community of Christians was an induction into eternal life. In Protestantism, however, the community is constituted by the voluntary assembly of those who bring their innately immortal souls with them. Ideally, such a political community should depend on the consent of the governed. Yet the more distinctly the autonomous individuality of personality (that which consents to be governed) emerges in subjectivity, and the more personality becomes the fundamental communal atom, the less reason there is to believe that such an entity can eternally survive. Personality seems a separation from, not an enhancement of, the older concept of the soul. Originally, despite its individualized discreteness, the soul is a communal notion, derived from God's unified entirety. The soul is in God as the body is in the secular community. To account for each person's unique individuality of personality (if this is assumed primary) requires the emergence of psychology as a discipline. Psychology is not simply the description and classification of temperaments, like the theory of humors had been, but an empirical accounting for the origins of individualized content of mind, for thought and belief. Psychology must always lead to abandoning the notion of an immortal essence: it will always discover the nonmetaphysical origins it seeks, since what it finds has been posited as a condition of the search. When self and soul were conceptually less distinct, even confused, immortality was more plausible.

If there is no warrant of a personal afterlife, then the personal self is irrevocably bound to one small portion of time. Eastern thought allows that such a self is a time-bound construction but believes that the self, accepting this, can abandon its time-bound illusion in favor of timelessness, although this process initiated by the self ultimately disintegrates it. Rather than making time fundamental and then limiting self to a segment of it, both the self and time are structurally congruent in Eastern thought. Although such a view might be made compatible with Western philosophical idealism, it goes further than idealism wishes: in the West, any ultimate relinquishing of self is not helpful but terrifying. When Hinduism becomes popular in Europe before and during modernism, Sankara's Vedanta, from around A.D. 800, proves the most attractive approach. A Vedanta that posits a "true self" (*atman*) allows one to forsake a false self. Through a misinterpretation (since *atman* is impersonal pure consciousness, without individuality), the Vedantic idea of a true "self" is reconciled with the idea that one reacquires what one gives up: you lose yourself in order to find yourself. This view implies a very Christian yet very uncapitalistic principle, that loss will in the long run turn out to be gain. Christianity always offers a remedy for the anxiety about the self's mortality, the ever-present suspicion that self and soul are not identical. Incidentally, the cure can work even for the nonbeliever, since actively accepting and actively denying the idea of personal immortality both, strangely enough, reduce the self's anxiety. Only indecision is painful.

The eventual price of modernity is having to face mortality without the Christian alternative. Modernism at first offers an aesthetic compromise to this dilemma, incorporating a variant of transcendentalism through its initial romanticism. Modernism begins as an attempt to preserve, through art, the idealism that it must relinquish if it is to thrive in the metropolitan environment that feeds it. (Modernists take this nourishment as if it were poison.) The course of modernism will be to perform a reductio ad absurdum on its own groundings, to iron-ize itself. Modernism unintentionally plays out and demonstrates for a modern technological society that transcendence cannot endure; it does this by making art the final bastion of transcendence under the terms of its own surrender. Afterward, options for the meaning of individual personality are placed fully inside time: in history, in economics, in nationalism, and in a secularized artistry where being famous replaces being saved. (Being a genius replaces sainthood.) Each of these areas yields various naturalisms—humanism, economism, Marxism, internationalism, critical formalism. The transcendental counterparts—Hegelianism in history, "spirituality" in art—will evanesce, with one important exception: race and blood in fascist nationalism.

Kant's strategy had been to reinstall Christian transcendence by preserving a rational philosophic grounding or access to ideas of free will, immortality, and the deity, for which religious grounding no longer sufficed. In fear of the deterministic and materialistic consequences of Enlightenment modernity, self and subjectivity had become the fundamental givens for Kant. What for the empiricists is undemonstrable, Kant transforms into the given that needs no demonstration. Kant dismisses Hume's assertion that introspection yields only a sequence of ideas, only content, never an uncontaminated selfhood as the vessel of that content. As empiricism puts physical law inherently inside the universe, instead of having it depend on the external volition of a deity, so Kant puts what once was the outcome of revelation fully inside the mind, making immanent what was once a communication. The romantics are those who, in the midst of a burgeoning modernity, turned both to Kant and to the idealism that follows in order to preserve access to some realm the methodology of modernity cannot describe. Romanticism proposes to link personality and individuality to something other than biological discreteness. While the ultimate "atoms" of matter may be everlasting, as Lucretius asserted, a composite is transient. In romanticism, therefore, the self cannot be a composite. Transcendence is preserved not as a gift (grace) to the self from its source but as a "faculty" whose function is to perform the transcendence. Isolating the function seems to verify its authenticity. Romanticism empowers and preserves the self through this faculty, the aesthetic version of which adds "creativity" and is often called "imagination." Transcendence exchanges its religious and philosophical verification for an aesthetic one, with which the artist can circumvent the limitations of the senses. Creativity can perform the transcendence; creativity is the transcendence.

It is in this sense that, in romanticism, art displaces religion: it provides individual selfhood with a rationale for claiming not only a conceptual knowledge of the eternal but a sensory manifestation and observation of the eternal. Art is an alternative incarnation of divine spirit. By transporting the Greek word for "perception," *aesthetik,* into the eighteenth century, the empiricist's limitations placed on the definition of "perception," taken from the Latin *perceptio,* can be both circumvented and counterbalanced: the transcendental truth can now also be "perceived."

The sense of being inhabited by transcendence—the sense that God is always present here where we are—diminished as the eighteenth century progressed, partly because of the growth of cities as the Industrial Revolution expanded. In the eighteenth century, sensual appetites were often represented in literary works as being indulged at a distance, perhaps at a country estate. The expanding middle class took pleasure then as now in imagining the upper class, despite its eloquence and sophistication, to be perverted, stupid, and egomaniacal.

This also counteracts what might otherwise be envy. (The counteraction to forbidden sensuality is sentimentality, constantly increasing through the late eighteenth century.[4]) As manufactured products (including houses) multiplied and became inexpensive, the city became the location where anyone, regardless of income or status or birth, could indulge the passions, in places easily identified—from brothels to taverns, from theaters to restaurants.

The indulgence of the passions is a special type of urban purchase: even when selfish or immoral, an urbanized indulgence need not be considered sinful. How is it that such passions of the self be indulged without the soul being tainted? Believing the soul can be sequestered from the marketplace neatly severs the soul from the urban self and its daily activities; the soul, put aside, diminishes, becoming a meager residue of what it once was. The self detaches from transcendence. By the nineteenth century it had become obvious that God did not live in the city. Even to those for whom transcendence had not been rendered superfluous by the Age of Reason, transcendence became evasive, ephemeral, sometimes accompanied by despondency. The heaviness of one's mortality could no longer be raised up by a faith that is more an exertion than a conviction.

In the midst of this transition, romanticism had begun to proclaim that transcendence remains real. The lives and works of artists will provide conclusive demonstration. Romanticism can then eventually separate itself from philosophical idealism, which becomes increasingly linked to a religiously conservative reaction to the Enlightenment. (The reactionary conservatism is transmuted into Hegelian political theory.) Of course, even if they fill the universe with pervasive spirit, romantic artists can also experience the loss of the traditional personified Judeo-Christian deity. Some romantic artists profoundly encounter that form of negative transcendence known best by its absence,[5] by the apprehension that the ground of being may be the void. But as ample compensation, poets and artists can now claim the entire transcendental territory for themselves.

The concept espoused by Goethe of a unified European literature written in diverse languages substitutes for European Christianity. (Montesquieu had much earlier envisioned Europe as one large nation.) The nineteenth-century writers do not, however, offer an unambiguous alternative to religion. Many continue to hope to preserve the transcendence that was once a natural occurrence before it became encrusted with now archaic institutionalization, codified dogma, and obsolete social relations. By substituting an intuitional "spirituality" for religious superstition and convention, they hoped to renew poetry, creativity, and awe. Art would outmode religion by spiritually fulfilling it in a new sacred incarnation; art itself is the immaterial embodied in the material.

In Judeo-Christianity what is now called "creativity" is certainly never listed among the virtues. Creativity is God's attribute. God also provides all the necessary texts, directly or through delegates, like the prophets; by granting Jesus personal divinity, the Christian texts are given priority over those of the earlier Hebrew prophets. In the Old Testament, God even provides the architectural directions for building the holy ark; Jesus is also a carpenter. The entire early Christian history of European art and literature is the gradual arrogation by writers and artists of God's textual and architectural responsibilities and prerogatives, in the name of a devotion that in fact would forbid this. By the time of Shakespeare and Rembrandt (forty-two years younger), the artistic manifesto need no longer contain a theology. By the time of modernism no behavior whatsoever, certainly not on the part of artists, will summon up the retaliatory wrath of God—which is exactly what the urban capitalists had also been demonstrating.

In romanticism, the privileged situating of artists at the margin of conventional society becomes, by an inversion of the common social geography, a privileged positioning at the center of social significance. Society itself, middle-class life in particular, is allegedly composed of merely peripheral activities, none of which has the enduring core from which the artist draws energy. The artist, therefore, should not merely guide society but should generate society. This romantic inversion of social geography, combined with the idealist inversion that places a once external revelation inside the mind, allows the transcendent again to be situated here in the midst of us. While the Old Testament God has been banished by empiricism to the remote empyrean, artists represent the transcendent in our midst; they walk among us, like Jesus.

By this procedure the romantic self retains the dignity and the mystery of the Christian self, and poetry confirms the religious truth, its essence if not its particulars. The myths are replaced by "myth" as a poetic concept. Metaphor writ large is symbol: an image becomes not simply an illuminative trope but an essential correspondence.

(Again, correspondence, unlike cause and effect, does not require time.) Although the correspondence offered by a metaphor contains an essential truth, the metaphor is a linguistic invention; like the creativity of God, metaphor simultaneously discloses and creates the truth; creation and revelation are poetically synonymous, a truth that is equivalent to the metaphor that seems to reveal it. A metaphor is a union surpassing the sum of its parts, and a myth is a metaphor extended and transfigured into narrative form. Myths are no longer literally true; instead, they signify truth in that special form the sole purpose of which is to create such signification. Dogma is no longer necessary.

• • •

Kantian aesthetics as a response to empiricism must also be considered a response to rising capitalism and its consumer ego. For Kant, the artwork does not function as an ordinary product: at least some portion of subjectivity escapes (at the final hour) from the union between empiricism and capitalism. Removed from the realm of products, art can be exempted from subordination to capitalism's aims. An artwork can be a physical, purchasable object yet something quite other than a commodity. The artwork does not have a purpose in the way fabricated products usually have a purpose. Unlike other commodities, an artwork is not intended to increase the convenience (*comoditas*) with which an outcome can be achieved. Art is its own outcome: what results from art is the experience of art. In the midst of emergent capitalism, art is not a product but an antiproduct. Art reaches through to the qualities of things-in-themselves that underlie, but are not available to, ordinary sensation and perception. Art calls attention to the structure, operations, and limitations of mentality. The relationship of subjectivity and the external world requires that things be used by minds. Humans labor in the world; innate mental structures make this possible. But art is not an aspect of this practical use—it is an attentiveness to the relationship itself pertaining between subjectivity and the world.

For the philosophical transcendentalist, the laws of nature investigated by science apply to appearance and manifestation. These laws do not describe the workings of subjectivity but result from the workings of subjectivity. Art, in this view, appears to be lawful but not determined: it contains principles of order and harmony. The "laws" of art are such that the appearance of any specific artwork is unpredictable—exactly the opposite of scientific confirmation. The artist cannot ultimately know the principles of order and harmony because they emerge from what lies behind or beyond the senses on which knowing rests. Art unites the subjectivity that configures the perceivable world, the content of the perceivable world, and the source of that subjectivity, which transcends the perceivable world. Art occurs when subjectivity returns to its origins rather than exercises its inherent functions. This requires a special faculty, which it is the privilege of artists to have. However, the only possible evidence for this faculty is the art that it makes possible. The positing of the faculty, then, involves a tautology, insofar as a mental phenomenon by itself generates the name of its cause.

This special aesthetic faculty is required to certify the viability of transcendence. Not only can this extraordinary faculty replace theophanic revelation: by circumventing empiricism, it also eludes the economic view of the world empiricism fosters. Aesthetic theory is the one remaining strategy available to the modern world for salvaging the transcendental that theology had once substantiated but no longer can sustain.

The romantics, however, understood (or misunderstood) this idealist intuitive faculty to be a transcendence performed by that very ego evolving within the empiricist climate. For Kant and the idealists, the general qualities of subjectivity are not equivalent to the properties of the unique ego. But it is the elevation of the ego functions that makes the romantics "romantic." In romanticism, the summit of the enhanced capabilities of the romantic ego is "genius," which involves a qualitative assessment, not (as for the empiricists) a quantitative measurement along a graduated scale (as wealth and social status are).

By making genius the summit of a quantifiable scale, the empiricists can view genius as a maximum quantity of intelligence (the IQ scale, for example), talent, or creativity, all applauded as socioeconomically useful aptitudes. Everyone has some measure or quantity of what is qualitatively the same intelligence or talent or creativity. (Like money: the rich have more, not a different kind.) Even ordinary people can find their place somewhere on the same scale that includes genius, in distinction from older exclusionary hierarchies of discrete plateaus. (One is either an aristocrat or absolutely not one.) "My" talent, intelligence, and creativity are properties of my-*self*, of ego and

personality, rather than of that medium from which the self has issued. My ego owns its capabilities. Individual talent is a form of capital; the self is entitled to keep all the profits from that use. Such an
idea would have been foreign in the Renaissance, and even to the
mercantilists; it would have been plausible though hardly irrefutable
during romanticism; yet it has become an undeniable truism in both
modernism and capitalism.

This is an extremely important turn of events. Combining the idea
of a romantic quality of genius that transcends everyday affairs and
customary socioeconomic life with the idea of a scale of talent within
everyday affairs, a talent taken to be a form of owned capital, makes
that "talent" superior to the capacity to produce a quantity of "labor,"
which once defined the worker. This creates a professional class, for
whom the educational system provides the intermediary adaptions for
entry. The current controversy that on the surface seems to be over
whether universities should focus on the traditional liberal arts and
sciences or be tailored to career specifications overlies a deeper one:
should inherent quantities of generalized aptitudes and intellectual
potentials be cultivated? Or should sets of skills be transmitted? The
latter keeps the student simply a unit of labor. Predicating incipient
aptitudes allows entry into the professions for those judged capable of
succeeding there. Upward mobility comes by releasing deterrents to
natural talent, as if humans, like flames, rise naturally. Capitalism,
then, is conceived of as the natural state of human affairs. All other
systems are inhibitory.

• • •

For the eighteenth-century neoclassicists the timeless was not the
same as an existent realm where there was no time. Certain truths,
statable as propositions, are perpetually valid and in that sense "eternal." Poetry can and should present such truths, poetry even ought to
present such truths, but they do not depend on poetry to be known.
The talent of the artist is the recognition of truths from outside the
domain of art and the communication of these truths in a special,
engaging way. For the neoclassicist, truths of morality, religion, and
"taste" are valid because the observations of reasonable people have
validated them over time. It takes time to acquire knowledge of the
timeless. Truth remains inside time.

In the transcendental setting, the truths contained in art are not statable in alternative propositions. Art points to what lies above or behind the utterable, the metaphysical underpinnings of consciousness. That metaphysical source of consciousness cannot be an object, since it grounds knowing objects; nor can it be rationality, for it is the medium in which rationality occurs. Having true artistic capacity is genius; skill is qualitatively distinct, improvable by training. Transcendentalism sees the division of the world into things as a partitioning grounded in a fundamental unity; logic yields integration. Empiricism, in contrast, sees the world as an aggregation of fundamental atoms and logic as an ordered scale; logic yields segregation.

To the neoclassicist, the essence of a thing is the natural properties determining its actions and relations in time. Nature is the sum total of the aggregation of discrete things. To the romantics, the essence of a thing is what has internally caused its manifestation. Nature is the name for the encompassing uni-form essence of the aggregation of all things. For the neoclassicist, as for the empiricist generally, if the laws of nature have a source higher than nature, then the laws have been invoked by the volition of a rational God. For the romantic, the laws of nature flow directly from the creative essence of God, who in that sense *is* nature, as well as is *in* nature. The romantics wish for time to have had an origin external to time. The romantic suspicion of science is promoted by the Newtonian concept of time as linearly infinite, originless duration, a narrow line in two directions.

In modernism, artistic intent is transferred from narrative, conceptual, and didactic poetry to poetry as visual metaphor. The aesthetic response moves away from the beauty of linguistic expression ("poetic diction") to the self-contained meaningfulness of images. First, there is the integration of French symbolism, which is a romanticism of the metropolis, a poetry in which the physicality of the romantics' "nature" has been rarefied away. (Urbanity is a mode of intellectuality, not physicality, because money itself is an absolutely pure concept, the only material signifier with limitless signifieds: anything can be purchased with it.) Metaphor is not simply poetic ornament but corresponds to essence.

More than this, metaphorical en-visioning (image-ry), grounded more in eyesight than in hearing, yields symbols that cannot be fully contained by language, although they are disclosed through language. In modernism, the visual escapes the bounds of the verbal. Painting loses narrative; poetry (as for the imagists) loses propositionality.[6] This allows the visual arts to be granted, in modernism, perhaps even a higher rank than poetry. Both verbal and visual art can stand, as self-sufficient images, both beside and against linguistic conceptualization, just as revelation (the "Word") once stood for the scholastics both beside and against Aristotelian logic. The image and the proposition stand to each other as faith and reason once had stood. This will be the ground of the formalist's dual-truth theory.

As individuality became increasingly psychologized (the transition from soul to subjectivity to individuated personality), romantic artists had become increasingly engaged in the idea of their selves as the bearers or disclosers of eternal truths: a metaphysical egotism. The intention of romanticism was to preserve a grounding for the self (transcendent, perhaps immortal) that empiricism was undermining and that post-Enlightenment Christianity could not by itself sustain. Romanticism differs from Kantianism in that the romantic poets are not fundamentally discussing the artwork: they are promoting an image of the artist. Romanticism requires the cultivation of an audience that believes not only in the skill or talent but also in the personal transcendent capacities of the artist. These capacities are often the underlying theme of the artwork. Renaissance artists shared communal collective knowledge but believed in an extraordinary form of *talent* to create beauty, a talent the artist had been granted by God. The romantic artist, however, has an extra-ordinary form of *knowledge* and is its source as well as its conveyor. The artist has not exactly had talent bestowed by God but inherently shares the creativity of God.

For the romantic, the state of the individual personality comes about through a spiritual rapport, the cultivation of an attunement to the transcendental. The artwork indicates where the truth resides, and this can be emotionally apprehended. Such a statement is nonsense to the empiricist, for whom truth is a deduction and the emotions, even where confirming, must be subordinated. For the romantic, verification is evidenced by the intensity of belief. The truth is not a proof that commands public consensus; substantiation is an individual act. For the empiricist, the individual personality comes about through learning (experience and training), which issues in a commitment to a moral and educational code, a set of general principles confirmed by rationality and governing conduct. From the romantic view, the ability to transform personality into objects of a certain sort is the unique genius of the artist. While talent is a propensity for adept behavior, a predisposition nearer to physicality than to spirituality, genius is an intrinsic structure of selfhood. Genius is not what one *has*, but what one *is*. Evidence of already being a genius begins with the seeking of genius. (Like salvation for the Calvinists: romantic artists often speak as if their artistic mission is predestined.)

To the empiricist, however, talent is an advanced form of a mental dexterity or a faculty that everyone possesses to some degree: the artwork is an abstraction of some part of all of us. Insofar as artists communicate truths of a general and universal nature, their personalities cannot dominate artworks. Classicism customarily abstracts the personality of the artist from the artwork, finding it an interesting but not an essential aesthetic component of talent. The part of the artist that is in touch with external truth is fundamentally a universalized rationality; mastering the skills of a craft results from mastering the rules validating the accepted practice, which are the same for everyone. (This is the supposition of the academies.) If some artists are much better than others, this can be attributed to the magnitude of an impersonal power of mentality; differences are more quantitative than qualitative. "Genius" is a quantitative term in empiricism, denoting the magnitude of talent.

In idealism, the personality of the philosopher or the artist also need not matter much, for intuition is not a personality trait. In romanticism, idealism's rarefied subjectivity is transformed into individuated ego. The artist's personality is an essential component of the work, for the art is the expression of that personality. It is not simply that the personality is seeking to approach truth; the personality is itself the method by which the truth is sought, by creating objects equivalent to that personality. The ego-personality seeks itself in the act of creating itself. Personal selfhood becomes a possible content— soon the major content—of art. This selfhood is not the self of traditional biography or of the didactic autobiographical confession, meant to describe rather than create the self. In romanticism, the personality is not (as for empiricism) the site of the inquiry but the process of the inquiry, whose procedural rules are grounded in an ultimately impersonal higher subjectivity, yet located in individuality.

In the transition from transcendental philosophical idealism to its artistic project, which is romanticism, the ego that is created results from economic structures founded within empiricism. The shift from mercantilism to capitalism involves a conceptual transition, changing priorities from the wealth of autocratically governed nations, where the subject is subsumed by an ethics of loyalty, to the wealth of individuals, whose citizenship legitimates the nation by an ethics of voluntary consent. Capitalist economic structures are immature when empiricism arises. The romantic personality emerges in a world increasingly dominated by the structures of empiricism and evolves by being situated in opposition to the empiricism that stimulates it. Yet capitalism transforms any countercultural movement into another product of the marketplace. The romantic eventually becomes integrated into the system of commercial exchange by means of the ego empiricism and capitalism have shown romanticism how to individuate. The art world becomes fully commercialized, and the artistic personality becomes an easily assumable role.

Because the artistic selfhood of the romantic has the potential to intermingle with the emerging ego of a combined Protestantism and capitalism, by the time of modernism a pronounced egocentricity is taken to be one defining characteristic of the artist. (One can even be an artist without producing any art.) When modernism evolves toward the dominance of critical formalism in literary high modernism, there will be a reaction against romanticism, and less personal theories of art will be advocated, although the advocates also exemplify the insistently egocentric personality they claim to refute. To this day, artists cultivate a personality based on the overlapping of or the confusion between transcendence and an intensity of ego growth, accompanied by what is clearly a mixture of fascination and repugnance for a positivistic (Anglo-American) psychology.

As psychological and evolutionary studies increase in the empiricist environment, the organism becomes viewed as an entity within the history of organisms generally. Mentality has been generated inside this history, as a dynamo generates electricity. Yet where does artistic talent and inspiration come from? If from the parents, why did they not possess it themselves? If from personal psychological factors, at what point can a combination of factors yield something not inherent in any one of those factors? If the causes of artistic inspiration can be discovered by psychology, then those causes will explain creativity, since discovering causes is what empiricist explanation is. But by putting the causal chain completely within natural history, the mystery disappears.

A theory might, for example, posit a talent innate in an individual organism but preceding the formation of selfhood. As the self forms, the physical/organic environment is such that the talent is expressed. But one then needs to ask how the self is formed subsequent to its talent. If the answer involves a psychological determinism, then the self is not basically responsible for its own talent.[7] Even if the self is Cartesian, a coherent immaterial entity living in the head, then while such an entity might possess talent, how or why remains a mystery. All artistic talent is exercised materially through the body (writing, painting, etc.); yet it cannot be argued that these bodily processes simply manifest what preexists in the mind. The artist does not know in advance of the creative act what precisely will emerge from it. Lastly, even if one supposes that the self has full responsibility for shaping itself, including the exercise of the effort to produce its own talent, this cannot account for genius—since the self is (apparently) powerless to generate genius if it is not latently there. In every case, reasons can be offered for retaining artistic creativity as an irresolvable mystery for empiricism.

There is also a difference between having genius and being a genius. In the romantic self that travels through the nineteenth century toward modernism, the latter concept prevails. Genius is not a possession but a state, not an assessment of talent but an existential category. Since modernist genius is defined like romantic genius, not only as talent but also as knowledge, the artistic ego claims superior insight into every facet of life, from poetry to politics. Yet that claim, currently still thriving, rests on a romanticism whose philosophical underpinnings generally had fallen into disfavor from the 1920s onward. The strength of modernism grows as the legitimations for that form of self on which its strength depends deteriorates.

Much of the modernist visual art is about this deterioration. The human figure and face are distorted, blurred, chopped up, and finally, in abstraction, disappear. This is not simply formal experimentation with planes, surfaces, and color; it is the expression of the romantic self in the process of being vanquished by a dominant empiricism that has forged a new self: the modern ego of consumer capitalism, an economic ego. Selfhood in literature becomes "fragmented." But artistic expression can only occur for the modernists by retaining romantic attitudes, since the modernist artist needs a selfhood to put in opposition to the economic system. Modernism, then, grows stronger while its romantic and idealist underpinnings grow weaker. As the self of consumerism becomes increasingly pronounced and distinct (hence isolated) in society, the romantic self deteriorates and shatters on the canvas.

Modernism is the process of this conflict. Transcendence struggles to assert itself despite its diminishing plausibility. The artist asserts individuality, uniqueness, mystical creativity, and spiritual insight while these have forfeited empirical meaning, until one arrives at a point of fully emergent but no longer grounded ego.

Capitalism contributes to this development. The ego base is shifted from religion to economics—to consumption. The "I" is directed toward a standard of living. As modernism inclines toward formalism in high modernism, modernist artists place their egos inside the forms of the artistic materials, just as economic humans place their egos inside the forms of financial transactions. In both cases, ego becomes structured in the form of things. A format for giving shape to the pure ego is invented that neither asks for nor relies upon the Christian underpinnings of self. These new forms allow ego to function as an autonomous entity within the autonomous time of science. Ego then requires natural internal energies to propel it. Matter had been assigned various internal forces throughout modernity: gravity, kinetic and potential energy, electromagnetic fields, and, most compellingly as modernism emerges, the discovery of the energy emitted by radioactivity. None of these are "things" in any ordinary sense, but each allows the behavior (the motions) of matter to be attributed to its own internal dynamics by recognizing that energy can be physically real, even if intangible. Similarly, the psychologists, biologists, economists, and sociologists provide the various vocabularies of ego energies—Smith's invisible hand, Freud's id, Bergson's *élan vital*, Darwin's urge for survival, Marx's class warfare, Weber's anomie, mesmerism, telepathy, animal magnetism, and so on.

The major discovery of the autonomous self is the implausibility of its presumed autonomy. The Enlightenment argued that rationality is the essential endowment of an autonomous self; yet rationality is precisely what undermines the autonomy of self by leading it toward the deterministic worldview of empiricist science. Rationality has released the freedom to discover the implausibility of free will.

The creation of self simultaneously creates the otherness that the self must depend on to establish itself. The self is at once dominant over otherness, which it incorporates into itself as its own thoughts and then manipulates as it pleases, yet dependent on otherness for its definition. Paradoxically, while there must already be an entity of self to have knowledge of otherness, the otherness is presumed to have existed before the self that discovers it. (In Eastern thought, self and otherness emerge simultaneously.) The self can only grow into the knowledge of itself by recognizing its separation from an otherness that the self is not. Every strengthening of selfhood correspondingly increases otherness, until one reaches the point, now stalemated, of the strongest possible ego facing the largest possible other. Since otherness is by far the larger entity—and, through science, daily growing larger on the scale of time and space—the self is increasingly terrified.

• • •

Early modernism holds that individuality is more than the parcel of mental energies generated by an organism whose biological cohesion generates and sustains selfhood. The coherence of individuality is also constituted as the continuous boundary around a portion of a universal immateriality (spirit), known and expressed through the body, but not causally dependent on matter. Quite the reverse: the manifestation of the material universe is dependent on this encompassing immateriality. Further, this immateriality is creative by its absolute nature. Creativity in the self is a replication of this.

From this perspective, human consciousness lies between and connects the material and immaterial. The contents of consciousness are images or signs for images (language), which are the materially real refashioned into immaterial substance, mentality. The formal properties of art relate to the essence of art just as the formal properties of the material world relate to its immaterial essence. The exterior formal properties of art, which the body perceives through the senses (color, sound, shape, texture), are the physical medium through which the inner forms of consciousness of the artist are linked to the inner forms of consciousness of the observer. The validity of the connection is demonstrated in proportion to the intensity of the aesthetic experience.

The profundity of modern art, like that of tragedy, is that this conception of the self is doomed for lack of evidence. Because it does not take the modernists long to understand this, the world that was to be a sanctuary becomes a stage. The weaker the grounding of selfhood, the stronger its public role, the greater the vulnerability, the greater the audacity. The self impersonates the qualities it desires. The vulnerability of the self and the importance of the entertainment industry increase together.

Within this crisis of modernist selfhood, the turn to critical formalism becomes most appealing. Formalism approaches the work as if an analysis of the ordering of the materials of which it is composed (its "immediate" causes in the Aristotelian sense) is sufficient for an assessment of its value. The narrative content of a literary or visual work is subsumed to form and becomes a minor concern. A work is designated critically significant as a consequence of a technical mastery and innovation such that Art itself, as a collection of aesthetic solutions and experiments, advances. In formalism, the history of art is a physical history, an anatomical history, like evolutionary theory in biology. Technical innovation alone, however, is insufficient: the criterion of meaningfulness is also required. Otherwise, random novelty and the bizarre would rival the genuinely important. In formalism, meaning is both communicated and caused by the medium. The world itself is understood to be unknowable except as it is organized (not merely perceived) by mental constructs. Moreover, it becomes unclear what the relationship might be between those constructs and some intrinsic organization of the universe. Formalism does not resolve this issue; on the contrary, formalist theory becomes a replacement for theories of art as truth when knowledge of the world becomes problematic.

For formalism, form in art is the sensory organization of matter abstracted as a category or pattern from its existence in time. Time can be excluded from an analysis of form, since the Sumerians, Greeks, Egyptians, Romans, Japanese, Chinese, and others were not simply "primitive" precursors of more advanced accomplishments: their work was fully mature and complete. Even the "primitive" Africans and Pacific Islanders had mastered art forms. But lest the artist be lost in time through the universalization of the principles of method, time is reintroduced as the sequencing of these time-less formal categories within the history of a specific culture, as if in any particular setting one "leads to" the other. Literary and art history become distinct from social, political, and economic history. They become self-contained causal histories (the Renaissance leads to mannerism which leads to the baroque which leads to the rococo, etc.), more than simply the narratives of sequential events and accomplishments.

Form is the truth about the artwork. This truth is not contained in the form (as if truth were a message carried by form) but is equivalent to the form—just as physical laws are the form but not, in the traditional sense, the essence of matter. The formalist equation of truth and form cannot, to be sure, satisfactorily displace the need for meaningfulness. This leads formalism to contrive, not quite legitimately, its dual-truth theory. Of the two sets of truths, science and art, only the latter is accompanied by meaning.

Time in art and literary history is the ordering of formalist categories that cannot be seen as causally related until after they occur. It becomes possible to argue for some constantly evolving inner principle of all art over time, as Hegel argued for the principal of evolving consciousness of spirit. Nevertheless, this no more reveals necessity than does the similar strategy of arguing for an inherently emergent principle or direction in biological evolution. A sequence can be fully determined, yet unpredictable in advance. The causal relations may only be traceable retrospectively. But if the order has not been necessary, how can meaning be attributed?

The formal patterns of art yield meaning in the same way that language yields meaning, through a contingent and arbitrary, even if historically grounded, vocabulary of signifiers. Those signifiers most attached to material reality, words designating things, seem sufficiently explicable through a physical description of how sensation works. Where meaning is representational, the aesthetic criteria usually include accuracy and lifelikeness. There is also, however, the presumption that representing the mind accurately does not require representing the world accurately and that it is not necessary for the best works of art to do both. This encourages the modernists' break from criteria that had rested for centuries in the techniques of accurate perspective and three-dimensional shadowing in painting. In literature, naturalism wanes—although the process is much slower and can never be complete, because so much of the audience for fiction demands "realism."

It is in psychological representation that formalist criticism seeks for meaning in the artwork, in a correspondence between the experience yielded by the artwork and a psychic structure whose reality the artwork verifies not only by stimulating it (which ordinary experience also can do) but by simultaneously clarifying it. Only certain (aesthetically privileged) persons can be authorized to ascribe such meaning: this becomes a most important modernist distinction between art and science. (No scientist is authorized to assign meaning to the facts and causal relations that comprise a scientific discipline.) Furthermore, no one need have made the universe as artists make artworks; but meaning cannot be attributed to what has not been "produced," as those who assign a meaning to the universe from a religious viewpoint readily understand.

Since every biological structure must be given an organic purpose, so with psychic structure: there must be needs for psychological stability, beauty, order, stimulation (sensory or mental), knowledge, transcendence, escape, or expression of the unconscious. For the empiricist, the origins of art are commonly attributed to its usefulness, described by anthropology: magic, instruction, ritual, entertainment, myth. Art functions both to advance social progress and to maintain social stability. In high literary modernism, too, art is said to satisfy some basic "psychological" need. Formalism further assumes that the more powerful and necessary the connection between the formal sensory properties of the artwork and these basic psychic mechanisms, the better is the artwork. Equally, artists must cause the aesthetic effect by the exercise of their unique abilities, rather than by imitation. One can borrow but not copy, use but not duplicate. Training and inspiration draw further apart. The artist must know the inner psychic process personally and directly. As verification of this knowledge, the great artist, beyond mastering the old forms, creates new forms.

Modernism did not begin with critical formalism; the turn to formalism is modernism's most significant transformation. When modernism began, the artwork might verify transcendent meaning also, beyond psychic mechanisms and the blatant material world. The interactions between the two were aesthetically sanctified, even if no longer sacred in the old theological way. Romanticism had relied upon a new epistemological capacity—the imaginative faculty discussed by Vico, Herder, and Coleridge. The long familiarity with the religious function of revelation, communion, and faith in religion had served as a ready-made paradigm for defining this aesthetic faculty: the aesthetic response is given the legitimating power once reserved for revelation. Indeed, it is even preferable to revelation because it places the potential for access to truth within human subjectivity and is not dependent on language alone, while revelation (not to be confused with the mystical experience) is basically a verbal message from the outside whose truth is legitimated by the identification of its source. When modernism begins by displacing the presumed objective detachment of impressionism and literary naturalism, the expression of artistic form is personal and unique—what the artist sees is not simply what is out there waiting to be seen. Yet the creative process is shared by all artists. Multifarious "truths" (the artists' distinctive visions) each separately merit the name "truth" because of their creative authenticity, not because they yield any consensus. Artistic form is taken as evidence of a universal transcendent impulse toward form itself, like God's need or urge to create order out of chaos, or like the impulse toward new forms in biological evolution. Art places the image of this living dynamic form in dead empiricist matter. Art is the impact of the sensory accompanied by a transcendence of the sensory. The aesthetic experience becomes infallible, like revelation, because the confirmation of its truth is equivalent to the means of its presentation.

But as modernism progresses, the artist cannot maintain this surety. (The symbolists, Van Gogh, Gauguin are long gone.) The aesthetic faculty is detached from quasi-religious inspiration and explicated in psychological terms. Pragmatism, psychoanalysis, behaviorism, introspectionism, and today cognition theory—each psychologizes art. As a consolation, for many artists art eventually becomes the expression of individuality, the truth is not a revelation about things but a disclosure about *me* (the artist). Art is a disclosure by way of confession. Point of view may be, but does not need to be, validated by public approval.

It will be characteristic of late modernism that many artists will seek to escape this psychologizing altogether, adhering to what they maintain are strictly impersonal formal criteria for artwork, as in minimalism, or the "new" novel, or conceptual art. But modern individualism already will have caught the artist in the same dilemma as the observer. As religious belief declines, ownership becomes essential to define selfhood; in capitalism, the dimensions of the self are verified by what it owns. The artistic self and the economic self are both verified by products—by the making of products and by the consuming of products. Form in the artwork is like inventory to the consumer. Yet the ego knows (or at least once knew) that defining self by economic possession is self-deception. Such an ego is fundamentally superfluous. In anxiety, the striving for production and for possession becomes more hectic as its goal becomes less attainable. Modern cities function to maintain this self-deception. I vigorously work to buy what you vigorously work to make, and vice versa, so that we cooperatively cre-

ate and substantiate each other's egos through often compulsive superfluous activity. Modernism had hoped to escape such an ego, even
as it collaborated in forging it.

• • •

Science works with the enthusiasm of the search for truth, the belief
that "truth" is a target with a valid ontological status. New theories are
improvements, not simply alternatives. Facts are ascertainable; theories
can be proven. Nevertheless, facts are contingent. The chain of cause
and effect has no beginning. The underlying structure of the system, the
laws described by formulas as well as the facts they determine, might
have been found different without consequences for humanity. Since
humans are here to do the investigating, whatever is discovered must
obviously be compatible with human existence. The consequences of
such a view for human self-definition must always be the same, regardless of the facts discovered. To include humanity in what the sciences
are authorized to investigate means the disappearance of the conscious
self (whether immaterial soul, mind, consciousness, or thought in the
Cartesian sense) as a unique kind of entity. Human existence is assumed
to be completely inside the physicality that characterizes everything else
science discovers. Although no set of facts can be incompatible with our
existence, nevertheless, the facts provide the *reason* for our existence.
We can imagine that, without the universe being as it is, we would not
be here.

If our existence is explained by facts that we have the ability to know,
then we also need to know that. We can be conscious of what we are
conscious of, and conscious of *that,* too. This leads to a seemingly infinite regress—to know that we know that we know, etc. There is always
presumed to be some level of consciousness higher than any content of
consciousness. The growth of science, when applied to humanity as an
object of science, undermines the self by placing the self as if it were an
object inside its own content. At each level of consciousness, the container of knowledge becomes contained by knowledge. This repetitive-
ly subordinates the very self that has undertaken science as a project.
The subject repeatedly reduces to its object. Psychology can then study
that object. As its discoveries grow, the self knows more and is less. The
optimism that accompanies science is matched by a social and personal
pessimism: the self wanes as the promise of its own fulfillment increases. The triumphs of reason sabotage the reasoner.

Capitalism pulls the ego away from its once presumed origins to leave it without metaphysical obligations. The new supporting frame it builds for itself is science—more exactly, the veracity of the senses; but since observation is an exercise of the ego, science can no longer ground ego as theology had once grounded selfhood. Self is gradually transformed to ego. The subject becomes an object. The existence of that object is then taken to precede the existence of the selfhood that is a subject to itself. The "person" is thought of as a physical object: I was born "me." That I think does not prove that I am (that the subject "I" is an entity); rather, that I am (physically) eventually comes to explain why I can be an ego that thinks. Ego achieves an ambivalent independence, because ego would rather have no origin at all. An origin only certifies its impermanence as an object.

Capitalism defends against the threatened disintegration of grounded selfhood by convincing its participants that owning is equivalent to being. (A most admired character trait becomes "self-possession.") Ownership implies, and seems to guarantee the autonomous existence of, the ego that owns.

To prevent this necessary derogation of selfhood by reason, reason had repeatedly been subordinated to other powers. Aristotelian reason is repeatedly constrained—Aquinas had constrained it as well, and as strategically, as Kant would. Such constraint legitimates retaining the stable, permanent, and irrevocable mind-based origin (God as thinker and planner) of Judeo-Christian individuality. In its optimism, the Enlightenment believes it will abolish its transcendental opponents and that reason (the rational ego) will conquer. But without the continuing vitality of its antagonist, winning is impossible for Enlightenment selfhood. The self is initially formed in a system of opposition: I-it, me-you, subject-object. Reason is the subject conquering, through subordination, the objects that have brought the reasoner into being. The ego tries to protect itself by dominating its origins in things. It masters knowledge. But those origins cannot be overcome in empiricism. Reason exercised in defense of a selfhood that reason must ultimately undermine yields the modern ego. The ego can travel one of two paths: either to its own enervation (the perplexed, docile, or tormented antiheroes of the modern novel, who are driven rather than motivated to action or inaction) or to a frenetic activity symptomatic of psychopathology (a workplace in which agitation and productivity have been confused).

The modernist irony is that the self is engaged in winning the battle that destroys it. Modern art does not fulfill its aim of replacing either religion or prophecy. By midcentury it will have fought long enough so that the ego will be stronger than ever, at least in the countries that win World War II. (The losers will quickly catch up.) Yet the ego will also be placed more in jeopardy than ever before. Unprecedented economic prosperity and educational opportunity go hand in hand with rising rates of clinical anxiety and depression. The combination of enthusiasm for the search for knowledge with the pessimism of what that knowledge implies for selfhood has led to the psychological dualities that characterize modern diagnoses. No longer are angels and devils engaged in a tug-of-war; the rope being tugged is the ultimate reality. Manic-depressiveness or anxiety-depression: these are psychology's unresolved versions of the dual-truth theorist's "reconciliation of opposites." Even for so-called normal people, vigorous work is punctuated by ingesting chemical depressants. Tranquilizers are consumed (not only as pills and liquids), yet tranquility is undesirable; satisfaction is both the goal and the major impediment to the goal. One's business increases the stress that the income from one's business is earned in order to relieve. Achievement augments the truth about the impossibility of the self's fulfillment.

The *concept* of the father in psychoanalysis has been derived from Time (Cronos/Chronos). But the *image* of the father in psychoanalysis is derived from the concept of selfhood as it was once imagined to be—unified, grounded, and powerful. This is the real Father before whom one stands in guilt. And if sometimes the Father looks like God, it is because he was once thought to be (made in) the image of God. Modern guilt is the inability to be the self that is nevertheless still imagined as constituting selfhood. We do not fully inhabit our selves: some vision of our self inhabits us. Where self was, ego now searches for it.

Perhaps one expects a renewed act of faith, a new grounding for self. Perhaps either a socialized capitalism or a capitalized socialism is intended as the new faith. Or perhaps there are no current contenders, no new faith for, or in, selfhood. This condition is now called postmodernity, which for this very reason knows no guilt.

The Modernist
Self in Capitalism

12

Romanticism had attempted to co-opt or to divert the evolving ego of an empiricist capitalism by claiming for a Kantian subject the same historical efficacy claimed for a Cartesian selfhood. The aesthetic ego was to supplant the capitalist ego by taking different models of virtue: the political genius and not the aristocrat, the poet and not the wealthy merchant. (Scientists were not in contention for such honors.) Ties with the writers' and artists' customary source of income were intentionally severed in the belief that these could be replaced by a general "audience" drawn from all classes. This attempt to give the aesthetic ego dominance over the capitalist ego concluded with the tables being turned on romanticism: the democratization of romantic art and literature turned out to be well suited to capitalism. Although capitalists have few sympathies with romantic daydreams, they have no difficulty marketing them. In modernism, this co-optation results in submission to the commercial art world and the turn to empiricist critical formalism.

The capitalist ego, basically the personality, has become the selfhood that artists now cultivate. However they claim to oppose capitalism, artists readily serve as archetypical examples of the modern economic ego: egotism employed in the production and marketing of a product—a double-sided product that is both the artwork and also the artist's personality—in a market ideally without constraints or censorship. (No anti-trust in art.) By the twentieth century, the artist is the entrepreneur par excellence, the conceptualizer, designer, manufacturer, distributor, and publicity agent for a unique product. To use the romantic organic metaphor that is also an industrial term, the artist becomes a "plant."

The altruistic interpretation of capitalism is liberalism. (Liberals originally believed that free market dynamics and minimum social controls would best improve humankind. The level of intervention demanded by liberal theory dramatically increased; now conservatives defend the free market and lament social engineering.) Liberal reform is designed to grant access to capital not only for the already wealthy (money concentrated in a family structure and kept there through inheritance, just like in the old aristocracy) but to people of commercial talent (*talentum:* a sum of money). Such talent is the ability to increase significantly the sum total of market transactions. Money thereby becomes more evenly distributed. Entrepreneurs reinvest one portion of profits to stimulate additional transactions; another portion they keep for their own purchases or to amass wealth (the potential to make purchases). Since a continually increasing amount of merchandise and money circulates, one person's gain need not be another's loss. There is virtually no limit to the quantity of new items (even land can be repeatedly divided into smaller parcels, as the suburbs illustrate, and vertically partitioned by apartments) or to the amount of new money. The supply of consumers is anticipated always to increase, through birth, through the opening of new markets, and through the stimulation of new desires in old customers.

There is also "talent" that can be employed, by others, to earn money, which is distinct from the talent to earn money. Such talent is itself a marketable product, which artists, entertainers, and athletes possess. For artists specifically, this talent becomes a credential for a type of qualified inheritance. People already in possession of money recognize people with talent and patronize them, adopt them (*patron,* from *pater*). The patron cannot predict the exact nature of the product the artist will produce, which distinguishes such investment from all others; trust is essential in the patrimonial relation. A cadre of professional connoisseurs develops, who earn money by brokering these relations. Merit is marketability, at prices that increase as the talent is more widely recognized. The product is identified by the proper name of the artist; the prominence of this name yields the price of the product and determines the value of future products bearing that name. The person of talent may become rich; but the funding source and the institutions established by that source always become even richer. Even if they do not sell the product, their net "worth" and their "value" (*esteem* and *estimate* have the same root) increases.

In a market economy, the artist may also operate as a merchant.[1] Merchants buy products or materials, incur expenses refashioning them and/or transporting them to the market, and sell the product for a price that covers their costs and adds a profit. The profit is the aim of starting the chain of production. But what exactly is the product of the artist? The value of the work seems to adhere not only to the object but also to its producer; the work primarily serves as a container for that talent. As the estimation of that talent increases, even the value of early work, perhaps already once sold, rises.

In its most unique form, where innovations not only surprise but, for whatever reason, astonish, the artist may be called a genius. Genius astonishes by producing what suddenly appears to be an advancement for art itself; hence the history of art can consist of a legitimate narrative. Each genius takes the next logical step (the logic legitimates the narrative—otherwise there is only the bizarre) without there having been any possibility of logically predicting it. Whether genius is a gift (if so, from whom?) or a power (if so, from where?), it is captured in the artwork. Dead matter takes the configuration of living spirit. Whether a work actually accomplishes this can remain in dispute; artists and critics both claim that those who differ with them lack insight.

A singular object whose value derives from embodying the abilities of a specified individual is, then, an artwork. (The qualification "singular" discriminates artworks from manufactured products, each copy having identical value.) This criterion applies even if the artist is actually unknown. Making an artwork is not the same as inventing a product, for the invention derives its value solely from the task it can perform. To know an artwork well is to know (in theory, at least) the artist's mind, since every artwork carries a narrative, a manifesto, a worldview. To know an invention well is not to know anything about the inventor. This is why the names of certain artists are illustrious, while the names of inventors, even of ubiquitous products—zippers, rubber tires, pencils—are known to very few. Although the artist works, no one asks that the artwork do work, as the invention must do. The artwork hides the labor necessary to produce it. All traces of labor, whether the artist's or the viewer's, ideally vanish during the aesthetic experience. In this way, the artwork becomes a denial of the dependence of truth on labor. Art need not work for a living: art is itself "living." Art is a denial of the economic system in which it functions, a denial of economic coercion. The writer and artist withdraw from the marketplace (perhaps as a "Bohemian") to study the characteristics of those who go to market.

Because art appears to be a release from labor, owning an important artwork can be a statement about one's place in a world where labor is not a necessity. The wealthy have escaped the exigencies of the labor by which one becomes wealthy. The leisure of wealth is the basis of prestige. Certain expenditures both signify and confirm such leisure. (A "Protestant ethic" once, but no longer, suggested some restraint in the matter.) Unlike the invention, the artwork does not gain or lose value by being put to or removed from work, even if the artwork is "put to work," of a sort, in a museum or a bank lobby. (An artlike object for which a utility is essential is "craft.") The value of the artwork is the visible representation of that which it contains but cannot directly show: the capabilities of its maker. These capabilities are implanted in the work by the artist's direct physical manipulation—a direct exercise of labor. (Reproducing the labor by precisely replicating the work does not yield an artwork but a copy.) Like a laying on of hands, the goal is to manifest what no amount of labor by itself can produce: talent or, beyond that, genius.

Simultaneously, writers and artists enact an extremely important commercial role because they produce merchandise that no else can produce. Without a constantly renewed supply of artworks, certain people would have their income eliminated or diminished: manufacturers of art products (paints, books); brokers and critics; the staffs of galleries, bookshops, theaters; teachers; critics; scholars; performers (actors, musicians); builders (museums, libraries); producers and directors (and one notes the long list of names and titles following the film); decorators; transporters; lawyers; administrators. Unlike artists, many of these employees have ongoing financial security. They altogether earn much more than artists. Prosperity in the art business depends on a constant supply of new works, but not (as it does for one artist) on any specific work or set of works.

Artists who generate the most commerce are the most venerated, precisely for that reason: they provide the primary product that supports all the rest. Fame is commercial applause. Yet very few artists will succeed commercially, while the average teacher, canvas manufacturer, agent, framer, bookbinder, or jukebox distributor earns consistent and usually reasonable wages. Knowing this, one must ask whether the romantic idea of the artist is now being preserved in a capitalist economy primarily for the labor it generates. The artist accepts this stereotypical profile, which justifies persistent dedication even in the face of poverty, ridicule, and misunderstanding. Artists are endowed with (or deluded by) the myth of achieving a transcendent truth and beauty beyond the grasp of—not to mention beyond the interest of—ordinary humankind. This myth nourishes the extremely large number of artists, most of whom work for free, that it takes to yield the minute proportion of artworks that support the art and literary marketplaces.

Working against overwhelming odds, artists wish to join the immortals. They are guided by assurances that great artists are never forgotten, assurances given by a society that places works in mammoth libraries and luxurious museums, in curricula staffed by a now-and-then honored professoriate, and in the public media—each of which celebrates works, artists, anniversaries, and movements, which are for the most part made available to the public for what seems to be for free. This stimulates commercial activity enormously more profitable than whatever is made to appear a gift. (The boards of directors of cultural institutions are themselves made up of successful businesspeople.) The modern artist hopes to achieve artistic immortality by contributing products to the most mortal of all activities, the marketplace. The immortality purportedly takes place in the museum, the library, and the classroom. The marketplace encourages this dream, building and maintaining institutions that hide the marketplace functions behind the facade of an economically useful romantic view of art. The museum and the public library are, after all, capitalist inventions like other "not-for-profit" corporations.[2]

• • •

For the transcendentalist, beauty is a nonphysical quality manifested by a creation and incorporated in it, pervading it. For the empiricist, beauty characterizes a response naturally generated by an interaction between intellect and certain forms. In both cases the artwork is imagined to avoid a full collaboration with commercial transactions, even though the marketplace provides the major criterion for "success." (The monetary value of the artwork is set only by demand, not supply, since there is only one of each original artwork.) Every artwork must be produced using materials, but the artworks are unlike other products because they are presumed intimately connected to what is thought exempt from social conformation—nature (for the empiricist) or spirit (for the transcendentalist). Whether the foundation of humankind is the history of the earth or of heaven, the artist escapes (theoretically) the normal daily economic constraints. Yet—unlike the hermit, mystic, mental patient, or prisoner—the artist must make things.

Of the artwork there is only one original, although there might be many reproductions. A marketable "product," on the other hand, consists of a large number of items, no one of which is the valued "original." (The prototype or the first one off the assembly line is primarily a souvenir.) While the primary criteria for evaluating the artwork exclude usefulness, whether as a lesson, implement, decoration, status symbol, or entertainment, this purported use-lessness of the artwork is also a use. Art provides the "aesthetic" experience, an escape or diversion. The possibility of that release convinces consumers that they have not been irrevocably trapped by economic conditions. Art presents itself as a superior alternative to the setting that makes art possible—as if art can overcome its origins, just as the modern personality strives to escape its physical-sexual parentage.[3] And although most artists eagerly discuss their monetary plight, they offer themselves as people enviably free from the degradations of economic coercion.

Escape from the economic pressures of life may be accomplished in other ways, through entertainment, sports (some are still disappointed that athletes are mercenaries), games, and sexuality. But the aesthetic experience is special, for one cannot simply go out to buy it. That is, while the artwork can be bought, the ability to extract its use cannot be bought but must be cultivated. This takes no money: an indigent can be a connoisseur. Here, too, artworks seem to surpass the bounds of the economic system. The artwork does not yield to the observer like an employee to the employer; rather, the observer must yield to it—one must give in to seduction, which in other cases is generally a misfortune.

The successful artwork is supposed to do the previously unimaginable. This makes the original "original" in both senses. Originality is not, however, alone a sufficient criterion. Significance demands the inclusion of meaning. The aesthetic response is the sign and authentication of that certain kind of meaning: meaning which, when experienced, serves as its own validation. A work without meaning attributed to it might be unprecedented yet inconsequential, even ludicrous.

Great art astonishes: we know we never could have thought of that. Novelty surprises: we wonder why we did not think of that. Art is the uncoerced creation of a commodity from the mind, a product whose function is to embody its own possibility. It has a use that surpasses the useful. It fills a part of the ego that could not have known itself empty, and that is not empty until it is being filled. This is why the history of art—certainly unlike the history of technology—always seems complete to (admittedly naive) observers during any particular segment of history.

The modern empiricist posits, as a component of humanism, that art responds to a general psychological need. Humans need to encounter structures that organize experience in encompassing categories of meaning, and art is one codification of meaning. Moreover, in certain areas meanings are tentative, ambiguous, or still in the process of emerging; people are confronted with alternatives. In such periods, art displays alternative moral and aesthetic values, often struggling with one another in a single work. To the empiricist as pragmatist, art is play, test, hypothesis: alternatives can be considered, enacted as possibilities in the imagination, free from immediate practical ramifications.[4] In addition, there is a natural human need for mental stimulation. Children in stimulating environments grow up smarter and, empiricists argue, more creative. Intelligence and creativity are desirable not only because they lead to the improvement of humankind but because to know one has these traits contributes to happiness. (The modern self most delights in its favorable self-assessment.) Psychologizing art also makes this service to human nature compatible with art's economic function, since filling human need is the sometimes dubious rationale given for the unconstrained sale of commodities.

For the empiricist, need is organically based—the mind is initially a tabula rasa and the content of mentality develops to mediate between the organism and the material world. For the transcendentalist, however, mentality and consciousness are not equivalent: sensory manifestations occur in the medium of consciousness (the unity of consciousness, or self, that Hume could not find). Since consciousness is a thing in the world, the world is more than material. Mentality is not situated between the organism and the world but between consciousness and the world. Consciousness has need, and mentality is its means. Art mediates between consciousnesses and the world and also calls the attention of consciousness to itself. Behind art is a consciousness exercised to put something new in the world for the very purpose of calling attention to the process of so doing. (In contrast, invention calls attention to its use, not its origin.) With art, we become conscious of the activity of consciousness in fulfilling its need, which is both what it wants to do and what it must, which confirms its autonomy.[5]

Again, art here seems to function outside normal market operations. In an updated classic economics, demand curves are either brought to the product by consumers or created by supply (depending on whether one thinks the consumer's ego fuels the marketplace or vice versa). In both approaches production is controlled by pre-existing expectations about creating consumer need, perhaps including the expectation of an inherent need to increase needs, in order to have something to work for, to be an employee for. The need for beauty and truth (meaningful art) has, however, been steadily decreasing in economical relevance, since beauty and truth are available "for free" in museums and libraries. Many artworks—buildings, monuments, and architectural sculpture—stand open all the time for public viewing. Beauty and truth are no longer directly related to economic well-being, so the consumer does not have to be overly concerned with them.

New consumer goods are publicized by identifying needs. Behaviors, too, become products. In entertainment and sports, for example, the criteria are external to the product: our expectations need to be met, and certain formulaic repetitions must occur for the product to satisfy. But people who look for artworks to fulfill their previous expectations are disparagingly called academicians or decorators, for an artwork must do the unpredictable, that which cannot be looked for but which is known to be genuine (neither a hoax nor a travesty) when it is found. For knowing an artwork is genuine, there are no necessary internal or external formal criteria. (Not even the intent of the producer.) An artwork is designated by those empowered to exercise criteria no one of which is mandatory.[6] The qualifications for authority are defined, although the authorities define for themselves what, specifically, their authority is over.

Gallery catalogs, reviews, criticism, and interviews are designed to indicate what need art will fulfill. These products may be offered as entertainment, instruction, or sometimes as themselves art. They advertise art by identifying art (it is what the publication so designates), by disclosing in advance the revelation the artwork will provide, and by explaining how to prepare oneself for that revelation. The public is assumed to need constant professional guidance, just as in so many other areas of personal life, whether child rearing, physical fitness, or cooking. One can no longer rely on the notion that the artwork appeals to natural intuitive responses: the audience must constantly be retrained. (Changes in aesthetic sensibilities and in employment skills proceed at a corresponding pace, always quickening, and persistent retraining is now an industry in both domains.) These products function to enhance expenditures on art, even in the guise of defending art's ultimate freedom from commercial concerns. Reviews of books, films, and art shows are placed in a special section of the newspaper, to which one can presumably turn for respite; but even that section contains mostly advertisements. University curricula, museum catalogs, and alternative galleries decry the commercialization of art, even as raising money becomes their own overriding concern. Like art itself, the products surrounding art claim to provide, or to be linked to, an elevation above the economic system that determines what these products are and how they are distributed. Consumers are invited to participate in an escape from what they are leaping into.

• • •

In capitalism an increasing number of employees are hired primarily to think, rather than to use the labor of their hands. The value of mental capabilities as a commodity for hire rests on conceptions of individuality. The Reformation encouraged the autonomy of selfhood for religious reasons, and the consumer ego of capitalism has derived its humanistic notions of the value of mental capabilities from this noncommercial tradition. Mentalities are not quite as easily interchangeable as pairs of hands. Each is, to some extent, unique. The individual must (to pun) "count." The educational system teaches how this is done.

As a general mechanistic epistemology, empiricism is least effective when dealing with value or uniqueness, especially when the two must be combined. In empiricism, the unique is a particular aggregation of nonunique components (as matter is composed of atoms). In the assessment of art, this customarily leads to a prescriptive formalism. Empiricist rules have designated guardians. In employment, similarly, skills—repetitive behaviors designed to have repeatable outcomes— are assumed to be quantitative composites; hence they can be taught. (The assembly line is a logical consequence of empiricism). Talent is the innate ability to do far more than one has been taught; aptitude is the ability to do with extreme competence what one has been taught. Eventually aptitude is elevated as the empiricist's commercial counterpart of talent and aligned with a semicreative function. The presumed uniqueness of the individual's specific exercise of a generalized aptitude defines a "professional." (Nonprofessional workers are all presumed to exercise learned skills in the same way.) In addition, the development of commercial expertise can be freed from any reliance on the circumstances of birth, allowing the financially skilled to displace the aristocrat, the saint, and the genius.

By the seventeenth century, the argument had been made that the moral virtues (basically those of the "gentleman," found early in Castiglione's *Courtier*) are "naturally" inherent in certain humans.[7] Empiricism expands this idea into a general human nature that is noble and good, counteracting the belief in humankind's fundamentally sinful nature. (Although the Protestant ethic, even in its weakened state, holds that hard work compensates for ontological unworthiness.) The baser manifestations of human behavior are considered as the residual inheritances of an animal nature or attributable to social corruption. But in the nineteenth century, after empiricism has been long established, just as the notion of the value of rationality had been previously derived by empiricism from classical and humanist sources, so is the notion of the value of talent borrowed from romanticism. Romanticism had redefined capabilities in the transcendental mode while empiricist capitalism (ostensibly no friend of romanticism) was rapidly increasing. The empiricist transforms these capabilities into a marketable quality.

Empiricist capitalism eventually appropriates the romantic notion of artistic talent as a uniquely personal quality. It applies that notion to what the mercantilists had seen as basically undifferentiated rational abilities—a matter of skill, not personality. The romantics, however, had intended to apply the notion to talents quite the opposite of, and superior to, rational abilities. The empiricist usually describes human capability in quantitative terms, as amounts of certain energies contained under pressure in an enclosed system. Energy can produce work, and it is stored in substances from which it can be released, to satisfy need. Just as energy resides in coal, petroleum, and electricity, so mental energy resides in the mind. The deployment of this energy in an orderly way, imposed by reason, yields valued cultural products.

Deployment in a disorderly, un-reasonable way results in emotional chaos. For the empiricist, order affords the boundaries within which energy is allowed to function, like in the self-enclosed engine that empiricism invents. For the romantic, the effusion of creative energy carries its own order with it. The order is inherent in the source from which it emanates, whether that source is psychological, transcendental, or in the bond between these two. Rationality is not the ultimate source or validation of art but an inhibition of it.

Artistic matters were of little interest to the practical mercantilists and new capitalists, except as attention to them might emulate the tastes of aristocrats. (There is the role of portraiture in establishing and confirming individual selfhood, but to have one's portrait painted is not equivalent to being interested in art.) Art always remains subsidiary within empiricism, and when romantic notions about art are pulled into the empiricist environment, there is no real integration. The artist rents a studio in the least valuable commercial space and is quickly evicted when the property value rises: art itself is such a tenant of empiricism. That enclave—and the geographical metaphor is Bohemia[8]—will be the site where modernism germinates.

In seventeenth- and eighteenth-century neoclassicism, artistic talent is a skill serving specific purposes that overtly concur with the interests of the ruling class. Political governance is legitimated by the avowed permanence of clear and obvious truths. Art is a certain refashioning of "truth" in modes of language that increase the receptivity to it by increasing the pleasure that accompanies it. Truth is external to art: the truth might be in the world without any particular work being in the world. The artist (the poet in particular) is instructor, moralizer, entertainer, and artisan. Although few possess such skills, it takes no metaphysics to account for them, only a theory of "natural" endowment enhanced by education and practice. The endowment is a quantitative measure. (Like money: the rich have more than the poor, but not a different kind.) The term *inspiration* in empiricism pays a compliment to the idea, not to any mystery in the process of contriving it.

The romantic defines artistic talent transcendentally. Certain truths are brought into the world by art and exist not only inside the artwork, but by virtue of it. The source of these truths is not accessible through the empiricist theory of aggregated sense perceptions, since higher truths make empiricism itself a subordinate epistemology.

(Hence romanticism is politically subversive.) The senses know only the appearance of the real. "Nature" is more than the name for what God has made; rather, nature is itself the unified system of primary cause, often personified. Nature "does," "instructs," and "determines." For the empiricist, nature as a whole is nonliving, but living things are produced within it (by it) and inhabit it. For the romantic, nature as a whole is alive.

"Talent" is not quite sufficient to explain the artist to the romantic. Talent must be accompanied by creativity, by inspiration, by imagination, "a synthetic and magical power," according to Coleridge. "Imagination," formerly not a hallowed term but a sometimes derogatory reference to the fanciful, achieves elevated stature. The artist's ability is not a physical substance naturally endowed (like eyesight). Aggregational criteria can be left to the empiricists. The physicality of the human body serves as an intermediary between two levels of immateriality, both of which are more important: individual consciousness and the source of that consciousness. The body is the container of the former and the manifestation of the latter.

The admixture of a romantic notion of talent and genius into the empiricist setting is insufficient to decompose or disorient the grounding empiricism, as the modernists will afterward learn. For a while, it appears that art might advance over neoclassicism, incorporating some romantic ideas, yet satisfactorily serving practical empiricist interests. The art envisioned by Matthew Arnold was to replace religion by paradoxically setting romantic inspiration on the foundation of the very rationality that romanticism had in its own view surpassed and then institutionalizing that inspiration in the educational system. In Victorian England, and throughout Europe in the midnineteenth century, romanticism is coerced to take this conservative turn. Many artists reject being set on that conservative foundation, since it supports (with Hegel's assistance) the new governmental and educational bureaucracies just as neoclassicism had supported monarchy.

The romantic compromise with empiricism can be evidenced by the importance of landscape painting. A landscape can be viewed and interpreted compatibly through the eyes of an empiricist eighteenth-century deist and those of a transcendental romantic, since for both "nature" is inspiring evidence of its cause, even if for different reasons. The landscape allows an empiricist art that simultaneously offers an escape from empiricism. Where empiricism is strongest, in midnine-

teenth-century England, France, and the United States, landscape
painting is the most popular genre. Such painting (whether the Hudson River school or impressionism) is simultaneously an outcome of
and a reaction to empiricism. In literature, naturalism in the novel,
resting on the environmental determinism of Hippolyte Taine,[9] will be
the attack upon and the revocation of this compromise; concurrently,
the symbolist movement in poetry will fortify it. Modernism as a
whole is an even more substantial, insistent, and durable attempt to
sustain the accommodation of romanticism to empiricism. Since modernism begins by rejecting any accommodation to the bourgeoisie,
however, there is no need or respect for landscape painting or even
for nature itself. Modernism is pure aesthetic urbanity.

The empiricist does reluctantly admit that talent is perhaps not yet
fully explicable, citing encouraging and always very recent research
in neurophysiology. But when artists blatantly reject the empiricist
limitations, empiricism reacts by marginalizing art altogether. Art becomes the specialty of a small group, often enlisted from among those
who see their function as preserving what has been fatuously ignored
by moneyed interests. The romantic artists had ultimately been disillusioned by the French Revolution, which had been distorted and incomplete. The modernists insist that a new revolution is needed, with
an artistic militancy, an "avant garde," to subvert those who are by
now too powerful to overthrow: the plutocracy.

Empiricism will retaliate by discarding art (in the romantic sense)
altogether. In its place arises the field of entertainment, where talent
can be adequately dominated by business interests. (In popular American entertainment, the stereotypical diabolical evildoer, frequently
Germanic, possesses exquisite aesthetic sensibility; he is sometimes
effeminate—especially in his taste for the "masterpieces" of European
impressionism, for a semi-abstract ersatz expressionism, and for good
French wine.) *Modern* becomes a term of reference to a decorative
style, the latest fashion. Some professional entertainers do have a talent possessed by only a few; they can serve as examples presumably
corresponding to artists. Nevertheless, entertainment talent can be
comfortably considered a dexterity and not an insight, physical not
conceptual, and certainly not transcendental. Entertainment is a category of working: thinking goes into the production and is not a component of the performance.

Observing what one admires but cannot hope to do yields enthusiasm and pleasure. (Admittedly, if one does hope to do it, envy may dominate.) Sports, spectacle, singing and dancing "acts," and fictional and nonfictional public narrative (television, film, books, even "news") become products in a system where the performance cannot be seen or heard for free. Admission must be paid, either directly (at the gate, in a store) or indirectly (by buying the product of a sponsor). Art is made "free" to the public, in museums and libraries, public monuments and public television, although this always involves public revenues and contributions from wealthy patrons or the corporations they control. Providing the public with entertainment is a way of earning money; providing it with art is a way of spending some of that money (although many businesses and numerous employees depend on art institutions). Yet there is an interdependence here. In the modern consumer economy, art is "free" to the public only in proportion to the increase in the gross national expenditure on entertainment.

Since the consumer ego is given a residue of history by the educational system, it can sense that it is as superfluous as the products it consumes. There is consuming with no ultimate consummation. The consumer ego knows it is an ephemeral phenomenon and strives to make itself permanent in the materiality of products. For the viewer, the purpose of and justification for entertainment is completely exhausted in the immediacy of the performance, whereas art requires both an external history (because it carries meaning) and a destiny. (The history of art is not art, but the history of entertainment is itself a variety of entertainment). The consumer, who evaluates most purchases on the supposition that their purpose is to provide pleasure, becomes a dabbler in transitory stimulations. Although preceding traditions are sheltered in the educational system, which both preserves and enfeebles them, the ego must co-opt these traditions and turn them into products. The ego erases the past by reinterpreting the function of the past as a service, as a prelude (by now inferred more than remembered) to the capitalism to which it was destined to give birth. While this superficially resembles the willful detachment of modernism from the causation of its own past, it is different. The modernists consciously empower themselves to reinterpret or cancel the past, while the consumer ego does this automatically. The modernist rejects the past, whereas the consumer forgets it.

At this point psychology discovers the unconscious, as if the unconscious had always been a universal mental constituent. This now-discoverable unconscious evolves only to the extent that there is more and more material that the ego would be frightened to know—the insights into its mortality and the transience it shares with the products it possesses. The geographical space of the unconscious occupies the empty region where the soul once was. In psychoanalysis, this anxiety is narrated as if it were the rejection of, and guilt toward, the literal father. But it is actually the self that humans once were (or thought they were) being resisted and cast off. Anxiety and guilt accompany a will exerting itself to create an ego whose only destiny is its dissolution.

In the consumer ego, the past is held in a tenuous suspension, floating on the solvent of daily concerns. The consumer ego loses the contents and also the sense of the past. The past is transformed into simulations, antiques, and scenery, real as pastime but not as past time. Nor can the consumer ego see very far into the future. Time has been stupendously condensed. Everyone wakes up daily into a world that they believe has very recently been changed and is soon about to change. To compensate, the modern ego assures itself that it is not superfluous, stressing the importance of nonmarket activities: religion, nature, family, friends, and learning. But this portion of the modern ego is a remnant, a dwindling anachronism that has not yet been converted to product. By the midtwentieth century, any creeds alternative to production and consumption are no more than poses and platitudes. Firm dedication to an alternative creed is considered fanaticism. Even the modernists cannot halt this process, and as the century progresses, artists become the entrepreneurs they excoriate.

Still, the ego cannot willingly yield to its superfluousness. The ego faces its dissolution with horror. It knows that earning and purchasing cannot be eternal activities, yet all the activities once presumed outside the marketplace are nevertheless gradually converted to products. The ego strives to fortify itself by strengthening the very fortifications that are the primary signs of its superfluousness. The Pluto in plutocracy—as an aphorism, not an etymology—is the god of death.

• • •

The empiricist theory that complex ideas are constituted by the aggregation of simple ideas, that advanced concepts are constructed of rudimentary ones, is repeatedly found inadequate to account for artistic creativity. There, it seems, the whole not only exceeds the sum of its parts but precedes it. Whether to give logical priority to the whole or to its parts becomes the critical decision. But this decision is also central to defining self, subjectivity, ego, and related concepts. Which concepts represent irreducible entireties, and which do not? The "I" of the Cartesian "cogito," what "apperceives" for Kant, the "soul" as customarily defined—each of these is presumed a unity with content "inside" it. The personality, clearly not an irreducible entity, can be identified as such a content. But as empiricism progresses, the mental entities that had formerly been granted the status of a unity become uninteresting. Their existence as immaterial essences has little relevance for the scientific elaboration of psychological theory. Whether God or soul exists or not, "association" or the conditioned reflex remain exactly the same. For empiricism, the former names of immaterial unities can even be thought of as erroneous unitary designations for collective, basically physical phenomena.[10] Consciousness emerges from the complex brain as a necessary consequence of ornate material structure, and the contents of consciousness are assembled through aggregations of sense perceptions. This makes the notion of consciousness less puzzling (although more marvelous). Ego and personality become derivative assemblages, and the apparent unity of a consciousness extended in time is seen as an effect rather than as an ultimate cause.

Describing ego and personality as assembled from parts originating as properties of organized inert matter, rather than as precipitations from or within immaterial entities or substances, allows ego to develop a material and procedural correspondence in the world of manufactured products. Products serve as an externalization of the structure of ego. The most developed, complex, and advanced ego is presumably the ego that has integrated the largest variety of experiences. The increased contents of memory (as if the mind could get "bigger") is taken as a quantifiable achievement. In a consumer society, the preoccupying experiences occur while one earns money contributing to the production or distribution of products or services and afterward enjoys what subsequently can be purchased. The accumulation of products becomes visible evidence of ego maturity. Those who own the most are most admired, not simply for the quantity of their possessions but for the evidence this apparently provides of exceptional abilities and intellect, of talent. This evidence is taken as if it might substantiate that the ego is a unified entity. One wants to be wealthy not only to live like the rich but to *be* rich, as if this can verify a previously existing ontological state.

In an economy based fundamentally on money transactions—the distinction between the Middle Ages and the Renaissance—many people can work to produce products (although for a long while most people's work is growing food), to make purchases, and to advance economically. Money is an intermediate stage of potency. (The theory of money lies behind the physicist's theory of potential energy.) But before the empiricists outmode unified entities of consciousness, those entities (such as the soul) provided an ontological priority that ego rested on or was attached to. While mortality was no less threatening to the ego, consolations were available. But empiricism has proved thoroughly convincing; although we might like to believe in the old metaphysical staples, we cannot. Our very selves insinuate that the immaterial entities are irrelevant.

Total product accumulation then becomes an external equivalent to ego development. The products one owns become, as it were, an exoskeleton of ego. Both the ego and its image are aggregational quantities. This allows a new correspondence of the internal and the external, a reversal: while once the material world was situated between two irreducible immaterialities, God and the human spirit, now the immaterial world of mentality is situated between two irreducible materialities, nature and products. Once a special case of the former circumstance, art becomes a special case of the latter. At the end of life, we leave behind assets—these assets being the conversion of all our possessions into a single number representing their monetary worth. That number also represents the extent of ego development.

The self-reflexive ego knows that spiritual immortality cannot be based on such reasoning. Immortality, too, becomes defined in terms of the endurance of products. Remembrances are accumulated in photographs, mementos, corporate records, the file cabinets of attorneys.[11] (The artist's hopes rest in the possibility of fame.) One's assets are passed on to subsequent generations, whose future purchases depend on us.

As in physics, mass and energy—products and money—are mutually convertible. Money is the most compact form of storing products: a bookkeeping notation takes up a minuscule amount of room, yet can in principle contain anything. This is not the same as the transference of aristocratic or feudal wealth, for entailed land would not be converted into money, and subsequently into other products. Nor could the money generated by other products necessarily be converted into land, whose possession was constrained by birthright or conquest. Yet money becomes the primary desirable asset. In mercantilist theory, the goal is the national aggregate accumulation of gold and silver. In capitalism, the emphasis moves to money held by private individuals with private interests. The land, the mansion on it, or any other item is of no fundamental significance; all are potential purchases—up for sale at the right price. What matters is a computed number—the notational conception of an "amount," what one amounts to.

Artists and artworks provide the exception. For the majority, ego must correspond to products made by others. If products, no matter how expensive, are manufactured by replication, many people can own one, but no one can own *it*. The empiricist approach from Lucretius onward, that uniqueness comes from different combinations of homogeneous atoms, can be applied to private possessions: individuality is a personal assortment of the available variety of reproducible consumer goods. People transform their energy, or talent, either into manufactured products or into services that leave behind no durable product. Like the products we buy, the products we make (which we did not originally invent) can be judged only in aggregational terms. How many; how often? This judgment is called "product-ivity." Both what we make and what we own add up to the number that represents their economic valuation. But they do not add up to anything: meaning does not increase with production, since there is not a quantum of meaning in each item.

The artist claims an alternative ego process. Any artwork depends on a unique act by a specific individual. The product the artist makes (the product that ego is turned into) is one of a kind. What the artist leaves behind, then, is not simply a number representing an aggregation, but a coherent entirety, a body of work, including its meaning, that corresponds to a complete irreplicable entity of ego. Most people work because they have to; the artist makes artworks purely voluntarily. No amount of money can cause a specific artwork, while industrial research and development aim at specific products. Artworks are a physically durable product, yet there is only one authentic one of each. The artist can be thought not to need to amass ordinary purchases to be the ego's insectlike exoskeleton. The artist externalizes selfhood by embodying personality in individual artworks.

(For renowned people, a biographer performs the role of permanently incarcerating the ego in a product. But the relationship between biography and its subject is not that of the artist and the artwork, since the ego of the biographical subject is not the cause of the biographical work. Certain autobiographies are enduring precisely because they can be classified as artworks. Even revelation and prophecy must take the form of art, must lend themselves to literary critique to be important.)

Art is often purported to endure longer than anything else humans make. The artist might imagine this endurance as a longevity of the ego. Writing is the most notable case, since its endurance does not depend on any particular physical instance of the work, all of which are "copies." Accordingly, literature was once considered the foremost art—indeed, the only "art." Paintings and statues could be classified as "art objects" once they became as potentially transportable as books, and media became long-lasting (like oil paint).

This slow transference of ego to the outside, to purchases, is now the central process of modern life. What exists inside is simply a self-assessment (praise or blame), for which there is no permanent external embodiment. The artist disdains such a transfer of ego, having found an alternative method: to produce a permanent embodiment, with its own criteria for self-assessment. In capitalism, the distance between the artist and everyone else widens. Art places a claim on the immortality that the ego has forsaken—although since art, too, is a physical product, staking that claim is a long way from being granted possession. The anxiety of the artist attests to this dilemma.

• • •

The simultaneous romanticizing and commodification of the female body evolved in concert with the consumer ego. At first, in Western society, the female body is part of the capital of the male or males who control or own it, who use it for simple labor—the creation of additional assets (including children). While these activities may involve a certain morality, they are believed to require no talent. In the Enlightenment, some argue that the woman owns her own body. The female body becomes a paradigmatic example of how internal ego structures, like self-esteem and public value, are equated with a physical externality. The woman has a body that others desire to "possess," and hence need to negotiate for. Dowries eventually become obsolete: the body is the dowry. Later, as the capitalist consumer ego grows, women are allowed to have talent, first of a domestic kind (not only being mothers, but being good mothers) and then of a professional kind (through access to education). The more this process advances, the more her body is designated both as the site of selfhood and as the container of her talent, like the male body. The woman who for centuries had been denied full selfhood is granted it only when that selfhood has generally become ego—that is, when self is no longer that immaterial entity once allied with soul.

Since consumer ego is externalized in the products that it owns, both male and female bodies become products. The shape of the body becomes standardized when it becomes evaluated like other products. Clothes can be ready-made, sold from racks arranged according to a few basic sizes and styles, in the expectation that the purchaser will take measures to assure that his or her body will fit those dimensions. (Fitting well into such clothes by being slender also saves cloth for the manufacturer.) The standardized body achieves individuality by continuing to accumulate variations of color, pattern, and design, never varying far from basic configurations. Fashion comes to operate like a form of modern art, centered first in Paris (like modernist painting) and later in London (like modernist writing). The wealthy possess the originals, while inexpensive copies circulate among the public like reproductions of artworks.

In this way the body becomes an end, not only a means—an external possession, a product. Once a mediator between the self and the world, being not quite fully of either, now the body is fully in and of the world. The mirror relentlessly confirms this. While clothes remain symbolic, the unclad body as it is imagined by others—an imagining encouraged by form-fitting designs—becomes increasingly significant. By the twentieth century the body competes with the clothes for prominence, and society is overtly and unrepressedly sexualized. (Freudianism, for which the body is always in hiding, consequently declines.) The female body can serve as the visible symbol of the quality of her selfhood; she is as good as she looks to men. Male bodies are also assigned this function, so that the male appearance—the imagined body—takes on increasing social importance as a visible confirmation of social and professional competence and stature. The ego owns and drives the body like an automobile.

•　•　•

Talent is a capital resource; the individual has something to sell other than the easily replicated manual labor. Talent is nature's recompense for having been born to parents without assets. The concept of a personified parental Nature determining or endowing us with our basic qualities becomes more popular as empiricism expands. Such an endowment requires no ancestors, no homage, no thank-yous. The artist demonstrates how success can be achieved despite lack of initial command over capitalist resources. Artists are usually among the family's younger children, even though (as in other fields) an oldest child is proportionately more likely to succeed. Eventually, everyone's aptitudes are presumed to be somewhat different. We all think of ourselves as unique commodities (as the uniqueness of everyone's DNA seems nowadays to prove), which validates not only our individuality but its comparative value. Ego and personality appear to operate as the managers of inner resources and are judged by success at handling the matter. For the first time since the expulsion from Eden, the ordinary person can perceive work not as a curse but as an opportunity.

Where our useful talent resembles that of others, we compete with them for acclaim, self-esteem, and money. The competition extends to noncommercial areas (flirtation, athletics) where success is also measurable and the ego to be congratulated for it. These simulate economic competitiveness in a less threatening and financially unintimidating trial run—just as art is simulated action for the pragmatist.

Persons with unique talents are in an enviable market position, assuming that their talent takes a socially desirable form. Eager purchasers make talent valuable, according to the law of supply and demand. "Higher" education functions to place a person in a group where membership indicates that innate talents and aptitudes (which educators claim to measure) have been developed in a way not shared by those outside the group. Professional associations can then control many conditions of employment. (The guild system assumed that admittance granted permission to learn and practice the craft; absent is the idea of a necessary preexisting aptitude.) Basing admission to the profession on aptitude, rather than on family or apprenticeship, makes the process "democratic." The label "professional" attests to the refinement of one's innate talent, separating the professional from those who have skills anyone can learn. People at the bottom of the economic and social scale are those who have some skills but neither talent nor money.

A more recent assertion, made to keep democracy and capitalism internally consistent and ostensibly fair, is that *every* person has innate talent, enough to be convertible into a product. Not to believe this now connotes intolerance.

A talent possessed by one person only is a special case. If the talent is considered admirable, the person is called creative. In terms of empiricist "natural" endowment, creativity is difficult to account for. Nature, after all, appears to transmit shared universal characteristics. Consequently, from Aristotle forward, theories of society have been based on common traits of citizens, not on their individual personalities. In nature, the unique is a physical aberration, a freak, often inviable. Unique talent in humans is an empiricist mystery. The Platonic and idealist solution supposes some transcendent cause or ground, often connected to the metaphor of a gift or a visitation; but while empiricism periodically absorbs this metaphor, its fundamental theory relies on the "association" of ideas and the mathematics of combinational probability (nowadays on the stupendous numbers of neuronal axons and dendrons). This might explain why novelty sporadically erupts, but not why the inconsequentially small number of ideas that advance civilization regularly emerge from among the inconceivably large number of possible combinations. Furthermore, important ideas do not arise at random but occur in specific geographical locations, whose importance strangely varies throughout history.

The artwork serves as the model for a special sort of product. While (like modern technology) the artist unites talent and physical production, the artist completes the process in a single act. Manufacturing is a repetitive process yielding numerous duplicates; the value of the artwork depends on its uniqueness—the least economical way of making any other product. As a product of the artist's talent or genius, the work derives from a fundamentally mental attribute. To confirm that talent, the artist needs to produce additional works. "Flukes" rarely count. The more the artist verifies talent, the more the values of individual works increase. The rarity of the work (the rarity of the talent) increases with additional products: an economic paradox.

(There is a distinction between the painting or statue and the literary work, since the financial success of the latter depends on reproduction. Nevertheless, an original work, the manuscript, contains the writer's genius. The publisher purchases this, while everyone else purchases a licensed copy. In literature granted the status of art, variations from the original text are corruptions; in other products, variations are usually enhancements or improvements.)

That many works by the same artistic hand legitimate the value of any single work has become the paradigm for those employed in the professions. A sequence of valuable ideas, not quite identical but related, is generated by the same talent and manifested, like art, in a certain style. Style is linked to personality; the person is said to have a style (of thinking, of personableness), and the product is also said to have style (design, efficiency, or attractiveness). Only in the nineteenth century, as this aesthetic paradigm influences the commercial workplace, does the literary word *style* take on this widely generalized meaning. This personal uniqueness alleviates the worker's subordination to the employer. One can now have a career; one can be a "free" agent, carrying one's "capital" of talent from place to place. Manual workers cannot do this. Their change of position means no change in pay or status, which is what separates labor and management (a different concept than ownership) and underlies the rationale for unions. Being "locked in" is the most intolerable condition for the professional; being "locked out" is the most intolerable condition for the worker.

Allowing everyone to believe in their special marketable talent will change the work environment by the third quarter of the twentieth century, reducing the reliance on unions and increasing the reliance on advancement through extended employment or education. Even if the actual work involves simple manual repetition, one can refer to one's "experience" (a mental attribute) and, claiming seniority, be paid more for it.

We have all come to resemble romantic artists in modern guise. In recent capitalism, the employee is conceived as the embodiment of a unique mentality from which will issue creative contributions to the economy. Nearly every product now in the market is not found in nature. Food is the largest economic factor only in "backward" countries. Nor do these products result from simple skills like weaving, sewing, and handcrafting, common to everyone who cares to learn. Empiricist capitalism has appropriated the idealist aesthetic that had once labeled the uniqueness of talent as "creativity" and associated it with divine creation. Scientific capitalism counteracts the romantics' attack by transforming romanticism's aesthetic notions into general descriptions of human personality in the work setting, which capitalism promotes as the site of self-definition. Notions of artistic insight transcending rationality are transferred to the description of practical rationality, a reclamation of the priority of Enlightenment reason. Creativity is not the transcendence of ordinary daily business (as for the romantics or the modernists) but an aptitude exercised precisely within daily business. Creativity is made somewhat less mysterious and more physiologically comprehensible (right-brain/left-brain theories, and the like). As the service economy replaces agricultural labor and manufacturing is "farmed" out to poor populations, employees can increasingly claim that their business achievements result from talent, aptitude, native intelligence (exactly the opposite of the intelligence of a "native"), and creativity.

The capitalist can even point to the artist as exemplary. After all, the admirable artwork is forged by the unique mentality of the artist, since innumerable people can merely draw or write well. It can even be argued that artistic freedom is a derivative of the political freedom that has enabled us to exercise our talents freely; consequently, what produces outstanding artists is capitalism itself. Even the fascists and the communists agreed on this: modern art is capitalist art.

That artists are available for this appropriation as exemplars of capitalism, that they lend themselves to it, characterizes later modernism. The artist illustrates how talent translates into unique products. The artist's dedication to the work, without assurance of financial reward, illustrates dedication in its purity—an abstraction of the conscientious continuous work typical of successful entrepreneurs, including inventors. Americans cite Thomas Edison as often as the romantics once pointed to Christopher Columbus. Following World War II, the expanding class of employed and self-employed professionals and executives will be trained on this model.

Of course, the modern artist—who not uncommonly disdains this system or at least feels aloof from it until welcomed into it—must not believe that the work is specifically directed toward economic rewards. Working for the money is prima facie evidence that one does not deserve it. Nevertheless, without the possibility of monetary success, one's dedications are simply hobbies. Like the Calvinist dilemma that piety cannot itself bring salvation although the sign of being destined for salvation is piety, so artists cannot work for rewards the receipt of which is the only sign that they deserve them. Yet the greater an artist's purported aloofness from the economic system, the more can the artwork's price be manipulated. That image is now part of the price. The purported aesthetic distance from commerce is precisely what most increases commercial value.

Even the egos of the employer and employee come to share in this structural ambiguity. The consumer ego very often thinks of its "true" self as existing where it spends the least amount of time. The mountains, the woods, the familiar sites of romantic inspiration that people often describe themselves as preferring are where everything is enjoyed and nothing is consumed. Work behavior is often described as if it were an assumed role, perhaps a game, something done intentionally because one wants to be adroit at the ways of the world. The ego wants to believe it has command of its role and not vice versa, although the latter is more likely the case.

• • •

As the spiritualized entity of Cartesian selfhood was weakening in the confrontation with materialism, ego was solidly building its boundaries. The mind takes on the structure of the walled medieval towns, in cities that no longer physically need that structure. As physical protective barriers come down, mental ones are erected: the seclusion of the ego (alienation), the nation and national languages, religious divisiveness, political revolution, the selectivity of work, marriage, and recreation—all provide the individual ego with ever-increasing categories for defining, and sheltering, its unique qualities.

The process has become immeasurably enhanced by the stupendous number of consumer products the distinct ego can use to assure itself that it is unlike any other. Although Cartesian selfhood is a separate entity (distinct, autonomously rational), its complete isolation was prevented by its immersion in a universe created by a reliable and amiable God. When such a self detaches from the meaning that a familiarity with the transcendent deity could provide, it becomes insecure and unstable, seeking new assurances. Material products corresponding to itself provide those assurances.

The transition is marked by shifting the base of self-conception from what had characterized Catholic Europe to what had come to characterize Protestant Europe. The Reformation of Christianity is actually a transformation, allowing for and adapting to a selfhood compatible with the expanding dominance of economic values. Protestantism predicates the absolute fundamental isolation and loneliness of the individual. The remedy once was God; it is now economic vitality.

• • •

The modern individual in the capitalist work setting has come to resemble the romantic artist. Each person claims a degree of talent and creativity as a resource to be freely exercised and freely bargained for. Products, like artworks, issue from the contributions of presumably unique personalities with distinctive aptitudes. This development is heavily indebted to modernism, which (as I have repeated many times in this book) has tried to maintain the romantic image of the artist in the midst of an empiricist environment, with mixed success.

A most important result of this circumstance is that the class conflict predicted by Marx has failed to occur in the way that Marx imagined it. Marx could not have known that what we now call modernism would emerge to provide a certain kind of employed individual with a self-image that capitalism itself had not originally encouraged.

The individualism customarily associated with the Renaissance, and hence with early capitalism, is an individualism that served the wealthy and not the poor. There were very few who occupied an intermediary position. The middle class later evolved to the point where it required a distinctive self-image whose content was not determined by emulating distinctions and mannerisms characteristic of the aristocracy. The peasantry had customarily been attached to the land by virtue of being born on it, often legally bound to it; but with industrialization the worker is not legally obliged to take a job at any predetermined site. But once a job is taken, the owners control the terms of employment through their control of wages.

This is the condition Marx analyzed. For Marx, the employer-employee or owner-worker relationship did not lend itself to structural change, because even though the employees' relation to the work was contractual, the contract carried no stipulations beyond the exchange of work for wages. No social or ethical contract existed. The exchange of money for labor is severed from all other social relations, a circumstance Marx advocated abolishing in its capitalist form. The alternative—that contractual employment could entail wider ethical and social stipulations that would serve the worker, even at the cost

of reduced profit to the owner—did not seem possible to the economists of the time, who did not foresee a day when there would not be
masses of the unemployed willing to work at subsistence levels. Owners had no reason to amend these circumstances, and workers were
powerless to do so.

But while the economic structure of capitalism does not lend itself to
change, the participants in the structure have changed. The class warfare predicted by Marx has not occurred because of the advent of this
process by which consumer ego has become a relatively autonomized
talent for the professional classes, an ever-widening category to which
anyone may now aspire. Although Marx recognized that technicians
and managers would configure the production process, he could not
envision them as more than the embodiment of capital's co-optation of
thought and science as a specific form of labor. But the widespread attribution of professionalism to all manner of work at all levels has
changed certain "relations" of production. Unions, which served the
worker as proletarian, have been unable to serve this wider function.
Freedom is now conceived as the ability to exercise, deploy, and invest
one's talent and to negotiate for the use of it. The employee's ability to
redefine selfhood and reconfigure self-image around this displacement
of physical force (labor) by inherent ego capacities, combined with the
romantically inspired sense that one's life has a social purpose and destiny within the work setting, has become the alternative outcome to the
conflict of labor and capital. Through the professionalized concept of
talent, joined to appropriate auxiliary structures in the work setting
(personnel policies, associations, governmental supervision), the workers no longer think of themselves as laborers, at least not in the sense
of proletarians. This ego reorientation evidently increases happiness or
the hope for happiness.

This paradigm is now proclaimed to be the free market system that
has bested Marxist socialism, although the capitalism that now exists,
while constituted as Marx defined it, does not operate as it did when
Marx analyzed it. Moreover, many of the workplace changes necessary to implement this "free" market economy have socialist origins.
(It long ago became quite clear that the freedom of the market and
the freedoms of those in it are frequently incompatible.) In the 1990s,
the Eastern and Western blocks seem to be drawing closer together
on their economic policies and perhaps even their economic structures.[12] Nevertheless, while the Western capitalist democracies in-

creasingly incorporated socialist economic recommendations, this was not to embrace socialism but to prevent any possible social upheaval inspired by socialism. The modifications were made as if capitalism believed it had generated them itself.

The participants in the system have not so much changed their economic relations as altered their psychological relations. The structure manifests itself in new attitudes, first arising in the Anglo-American environment. (While one might have, in English, a "profession" as early as the sixteenth century, the noun *professional* enters the language in Marx's lifetime.) For example, the capitalist concedes that it is sound business practice to attract talent rather than labor, minds rather than solely bodies. Even where manual labor is employed, the professional class is given latitude by the owners to manage it. Retaining the specific manager is often more important than retaining any specific laborer, and managerial strategies are influenced by the career aspirations of the professionals. For the manager to acknowledge the workers' mentality creates the hierarchical scale of mental expertise on which both laborer and manager place themselves, since they are, after all, both employees. Only through their mutual acknowledgment of the criterion of mental ability can the managers be set socially and economically above the workers. The capitalist, too, has come to accept the definitions the professional class has given to itself. Even when their immediate interests conflict, the "bourgeoisie" and the workers now psychologically depend upon one another not only for their economic well-being but for their selfhoods. The bourgeoisie is not exactly bourgeois any more.

Marx's view of the potentials of a liberated human nature owes much to the interaction of romanticism and idealism, which he set against capitalism by the remarkable strategy of separating capitalism from empiricism. He rejected the assumption that the union of the two is necessary or natural, rejected the assumption that the discovery of empiricist economic "laws" had already validated capitalism as the system best designed to increase human happiness. Rather than placing socialism in opposition to empiricism, which was the initial strategy he derived from a nonempiricist Hegelianism, Marx later attaches empiricism to socialism by making capitalism a stage or episode inside a lawfully determined causal historical sequence leading to socialism. The "materialism" in dialectical materialism is an arrogated empiricism, expanded by the nineteenth century to include law-driven evolutionary causality.

Capitalism is not a necessary consequence of Enlightenment thinking. Nevertheless, Adam Smith's "invisible hand," the law of supply and demand, has been a convenient substitute for the noneconomic deterministic forces of time, history, and religion that modernity sought to obviate. While the invisible hand places determinism (law) in the midst of human freedom, it does so seemingly without violating that freedom. This is a perfect amalgamation of the empiricist paradox that while all events in the universe are strictly determined, an exemption of one sort or another can be made for human behavior. We act freely, although the aggregation of all these free acts can be exactly described by a mathematical formula, so that while we individually determine our acts one at a time, we are not in control of their aggregated results. My selfishness actually works to your benefit, and yours to mine.

The law of supply and demand requires the empiricist version of time: the two curves are presumed to exist synchronically and independently at each moment, and economic time is a sequence of these synchronous graphs, like the ticking of a clock. Capitalism is inextricably linked to time, and as time moves forward, so capitalism must ride along inside it or stagnate. This is the basis of the Marxist critique: capitalism cannot stabilize; it must grow or collapse; it cannot master time and reach equilibrium. In Marxist socialism, prices, wages, etc., are to be generated not solely by the flow of time inside a formula that depends on time but by permanent, planned human relations. Capitalism, however, insists that it can and will reach permanence, as a form (to use a biological analogy) of symbiosis: each citizen is conceived of as an entity with its own self-generated interests; and the system is their mutually beneficial cooperation, enacted with a daily consent. Change and growth need never end: change is increasing the number of people participating in the symbiosis.

The biological metaphor for the stability socialism hopes to achieve is, alternatively, homeostasis (a structural integrity based on a constant metabolism). The system is a fundamental unity, of which the members are components; they do not simply join or consent to the system; rather they are produced by the system. Growth, even if chosen as a benefit, is not necessary to the system. Socialism denies that capitalism can continually grow; capitalism denies that socialism can ever stabilize.

The aesthetics derived from romanticism relies on an "inspiration" that becomes a possible, even if impractical, alternative economic strategy. Inspiration (hence talent) is externalized and eternal-ized, both as a natural source of creative capital and as the "law" that yields creativity in artistic form. Like an "invisible hand," inspiration is both the force and the shape it takes. Otherwise, inspiration would be only a subjective and a historical event, and the artist could not claim transcendence.

Modernism revitalizes this aesthetic "economy" in its own antagonism to capitalism, although it cannot separate capitalism from empiricism (deductive reason, science, technology) as Marxism does. Capitalism then arrogates modernism's originally romantic aesthetic by making modernism a component of capitalism, which is why the Marxists repudiated modern art. But by encapsulating modernism, capitalism unwittingly adapted to modernism's attempted reconciliation of the capitalist ego and the romantic self—the transformation of romantic *self*-centeredness into modernist *ego*-centricity. By the mid-twentieth century, the responsibility for the transmission of "culture" is, after all, controlled in the classroom by those for whom modernism is most appealing.

In modernism we can find the immediate source of the attitudes concerning the creative self now embedded in the educational system and used to shape the egos of future professionals. Everyone now is a potential professional. These attitudes are no longer merely opinions of the self, but a constituent of ego. They—and consequently modernism itself—are ultimately responsible for counteracting Marx's predicted revolution inside capitalism.

Notes

Chapter 1: Modernity and Modernism

1. Within the extensive literature attempting to define modernism, the distinction between modernity and modernism, variously defined, has periodically been made; e.g., in Matei Calinescu, *Five Faces of Modernity* (Bloomington: Indiana University Press, 1977), and Renato Poggioli, *The Theory of the Avant-Garde* (Cambridge: Harvard University Press, 1968; first published in Italian, 1962). Calinescu distinguishes two types of "modernity" along the lines that modernity and modernism are distinguished here. A related comparison is elaborated in Daniel Bell, *The Cultural Contradictions of Capitalism* (New York: Basic Books, 1976).

From the 1930s modernism as a cultural and aesthetic phenomenon has been addressed as a coherent movement. See e.g., Edmund Wilson, *Axel's Castle* (London: Scribners, 1931); Jose Ortega y Gasset, *The Modern Theme* (New York: Norton, 1933; trans. of *El tema de nuestro tiempo* [1931]); and Herbert Read, *Art Now* (London: Faber and Faber, 1933). Of the many important works that followed through the 1970s, a few illustrative ones are Jacques Barzun, *Classic, Romantic, and Modern* (New York: Doubleday, 1961); Peter Faulkner, *Modernism* (London: Methuen, 1977); Northrop Frye, *The Modern Century* (Toronto: University of Toronto Press, 1968); Irving Howe, *The Decline of the New* (New York: Harcourt, Brace, and World, 1970); Louis Kampf, *On Modernism* (Cambridge: MIT Press, 1967); Joseph Wood Krutch, *The Measure of Man* (Indianapolis: Bobbs-Merrill, 1954); Stephen Spender, *The Struggle of the Modern* (London: Hamilton, 1963); Wylie Sypher, *Loss of the Self in Modern Art and Literature* (New York: Random House, 1962); Lionel Trilling, *Mind in the Modern World* (New York: Viking, 1973). In addition, innumerable studies address specific movements, genres, and countries. A helpful bibliography can be found in Malcolm Bradbury and James McFarlane, eds., *Modernism* (New York: Penguin, 1976; reprintings have updated the bibliography through around 1980). There are even more numerous studies of individual artists, authors, thinkers, critics, theories, and works. There is a good introductory bibliography on modernism and related subjects in Norman F. Cantor, *Twenti-*

eth Century Culture (New York: Peter Lang, 1988). Recent literature also looks at modernism as a movement turned into or superseded by postmodernism. It nowadays requires some restraint to leave Derrida, Lacan, Foucault, Baudrillard, Barthes, Lyotard, et al. out of any discussion. Good bibliographies follow each essay in Bryan Turner, ed., *Theories of Modernity and Post-Modernity* (London: Sage, 1990). For structuralism and post-structuralism in literary theory, there is a bibliography in my *From the New Criticism to Deconstruction: The Reception of Structuralism and Post-Structuralism* (Urbana: University of Illinois Press, 1988).

2. Freud published *The Interpretation of Dreams* in 1900. Modernism has at times allied itself either with a psychology of the unconscious or with the more empiricist behaviorism that proliferated after J. B. Watson's *Behaviorism* (1924), although the two approaches are antagonistic. Modernists on the political Left have usually been attracted to theories of the symbolic unconscious stressing the distinctions between thoughts and their hidden causes. Modernists on the political Right have welcomed modified behavioral theories stressing the function of art as the conscious and intentional organization of sensation, perception, and emotion.

3. The transcendental logic is to "examine the origin of our cognitions of objects so far as that origin cannot be ascribed to the objects themselves" (Immanuel Kant, *Critique of Pure Reason,* 2d ed., trans. J. M. D. Meiklejohn [New York: Dutton, 1950], introduction, sec. 2). Kant refutes what he calls material idealism—the idea that objects existing "in space without us" is "doubtful and undemonstrable" or "false and impossible" (book 2, chap. 2, sec. 3). Kant had Berkeley in mind and could not anticipate the more complex idealism that would arrogate him as its precursor.

Johann Gottlieb Fichte's idealism is first explicated in *Basis of the Entire Theory of Science* (1794). See Fichte, *Science of Knowledge,* trans. P. Heath (New York: Cambridge University Press, 1982). Fichte's notion of "ego" is a transcendental ego that is intuited since it is beyond objectification, not the psychoanalyst's "ego" or personalized "I." For G. W. F. Hegel on the Absolute, see *Encyclopedia of Philosophy,* trans. G. E. Mueller (New York: Philosophical Library, 1959), esp. part 3, and the so-called Greater Logic, *Science of Logic, 1812–16,* trans. A. V. Miller (Atlantic Highlands, N.J.: Humanities Press International, 1969).

4. In the nineteenth century, certain thinkers hoped to return to the Kantian philosophy as an ally of scientific investigation, rejecting what they saw as the irrational distortions imposed upon Kant by idealism. The movement begins with Hermann von Helmholtz and F. A. Lange. A subsequent variety of related German approaches includes the work of Wilhelm Windelband. In sociology, Georg Simmel and Max Weber represent the movement.

5. Some relevant texts are Friedrich von Schiller, *On the Aesthetic Education of Man, in a Series of Letters* (1795), trans. E. M. Wilkinson and L. A. Willoughby (Oxford: Oxford University Press, 1967), and Friedrich Schlegel, *Dialogue on Poetry* (1800), trans. E. Behler and R. Struc (University Park: Pennsylvania State University Press, 1968). For Novalis (Friedrich von Hardenberg), see

Hymns to the Night and Other Selected Writings, trans. C. E. Passage (New York: Liberal Arts, 1990). Also, Friedrich Wilhelm von Schelling, *On the Relation of the Plastic Arts to Nature* (1807), in Hazard Adams, *Critical Theory since Plato* (New York: Harcourt, Brace, Jovanovich, 1971), 446–58; Hegel, *Aesthetics* (1835), trans. T. M. Knox (Oxford: Clarendon Press, 1975), a collection made up from manuscript notes of lectures given from 1820 forward.

6. Some typical expressions of this theme in the United States run throughout *America and Alfred Stieglitz,* ed. Waldo Frank, Lewis Mumford, Dorothy Norman, Paul Rosenfeld, and Harold Rugg (New York: Literary Guild, 1934). Contributors include William Carlos Williams, Lewis Mumford, Gertrude Stein, Paul Strand, and Jean Toomer.

7. The work of Saint-Simon, Fourier, and Comte illustrates how history as progress toward maximizing human happiness might be fulfilled through the idea of a permanent community on fixed and enduring principles. In the midnineteenth century, ideal communities were founded in the United States by communists, Christian socialists, Owenites, Fourierists, Icarians, etc. Many Europeans emigrated for that purpose.

8. Two of the important texts defending the moderns are, in France, Charles Perrault, *Parallele des anciens et des modernes,* in four parts between 1688 and 1696, and, in England, Jonathan Swift's *Battle of the Books,* written ca. 1696–98, although not published until 1704.

9. Descartes, *Meditations on the First Philosophy* (1641), Meditations 3 and 4, provide proofs of the existence of God. In the *Essay Concerning Human Understanding* (1690), Locke relies on a version of the cosmological argument that every phenomenon must have a cause: since I obviously exist, there must be a cause for it, and so on, back to a grounding cause.

10. Conservative reactions after the defeat of Napoleon were widespread. There was a suspicion of journalism, for example, especially of attacks on social abuses in the Voltairean manner and of liberal professors, who lost their positions. Even in England the Six Act was passed in 1819, setting restrictions on gatherings and publications, although the act had little actual effect.

11. Modernism's ultimate reliance on aesthetic values to the exclusion of spiritual values is, according to Suzi Gablik, the weakness that condemns it. See *Has Modernism Failed?* (New York: Thames and Hudson, 1984).

12. Timothy Reiss, *The Discourse of Modernism* (Ithaca: Cornell University Press, 1982), discusses Jean-Pierre Vernant's assertion that the theory of the will in Aristotle did not include intellectual deduction, in the sense of planning prior to the exercise of volition, but meant only actions done without coercion from without. The idea of a "free will" in the now-common usage, the argument continues, did not enter the Greek vocabulary until around the first century B.C.

13. In the *Discourse on Method,* Descartes states (in part 2) that he "will accept nothing as true which I did not clearly recognize to be so." If "we abstain from receiving anything as true which is not so, and always retain the order which is necessary in order to deduce the one conclusion from the other, there can be nothing so remote that we cannot reach it, nor so recondite that

we cannot discover it" (*Descartes: Selections*, ed. R. M. Eaton [New York: Scribners, 1955]).

14. Thomas Hobbes's *Leviathan* was first published in 1651, nearly forty years before Locke's *Essay.*

15. Hume's *Treatise of Human Nature* was written in 1737. "This skeptical doubt is a malady, which can never be radically cured. . . . 'Tis impossible upon any system to defend either our understanding or senses; and we but expose them farther when we endeavor to justify them in that manner" (part 4, sec. 2).

16. The monism of Advaita Vedanta, based on the Vedic commentaries of Sankara, the eighth-century Indian philosopher, is of particular relevance here, since it was the most attractive form of Indian philosophy in the nineteenth century. See Karl H. Potter, *Presuppositions of Indian Philosophy* (New York: Prentice-Hall, 1963).

17. All Enlightenment thinkers did not support the optimistic exclusion of human will from strict causation; consider Helvétius, La Mettrie, and d'Holbach. Whatever the specific arguments, room was always made for intentional human progress.

18. God's persistent endeavor could also be supplemented by the work of angels. Both St. Bonaventure and St. Thomas Aquinas held this belief in the thirteenth century. Isaac Newton, in the *Principia* (1687), allowed that God could intervene from time to time to make small rectifying adjustments in the planets' orbits. Around the turn of the nineteenth century, Laplace showed that such small modifications were unnecessary. The Cartesians often attacked Newton's theory because it could not explain why the planets were in motion in the first place, even if gravity existed.

19. "The conditions of the *possibility of experience* in general are at the same time conditions of the *possibility* of the *objects* of *experience,* and have, for that reason, objective validity in an *a priori* synthetical judgment" (*Critique of Pure Reason,* book 2, sec. 2).

20. In the *Critique of Practical Reason,* Kant allows the moral sense, or reason, to serve as a basis by which one is led, necessarily, to the ideas of God and free will, which Kant offers as a special kind of proof. While he had once refuted all logical proofs of God's existence, he argues that "We *ought* to endeavor to promote the highest good (which therefore must be possible). Therefore we must *postulate* the existence of a cause of the whole of nature, which is different than nature, and which contains the ground . . . of happiness and morality" (trans. T. K. Abbot [London: Lippincott, 1905], 221).

21. It is Fichte's position that the human spirit fulfills itself by moral striving. Since striving requires a resistance, the world serves the absolute ego as the setting for, as well as the impediment to, its active endeavor toward its own freedom. The idea that the resistance emanates from the same divine source that shall overcome it is earlier found in Jacob Boehme.

22. Hegel's transformation of freedom from a concept to a force is particularly evident in his *Reason in History* (trans. R. S. Hartman [New York: Liberal Arts, 1953]). "Consciousness in itself, freedom abstractly considered, is the formal aspect of the activity of the absolute Idea" (33).

23. As early as the twelfth century, the monastic artist Theophilus wrote, "Let no one glorify himself and not another but let him humbly render thanks to God" (quoted in Andrew Martindale, *The Rise of the Artist* [New York: McGraw Hill, 1972], 57).

24. Throughout the history of Christianity, art has been used to signify the transcendent, and even to evoke it. In the eighteenth century, before idealism and romanticism are fully developed as radical alternatives to traditional orthodoxy, there are numbers of proposals to integrate the common orthodoxy with a religious aesthetic, especially in Germany. Chateaubriand, at the beginning of the nineteenth century, exemplifies this approach in France.

25. For Friedrich Schlegel, the artist discovers his own participation in divinity through the discovery of individuality through creativity. For Schelling, the human mind realizes its infinite nature in art. For Novalis, poetry reveals the infinite that grounds meaning; the artist is like God, a creator, mediating between the finite and the infinite, freely transforming the world, not merely accepting its empirical reality. For Schiller, too, art allows the world to be freely constructed in order to be known in forms not subordinated to rational materialism.

26. See J. Hillis Miller, *The Disappearance of God* (Cambridge: Harvard University Press, 1963).

27. The Anglo-American lineage for this view passes from Coleridge to Carlyle to Emerson and Thoreau.

28. There was good reason to believe Hegel was right about the emergence of freedom. Slavery was abolished in the British colonies in 1833, in the French colonies in 1848, and later in the colonies of Portugal and the Netherlands. Slavery was also abolished in Columbia in the 1820s, in Mexico in 1829, in Argentina in 1853, in Venezuela in 1854, in Peru in 1856, and in the United States in 1863.

29. Even in England, the bastion of empiricism, idealism was formidable, especially through the work of T. H. Green, Bernard Bosanquet, and F. H. Bradley, whose important *Appearance and Reality* appeared in 1893. T. S. Eliot did his doctoral dissertation on Bradley.

30. Russell discusses his own transformation in *Autobiography of Bertrand Russell*, 3 vols. (Boston: Little Brown, 1967–69), vol. 1.

31. See Bergson, *An Introduction to Metaphysics* (1903), trans. T. E. Hulme (New York: Liberal Arts, 1949). For Croce, the artist intuits a preperceptual nature; because this intuition is by some direct means made an object through its expression in art, the intuition and the expression are congruent. See *Aesthetic as Science of Expression and General Linguistic* (1902), trans. C. Lyas (Cambridge: Cambridge University Press, 1992).

32. Bergson's *Creative Evolution* (1907), trans. A. Mitchell (1911; rpt., Westport, Conn.: Greenwood Press, 1975).

33. Ampere's classic paper *Experiments on the New Electrodynamical Phenomena* appeared in 1822, when Hegel was in his fifties. Of course, it took some decades for field theory to mature.

34. Gertrude Stein and the group that gathered around her experimented with and published the results of automatic writing, done with the arm in a

loose suspended sling. When Stein was at Radcliffe, one of her professors was William James. Automatic writing was commonplace among the surrealists.

35. Eugene Chevreul's *The Principles of Harmony and Contrast of Colors* (1839) discussed how colors placed in proximity influence one another. That a color could be created by having the viewer's eye construct it from patches of primary colors, rendering the color more brilliant, was a scientific as well as an aesthetic insight. In the spirit of the age, the impressionists cultivated scientific interests. Pissarro and, later, Seurat read the work of Hermann Helmholtz and James Clerk Maxwell. Ogden Rood's *Modern Chromatics* (1879) influenced Seurat, Delaunay, and Kupka. One also notes Brisset, a philologist who based a theory of language on the pun, which some dadaists were attracted to. A full study of these matters (excluding Brisset) appears in Paul Vitz and Arnold Glimcher, *Modern Art and Modern Science* (New York: Praeger, 1984).

36. Edmund Wilson attributes the source of modernism to symbolism in *Axel's Castle* (1931). Axel is the tormented German aristocrat in the symbolic play (*Axel*) of Villiers de L'Isle-Adam.

37. In *The Postmodern Condition* (Minneapolis: University of Minnesota Press, 1984), Jean-Francois Lyotard posits that the "grand narratives" of the Enlightenment have been declining and are now moribund. Even should this be the case, these narratives are modernity's, not modernism's, for in modernism the relinquishing of narrative is never a disaster, only an aesthetic experiment. If "postmodernity" is also "postmodernism" (which is unlikely, although many writers use the one term for both meanings), it would be because modernism can be no more vital than the surrounding "medium" of modernity, in which modernism has prospered by an assault of a kind that ultimately makes it a collaborator. Modernism's failure might be seen as an indirect result of modernity's irresoluteness and decline. The view taken here, however, is that modernity is still thriving, although in France, England, and the United States during the late 1970s and early 1980s there was much reason for intellectuals on the political Left to be dejected. But even should modernity continue to thrive, as seems likely (and perhaps Jürgen Habermas is correct: the Enlightenment project still needs to be fulfilled), modernism will have concluded.

Chapter 2: Modern Art and Literature: Early Phases

1. In 1883, the Danish critic Georg Brandes published a series of exceptionally well-received essays entitled *Men of the Modern Breakthrough* (*Det moderne Gjennembruds Maend*), in which he gave substantial attention to Ibsen. Generally, certain midnineteenth-century authors were by the end of the century considered "modern": Ibsen, Flaubert, Strindberg, Nietzsche, Kierkegaard.

2. See David Perkins, *A History of Modern Poetry: From the 1890s to the High Modernist Mode* (Cambridge: Harvard University Press, 1976), for poets writing in English; also Marjorie Perloff, *Poetic License* (Evanston: Northwestern University Press, 1990).

3. The Salon de Refusés was established on the whim of Louis Napoleon,

who visited the Salon and ordered the rejected works (three-fifths of those submitted) hung in a separate place. Manet's *Dejeuner sur l'Herbe* received widespread notice, annoying the critics as much as the exhibit of Manet paintings earlier that year. Baudelaire's essay on his friend Manet is among the favorable responses. See the collection of reviews by Baudelaire in *Art in Paris, 1845–1862*, trans. and ed. Jonathan Mayne (London: Phaidon, 1965).

4. Kant's statement is in his *Kritik der Unteilskraft*, quoted in Hugh Honour, *Neo-Classicism* (London: Penguin, 1968), 114.

5. The primary/secondary distinction is Galileo's, used by Descartes and accepted by Locke. Berkeley rejects the distinction, as have many writers since.

6. Symons's *The Symbolist Movement in Literature* was first published in 1899, revised and republished in 1919. Pound and Eliot learned much from the symbolists; and Eliot's having been led to the poetry of Jules Laforgue through Symons's book is usually considered an important event. Pound, however, had little tolerance for the symbolists' longings for the rarefied infinite and absolute. Eliot, of a different sensibility than Pound, converted to Catholicism in 1927. See Perry Meisel, *The Myth of the Modern* (New Haven: Yale University Press, 1987), and Louis Menand, *Discovering Modernism* (Oxford: Oxford University Press, 1987).

7. The British pre-Raphaelite painters began as a group in 1848 and included Dante Gabriel Rosetti, J. E. Millais, Edward Burne-Jones, and William Holman Hunt. Hunt exhibited work in Paris in 1855 (Timothy Hilton, *The Pre-Raphaelites* [New York: Oxford University Press, 1970]).

8. *The Complete Letters of Vincent Van Gogh*, 2d ed. (Boston: New York Graphic Society, 1981).

9. See *Cézanne by Himself: Drawings, Paintings, Writings*, ed. Richard Kendall (Boston: Little, Brown, 1988).

10. In the early eighteenth century, George Berkeley argued that an object's essence is equivalent to its perception, since whenever any object is imagined, the existence of an observer looking at it is presumed in thought. Berkeley therefore rejects the distinction between primary and secondary qualities: all properties of objects result from the perception of them, and what objects are without anyone looking at them is a nonsensical question. Here, then, is a precursor of the modernist connection between turning away from the "primary" qualities and what is, for early modernism, the aesthetic principle that seeing is itself the cognition of essence.

11. For the prioritizing of the visual as a mode of thought, even to the extent that there need not be any dependency on language, see Rudolf Arnheim, *Visual Thinking* (Berkeley: University of California Press, 1969), 68, 101–2, 236–37.

12. Lawrence Gowing writes, "No single touch of paint corresponded to any specific object" in Turner's later painting (*Turner: Imagination and Reality* [New York: Doubleday, 1966], 16). The possible influence of Turner and Constable on impressionism is based on Monet's and Pissarro's presence in London during 1870, where they saw these painters' works.

13. Wolfgang Kohler published his influential work on the mentality of apes in 1917. His *Gestalt Psychology* appeared in 1929. See *Documents of Gestalt Psychology*, ed. Mary Henle (Berkeley: University of California Press, 1961).

14. The surrealists also were attentive to the work of psychic mediums and experimented with techniques of psychic automatism. The surrealist artist is as much the observer of the work as its creator, said Max Ernst: the artist watches the work emerge, often without even having to assist it very much. Breton, incidentally, visited Freud in Vienna in 1921.

15. For general, well-illustrated summaries of movements in modernist painting, see Sam Hunter and John Jacobus, *Modern Art* (New York: Abrams, 1985); John Russell, *The Meaning of Modern Art* (New York: Museum of Modern Art, 1981); H. H. Arnason, *History of Modern Art* (New York: Abrams, 1978); *Modern Art and Modernism*, ed. F. Franscina and C. Harrison (New York: Harper and Row, 1982).

16. Husserl warns against psychologizing in the Prolegomena of *Logical Investigations*, trans. J. N. Findlay (London: Routledge and Kegan Paul, 1970).

17. Ludwig Feuerbach's *Thoughts on Death and Immortality* (1830) denies the possibility of immortality because the very nature of humans, of God, and of the relation between them makes immortality logically infeasible. In the twentieth century, existentialism has theistic adherents (Tillich or Buber) and atheistic adherents (Sartre), but an inescapable mortality is philosophy's central tenet for both.

Heidegger's discussions of death and of time are in sections 45–53 and 61–71 of *Being and Time*, trans. J. Macquarrie and E. Robinson (New York: Harper, 1962).

18. Much attention was given to the dehumanization caused by modern technological change and the intensifying urban environment. In the United States, there is Lewis Mumford, *The Condition of Man* (New York: Harcourt Brace, 1944).

19. To see the issue as a matter of vocabulary is more critical than it may at first appear. The rules of grammar—whether grammar is strictly a conventional code or derives, as Noam Chomsky contends (*Syntactic Structures* [The Hague: Mouton, 1957]), from innate brain structures—define which sentences in a language are formally correct and which are incorrect, regardless of what they mean. Users of the language usually can immediately distinguish between correct and incorrect sentences. But in art there is no grammar that disallows expressions (artworks) of a certain kind because they are incorrect. The visual and literary arts have a vocabulary, but not a grammar one can violate, even if conventions can be violated. (On related matters, see Terence Hawkes, *Structuralism and Semiotics* [Berkeley: University of California Press, 1977].)

20. A number of the sources concerning artistic manifestos, including spiritual ones, appear in Herschel B. Chipp, *Theories of Modern Art: A Sourcebook* (Berkeley: University of California Press, 1968). See esp. Wassily Kandinsky, *Concerning the Spiritual in Art* (1912; rpt., New York: Wittenborn, 1947); Roger Lipsey, *An Art of Our Own: The Spiritual in Twentieth Century Art* (Boston: Sham-

bhala, 1988), and *The Spiritual in Art: Abstract Painting, 1890–1985* (New York: Abbeville, 1986).

21. The use of *interpretation* as a word indicating a proper signification or meaning goes back to the fifteenth century. New is the idea that the world as a whole is a text subject to interpretation and that such an interpretation can be a "personal" one.

22. John Keats's concept of "negative capability" appears in a letter written in 1817. (See *The Letters of John Keats,* ed. Maurice Forman [New York: Oxford University Press, 1952].)

23. Pound's imagist manifesto says, "The natural object is always the *adequate* symbol. . . . Go in fear of abstractions" (quoted in Malcolm Bradbury and James McFarlane, eds., *Modernism: 1890–1930* [London: Penguin, 1976], 231).

The Bloomsbury group (Lytton Strachey, E. M. Forster, Clive Bell, Virginia Woolf, G. E. Moore, John Maynard Keynes, et al.) lasted for about twenty years, from 1910 to 1930.

24. In biblical studies, *exegesis* had been defined as interpretation and *hermeneutics* as the development of the principles on which interpretation would be conducted. The latter term, extended beyond biblical studies, came to indicate that the principles of interpretation must acknowledge that the purposes and intentions of the interpreter shape the interpreter's position in regard to what is perceived as reality. Interpretation cannot simply be "objective," especially when one looks at social phenomena, including texts. The texts themselves have been produced by authors necessarily also embedded in a context of culturally determined meanings and forms, perhaps not (at first) shared by the interpreter. Interpretation is an interaction with what is being interpreted, and the interpreter cannot be extricated from the text under scrutiny. These matters are discussed in Roy Howard, *Three Faces of Hermeneutics* (Berkeley: University of California Press, 1982).

25. In *The Well-Wrought Urn* (New York: Harcourt Brace, 1956), Cleanth Brooks writes that in a poem we do not find "an idea or set of ideas, which the poet has communicated. . . . The poem itself is the *only* medium that communicates the particular 'what' that is communicated" (74).

26. For a profusely illustrated history of photorealism, see Louis K. Meisel, *Photorealism* (New York: Abrams, 1872); also Frank H. Goodyear, *Contemporary American Realism since 1960* (Boston: New York Graphic Society, 1981).

27. Attacking the scientific relevance and reputation of Freud is now a small empiricist industry as Freudianism loses its immense influence. However, Freud and his theories have taken on a new life in French post-structuralism. See the work of Jacques Lacan, for example (*Ecrits: A Selection,* trans. A. Sheridan [New York: Norton, 1977]). That Freud has not been granted the empiricist stature that was his aim has in fact encouraged his availability for the Continental philosophy grounded in phenomenology.

28. The term *transparent technology* is in Hugh Kenner, *The Mechanic Muse* (New York: Oxford University Press, 1987).

29. In 1839 Dominique Francois Arago delivered a report to the Chamber of Deputies in Paris in which he lauded the potential scientific uses of pho-

tography and its "economic advantages which, incidentally, seldom go hand in hand in the arts with the perfection of production" (23). That is, in the arts the costs rise with "perfection," but the perfect accuracy of photography is achieved at a small cost. Arago made a similar report to the French Academy of Sciences. Louise Daguerre wrote that the photographic process "is not merely an instrument to draw nature; on the contrary, it is a chemical and physical process which gives her the power to reproduce itself" (13). Both views are included in Alan Trachtenberg, ed., *Classic Essays on Photography* (New Haven: Yale University Press, 1980).

30. Alfred Stieglitz's life work was to be himself the undeniable demonstration of genius in photography. He edited *Camera Work,* which appeared, on a sometimes irregular schedule, between 1902 and 1917 and which contained the work of many photographers who firmly established the medium as an art form. The small galleries he personally maintained and himself staffed in New York premiered in the United States the work of Matisse, Picasso, Rodin (drawings), Picabia, and others. These exhibits were the most significant American preparation for the Armory Show in 1917.

31. Arnold Hauser writes that the humanists saw the artists as reinforcing their own views and their own hard-earned status. This "mutual relationship first gave rise to that conception of the unity of the arts . . . unknown before the Renaissance" (*The Social History of Art* [New York: Vintage Book/Random House, n.d.], 2:62).

32. The theory of "complementarity"—that light is both a particle and a wave—is Niels Bohr's. In a specific experiment light will appear either as a particle or as a wave. The way we choose to observe it determines what it will be found to be. This reinforces a Kantian view of quantum physics.

33. Mendeleyev's periodic table followed John Dalton's development of the idea of atomic weights. Mendeleyev's final version was published in 1871.

34. Pointing to the limitations entailed by the use of a camera is sometimes considered insulting to photography. When Rudolf Arnheim pointed to the "powerful material constraints" of the camera ("On the Nature of Photography," *Critical Inquiry* [Sept. 1974]), he was heatedly refuted by Joel Snyder and Neil Walsh ("Photography, Vision, and Representation," *Critical Inquiry* [Sept. 1975]).

35. George Eastman, the founder of Eastman Kodak, coated a pliable material with the photographic emulsion so that a long length of film could be rolled up and pulled by a take-up roller a segment at a time behind the lens.

36. Various forms of artwork use photographic materials to produce images. "Photography" here refers to an image resulting from, in the common terminology, "taking a picture": the image in the photograph is *of* something (some thing) external to the camera. Painting with light on light-sensitive materials is not photography, even if one insists on noting that the word *photography* might include this in a literal interpretation ("light drawing").

37. Baudelaire was not impressed. In a review of the Salon of 1890, he said that "in these deplorable times" those who believe art must be "an exact reproduction of nature" have been heard by an "avenging God [who] has

heard the prayer of this multitude: Daguerre was his messiah" (Trachtenberg, 86–87). Matisse declared that photography had freed him, and painting generally, from the need to "copy" things.

38. By the late seventeenth century Dutch painting is clearly an excerpt of a reality extending beyond the frame. Dutch "genre" painting in general employs the technique. See J. R. Martin, *Baroque* (New York: Harper and Row, 1977).

39. On the absence of surface tactility in photography, see Richard Hennessey, "What's All This about Photography?" *Artforum* 17, no. 9 (May 1979).

40. "The mistake which has led so much theorizing on art into the bog is in thinking that there must be means of representing 'appearances' or even 'space' *as such*" (E. H. Gombrich, *Art and Illusion* [Princeton: Princeton University Press, 1960], 261; emphasis mine). Also, the art of perspective "wants the image to *appear* like the object. . . . It does not claim to show how things appear to us, for it is hard to see what such a claim could mean" (257; emphasis mine).

41. In the best-known work of the International Gothic, the *Tres Riches Heures* made by the Limbourg brothers in the early 1400s for the Duke of Berry in the Court of Burgundy, human figures set behind one another look almost like cutouts, one pasted partially over the other.

42. The technique of indicating depth by comparative size alone was much admired at the time in Katsushika Hokusai's series "Thirty-six Views of Mt. Fuji." See Kirk Varnedoe, *A Fine Disregard: What Makes Modern Art Modern* (New York: Abrams, 1990), chap. 2.

43. "Let anyone consider those arguments which are thought manifestly to prove that colors and tastes exist only in the mind, and he shall find that they may with equal force be brought to prove the same thing of extension, figure, and motion" (George Berkeley, *The Principles of Human Knowledge*, part 1, par. 15).

Chapter 3: Modern Art and Literature: Later Phases

1. For bibliography in American literature, see *Literary History of the United States*, ed. R. E. Spiller, W. Thorp, et al. (New York: Macmillan, 1967). The bibliography is in two volumes, and there is a 1972 supplement. Numerous theoretical works are referred to in the endnotes to Vincent B. Leitch, *American Literary Criticism from the Thirties to the Eighties* (New York: Columbia University Press, 1988). See also the bibliographical volumes in the multivolume collection of critical essays *Twentieth Century American Literature*, ed. Harold Bloom (New York: Chelsea House, 1988). For theoretical works in literary criticism, *International Bibliography of Literary Theory and Criticism*, ed. Ralph Cohen (Baltimore: Johns Hopkins University Press, 1988), includes chapters on works written in English. There is a good bibliography in *Image and Ideology in Modern/Postmodern Discourse*, ed. David B. Downing and Susan Bazargan (Albany: State University of New York Press, 1991).

2. The Bauhaus School, founded by Walter Gropius, generated the inter-

national style characterized by the architecture of Gropius, Mies van der Rohe, Le Corbusier, and Philip Johnson. The Bauhaus School was closed in 1933 by Hitler, who considered it a center of international communism. The Museum of Modern Art held the International Style Exhibition in 1932, an event seen as substantiating the legitimacy of modern art in the United States. The museum opened in 1929, the year of the stock market crash (although no causal relationship is suggested), twelve years after the Armory Show.

3. The Salon Carré of the Louvre was begun in 1667; it was on a regular schedule by the 1740s. As the eighteenth century progressed, more than seven hundred people a day visited the salon. This stimulated the growth of a large art market. Artists became adroit entrepreneurs of respectable distinction.

4. T. S. Eliot's famous "objective correlative" addresses this means of translation. "The only way of expressing emotion in the form of art is by finding an 'objective correlative'; in other words a set of objects, a situation, a chain of events, which shall be the formula for the particular emotion; such that, when the external facts, which must terminate in sensory experience, are given, the emotion is immediately evoked." The definition appears in the essay "Hamlet and His Problems," in *The Sacred Wood* (London: Methuen, 1921; rpt., New York: Barnes and Noble, 1960), 100.

5. The New Criticism dominated literary analysis in English from the 1940s to the 1970s, when the structuralist movement demanded equal attention. Leading figures are Cleanth Brooks, John Crowe Ransom (who gave the movement its name), Allen Tate, Robert Penn Warren, Yvor Winters, and W. K. Wimsatt.

6. A definitive essay here is T. E. Hulme, "Romanticism and Classicism," which was published in *Speculations* (1924) but was written ten years earlier. "The romantic, because he thinks man infinite, must always be talking about the infinite," Hulme writes. "In the classic attitude, you never seem to swing right along to the infinite nothing." (In Hazard Adams, ed., *Critical Theory since Plato* [New York: Harcourt, Brace, Jovanovich, 1971], 767–68.)

7. Fear of a possible revolution in the United States after World War I contributed to the growth of a generation of expatriates, who (socialists or not) sought a wider scope of intellectual tolerance in Europe. Earlier travelers abroad were not exactly expatriates, even if they lived in Europe for some time: they were seeking cultural enrichment. The later expatriates were fleeing as much as they were seeking. Those who went to France were more likely to be on the Left, while those who went to England were more likely to be on the Right. And Henry James had shown all of them how one might leave one's own country to achieve literary fame.

8. Rimbaud is central here, especially the two "Lettres du voyant" (1871).

9. Here, too, T. S. Eliot has been most influential. "What happens is a continual surrender of himself as he is at the moment to something which is more valuable. The progress of an artist is the continual extinction of personality" ("Tradition and the Individual Talent," in *The Sacred Wood*, 52–53).

10. In Russian formalism, literary art defamiliarizes or makes novel its vocabulary (the concept is Victor Schlovsky's), thereby making its subject, in

part, the calling attention of language to itself. Accordingly, literature has an autonomous stylistic history, a notion that was unacceptable to the Marxists. See Victor Erlich, *Russian Formalism* (1955; rpt., New Haven: Yale University Press, 1965), 147. Roman Jakobson took the formalist method to found Prague structuralism. See also Northrop Frye, *Anatomy of Criticism* (1957; rpt., Princeton: Princeton University Press, 1973).

For painting, the sources of formalist criticism include Alois Riegl, Heinrich Wölfflinn, and Aby Warburg, all writing in Germany before World War I (see Michael Podro, *The Critical Historians of Art* [New Haven: Yale University Press, 1982]). Writing through the 1920s was Erwin Panofsky. These writers are, to be sure, hardly modernists.

For Roger Fry, see his *Vision and Design* (1921; rpt., New York: Brentano's, 1960). For Clement Greenberg, *The Collected Essays and Criticism* (Chicago: University of Chicago Press, 1986).

11. Literary criticism is "a species of knowledge" requiring a "coherent scheme which must be rational" (Rene Wellek and Austin Warren, *Theory of Literature* [New York: Harcourt, Brace, 1942], 15–16).

12. This early approach, where the history of art has not yet been extricated from sociopolitical history, relies on Hegel, who in his *Aesthetics* asserts that in each age art reflects the specific relationships that define the contemporaneous world.

13. This statement refers to work settings generally, from engineering facilities to new-car showrooms. In some professions, a conservative nonmodernism represents (or has until recently) status: in the attorney's office, for example, compared with the modern physician's office. In cases where the professional office is "traditional" and (an essential qualification) the profession is highly paid, the home is usually furnished insistently modern. The traditional office will be inside a modern building, while the expensive home with modern furnishings will be in a traditional neighborhood.

14. In capitalism, the ends of production, the actual products, are supposed to be independently determined entirely by market demand. Planning production based on forecasted needs determined by social values is rejected. Hence the happy I-told-you-so responses to the economic difficulties that arise in communist economies. The case of Japan, however, where very long-range planning is guided by the government, gives the West cause for continual consternation.

15. Recently (1990–91), there have been the cases of Robert Mapplethorpe's photographs of nudity, genitalia, sexual acts beyond the pedestrian, and homoerotica and Albert Serres's crucifixion cross immersed in urine confessed to be his own. But one could likely point to similar cases every other year or so since Manet exhibited *Dejeuner sur l'Herbe*, including the famous opening of Stravinsky's *The Rite of Spring*.

16. Because New Critical formalism was politically quite docile—and whatever political principles the best-known New Critics held were "southern agrarian"—many assumed that the structuralism emerging from Saussure and Claude Lévi-Strauss and flowing into literary criticism would be insepar-

able not only from political critique, of which there is all sorts, but from political action. Such has not proved the case. See Edward Said, *Beginnings* (New York: Columbia Universiy Press, 1985).

Formalism in the visual arts was not to be fully accepted into criticism, especially academic criticism, except by severing the critical method from the originally socialist attachments, such as those of Greenberg, so formalism could be conveniently detached from the Left. This accomplished, formalism subsequently pervades criticism in the visual arts as thoroughly as in literature and is permitted to flourish in the university.

17. Cubism rejected literary and symbolic content, exactly the opposite of what would be surrealism's position. (See John Golding's essay on cubism in Tony Richardson and Nikos Stangos, *Concepts of Modern Art* [New York: Harper and Row, 1974]). That is why surrealism is, in this study, assigned to high modernism.

18. It was Greenberg who arrogated abstract expressionism for formalism, as a way of partitioning a territory for what he called "American art." This critical strategy helped shift the center of visual modernism across the Atlantic Ocean.

19. T. E. Hulme has already been mentioned (chap. 3, n. 6). For the painters, romanticism was largely associated with a specific variety of techniques, with a certain set of methods rather than with a worldview that they were rejecting. (In fact, painters mostly shared the romantic worldview.) Hence, the painters had no need to insist upon being classical, as opposed to romantic.

20. On absurdity, see Jean-Paul Sartre, *Being and Nothingness*, trans. H. Barnes (New York: Washington Square Press, 1966), part 2, chap. 1. The theistic existentialists (Karl Jaspers, for example) do not find the world absurd; for them, it does have a secure grounding in being, although mortality weighs no less heavily for that reason. See Jaspers, *The Origin and Goal of History*, trans. M. Bullock (New Haven: Yale University Press, 1953).

21. One should recall the substantial attention given to Hans Vaihinger's *Philosophy of 'As If'*, trans. C. K. Ogden (London: K. Paul, Trench, Trubner, 1924). There is an interesting discussion of Stevens and others, in regard to "fictions," in Frank Lentricchia, *After the New Criticism* (Chicago: University of Chicago Press, 1980), 28–30.

22. In *The Anxiety of Influence* (New York: Oxford University Press, 1973) Harold Bloom has elaborated the thesis that poets compete with past poets. Fame can be granted to one only at the expense of another, since there is only so much room in the canon and the hierarchy of genius is a ladder at each point apparently only one rung wide. For example, the high modernists displaced the romantics with the Elizabethans or Goethe or Dante or the "metaphysical" poets like Donne. Of course, the comparison inherent in the displacement awards the romantics the stature one would deny them while overcoming them. The painters respond in the same way to Delacroix, Manet, Degas, and the impressionists, as do the musicians to Beethoven, Brahms, Schumann, and Chopin.

Chapter 4: Modernism and Empiricism

1. The "rights" referred to here are natural rights, which Locke advocated: not simply legal or social constructs or codified power relationships, but naturally inherent prerogatives superior to the legalities of any specific social arrangement. In an empiricist theory, these resemble the natural laws of the material universe ("the laws of Nature and of Nature's God," in the words of the Declaration of Independence, following Locke). Since the Hegelians give history freedom as its destination, they too adhere to a theory of inherent rights—although theirs is not, obviously, an empiricist theory: the rights may be "natural," but not quite in the Lockean sense.

While *nomos* refers generally to law and custom, the Greek sophists elevated it to a universal principle, above physical nature.

2. Of course, since Adam was also formed from the ground and the Bible does not say specifically how life was put into the animals, it might be argued that Adam is the first animal, especially since, when God wishes to provide a "help meet" for Adam, it is (more) animals that he makes. Eve is a later afterthought, once the animals apparently do not provide Adam sufficient companionship (Gen. 2:19–23).

3. In *An Enquiry Concerning Human Understanding*, sec. 10, Hume writes concerning the possibility of miracles: "A miracle is a violation of the laws of nature; and as a firm and unalterable experience has established these laws, the proof against a miracle . . . is as entire as any argument from experience can possibly be imagined."

4. Descartes writes in the Fourth Meditation: "God . . . whose idea is in me . . . cannot be a deceiver, since the light of nature teaches us that fraud and deception necessarily proceed from some defect" (*Descartes: Selections*, ed. R. Eaton [New York: Scribners, 1955], 126).

5. "The decrees and mandates of God, and consequently His providence," says Spinoza in the *Ethics*, "are merely the order of nature . . . [even though scripture] describes an event as accomplished by God or God's will" (*The Philosophy of Spinoza*, ed. J. Ratner [New York: Modern Library, 1927], 113). Also in the *Ethics*: "The mind is a certain and determinate mode of thought, and therefore it cannot be the free cause of its own actions" (191).

6. This pantheistic interpretation (an egregious misinterpretation, some would have it) of Spinoza marks his rediscovery by Goethe, Schelling, and, as a result of their influence, Coleridge. Despite that veneration, Jacobi was one romantic philosopher who rejected Spinoza, in response to Lessing's having told him that Spinoza was the greatest of all philosophers. On the influence of Spinoza, see Yirmiyahu Yovel, *Spinoza and Other Heretics* (Princeton: Princeton University Press, 1989).

7. "The cause of sense is the external body or object which presses the organ proper to each sense . . . which pressure, by the mediation of the nerves and other strings and membranes of the body continue inward to the brain and heart" (Hobbes, *Leviathan* [1651], ed. H. W. Schneider [New York: Dutton, 1951], 25).

8. Aristotle recognized the similarity between humans and monkeys. Galen actually dissected monkeys. The similarity was usually seen as an interesting coincidence. In 1758, Linnaeus classified humans as primates (with apes, monkeys, bats, and lemurs), although during the following century almost everyone else put humans in a separate order, until the time following Darwin.

9. This subject can no longer be mentioned without appropriate homage to Arthur Lovejoy's *The Great Chain of Being* (Cambridge: Harvard University Press, 1936).

10. Leibniz takes Spinoza's concept of a single substance with two "aspects," mind and matter proceeding conjointly, and provides the metaphysics with an actual mechanics (or physics) of operation. Leibniz is enough Spinoza's junior to integrate Galileo's work. (Galileo was still alive when Spinoza was born.) In the *Monadology* Leibniz explains that "the soul follows its own laws, and the body likewise follows its own laws. They are fitted to each other in virtue of the preestablished harmony" (*Leibniz,* trans. G. R. Montgomery [LaSalle, Ill.: Open Court Press, 1953], 268).

11. One thinks here of the so frequently hostile responses to the speculations of John Eccles, the neurobiologist, in his *The Human Psyche* (New York: Springer, 1980), for example.

12. China was particularly intriguing, and much attention was given to Confucius, who lived five hundred years before Christ. The Jesuits made strong claims that the thought of China and of Christianity were readily reconcilable, although the Jesuits were condemned for this around 1700. Freethinkers argued that the case of the Chinese proved that pagans could be moral and admirable, perhaps more so than Christians. They saw Confucius more like Spinoza, who was considered an atheist by the European orthodox. See Paul Hazard, *The European Mind, 1680–1715* (New York: New American Library, 1963), chap. 1.

13. In 1786, William Jones announced that he had discovered good reason to believe that Greek, Latin, and Sanskrit had the same source, a source probably shared by the Germanic and Celtic languages. In the early nineteenth century, the work of Rasmus Rask and Jacob Grimm added confirmation to the hypothesis. See Philip Baldi, *An Introduction to Indo-European Languages* (Carbondale: Southern Illinois University Press, 1983).

Comparative religion was aided by the increasing rigors of biblical scholarship. Modern textual, linguistic, and historical investigation of the Bible may be said to begin as early as V. A. Bengel's edition of the Greek text of the New Testament in the early eighteenth century. In the nineteenth century, these methods became prevalent in serious scholarship. Karl Lachmann prepared a text of the entire Old Testament and Ferdinand Bauer a New Testament. Also, toward the end of the century there is Julius Wellhausen's study on the sources of the Pentateuch. See *The Cambridge History of the Bible,* 3 vols. (New York: Cambridge University Press, 1963–70).

14. The correspondence between European idealism and Hinduism, especially Advaita Vedanta, is striking. Herder read the Upanishads; through him

Schopenhauer was introduced to this portion of the Vedas. Indian thought persistently contributes to the phenomenology that extends from Hegel through Nietzsche to Heidegger. The English domination of India provides one conduit in the nineteenth century. Outside mainstream philosophy, Hinduism provoked the substantial theosophical movement of H. P. Blavatsky and the work of G. I. Gurdjieff. One recalls Thoreau's references to Indian literature in *Walden*, which he encountered in books from Emerson's library.

15. In the Renaissance, Marsilio Ficino wrote to Paul of Middleburg that the age, especially in Florence, "has recalled the Platonic teaching from darkness into light" (quoted in Peter Murray and Linda Murray, *The Art of the Renaissance* [New York: Oxford University Press, 1963]), 167.

16. In the Middle Ages, God was sometimes portrayed, albeit infrequently, as an architect with a huge pair of dividers. That image is now familiar from William Blake's painting.

17. Employing the word *passion* to refer to Jesus on the cross or the suffering of martyrs is a very old usage and most likely the oldest usage of the term in English, which took the word from Old French. The "link" mentioned in the text would not have been at all remote to the romantics.

18. Alfred North Whitehead at one point called his thought "the philosophy of organism." Nature's largest systems are comprised of smaller systems, each system having an internally coherent structure, yet all interacting over space and time. As in the human being, with its strata of organs, systems, body, and mind, the whole is more than the sum of its parts. The sciences of each system individually cannot, therefore, add up to an exhaustive description of the world. See his *Process and Reality* (1929).

19. Johann Winckelmann, writing around 1755 (*Writings on Art*, ed. D. Irwin [London: Phaedon, 1972]), believed that only by following in the steps of the Greeks would the modern European world achieve greatness. This position depends upon judging the works of the Greeks on aesthetic criteria, seeing them as art rather than as (also) information. Aestheticizing a phenomenon so that it yields a meaning superior to its ostensible content is used both by neoclassicism and romanticism. For neoclassicism, the technique is allegorical; for romanticism, the technique is mythological.

20. E.g., Kenneth Burke, whose earliest writings are published in the 1930s. See *Language as Symbolic Action* (Berkeley: University of California Press, 1966).

21. H. G. Wells's *Outline of History* (1925) was for many years a best-seller.

22. The Theosophical Society in the United States was founded in 1875.

23. Charles Sherrington coined the term *synapse*; see *The Integrative Action of the Nervous System* (1906).

24. Specific examples of late nineteenth-century painters of dreamlike fantasy and near hallucination, some voluptuous and others tormenting, are Arnold Böcklin, Jean Delville, James Ensor, and Edvard Munch, all painting in the 1890s. Hieronymus Bosch and, three hundred years later, William Blake often seem like precursors. Literary symbolism clearly influences painting, having transformed the world into a veil to be poetically lifted. (For the ro-

mantics, the world itself was not the veil.) By early in the twentieth century, there is the subjective antinaturalism of German expressionism (Kandinsky, Marc, Klee), itself already a modernist movement, with its roots in the Berlin secession of the early 1890s.

25. On the Gnostic demiurge, see Giovanni Filoramo, *A History of Gnosticism*, trans. A. Alcock (London: Blackwell, 1990).

26. I. A. Richards was the literary critic especially influential in promoting behaviorism. His *Principles of Literary Criticism* appeared in 1925, the year after James B. Watson's *Behaviorism*. Richards moved toward other approaches when it became apparent how inhospitable behaviorism was to whatever makes literature so compelling to those who spend their lives thinking about it.

For a discussion of psychology in the twentieth century see Peter Berger, "Towards a Sociological Understanding of Psychoanalysis," in his *Facing Up to Modernity* (New York: Basic Books, 1977).

27. Pragmatism and humanism are not identical. Some argue that pragmatism actually intends to fulfill the project of romanticism, which humanism certainly does not intend. In addition, some recent pragmatists describe the experience of art as being the primary way of reaching moral positions, without requiring that the truth in art be stable in other forms. See Giles Gunn, *The Culture of Criticism and the Criticism of Culture* (New York: Oxford University Press, 1987); Richard Rorty, *Consequences of Pragmatism* (Minneapolis: University of Minnesota Press, 1982); and Joseph Kupfer, *Experience as Art* (Albany: SUNY Press, 1983).

28. Thomas Kuhn, *The Structure of Scientific Revolutions*, 2d ed. (Chicago: University of Chicago Press, 1970).

29. For John Dewey's approach to art see chap. 4 of *The Quest for Certainty* (1929; rpt., New York: Macmillan, 1960).

In one aspect of humanism, the New Humanist movement, Irving Babbitt attacked the romantic outlook, together with the realism and naturalism in the arts for which he thought romanticism was also responsible. His *Rousseau and Romanticism* appeared in 1919. He advocated the "classical" virtues in art—balance and moderation, a position that influenced high modernist writers like T. S. Eliot.

30. Johann Gottfried von Herder, *On the Origin of Language*, trans. J. H. Moran and A. Gode (New York: Ungar, 1966). In his "Essay on the Origins of Language," Rousseau writes, "As emotions were the first motives which induced humans to speak, the first utterances were tropes. Figurative language was the first to be born."

31. "Nature has observed this principle like a mother, that the actions she makes requisite for our needs also give us pleasure; and she attracts us to them not only through reason, but also through appetite" (Montaigne, "On Education," in *Complete Essays of Montaigne*, trans. D. M. Frame [Stanford: Stanford University Press, 1965], 118).

32. The meaning of what the artist is going to say "does not exist anywhere—not in things, which as yet have no meaning, nor in the artist him-

self, in his unformulated life" (Maurice Merleau-Ponty, *Sense and Nonsense*, trans. H. Dreyfus [Evanston: Northwestern University Press, 1964], 19).

33. Michel Foucault, *The Archaeology of Knowledge*, trans. A. M. Sheridan Smith (New York: Pantheon, 1972).

34. The theory of humors can be traced back to Empedocles' belief in the influences of cosmic elements, which influenced Hippocrates' notion of the "balance" of basic bodily fluids. Both psychoanalysis and, later, Ernst Kretchmer's relation of body types and personality in the 1920s also create personality classifications that are categories of things made to fit categories of selves.

35. The condemnation occurs at the Council of Trent. Art and religion go their own way in mannerism. See John K. G. Shearman, *Mannerism* (London: Penguin, 1967); Linda Murray, *The High Renaissance and Mannerism* (Oxford: Oxford University Press, 1977).

36. Real, almost palpable physical light appears in (is represented in) baroque painting. Objects are not only illuminated, but this light falls on them. See Germain Bazin, *The Baroque*, trans. P. Wardroper (Greenwich, Conn.: New York Graphic Society, 1968).

Chapter 5: Science and Modernity

1. Whether or not the elevation of reason was compatible with religious piety was continuously disputed during the seventeenth century. Some argued that Cartesianism, if accepted, would ultimately erode religious belief (as it has). The attacks on the rationalist freethinkers (usually living in Holland) are most interesting in the writings of Jacques Bossuet at the beginning of the seventeenth century and Nicholas de Malebranche toward the end.

2. Erwin Panofsky addressed these general issues of the aesthetic relations of sign, symbol, object, and world in *Early Netherlandish Painting* (Cambridge: Harvard University Press, 1953).

3. For Marx, alienation is the condition under capitalism of the worker, whose labor has been turned into a commodity and, consequently, whose body is simply a machine of production. For Emile Durkheim, anomie is caused by the erosion of a former sense of community and shared norms, replaced by unconstrained individualism and rationalism—an unfortunate aspect of modern times. Similar ideas can be found in other nineteenth-century thinkers. Max Weber and Ferdinand Tonnies, for example, were unhappy with and attempted to account for the aspects of modern life taking shape during their lifetimes.

4. Jean-Baptiste Lamarck argued (in *Zoological Philosophy* [1809]) that behaviors frequently repeated during an animal's lifetime would not only be strengthened as a tendency but would be somehow recorded in the reproductive cells to be passed on to offspring. Gregor Mendel's experiments with garden peas in the 1850s and 1860s provided evidence for the genetic transmission of traits, although when he first announced his findings they had no effect. Around 1900 the experiments were recognized to contain the key to what is now standard genetic theory.

5. Cartesian "analytic" geometry includes the plotting of algebraic curves on two coordinates on a flat plane. Solid geometry comes from adding a third coordinate at right angles to the other two (i.e., a third dimension). Leibniz and Newton invent calculus separately, although Newton is better known for it because his mathematical notation became standard. (Newton published *Method of Fluxions* in 1671; Leibniz's first essay on calculus appeared in 1684.) By the 1890s Hermann Minkowsky, a Russian mathematician (who, incidentally, conceived of the four-dimensional space—the ordinary three plus time—upon which Einstein built), demonstrates that proofs in basic number theory can all be configured in geometrical format.

6. The only book published in Spinoza's own name in his lifetime was *Principles of Descartes' Philosophy Geometrically Demonstrated.*

7. What is now called the scientific method was suggested as early as the late twelfth century by Robert Grosseteste, at Oxford University. He advocated reaching general laws through direct observation. His pupil, Roger Bacon, used the term *experimental method* (in Latin, of course) and well understood that descriptive mathematics was essential to the method. Galileo, preferring circular orbits, never agreed with Kepler that the planets travel in ellipses.

8. Michel Foucault's *The Archaeology of Knowledge* renewed everyone's interest in such matters.

9. That animal motion is a form of mechanics was obvious. Since economics meant a theory of prices and prices are numbers, economics readily lent itself to mathematics. Genetic theory became susceptible to mathematics when the transmission of genetic material could be seen as the mechanical distribution of isolated genetic units or particles according to very simple probability tables. Genes nowadays have a complicated mathematical life quite detached from their carriers. Durkheim's paradigmatic study of suicide was published in 1897.

10. Antoine Lavoisier, usually described as the founder of chemistry, did his work on combustion in the 1770s. Around the same time Cavendish discovered hydrogen, Rutherford discovered nitrogen, and Priestly discovered oxygen (the gas that Lavoisier used). As for electromagnetism, in 1820 Orsted showed that electric current passing through a wire yielded a magnetic field. In a very short time, Ampere provided the mathematics of the phenomenon.

11. "A close, naked natural way of speaking; positive expressions; clear senses; bringing all things as near the mathematical plainness as they can" (Thomas Sprat, *History of the Royal Society* [1667], ed. J. I. Cope and H. W. Jones [St. Louis: Washington University Press, 1958, 126]).

12. The Cartesians attacked Newtonian theory. Although it did account for the paths taken by the planets, it could not account for where motion originates. It cannot be a property of bodies themselves, which can be stopped. Since force comes from motion, there must have been an origin for that force outside the Newtonian scheme.

13. This does not mean that the paths of the planets were exactly circular. Rather, a system of small circular motions (epicycles) are transposed against the inherently circular orbital motion so that the mathematical results are the

actual observed motion of the planet. Since the planets actually travel in ellipses, the calculations based on circles took much ingenuity. In fact, by having the planets revolve around the sun, Copernicus used more epicycles than Ptolemy. Still the sun ends up off to one side of the center of the earth's orbit.

14. Newton wrote to Richard Bentley: "For the *cause* of gravity is what I do not pretend to know. . . . It is *inconceivable* that inanimate brute matter should, without the mediation of something else, which is *not material,* operate upon, and effect other matter without mutual contact" (quoted in William Wightman, *The Growth of Scientific Ideas* [New Haven: Yale University Press, 1953], 101; emphases mine).

15. Ferdinand de Saussure, *Course in General Linguistics,* trans. R. Harris (London: Duckworth, 1973).

16. In trying to account for the changes undergone by the earth, the catastrophic theory is actually the older one, proposed by Abraham Werner in the late eighteenth century. James Hutton's uniformitarian theory followed, and afterward, the best known of them, Charles Lyell's gradualism.

17. See chap. 4, n. 8. The human being (genus *Homo*) is one of about one hundred genera in the phylum *Chordata,* itself one of the thirty-three phyla of the kingdom *Animalia.* In Lynn Margulis and Karlene Schwartz, *Five Kingdoms: An Illustrated Guide to the Phyla of Life on Earth* (San Francisco: Freeman, 1982), the picture of the typical *Chordata* is not a human but a salamander.

18. The Copenhagen model of quantum physics, currently with more adherents than any other, asserts that we cannot know whether our ideas about reality (our descriptions of reality) actually correspond to reality. Even to ask that question is pointless.

19. Max Planck, Werner Heisenberg, and Max Born were Germans; Schrödinger was Austrian. It is not being suggested here that the early quantum physicists were all German nationals or that they were all sympathetic to German political causes. Niels Bohr was Danish, received his doctorate in Copenhagen, studied in England, publicly opposed the Nazis, and worked at Los Alamos. Louis de Broglie was French and spent his career in France. Nevertheless, the philosophically Germanic origins of the discipline are unmistakable.

20. It is sometimes argued that the view of the Copenhagen school of quantum physics can be best associated with philosophical pragmatism, traceable back to William James. The Copenhagen quantum theorists stress that the success of the theory in accounting for and predicting observations is not equivalent to a guarantee that the terms used in the theory (specifically, the names of the particles) actually correspond to whatever actually exists at the smallest level. After all, no matter how sophisticated the instruments, this can never be observed directly. Locating the lineage of quantum physics in pragmatism is probably a sign of where one's basic patriotism lies. There are also those who see pragmatism as basically indebted to Kant in the first place.

The influence on the Anglo-Americans of thinkers, who, it is argued here, recuperate for the Germanic tradition in intellectual spheres what was relinquished in the political sphere is an interesting history on its own. It also involves the role of German-speaking Jewish thinkers. Marx, Freud, and Einstein (a by now familiar trio) immediately come to mind; and it is notable how Einstein all his life denied the correctness of quantum physics.

Chapter 6: A Matter of Time

1. That God's perpetual rule by decree or volition was replaced by the rule of inviolable law suggests the general replacement of rule by personal domination: the turn to autonomous legality, the rule of law considered independent of those subject to it (as in a theory of natural rights). The replacement of monarchical imposition, or its diminution by constitutional legislation, has the same conceptual structure as the theological change.

2. Aristotle, *Poetics*, 1450b (Oxford University Press translation).

3. In 1862, Kelvin estimated the age of the earth at 100 million years. By 1899, he had revised the figure downward to 20–40 million years.

4. Georg Cantor's theory of infinity was developed during the 1890s. *Contribution to the Founding of the Theory of Transfinite Numbers* was published in 1915.

5. With the introduction of clocks in the thirteenth century, the "seasonal" hours, which varied in length according to the time of year, were regimented. Minute hands were not in general use until the seventeenth century, and at around the same time the pendulum was able to keep track of seconds.

6. See Frank E. Manuel, *The Prophets of Paris* (Cambridge: Harvard University Press, 1962), esp. Fourier's idea for the phalanstery.

7. For the baroque outlook on time, see J. R. Martin, *Baroque* (New York: Harper and Row, 1977), chap. 6.

8. Jacques Derrida, *Of Grammatology*, trans. Gayatri Spivak (Baltimore: Johns Hopkins University Press, 1976), and *Margins of Philosophy*, trans. Alan Bass (Chicago: University of Chicago Press, 1982).

9. Henri Bergson, *Time and Free Will*, trans. R. L. Pogson (New York: Macmillan, 1921).

10. The finite speed of light was demonstrated by the Danish astronomer Olaf Christensen Romer (1644–1710). Romer was at the University of Paris when he made the observations and calculations.

11. Social legislation in the nineteeth century was often introduced to counter the revolutionary force and intent of socialism. Nevertheless, the legislation itself was usually inspired by the socialist promise.

12. This issuing of freedom in modernism is an appropriation of Freudian psychoanalysis, which is used as if it might serve as an empirical base for a nonempirical art, like surrealism. The optimistic transformations of Freud's fundamental pessimism grow as modernism shifts toward the United States.

13. Not all neoclassicists were intolerant of independent deviation. David appears to have had a tolerant view toward pupils. Nevertheless, the relaxation of regimented discipline increases as the nineteenth century advances.

14. The movement described here is what allows for the emergence of sociology. Republicanism was for a long time considered suitable only for

small territories, until the United States provided a contrary example. Also, in the eighteenth century it was considered a weak form of government: that the colonies could defeat a monarchy in war (both in the American Revolutionary War and in the War of 1812) substantiated the potential strength of democratic republicanism.

15. Hamlet's dilemma of will was early described by Samuel Taylor Coleridge. (See *Shakespearean Criticism*, ed. T. M. Raysor [New York: Dutton, 1930].)

16. James Macpherson published his own poems falsely attributed to one "Ossian," a third-century Gallic (Celtic) poet, in 1760. Thomas Chatterton, with similar deceit, attributed his poems to Thomas Rowley, a purported fifteenth-century monk of Bristol. Thomas Percy published Percy's Relics, an (honest) collection of old English poems, in 1765. There is, as well, Herder's publication of German folk songs, *Volkslieder*, in 1778–79.

17. The idea that the painter is not simply a crafter but like the poet is sometimes traced back to Leonardo do Vinci, who according to Vasari applied the term *genius* to himself. (Aristotle had excluded artisans from citizenship.) Also, Ficino's description of the poet as both melancholy (according to Aristotle) and frenzied (according to Plato) was applied to painters by Vasari. See Peter Burke, *The Italian Renaissance* (Princeton: Princeton University Press, 1986), 193, where it is also noted that the terms applied to painting (*elegance, loveliness, sweetness, grace*) were terms applied to lyric poetry, not to the higher epic poetry.

18. In Old English law, any compensation for loaning money was considered usury. In the Middle Ages, the Christian church prohibited charging interest on loans as a sin. The Muslim Koran prohibits interest on loans.

19. There is the theosophical-metaphysical use of time as the fourth dimension in P. D. Ouspensky's *Tertium Organum* (1920; rpt., New York: Knopf, 1922).

20. Delacroix first proposed that black was no longer necessary, and many impressionists adopted the advice. Renoir was one who did not.

21. Eadweard Muybridge made photographs in 1872 and afterward displayed animals and humans in motion through a technique of rapidly sequential pictures. (His first challenge was to demonstrate that a trotting horse at times has all four feet off the ground.) These motion studies influenced those pictorial movements, like cubism, where a number of views or motions are incorporated onto a single canvas in a single figure.

22. See Rudolf Arnheim, *Entropy and Art* (Berkeley: University of California Press, 1971).

Chapter 7: Time Concerns

1. "Spending" time properly, considering time as "precious," not to be "wasted," is part of the ethic of achievement found in the Renaissance dialogues of Leon Battista Alberti, published from 1432 onward. The idea can also be found from time to time in Erasmus.

2. Pascal's wager, in *Pensées,* actually functions as a capitalist metaphor: a gamble as an investment. Pascal's frequent lugubriousness may be attributable to his apprehension that one cannot get to heaven through such theological capitalism.

3. Eventually there was the unearthing of painted walls and other works from Herculaneum and Pompeii, discovered in 1738 and 1748 respectively. But the quality of these works was very disappointing.

4. Thomas Aquinas was canonized in 1323, forty-nine years after his death.

5. The Dutch were innovators in mass production, even when it came to artworks. (It can be argued that the Japanese learned their strategies of production from the Dutch.) The average price of a Salomon van Ruisdael landscape or or a Steen genre painting was 25 percent of the weekly wages of a Leiden textile worker. (See Carlo Cipolla, *Before the Industrial Revolution* [New York: Norton, 1966], 256.) By the midseventeenth century in Holland, farmers and shopkeepers bought art (George Clark, *Early Modern Europe, 1450–1720* [New York: Galaxy, 1960]).

6. The compatibility of Aristotle and Christianity might even be urged because Aristotle allowed, in the *Nicomachean Ethics,* that nature could (might) have a purpose.

7. Cf. Aquinas: "Now God wills some things to be done necessarily, some contingently, so that there be a right order in things for the perfection of the universe. Therefore, to some effects He has attached unfailing necessary causes from which the effects follow necessarily; but to others defectible and contingent causes" (*Summa,* question 19, article 8).

8. The subject of early intelligence and the mind of the child is addressed, diversely, in the works of Jacob Bronowski, Bronislaw Malinowski, Claude Lévi-Strauss, and Lucien Lévy-Bruhl.

9. Michelet first used the term *Renaissance* in 1855. Jacob Burckhardt's *Civilization of the Renaissance* in Italy was published in 1860.

10. Phoebe Pool, *Impressionism* (New York: Praeger, 1967), 46.

11. Chateaubriand makes such an argument in *The Genius of Christianity* (1802).

12. Monet and Pissarro would have seen the work of Turner and Constable in London in 1870. The pre-Raphaelite William H. Hunt exhibit occurred in Paris in 1855.

13. Children's art was included in the publications of the Blaue Reiter group, in Munich, around 1912 and thereafter.

14. The most lasting image of this impotence has been that of the Fisher King in T. S. Eliot's *The Waste Land.*

15. Reducing or tracing back the complexity of thought to the rudimentary can be done on physical grounds by using the notion of primary atomistic sensations, as Bertrand Russell does, or on linguistic grounds, as in Wittgenstein's notion (in the *Tractatus)* of primary basic propositions or sentences.

16. "In the id, there is nothing corresponding to the idea of time" (Sigmund Freud, *New Introductory Lectures on Psycho-Analysis* [New York: Norton, 1933], 104).

17. *Wit and Its Relation to the Unconscious* was published in 1905.

18. The relationship of Cronos (the God's name) and Chronos (time) rests on a pun. The initial sounds of the two words are distinct phonemes in Greek, although the second, the guttural (velar), is not used in English.

In linking the two terms I have relied on the following evidence. First, the name *Cronos* was used in Athens to mean an "old dotard" or "old fool." This suggests to me that the idea of time (Chronos) was attached to the name (Cronos) to yield a derogatory reference to a time of life (old age). The term *Chronos* (time) refers to a certain time of life in some ancient Greek compound words. Further, since the era of Cronos generally was referred to as a "golden age" (i.e., it originally carried no negative connotation), I assume this, too, suggests that the derogatory term resulted from a blending of the two terms. Second, the name *Cronos* also referred to the god Saturn, the god of planting or of seed; in an agricultural environment the cycles of planting, etc. would inextricably be bound to the passing of time (Chronos), especially in a society where time and history were conceived to be cyclical. Third, the *Greek-English Lexicon*, 9th ed. (London: Oxford University Press), cites a line in Aristotle where Cronos is used in a way that yields the interpretation "= Chronos." Reference is made there (p. 998) to another line in Aristotle supporting the connection.

19. Freud discusses the relation of art and society in *The Future of an Illusion* (1927).

20. The American psychoanalytic optimism undoubtedly peaked with transactional analysis.

21. That the Mafia is an extended family structured for production is precisely what makes it unmanageable by capitalism. For a discussion of the modern family, see Christopher Lasch, *Haven in a Heartless World* (New York: Basic Books, 1977).

22. John C. Greene, *Science, Ideology, and World View* (Berkeley: University of California Press, 1981); Stephen J. Gould, *Ever since Darwin* (New York: Norton, 1977).

23. The rebellion of the sons against the father as an actual historical act is defended in Freud's *Moses and Monotheism* (1939).

24. Robert C. Bannister, *Social Darwinism* (Philadelphia: Temple University Press, 1979).

25. Claude Lévi-Strauss addresses a related idea: the conflict between the "chthonous" and "autochthonous" (the earth-generated and the self-generated) concepts of human origins. See *Structural Anthropology*, trans. C. Jacobson and B. Grundfest (New York: Basic Books, 1963).

26. Leeuwenhoek began his observations around 1674. That the senses must be confined to a small range to keep reality manageable is also of literary use: in Poe, overrefinement of the senses is symptomatic of madness. Recall, as well, Alexander Pope's line "to die of aromatic pleasure from a rose." Aldous Huxley's *Doors of Perception*, the once-popular report in the 1960s of his experiences with mescaline, is also structured on the premise that evolution has limited the scope of the senses for reasons of practical survival.

Chapter 8: Modernism Left and Right

1. The "strong" force in the nucleus is said to depend on the exchange of gluons; gravity is said to involve the exchange of gravitons.

2. The "iron law" of wages was formulated by David Ricardo in *The Principles of Political Economy and Taxation* (1817), where he argued that any attempts to improve the wages of workers would be futile.

3. On the matter of the oppressed and their liberation, Hegel's section on "lordship and bondage" in *The Phenomenology of Mind* (1806) influenced Marx (Trans. J. B. Baillie [New York: Harper, 1967], 228–40).

4. The stories of Baudelaire's continuing financial contestation with his mother, who held his inheritance hostage, of Cézanne's refusing the ambitions of his family for him to enter law, of Monet's eventual rejection by his family, of Vincent Van Gogh's life compared with that of his brother Theo are illustrative of this still quite common theme. The issues separating the later nineteenth-century artist and writer from the family often concern life-style.

5. In the *Treatises of Civil Government* Locke argues that although God did not originally divide the world among individuals, God surely condones any division based on people keeping what they gain by their labor.

6. Under Louis XIV, Charles Le Brun became the *premier peintre du roi*, appointed by the king as the permanent director of the Royal Academy of Painting and Sculpture.

7. Pound's support of Mussolini, on whose behalf Pound did radio broadcasts, is a notorious case. Many of Eliot's views came from Charles Maurras, including his advocacy of an inherited aristocracy and (much discussed in recent years) his opinion of Jews. Lawrence believed that a reliance on "blood" (instinct, emotion) would be preferable to a reliance on an outmoded rationality that he associated with English convention, although, to be sure, when he was first formulating his views he could hardly have imagined how such an idea would be used by the late 1930s. Still, he was sympathetic to the Germans, or at least understanding of them, during World War I.

8. Some Futurists participated in the founding of Italian fascism. In 1919, Marinetti spent three weeks in jail with Mussolini.

9. Emile Nolde was a member of the Nazi party. Goebbels, who once hung Nolde's paintings in his office and expressed admiration for Edvard Munch, wrote a novel in 1933 that contained the statement "Today we are all Expressionists. . . . Its power and secret are in its passion." In 1937, Nolde's painting was condemned by the Nazis as degenerate (Jean Clay, *Modern Art: 1890–1918* [Secaucus: Wellfleet Press, 1978]). When Hitler was starting his political career, he identified himself as a "painter" (see chap. 10).

10. Gerald Graff, *Literature against Itself* (University of Chicago Press, 1979), discusses this partitioning of the field of truth.

Chapter 9: The Politics of Empiricism and Transcendentalism

1. G. E. Moore's *Principia Ethica* was published in 1903. Moore was a member of the Bloomsbury group.

Chapter 10: The Politics of Fascism

1. Alan Bullock, *Hitler* (New York: Harper, 1960). On German fascism, see Hans Mommsen, *From Weimar to Auschwitz* (Princeton: Princeton University Press, 1991).

2. See Paul Raabe, ed., *The Era of German Expressionism*, trans. J. M. Ritchie (Woodstock, N.Y.: Overlook Press, 1974).

3. "Suppose . . . we succeeded in explaining our entire instinctive life as the development and ramification of *one* basic form of the will—namely, of the will to power" (*Beyond Good and Evil*, in *Basic Writings of Nietzsche*, trans. W. Kaufmann [New York: Modern Library, 1968], 238).

4. On Italy's fascism, the relation to Dalmatia and Fiume, and related matters, see Gaetano Salvemini, *The Origins of Fascism in Italy* (New York: Harper and Row, 1973), and Alexander De Grand, *Italian Fascism* (Lincoln: University of Nebraska Press, 1982).

5. On Hitler in Munich, see Robert Payne, *The Life and Death of Adolf Hitler* (New York: Praeger, 1973), also F. L. Carsten, *The Rise of Fascism* (Berkeley: University of California Press, 1967), as well as *Radical Perspectives on the Rise of Fascism in Germany*, ed. M. Dobkowski and I. Wallimann (New York: Monthly Review Press, 1989).

6. General Georges Boulanger was active in France in the 1880s. Charles Maurras was first active in France around the turn of the century; his *The Future of Intelligence* was published in 1905. In the forties he supported the Petain government in Vichy during the German occupation.

7. On Lagarde, Langbehn, and Van den Bruck, see Fritz Stern, *The Politics of Cultural Despair* (Berkeley: University of California Press, 1961).

8. On the circumstances leading up to the war, see D. C. Watt, *How War Came* (New York: Pantheon, 1989).

9. The program of the National Socialist German Workers' party announced by Hitler in 1920 included the abolition of income not earned by work (which for centuries had been a way of referring to interest on loans) as well as a specific reference to "breaking the shackles of interest" (a clause quoting the title of a pamphlet by Gottfried Feder).

10. On the sociobiology controversy see E. O. Wilson, *Sociobiology: The New Synthesis* (Cambridge: Harvard University Press, 1975), and M. S. Gregory, A. Silvers, and D. Sutch, eds., *Sociobiology and Human Nature* (San Francisco: Jossey-Bass, 1978).

Chapter 11: The Sources of the Modernist Self

1. The fields of logic and mathematics come together in the nineteenth century. George Boole's *Mathematical Analysis of Logic* and Augustus De Morgan's *Formal Logic* both appeared in 1847.

2. Brook Farm lasted from 1841 to 1847, located near Roxbury, Massachusetts. Nathaniel Hawthorne was among the initial shareholders.

3. The Black Death, a bubonic plague, came to Europe in 1348. Periods of quiescence were followed by new outbreaks during the subsequent three cen-

turies. The outbreaks became increasingly localized. The Great Plague, during 1664–65, was mostly limited to London.

4. Sentimentality is a component of eighteenth-century "sensibility." Louis Bredvold suggests that "more tears were shed" in the eighteenth century than in the nineteenth (*The Natural History of Sensibility* [Detroit: Wayne State University Press, 1962], 5). For the reaction against the extremes of sensibility, see *Sensibility in Transformation,* ed. Sydny Conger (Rutherford: Fairleigh Dickinson University Press, 1990).

5. See chap. 1, n. 26.

6. See chap. 2, n. 23.

7. The individual "has no ultimate responsibility for a [biological] species trait or a cultural practice, even though it was he who underwent the mutation or introduced the practice" (B. F. Skinner, *Beyond Freedom and Dignity* [New York: Knopf, 1971], 209).

Chapter 12: The Modernist Self in Capitalism

1. On the American artist as entrepreneur in the eighteenth and early nineteenth centuries see Neil Harris, *The Artist in American Society* (Chicago: University of Chicago Press, 1962). While "a few artists grew bitterly hostile to business values and . . . materialism . . . [most] neither noticed nor minded their absorption into the business world" (65–66).

2. The first "museum" available to the public was Oxford University's Ashmolean Museum, opened in 1687. During the eighteenth century, the idea of a collection owned by the citizenry and opened to them became part of Enlightenment thinking. Diderot proposed a national museum for France in 1765. It was in England in the midnineteenth century when the museum began to be seen as a way to socialize the expanding urban population by providing culture and diversion. In the United States, the Smithsonian Museum was founded by federal legislation in 1846.

3. For a discussion of the rejection of one's physical-sexual origin, see chapter 7.

4. "In the arts . . . we can not only modify our own attitude so as to effect useful preparation for what is to happen, but we can modify the happening itself" (John Dewey, *The Quest for Certainty* [New York: Minton, Balch, 1929], 132).

5. That literature is not only a mode of expression but is that specific form of language that calls attention to the functioning of language itself, bringing into the fore of consciousness the linguistic processes that underlie consciousness, is a central theme of the "structuralism" that influenced literary studies in the 1960s and 1970s. See chapter 5 in my *From the New Criticism to Deconstruction.*

6. For a discussion of the relation between critical criteria and authority in literature, see John Ellis, *The Theory of Literary Criticism* (Berkeley: University of California Press, 1974).

7. Castiglione's *Cortegiano* appeared in 1528. Castiglione praised the social

refinements of the courtier (dancing, fighting, lovemaking, agility, strength), but also demanded the moral virtues—allegiance (since the courtier would be in service to a prince), uncompromising standards, integrity, and dignity. These latter contribute to the elevated empiricist conception of human nature. Over time, courtly social refinement fell into distinct areas of etiquette and courtesy. The former no longer needs to be connected with moral commitment.

8. For a history of aesthetic Bohemia, see Jerrold Seigel, *Bohemian Paris* (New York: Penguin, 1986).

9. In his introduction to *History of English Literature* (1863–64), Taine argues that a society's structures and institutions, as well as its cultural objects, are causally determined by *la race, le milieu,* and *le moment.*

10. See Gilbert Ryle's discussion of the "category mistake" (*The Concept of Mind* [London: Hutchinson, 1949], chap 1).

11. Considering memory to be a form of physical "storage" allows the computer's storage of data and directions to be called "memory." Increasingly, memory is not human recollection, but a substitute for it. Something can be placed in "memory" (like a subtotal on a calculator) so that it does not have to be remembered.

12. The recent fall of communist governments in the former Soviet Union and elsewhere in Eastern Europe is often described as if this signified the ultimate victory of capitalism over socialism. It is too soon to say exactly what kinds of structures will evolve in the former communist states. Nor does it seem likely that capitalism has finished evolving. The point here is that by 1991, neither capitalism nor socialism existed as they were when the theoretical disputes began in the nineteenth century. Capitalism no longer simply means freedom of the marketplace; democracy has placed many constraints upon capitalism, and not all of these modifications originated from inside the theory of capitalism. And communism is (was) hardly socialism as Marx envisioned it. The bridge crossed by Poland, Czechoslovakia, etc., was shorter than many imagined.

Index

- Takes too big a view? "Empiricism" since 1600
too wide + all-inclusive a frame? Emptily schematic...
- p. xi, top – leads to huge, ridiculous claims?

ART BERMAN is a professor in the division of language, literature, and communication at the Rochester Institute of Technology. He has previously published *From the New Criticism to Deconstruction: The Reception of Structuralism and Post-Structuralism.*